Modelling Nature-based Solutions

Integrating Computational and Participatory Scenario Modelling for Environmental Management and Planning

Nature-based Solutions (NBS) are essential to ensure a sustainable society and healthy ecosystem over the coming decades. However, the systems to be managed are both broad and complex, requiring an integrated understanding of both biophysical systems, such as soils and water, and economic and social systems, such as urban development and human behaviour. This edited book joins these domains of knowledge together from an applied perspective and considers how computer science can help. It takes a strategic look at the benefits and barriers to using modelling within environmental management and planning practice. It delves further by providing an in-depth comparative review of a wide range of models from a variety of scientific disciplines of interest with examples of their use for NBS. As such, this illustrated guide is designed to help students, researchers and practitioners navigate the huge range of modelling options available and develop the common understanding to work interdisciplinarily.

DR NEIL SANG is a researcher in Geographical Information Science (GIS) at the Department of Landscape Architecture, Planning and Management, Swedish University of Agricultural Sciences (SLU). His research interests are broad, spanning a range of modelling approaches such as GIS, optimisation and AI, simulation modelling, remote sensing, citizen science and GeoDesign. Formerly at the James Hutton Institute (UK), he has worked in a wide range of subject areas within socio-environmental science.

Modelling Nature-based Solutions

Integrating Computational and Participatory Scenario Modelling for Environmental Management and Planning

Edited by

NEIL SANG
Swedish University of Agricultural Sciences

CAMBRIDGE
UNIVERSITY PRESS

CAMBRIDGE
UNIVERSITY PRESS

University Printing House, Cambridge CB2 8BS, United Kingdom

One Liberty Plaza, 20th Floor, New York, NY 10006, USA

477 Williamstown Road, Port Melbourne, VIC 3207, Australia

314–321, 3rd Floor, Plot 3, Splendor Forum, Jasola District Centre, New Delhi – 110025, India

79 Anson Road, #06–04/06, Singapore 079906

Cambridge University Press is part of the University of Cambridge.

It furthers the University's mission by disseminating knowledge in the pursuit of education, learning, and research at the highest international levels of excellence.

www.cambridge.org
Information on this title: www.cambridge.org/9781108428934
DOI: 10.1017/9781108553827

First published 2020

Printed in the United Kingdom by TJ International Ltd. Padstow Cornwall

A catalogue record for this publication is available from the British Library.

Library of Congress Cataloging-in-Publication Data
Names: Sang, Neil, 1977– editor.
Title: Modelling nature-based solutions : integrating computational and participatory scenario modelling for environmental management and planning / edited by Neil Sang.
Description: Cambridge ; New York, NY : Cambridge University Press, 2020. | Includes bibliographical references and index.
Identifiers: LCCN 2019045024 (print) | LCCN 2019045025 (ebook) | ISBN 9781108428934 (hardback) | ISBN 9781108553827 (epub)
Subjects: LCSH: Environmental management – Computer simulation. | Environmental management – Data processing. | Environmental protection – Planning – Computer simulation. | Environmental protection – Planning – Data processing. | Sustainability.
Classification: LCC GE300 .M649 2020 (print) | LCC GE300 (ebook) | DDC 333.701/13–dc23
LC record available at https://lccn.loc.gov/2019045024
LC ebook record available at https://lccn.loc.gov/2019045025

ISBN 978-1-108-42893-4 Hardback

Contents

The colour plate section can be found between pages 180 and 181

Contributors

Matthew Aitkenhead
James Hutton Institute, Aberdeen, UK

Ioanna Akoumianaki
James Hutton Institute, Aberdeen, UK

Iain Brown
Independent Scientist, (Formerly Centre of Expertise on Climate Change and Centre of Expertise for Water (CREW)), James Hutton Institute, Aberdeen, UK

Arthur Capet
Modelling for Aquatic Systems (MAST) Group, Liège University, Liège, Belgium

Johanna Deak Sjöman
Swedish University of Agricultural Sciences, Alnarp, Sweden

Gillian Donaldson-Selby
James Hutton Institute, Aberdeen, UK

Sarah Dunn
Independent Scientist, (Formerly) James Hutton Institute, Aberdeen, UK

Jiaqi Ge
School of Geography, University of Leeds, Leeds, UK

Sarah Gottwald
PlanSmart Research Group, Leibniz University, Hannover, Germany

Ron Janssen
School of Business and Economics, Spatial Economics, Vrije Universiteit Amsterdam, Amsterdam, Netherlands

Erik Johansson
Lund University, Lund, Sweden

David Miller
Integrated Land Use Systems Group, James Hutton Institute, Aberdeen, UK

José Muñoz-Rojas
Scientist in Rural Landscape Dynamics, ICAAM Universidade de Évora, Évora, Portugal

Åsa Ode-Sang
Department of Landscape Planning and Management, Swedish University of Agricultural Sciences, Alnarp, Sweden

Gary Polhill
Information and Computational Sciences Group, James Hutton Institute, Aberdeen, UK

Christopher Raymond
Helsinki Institute of Sustainability Science (HELSUS), Faculty of Biological and Environmental Sciences, Faculty of Agriculture and Forestry Sciences, University of Helsinki, Helsinki, Finland, and

Department of Landscape Architecture, Planning and Management,
Swedish University of Agricultural Sciences, Alnarp, Sweden

Neil Sang
Swedish University of Agricultural Sciences, Alnarp, Sweden

Chen Wang
James Hutton Institute, Aberdeen, UK

Foreword

Modelling Nature-based Solutions: Integrating Computational and Participatory Scenario Modelling for Environmental Management and Planning is an important book. It examines issues involved in deciding how to plan for the profound, complex, uncertain and contentious changes which are expected to occur in the coming generations related to climate and demographic change. It focuses on human and scientific aspects related to the United Nations Development Goals, and especially on the key natural systems of soil, water and green infrastructure. In each of these, modelling methods applicable to planning vary, and there are choices related to an appropriate balance between scientific accuracy and public understanding which must be made – and these are not simple choices.

Originally conceived as being specifically directed to Swedish circumstances, the themes discussed in the book have broad global implications, as all countries will have to consider similar issues. Yet even then, these decisions are likely to be insufficient, as the natural systems which need to be planned and managed at the national level do not respect political boundaries. As the authors point out, we are faced with a 'wicked problem'. Nonetheless, and with an awareness of the complexity facing the world, it is a problem which needs feasible solutions. The authors provide an illuminating contribution towards that end.

Carl Steinitz
Wiley Professor of Landscape Architecture and Planning Emeritus
Harvard University

Honorary Professor
Centre for Advanced Spatial Analysis,
University College London

Acknowledgements

Parts of this book are based on updating and reworking of the report *A Review on the State of the Art in Scenario Modelling for Environmental Management* (edited by Sang & Ode-Sang, 2015), reproduced with the kind permission of the Swedish Environmental Protection Agency (Naturvårdsverket). Part of the research reported here was undertaken in the Skåne Local Interaction Platform of Mistra Urban Futures, the financial support of which is gratefully acknowledged. As editor I would like to thank the contributors for their work and also thank the James Hutton Institute for my own training in modelling for interdisciplinary projects, experience which left me with a deep respect for the skills and knowledge of scientists, practitioners and stakeholders across different fields of endeavour.

I hope this book will be of interest to modellers, practitioners, students and stakeholders from a range of fields and that we have succeeded in making the subject accessible. I reflect that my own modelling knowledge is built on foundations in mathematics, language and critical thinking from teachers in many disciplines from postgraduate to school level, many of whom had probably never heard of GIS. These skills are the fundamental prerequisites for a healthy conversation around evidence-based policy to address socio-environmental issues and that they are in fact widely taught should be a source of encouragement; so I would also like to thank the teachers who lay those foundations.

Introduction

Neil Sang

This book began life as a review of environmental scenario modelling undertaken by the Swedish University of Agricultural Science (SLU) on behalf of the Swedish Environmental Protection Agency (Naturvårdsverket) and the Swedish Agency for Marine and Water Management (Havs och vattenmyndigheten) (Sang & Ode-Sang, 2015). That report focused on several categories of problems which together represent coupled systems with impact on the 16 Environmental Goals set out by the Swedish Government (Prop. 2009/10:155) as its legislative response to domestic and international environmental obligations such as the UN Sustainable Development Goals (United Nations, 2015a). The book extends that core to provide global context, via a set of case studies drawn from around the world and to look beyond simply modelling the problem to how such models can help identify solutions, particularly where these rely on natural processes, i.e. nature-based solutions (NBS).

WORKING MODELS FOR WICKED PROBLEMS

The recent special report from the Intergovernmental Panel on Climate Change (IPCC, 2018) represented a notable shortening of the time frame by which climate change is expected to have serious impacts. Models which had to date tended to focus on a 100-year horizon or longer now predict significant effects by as early as 2050, well within a typical strategic planning remit. The IPCC report also gathered together research on the potential impact of climate change for human and natural systems touching on every aspect of the eco-system services which sustain quality of life for people, such as: the marine environment and fishing resources; freshwater ecology and water resources for drinking and irrigation; impacts on biodiversity, agricultural systems and food security; as well as direct threats to human life from extreme weather – as further emphasised by the Fourth National Climate Assessment from the USA (USGCRP, 2018).

Sea-level rise (SLR) clearly has huge significance for the population it will displace, with many major cities already facing difficult decisions as to what can (or should) be protected and what must be given up to the sea. However, its role as the central message for the impact of climate change has perhaps served to obscure from public discourse the complexity and intractability of the many other issues related to climate change but also other drivers. It is in the combination of pressures, some with contradictory mitigation options, that the real difficulty lies. For example, if the only issue were SLR, then a planned 'retreat' to higher ground over the course of a century might seem like a reasonable solution. However, if the land which this would urbanise is prime agricultural land and food security is also a major concern, then the decision becomes rather harder. To compound this, in addition to climate change, there are other trends to contend with over the same timescale such as population growth (United Nations, 2015b) and urbanisation (CCFLA, 2015). In the past, urban expansion while protecting other land resources might have been met by land reclamation from the sea, yet SLR makes that more expensive and contentious (Nicholls, 1995) and further impacts biodiversity and related ecosystem services (Yu et al., 2017) already under pressure from climate change (Bakker et al., 2016), as does conversion of existing land to agriculture (OECD, 2008; Kanianska, 2016). 'Caught between urban sprawl and the deep blue sea' densification of cities might seem an obvious strategy to accommodate more people. However, the higher risk of extreme temperatures (Mora et al., 2017) means this must be achieved without exacerbating the urban heat island effect (Musco, 2016).

It is to deal with this kind of 'wicked' problem, where the complexity is impossible to intuitively grasp and the trade-offs significant, that planners are increasingly turning to computer models to help. That alone would suggest this book to be apposite reading, but there is actually a far harder planning problem to be found in the gaps between these intersecting scenarios: uncertainty. The scenarios of global drivers contain considerable uncertainty even within the scientific consensus. Furthermore, even if the chances of a particular scenario are in general quite well modelled, the risk of a 10-year, 100-year or 1000-year event are still probabilities; when they may happen is uncertain. So planners are faced with highly contentious problems around how much resources to commit today in order to create resilience to future events. For some of these issues, such as storm damage, a balance can be struck between protective measures such as sea walls and short-term emergency response measures. Other issues, such as planning for migration, are different in that they may present as non-linear but gradual changes in typical annual migration rates or a sudden event such as refugees fleeing a war or natural disaster. Both require a wide variety of facilities such as accommodation, health care, schools and so on, facilities which are likely to need long-term investment. Spatial planning of our landscape and cities takes time, yet it is increasingly clear that the scenarios to plan for are changing more rapidly and have greater uncertainty than in the past, while solutions must operate within a narrowing envelope of options.

Decisions such as what to protect from SLR and what to abandon are highly contentious politically, particularly if it involves asking people already lacking in resources to commit these for (maybe someone else's) possible benefit some years into the future. NBS can help to overcome such issues by offering rapidly realised benefits such as food or income, while also mitigating environmental problems for the future. However, 'win–win' solutions are not always obvious. So if the 'best-laid plans' are not to be simply overtaken by more immediate interests, it is important that models which help decision-makers understand the challenges also help them achieve consensus around a course of action. That is why it was considered so important that this book includes the societal dimension, in terms of how to communicate models, how to model societal responses and how to integrate models into a participatory process through methods such as geodesign

(Steinitz, 2012) to find consensus around plans with sufficient detail to be workable and sustained over time.

The book opens with a chapter sharing the extensive experience of Miller et al. as to how stakeholders ranging from government organisations to ordinary citizens can become part of understanding problems and planning solutions with the help of modelling and visualisation techniques. Chapter 2 (Ge and Polhill) then considers how human behaviour can be included within models of the systems to learn how the whole system can be directed towards some desired outcome. Chapters 3, 4 and 5 review in detail available models for three key biophysical systems – soil (Aitkenhead), freshwater (Dunn) and marine (Akoumianaki and Capet). Chapter 6 picks up several of the same themes as these, but takes a more specifically planning-focused view, looking at issues relating to both fresh- and sea water flooding (Sang). Deak Sjöman and Johansson (Chapter 7) look at similar NBS to Chapter 6 (i.e. green infrastructure), but show how it can be utilised in relation to urban climate management and thus apply a quite different set of models to the same NBS.

By this point, a potentially bewildering range of models has been set before the reader (see Appendix for a list), Chapter 8 (Sang and Aitkenhead) looks at how the overall process may be supported by a spatial data infrastructure as well as the use of data mining as an alternative (potentially more generic) approach to modelling a range of issues.

Chapter 9 (Gottwald, Janssen and Raymond) looks to the future of planning, considering how this knowledge might be brought together to include both modelling and public participation within a geodesign process to solve 'wicked' problems in spatial planning and environmental management. In particular, this chapter exemplifies the value which may be obtained from using simpler models within a participatory setting.

In addressing models relevant to this broad range of subjects, many mainstream modelling methodologies are discussed. However, the reviewers were asked to focus on models which would be likely to be of particular relevance to an applied policy setting across a range of scales. The review should be read in this light; it is not intended to form a comprehensive collation of all models on a given subject, and the emphasis is on practical, rather than experimental, options. Where reviewers have provided recommendations or other evaluations of particular models this is their professional opinion given within this context.

THE SCALE OF THE PROBLEM: UNCERTAINTY, COMPLEXITY AND CONFLICT IN ECOSYSTEM SERVICES

For at least 20 years there has been a growing political recognition of the interdependence between different ecosystems and humanity's dependence on Ecosystem Services (ES), as encoded within the Convention on Biological Diversity (CBD, 1994), Arhus Convention (UNECE, 1998) and the European Landscape Convention (Council of Europe, 2000). This has focused interest on understanding systems at the landscape scale, that being the entire system over an 'area, as perceived by people, whose character is the result of the action and interaction of natural and/or human factors' (Council of Europe, 2000). The Millennium Ecosystem Assessment sought to provide a picture of the current state of ES around the world as to the existing degree of environmental degradation, but also its likely resilience to future scenarios (Peterson et al., 2003; Hassan et al., 2005). In parallel to this 'policy'-level interest, increasing knowledge of the environmental processes in combination with rapidly increasing computer power has allowed systems to be modelled in much greater detail and over much larger scales than was possible only a decade ago. These models may explore large data sets ('data mining') to find subtle relationships or may simulate biophysical processes such as flooding, soil nutrient flow or crop growth to provide information on a detailed scale or to assess the strategic impact of future scenarios (Aitkenhead et al., 2011; Demir & Krajewski, 2013; Negm et al., 2014). It has also been increasingly recognised that people are part of these systems, are important drivers of change, and that solving complex environmental problems may be more effectively achieved by understanding people's motivations and attitudes and influencing public opinion (Peterson et al., 2003).

Figure I.1 provides an illustration of how different components of a system may be addressed by different types of models, with the output of some providing inputs in terms of scenarios on which other models may run. However, even this simple situation shows how complexity quickly accrues at the landscape scale. For example, climate change may be taken as an externality, with current trends providing some basic scenarios, or alternative climate scenarios may be developed based on statistical trends plus expert knowledge encoded into simulations. This choice influences the freshwater and marine systems and both options carry their own potential sources of error. Historical data may not hold true in the future, while expertise may be incorrect; in both cases the levels of rainfall or SLR will also reflect some imprecision. These errors thus propagate to the flood models and the predicted impact of flooding on a range of other risks from food security and electricity supply to soil loss and biodiversity. Thus, models need to be selected which provide effective knowledge about individual systems, but an alternative might be selected in order to minimise error propagation at an integrated landscape scale.

Attention must therefore be paid to the purpose of the model. For example, will anthropogenic effects be encoded and incorporated within the model, where one may face issues of quantifying vague data, or will the model be used to inform stakeholder opinion, where the risk is that those with less expertise may see precision as validity.

Figure I.2 shows a 'meta-model' of the system illustrated in Figure I.1, with a focus on the role of the modelling stages as illustrated by the colour of the links between landscape issues. For example, CO_2 emissions may be a driver of climate change; which emission scenarios to use could be established via participatory methods; the climate model output then acts as one driver of models as to future land use and thus production of food, which acts as a limiter to how large an

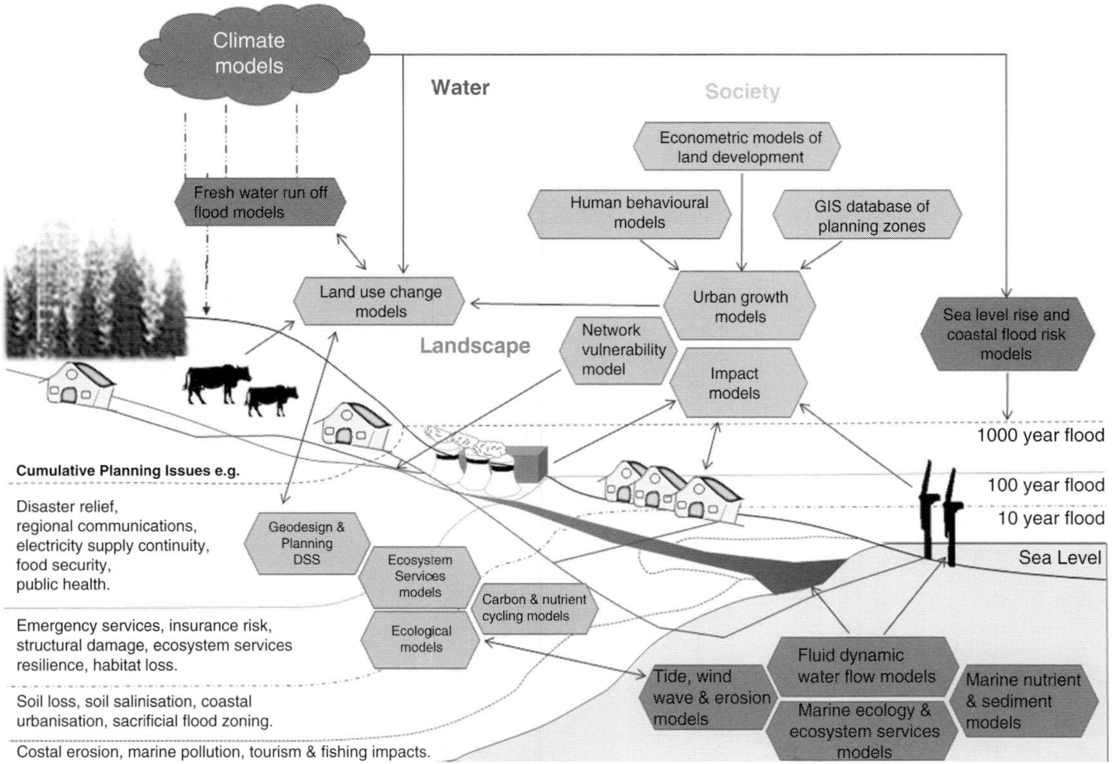

FIGURE I.1 A coupled socio-environmental system. (A black and white version of this figure will appear in some formats. For the colour version, please refer to the plate section.)

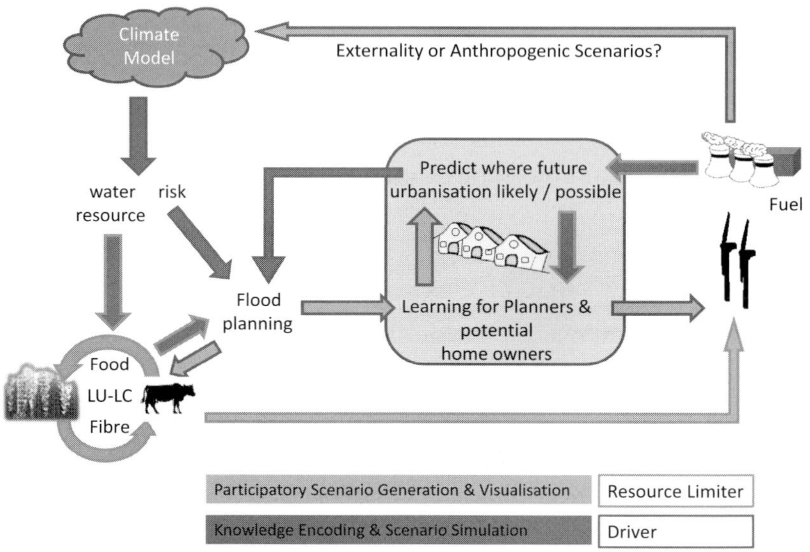

FIGURE I.2 A meta-model of a coupled socio-environmental system. (A black and white version of this figure will appear in some formats. For the colour version, please refer to the plate section.)

urban population can be sustained affecting future energy needs and thus emissions, and so on.

Both of these figures are forms of conceptual model, sitting at different levels of complexity, emphasising different aspects of the same system and serving different ends. The first might serve as a schematic for how proposed models will be integrated and the questions, uncertainties and feedback links they will address. The second may support discussion with policy makers as to what ecosystem services are at stake and how they might be protected. The same conceptual model is unlikely to serve both purposes well. Computer models, while necessarily more complex (in order to be specific in their predictions), nonetheless must also reflect a particular higher-level conceptualisation in order to serve a particular audience or purpose, and so exclude some aspects in order to emphasise others. From an NBS point of view that might, for example, mean focusing on those natural elements of direct relevance to people, but in a complex natural web of functions defining what is especially relevant is difficult. Sometimes that might be achieved by encoding expert knowledge into the model about how a system works, or finding statistical thresholds beyond which a system changes, or by simply asking people what they consider to be most important. Whichever method is used, different and potentially conflicting priorities arise. Modelling can help to make such considerations unambiguous and to understand the implications a given decision may have for the system as a whole.

PRECISION, PARTICIPATION AND PRAGMATISM

The book is parenthesised by chapters focusing on public participation and planning. Chapter 1 explores in depth the various methods by which public participation has been included within the modelling process itself and how modern visualisation technology is making the subject matter more intuitive and engaging. The aim is to generate a scenario are based on discussions between experts and other stakeholders as to what factors should be considered and what outputs shown (for example, the worst or best case).

Knowledge encoding is where information is first gathered, e.g. from statistical databases or via stakeholder consultation, and then its implications distilled and encoded into a modelling method. The method may be simple (e.g. GIS overlay) or complex (e.g. cellular automata), but the underlying principle is to generate an explicit and repeatable model leading to a scenario which is as representative of our knowledge as possible. That is not necessarily the same as objectivity – models may take one or indeed many perspectives on a problem – but it does mean that the evidence base is explicit and open to question. Social Science and increasingly the humanities have become integral parts of the modelling process, be that in providing methods to understand different sectors of public opinion (Peterson et al., 2003; Sang & Birnie, 2008), or building expert knowledge into models (Pricea et al., 2012), or even simulating human and wildlife decision-making through cellular automata or agent-based models (ABMs) (McLanea et al., 2011). Chapter 2 specifically addresses how ABMs represent decision-making, what ABMs show and how they are being used to address environmental management. It is notable that all chapters emphasise the important role stakeholders have to play in improving the accuracy or relevance of the models they review. Combining socio-economic and biophysical models has also become an important potential tool in policy and planning by allowing examples of future scenarios to be developed based on robust evidence, and communicated through intuitive visualisations (Miller & Morrice, 2006). In this way, stakeholders can be shown the potential impact of developments, or potential future problems if we (collectively) fail to adapt our behaviour to use common pool resources sustainably (Ostrom et al., 1994).

The emphasis on the human dimension throughout this book is not at the expense of attention to detail on the modelling of natural phenomena. Chapter 3 is a highly detailed review of soil modelling. One of the most prolific fields of modelling, soil models range from pragmatic 'rules of thumb' about likely typical soil categories to highly sophisticated models for the interaction between specific soil characteristics and physical and biotic forces. This chapter provides key examples of the principal methods plus the likely requirements to implement each and considers the implications of this for their relevance to application in determining real intervention with NBS. Chapter 4 provides a deep analysis of modelling NBS for managing freshwater resources covering the principal advantages and issues for different modelling approaches across a range of different scales for several NBS including provision of safe drinking water, integrated river basin management, stream chemistry and pollution management. Chapter 5 explores marine models and ecosystem services assessment frameworks for enhancing coastal adaptation and ensuring ocean sustainability. Modelling marine ecosystem change and processes faces particular difficulties. In addition, there is a scarcity of comparisons between outcomes from nature-based coastal defences and 'hard' or 'grey' engineering solutions (e.g. dikes and seawalls) for coastal protection, which are predominantly applied. Understanding these challenges can help to better understand the trade-offs between environmental, economic and social components of marine social–ecological systems. To this end, Chapter 5 reviews and evaluates models supporting decision-making on nature-based coastal protection and blue carbon sequestration and storage based on their ease of use, complexity and cost. Chapter 6 deals with both sea water and freshwater in relation to flooding. While many of the dangers flooding presents do relate to topics such as pollution, these are addressed in the previous chapters; here, the emphasis is on modelling the impact of the water itself. This apparently simple problem has, in fact, many dimensions both literally and figuratively, and there are a range of approaches of increasing complexity. Recognising the emphasis of the book on the pragmatic application of models, the capabilities and limits of simpler models are explored before moving on to more complex options. NBS approaches to flood risk reduction, such as Low Impact Drainage and Urban Forestry, often provide multiple other ecosystem services such as micro climate effects. Chapter 7 explores how the local climate can be modelled for urban areas, looking at important nuances within the most common models with significant implications for predicting how effective NBS may be. Given predictions for days exceeding potentially fatal 'wet bulb' temperatures (Mora et al., 2017), understanding how much cooling to expect from NBS approaches is essential, yet quality of life deteriorates well before that critical level. So it is particularly welcome that the chapter brings in the human dimension again through consideration of perceived comfort.

However, understanding what ES our environment provides and the problems to be faced is not the same as knowing how to effect the necessary change. Understanding how to foster greater support for NBS measures, how to 'nudge' human behaviour towards sustainability and how that behaviour may change given the coming stressors, and indeed how to communicate these complex issues to stakeholders, is crucial. In particular, there is a need for approaches which can find not only compromises that allow solutions to be implemented and sustained, but also approaches to build a sense of common purpose and mutual advantage in protecting the ecosystem upon which we depend. In the abstract case this is easily supported, but when broken down to individual decisions which impact essential interests it is much harder to achieve. Chapter 9 explores geodesign not only as a means to improve decision-making with support from models but as an approach which, while not replacing the need for professional mediation, provides a means to foster communication by using maps and models to break down the boundaries of knowledge, experience and perspective between groups of stakeholders.

A MULTI-SCALE APPROACH

Some of the most comprehensive modelling approaches, which build together socio-economic and biophysical models into an integrated system, are simply too hard to implement or understand to be feasibly employed by most of the agencies who might need their guidance. This 'utility gap' is often underpinned by limitations of data availability, the cost of specialist equipment or software and licensing issues. However, the most difficult issue to address can be the lack of the range of skills needed to implement and interpret the results, which is itself a fundamental part of the modelling process. One reason why skills become such a critical issue is the sheer range of modelling methods and scenario contexts to be considered. Knowledge is needed within various technical subjects such as computer science, geo-information science, visualisation or web design and socio-economic disciplines such as stakeholder engagement, governance, sociology, agro-economics and demography, as well as biophysical sciences from meteorology to soil science and ecology to chemistry (to name but a few). These then need to engage in teams with domain expertise such as management of mountainous regions, transport planning or marine planning.

Furthermore, the scale of application is critical both in terms of the data which might be available and the nature of the questions to be asked. National agencies may be most interested in methods which can be computed nationally and provide suitable statistics at that scale. Local government, on the other hand, may be able to provide more detailed data and use more spatially intensive modelling techniques, but they are also more likely to need precise spatial output, perhaps for visualisation for stakeholder engagement as part of the scenario development process (Figure I.3).

So is it feasible to expect each region to maintain its own scenario modelling expertise? Any review of landscape-scale scenario modelling needs to take into account the organisational structure within which models may be implemented and the opportunity for them to have a realistic impact on policy. Models need to be evaluated not only in terms of their ability to accurately describe systems, or predict future scenarios, but also in terms of their feasibility and whether actors in that system such as planners and members of the public can understand and trust the scenarios generated. Given the wide range of contexts in which models discussed here might be used

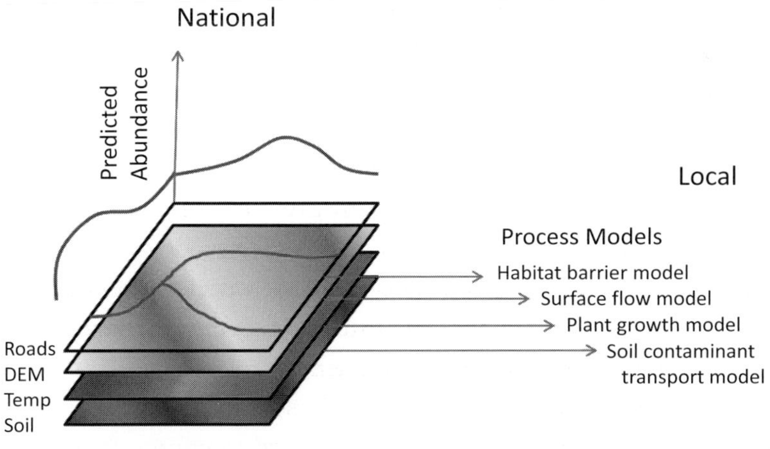

FIGURE I.3 Spatial scale, modelling approach and example applications. DEM, digital elevation model. (A black and white version of this figure will appear in some formats. For the colour version, please refer to the plate section.)

it is impossible to be definitive, but the authors have all tried to provide some sense of how practicable the models discussed are.

While scale of application is a critical decision, it may also become necessary to employ models which extrapolate results from detailed case studies to larger areas. Thus, spatial sampling methodology is a vital part of the overall scenario development process, in particular to ensure that 'spatial minorities' are represented (Sang & Birnie, 2008). The question must therefore extend beyond what models might be feasibly used at present to what spatial data infrastructure [e.g. INSPIRE EC 2007 (EC, 2007)] is needed to enable widespread use of more sophisticated scenario models and how the modelling resources available can be organised to best effect. Chapter 8 looks at the importance of spatial data infrastructures in making modelling activities more financially and logistically feasible. Chapter 8 also considers how so-called 'data mining', 'big data' or 'artificial intelligence' approaches might provide more generic alternatives to some of the models reviewed elsewhere in the book and so help to use expertise more efficiently. It is perhaps interesting to note that data mining itself often draws inspiration from nature as to effective means of problem solving. For example, both genetic algorithms and artificial neural networks draw inspiration from nature's approach to problem solving: test small alterations, see what works and balance this choice between optimising for that which is ideal now and retaining the flexibility to adapt in future. Indeed, that maxim (if such it is) might serve as a general guide to how to approach modelling and implementing NBS.

This iterative, stepwise method towards 'annealing' some solution is in keeping with the underpinning tenets of geodesign (Steinitz, 2012), as exemplified by Chapter 9. Geodesign seeks to bridge the utility gap with a combination of intuitive computer interfaces to scientific models and methods for managing negotiation around complex contended problems. Models deployed within such a process therefore need to provide objective impact assessment sufficient to inform on the subject matter without unnecessarily delaying or superseding the agency of the decision-makers. There is thus a common purpose between the most complex integrated assessment models and the simplest models to be deployed within geodesign processes. They are both models which help the right questions to be asked, rather than models intended to supply definitive answers.

Chapter 10 looks at the relationship between the organisational level of potential applications (from operational to strategic decision-making) and questions of model accuracy, spatio-temporal precision, feasibility and credibility. It takes a multi-level view of the issue with different modelling approaches having characteristics which are particularly relevant to different scales and degrees of abstraction. Which modelling approach is both relevant *and* feasible is dependent on context and model complexity can itself become a barrier to use, so there is an urgent need for a concerted effort towards ensuring modelling knowledge is applied in practice.

PROCEED WITH CAUTION

A model is only as good as the science which underpins it and how well that scientific knowledge is encoded within the model. Furthermore, the best predictions will only be achieved when correctly calibrated, which also entails the operator appreciating the end goal to be not only prediction of a system's response to a given degree of confidence, but providing actionable information for decision-makers.

> Science is perhaps a victim of its own success. In recent decades it has acquired the conceptual and computational tools to move beyond the small number of processes that are truly Newtonian and look at the complex phenomena that make up most of nature – such as climate, earthquakes and landslides, living organisms and ecosystems. Here, feedback effects often make behaviour 'nonlinear' – small influences can have big consequences, so nature's inherent randomness may be unpredictably amplified ... But it is hard to get an intuitive picture of such processes that ... happen on many different time scales, and the degree of predictability differs for each. (Ball, 2014)

Modelling, particularly when combined with maps and other visualisation, can help provide that intuitive picture. However while 'in science being "wrong" is often at least as important as being "right"' (Ball, 2014), in environmental management and planning, confidence in model output is critical. Yet the range of agency decision-makers have to intervene may in fact be relatively crude in relation to the precision of model output, in which case simpler modelling approaches which allow a broader range of scenarios to be considered may (in some cases) be more effective and provide greater confidence as to a course of action than precise but unwieldy simulations on a narrower range of scenarios.

Equally, decision-makers need to recognise that error margins often reflect not only limitations to the model but a real range of possibilities; methods are needed to plan for this uncertainty. In both cases, developing linguistic and conceptual common ground between scientists, technical specialists, planners and citizens is vital if models are to be effectively deployed and potentially serious misunderstandings avoided. However, scientific uncertainty as to the precision of predictions from computer models should not be mistaken for lack of a clear trend and scientific consensus as to the serious implications of even the least worst-case scenarios facing society in terms of environmental management and planning. Nor should uncertainty in the respective knowledge bases or the vagaries of communicating complexities between professions and with other stakeholders be considered sufficient excuse to stay within our disciplinary and professional comfort zones. Indeed, the absence of certainty is precisely why interdisciplinary approaches are needed. Wide though the error margins may sometimes be, the trend is clear: 'change is coming, whether you like it or not' (Thunberg, 2018).

ACKNOWLEDGEMENTS

This introduction and Chapters 1–8 and 10 are built upon work carried out by the Swedish University of Agricultural Science (Alnarp, Sweden) and the James Hutton Institute (Aberdeen, UK) for the Swedish Environmental Protection Agency (Naturvårdsverket) under contract number 802-0328-13 and published in the report by Sang and Ode-Sang (2015).

REFERENCES

Aitkenhead, M. J., Albanito, F., Jones, M. B. & Black, H. I. J. 2011. Development and testing of a process-based soil model (MOSES) for ecosystem services. *European Journal of Soil Science*, 222, 3795–3810.

Bakker, J. P., Baas, A. C. W., Bartholdy, J., Jones, L., Ruessink, G., Temmerman, S., et al. 2016. Environmental impacts – coastal ecosystems. *In*: Quante, M. & Colijn, F. (eds.) *North Sea Region Climate Change Assessment*. Cham: Springer International Publishing.

Ball, P. 2014. 'Caution should be the watchword for scientists trying to predict the future', *Guardian*, Wednesday 12 November 2014.

CBD. 1994. Convention on Biological Diversity. www.cbd.int/convention/articles/default.shtml?a=cbd-00

CCFLA. 2015. *State of City Climate Finance 2015*. New York, NY: Cities Climate Finance Leadership Alliance (CCFLA).

Council of Europe. 2000. European Landscape Convention: Committee of Ministers of the Council of Europe. Florence.

Demir, I. & Krajewski, W. F. 2013. Towards an integrated Flood Information System: centralized data access, analysis, and visualization. *Environmental Modelling & Software*, 50, 77–84.

EC. 2007. Directive 2007/2/EC of the European Parliament and of the Council of 14 March 2007 establishing an Infrastructure for Spatial Information in the European Community (INSPIRE).

Hassan, R., Scholes, R. & Ash, N. (eds.) 2005. *Ecosystems and Human Well-being: Current State and Trends: Findings of the Condition and Trends Working Group*. The Millennium Ecosystem Assessment Series. Washington, DC: Island Press.

IPCC. 2018. Global warming of 1.5 C. *In*: Masson-Delmotte, V., Zhai, P., Pörtner, H-O., Roberts, D., Skea, J., Shukla, P., et al. (eds.). Geneva: Intergovernmental Panel on Climate Change.

Kanianska, R. 2016. Agriculture and its impact on land-use, environment, and ecosystem services. *In*: Almusaed, A. (ed.) *Landscape Ecology – the Influences of Land Use and Anthropogenic Impacts of Landscape Creation*. London: IntechOpen.

McLane, A., Semeniuk, C., McDemid, G. & Marceau, D. 2011. The role of agent-based models in wildlife ecology and management. *Ecological Modelling*, 222, 1544–1556.

Miller, D. & Morrice, J. 2006. *Visualisation Tools for Public Participation in the Management of Landscape Change*. Aberdeen: The Macaulay Land Use Research Institute.

Mora, C., Dousset, B., Caldwell, I. R., Powell, F. E., Geronimo, R. C., Bielecki, C. R., et al. 2017. Global risk of deadly heat. *Nature Climate Change*, 7, 501.

Musco, F. 2016. *Counteracting Urban Heat Island Effects in a Global Climate Change Scenario*. Cham: Springer International Publishing.

Negm, L. M., Youssef, M. A., Skaggs, R. W., Chescheir, G. M. & Jones, J. 2014. DRAINMOD-DSSAT model for simulating hydrology, soil carbon and nitrogen dynamics, and crop growth for drained crop land. *Agricultural Water Management*, 137, 30–45.

Nicholls, R. J. 1995. Coastal megacities and climate change. *GeoJournal*, 37, 369–379.

OECD. 2008. *Environmental Performance of Agriculture in OECD Countries since 1990*. Paris: OECD.

Ostrom, E., Gardner, R. & Walker, J. 1994. *Rules, Games, & Common Pool Resources*. Ann Arbor, MI: The University of Michigan Press.

Peterson, G. D., Cumming, G. S. & Carpenter, S. R. 2003. Scenario planning: a tool for conservation in an uncertain world. *Conservation Biology*, 17, 358–366.

Price, J., Silbernagel, J., Miller, N., Swaty, R., White, M. & Nixon, K. 2012. Eliciting expert knowledge to inform landscape modeling of conservation scenarios. *Ecological Modelling*, 229, 76–87.

PROP. 2009/10:155 Svenska miljömål – för ett effektivare miljöarbete. Stockholm.

Sang, N. & Birnie, R. 2008. Spatial sampling and public opinion in environmental management: a case study of the Ythan catchment. *Land Use Policy*, 25, 30–42.

Sang, N. & Ode-Sang, A., 2015. *A Review on the State of the Art in Scenario Modelling for Environmental Management*. Stockholm: Naturvårdsverket.

Steinitz, C. 2012. *A Framework for Geodesign: Changing Geography by Design*. Redlands, CA: Esri.

Thunberg, G. 2018. *Climate Justice Now*. Poland: COP24. Reported in full by Gül Tüysüz for CNN.

UNECE. 1998. Convention on Access to Information, Public Participation in Decision-making and Access to Justice in Environmental Matters. Århus.

United Nations. 2015a. *Transforming Our World: The 2030 Agenda for Sustainable Development*. New York, NY: UN.

United Nations. 2015b. *World Population Prospects: The 2015 Revision, Key Findings and Advance*. New York, NY: UN.

Yu, S., Cui, B., Gibbons, P., Yan, J., Ma, X., Xie, T., et al. 2017. Towards a biodiversity offsetting approach for coastal land reclamation: coastal management implications. *Biological Conservation*, 214, 35–45.

1 Landscape Modelling and Stakeholder Engagement: Participatory Approaches and Landscape Visualisation

David Miller, Åsa Ode-Sang, Iain Brown, José Muñoz-Rojas, Chen Wang and Gillian Donaldson-Selby

1.1 INTRODUCTION

Landscapes are defined as 'an area, as perceived by people, whose character is the result of the action and interaction of natural and/or human factors' (Council of Europe, 2000). Cultural landscapes are defined by the UNESCO World Heritage Convention (1992) as distinct geographical areas or properties uniquely 'represent[ing] the combined work of nature and of man'. It also describes cultural landscapes as a 'diversity of manifestations of the interaction between humankind and its natural environment', and that the protection of traditional cultural landscapes can contribute to maintaining biological diversity. Indeed, Pilgrim and Pretty (2010) propose that the resilience of ecocultural systems is at its strongest when biological and cultural diversity can be considered as an interdependent whole.

Since the publication of the Millennium Ecosystem Assessment (MEA, 2005), ecosystem services (ES) have been steadily incorporated into international, national and regional policies across numerous sectors and are being embedded into natural resource management and planning. ES are the benefits people obtain from ecosystems that, in the case of regulating, provisioning or cultural services, deliver goods. Goods are 'all use and non-use, material and non-material outputs from ecosystems that have value for people' (UK NEA, 2011), and cultural services are the non-material benefits people obtain from ecosystems through spiritual enrichment, cognitive development, reflection, recreation and aesthetic experiences (MEA, 2005).

Several ES frameworks (conceptual and decision-making) have been developed to incorporate the ecology and economics of ecosystems into natural resource policy, planning and management (De Groot et al., 2002; UK NEA, 2011). Cultural services, such as the artistic, aesthetic or spiritual benefits associated with ecosystems, are included in many such frameworks and typologies currently being used and debated (Daniel et al., 2012). Landscapes are key elements of such services and central to their delivery (Dickinson & Hobbs, 2017).

Pathways of changes in landscapes and the services they provide can be explored through the use of scenarios that represent different storylines of change. These can be quantified to convert the storylines into spatially explicit representations combining multiple drivers such as climate change, policy or socio-economic factors into patterns of land-use change (Brown & Castellazzi, 2014). Such representations can include mechanisms for use in the mitigation and adaptation of drivers such as climate change.

Nature-based solutions (NBS) are being adopted as a core policy response that delivers multiple benefits of mitigation and adaptation of climate change which also has the functions of promoting a green economy and addressing societal challenges of human health and well-being, degradation and loss of natural capital, disaster risk reduction, social cohesion and poverty alleviation (Pauleit et al., 2017).

Representing such scenarios with landscape visualisation tools enables an exploration of alternative futures for different purposes. These include modelling of public preferences with respect to landscapes under different scenarios, dialogue with domain experts on the characteristics of change (e.g. rate, extent, interactions between features, etc.), raising awareness of the prospects of change among stakeholders of differing levels of expertise, and the scope and outputs of implementation of policy interventions, such as NBS.

1.2 LANDSCAPE CONCEPTUAL FRAMEWORK

Tveit et al. (2006) present a framework for the assessment of landscape visual character (the 'VisuLands framework'). The framework links landscape indicators to theories of landscape aesthetics and landscape perception, providing a comprehensive approach to visual landscape assessment. The framework identifies key concepts of landscape aesthetics.

1. Stewardship (sense of order/care, human presence by active landscape management).
2. Coherence (unity of a scene, repeating patterns of colour and texture, correspondence between land use and natural conditions).
3. Disturbance (lack of contextual fit and coherence, constructions and interventions).
4. Historicity (historical continuity and historical richness, different time layers, amount and diversity of cultural elements).
5. Naturalness (closeness of landscape to perceived natural state).
6. Visual scale/openness (landscape rooms/perceptual units).
7. Complexity (diversity, richness of landscape elements and features, interspersion of pattern).
8. Imageability (qualities of a landscape present in totality or through elements; landmarks and special features, natural and cultural, making the landscape create a strong visual image in the observer, making landscapes distinguishable and memorable).
9. Ephemera (changes with season and weather).

The framework was developed further by Ode et al. (2008), identifying a range of currently used indicators for visual landscape assessment. Fry et al. (2009) explored the conceptual common ground between visual landscape character and key ecological aspects, identifying a range of landscape indicators relevant for both visual and cultural functions and ecological function. This framework provides a basis for assessing the potential impacts of drivers of change with respect to landscapes (e.g. Ode & Miller, 2011; Tveit & Ode-Sang, 2014). However, the identification of indicators which relate to cultural services such as sense of place, identity or spiritual qualities of

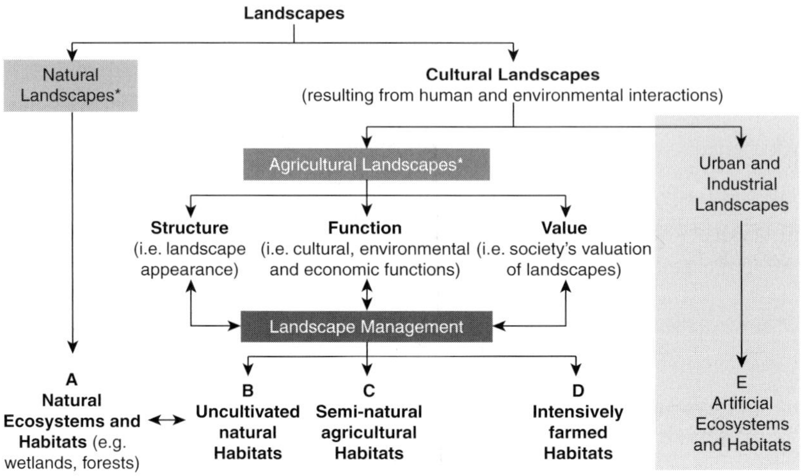

FIGURE 1.1 Defining cultural and natural landscapes: the agricultural context (modified from OECD, 2001).

landscapes is challenging, and thus far no common and meaningful indicator system has been developed.

The OECD (2001) presented an agricultural context for defining landscapes (Figure 1.1). They classify landscapes by reference to the presence of human intervention. Agricultural landscapes are conceptually linked to landscape management through structure, function and value. Ecological indicators within landscape planning have their foundation and theoretical base in landscape ecology. This is related to three fundamental components of landscape: structure, function and change (Forman, 1995). Identifying the main structural elements in the landscape and their relationship with ecological processes is essential for our understanding of how landscape change will affect species and ecological communities and hence ecosystems (Turner et al., 1999). Understanding the relationships between structure and function also enables the prediction of ecological consequences of proposed spatial solution(s). These directly link to the groupings of ecosystems and habitat types (A–E, Figure 1.1). Value has different components, two of which can be distinguished in this framework from Unwin (1975): landscape value, the investigation and measurement of value judgements or preferences in

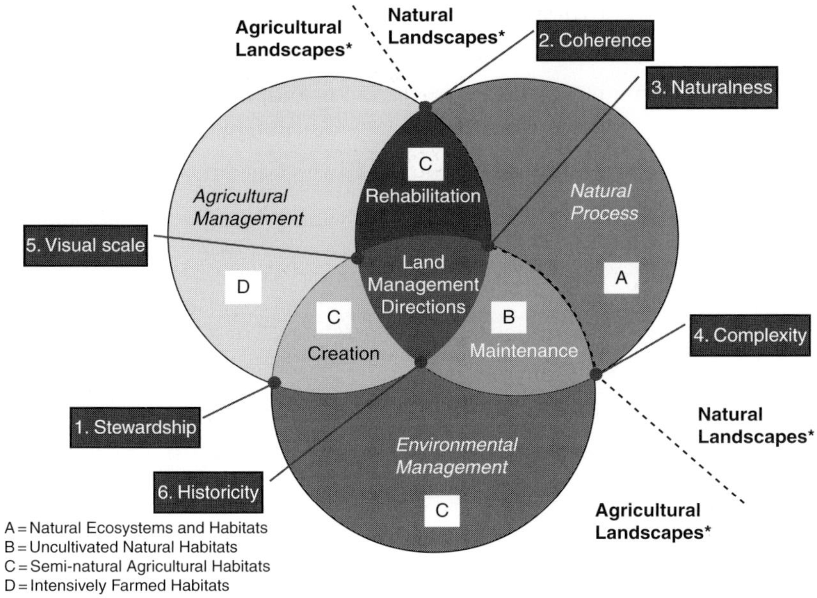

FIGURE 1.2 Conceptual interactions between processes of change in rural areas and selected landscape concepts (modified from Fry et al., 2009).

the visual landscape; and landscape evaluation, an assessment of the quality of the objective visual landscape in terms of individual or societal preferences for different landscape types.

This classification of landscapes provides a basis for associating landscapes and their characteristics with particular types of management practice and pressures for change. The nature of management practices may change through time, with consequences for the functions and aesthetics of landscapes.

The UK Foresight Land Use Project (2010) highlighted the importance of an integrated land systems perspective for understanding the complex relationships between society, land and landscape. Similarly, the 4th SCAR Foresight Exercise of the European Commission (2015) in its study of bioeconomy scenarios identified the need for a territorial approach to land use to assess how to make a multifunctional landscape more sustainable. Figure 1.2 shows a representation of the set of landscape concepts with respect to the OECD classification of landscapes. This combination provides a basis for analysing changes in socio-economic or biophysical changes to be translated into a landscape framework, with which scientific tests relating to landscape impacts can be planned and representations of land uses designed.

1.3 PROSPECTIVE CHANGES IN LAND USE

Driving forces continuously modify the 'state' of a landscape, making them neither stable nor constant, but dynamic, evolving features. Change has always been integral to landscapes (rural and urban) but 'it now seems more intensified in terms of pace and persistence' (Halfacree, 2006). Rural landscapes experience rapid (traumatic) and slow, continuous (but cumulatively large-scale) change (Antrop, 2004). Two trends are discernible, which are policy-induced processes of intensification and extensification (Vos & Klijn, 2000), which in turn directly or indirectly influence the character of the landscape (Miller et al., 2018).

Both of these processes can potentially degrade landscapes and features, as has been documented from many regions (e.g. Slovakia, Pyrenees, Norway; Fjellstad & Dramstad, 1999; Green & Vos, 2001).

Agricultural intensification may lead to disturbance and damage of cultural heritage objects, soil erosion, flooding, pollution and reduced quality of landscape experience. Land abandonment, followed by scrub encroachment and woodland growth, may reduce perception of landscape quality and accessibility. Precisely which processes of landscape change are dominant, and the consequences of these changes, can vary under different geographic and climatic conditions.

Antrop (2005) has stressed the importance of understanding which land uses are changing, how quickly, by how much and how this relates to historical legacies. He recognises that drivers of change have different dynamics and effects over time, and that

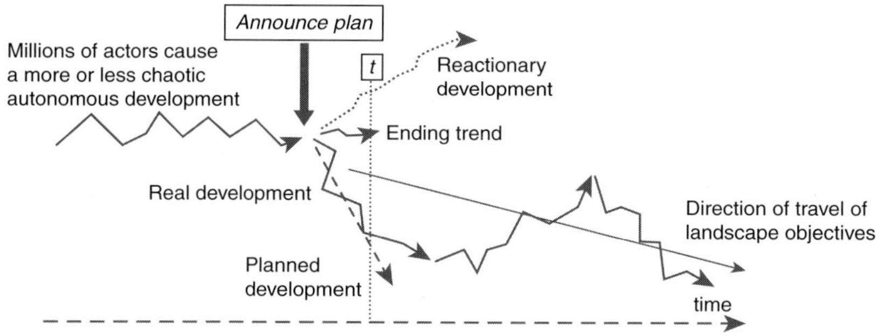

FIGURE 1.3 Autonomous development and process of planning (modified from Antrop, 2005).

actual and planned change may follow different pathways (Figure 1.3).

Landscape is often perceived as the backdrop to events and less often as having its own history and traces of former land use, which is required to understand *landscape as space* (Nord, 2009). Tools which enable greater understanding of the time periods through which landscapes evolve include Landscape Character Assessments (LCA), which is a set of techniques and procedures used to classify, describe and understand the evolution and physical and cultural characteristics of landscape. A complementary classification system is that of the Historic Landscape Characterisation (HLC) methodology used in Scotland, England and Wales (Fairclough & McInnes, 2002; Aldred & Fairclough, 2003), which was developed to provide a comprehensive understanding of the historic environment and establish an overall framework in which discrete heritage assets may be located (Clark et al., 2004).

Methodologically, these two groups of techniques have many things in common and are in line with international initiatives such as the Dobris Assessment (Stanners & Bourdeau, 1995) and the European Landscape Convention (ELC) (Council of Europe, 2000), which advocate protection of natural and cultural heritage at the landscape level. In particular, the ELC states that 'the landscape contributes to the formation of local cultures and that it is a basic component of the European natural and cultural heritage, contributing to human well-being and consolidation of the European identity'. In its National Measures, the ELC obliges signatory states to promote the 'participation of communities and public authorities in decisions affecting the landscape of the region or locality'.

In many cases, landscape changes can significantly reduce biodiversity, cultural value and sense of place (Naveh, 2007; UK NEA, 2011). Knowledge about the direct and indirect impacts of environmental and human influences on landscapes will improve understanding of the roles of landscape components and wider cultural significance, and inform strategies for protection, mitigation of risks and increased landscape resilience to change. The use of scenario development and modelling can help develop such understanding and so inform strategies for the protection and enhancement of cultural landscapes.

Understanding historical changes in landscape can inform the development of policies, strategies and monitoring frameworks for the effective management of cultural landscapes. This also requires consideration of prospective futures. Nassauer (1995) proposed working with 'possible landscapes', bringing multidisciplinary perspectives to bear when considering human behaviour in ecological systems. The use of such multiple perspectives provides one means of developing credible scenarios of alternative futures, drawing on expertise in the biophysical and socio-economic sciences.

1.4 SCENARIO ANALYSIS

1.4.1 Overview

Scenarios are 'plausible descriptions of how the future may develop, based on a coherent and internally consistent set of assumptions about key relationships and driving forces' (Nakicenovic & Swart, 2000).

They are not forecasts, predictions, projections or plans of the future for a given time period (van der Heijden et al., 2002).

Scenario analysis provides one tool for considering the implications of a plan or management decision across a range of future possibilities (Steinitz et al., 2003), and is therefore also a valuable analytical device for spatial planning (Couclelis, 2005), enabling practitioners to engage with the process of developing coherent storylines that are applicable at a range of scales.

The use of scenarios for strategic planning began to be formalised for the analysis of war games post–World War II (van der Heijden, 1966) and has been used in business situations (such as Royal Dutch Shell; Wack, 1985), politics (e.g. Kahane, 1998) and environmental assessments (e.g. Gallopin et al., 1997). A description of their use and evolution is presented in the Scenarios Working Group of the Millennium Ecosystem Assessment (www.unep.org/maweb/en/Scenarios.aspx) and the UNEP GEO-3 Scenarios (Potting & Bakkes, 2004) and a review of scenario development by Rothman (2008).

The development and use of scenarios enables evaluation of different decision choices (in policy or business) and the range of alternative outcomes and associated pathways (e.g. Ringland, 1998). These may be described in terms of destinies, because current state and development pathways set limits on possible futures, and choices, which will influence the differences between potential futures. Ringland (1998) summarises their roles as:

(i) Consequence assessment: assessing the implications of present action, decisions, policies, etc.
(ii) Early warning and guidance: detecting and avoiding problems before they occur.
(iii) Proactive strategy formulation: considering the present implications of possible future events.
(iv) Normative scenarios: envisioning aspects of possible or desired future.

Therefore, scenarios provide a context for exploring the development of policies and plans under alternative futures, both socio-

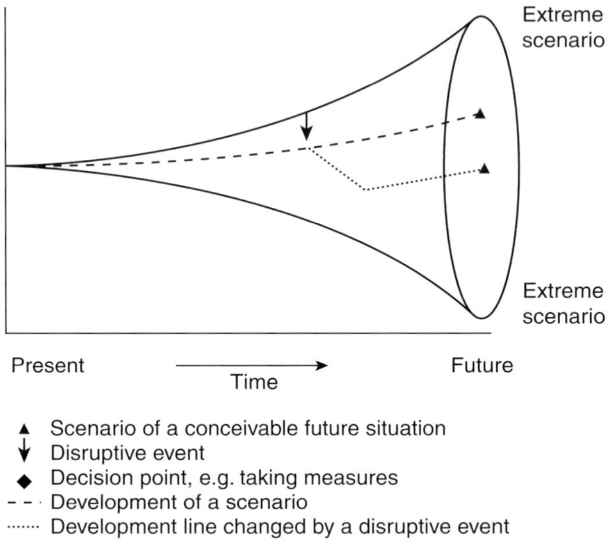

FIGURE 1.4 Conceptual representation of the effect of a disruptive event on a range of possible scenarios (modified from von Reibnitz, 1988).

economic (e.g. economic conditions) and biophysical (e.g. climate change). Consideration of possible but extreme pathways of change enables the testing of the sensitivity of change to disruptive events (e.g. disease outbreak, civil unrest, business failure) and the timing of decision-making events (e.g. political elections, meetings of company Boards, actions of individuals). Von Reibnitz (1988) presents this in Figure 1.4.

Van Notten et al. (2003; Table 1.1) developed a typology of scenarios, listing the characteristics of 14 types and their alignment with identified overall themes of scenario development (project goal, process design, scenario content).

This typology provides a basis for assessing the choice of methodology with respect to the purpose of the task to hand. The discussions of change in Figures 1.3 and 1.4, whether relating to landscape (Antrop, 2005) or conceptually (von Reibnitz, 1988), communicate the same message of recognition of the importance

Table 1.1 *Typology of scenarios (Van Notten et al., 2003)*

Overarching themes		Scenario	Characteristics
A	Project goal: exploration vs. decision support	I	Inclusion of norms: descriptive vs. normative
		II	Vantage point: forecasting vs. backcasting
		III	Subject: issue-based, area-based, institution-based
		IV	Timescale: long-term vs. short-term
		V	Spatial scale: global/supranational vs. national/local
B	Process design: intuitive vs. formal	VI	Data: qualitative vs. quantitative
		VII	Method of data collection: participatory vs. desk research
		VIII	Resources: extensive vs. limited
		IX	Institutional conditions: open vs. constrained
C	Scenario content: complex vs. simple	X	Temporal nature: claim vs. snapshot
		XI	Variables: heterogeneous vs. homogeneous
		XII	Dynamics: peripheral vs. trend
		XIII	Level of deviation: alternative vs. conventional
		XIV	Level of integration: high vs. low

of pathways of change, reflecting key trigger points which then redirect processes, such as those which affect land use and landscape. The nature of such triggers may be ones which are planned and controlled, such as decisions which represent a change in policy or in its implementation (e.g. permission for a development), or unplanned and unexpected, such as a natural disaster or extreme event (e.g. flash flood).

Climate change scenarios suggest an increasing vulnerability of cities to water scarcity, flooding, heatwaves and increase of related costs of infrastructure, hazard management and health systems (Gupta & Gregg, 2012). The EEA (2009) notes that 26 European river basins are already under permanent water stress, while another 43 experience it seasonally. According to projections, the numbers are going to increase by about 30% by 2030. Although rare in nature, 'low-probability high-impact events' (e.g. Alcamo et al., 2006), such as large-scale floods and disease outbreaks, are usefully employed within scenario analysis to highlight the extreme outcomes of events. These 'shock' scenarios can be used to investigate the resilience of existing land systems and the prospective impacts on landscapes. Their impacts can be translated through theoretical effects on the landscape concepts, or based upon empirical evidence.

For example, extreme flood events may modify river channels, removing surface vegetation and damaging built infrastructure, reducing the sense of order and care, and active management, and so reducing levels of stewardship and increasing levels of disturbance. These would lead to negative impressions of landscape. However, such changes could be ephemeral in nature, with repeat flooding adding to the historical imprints on the landscape (e.g. oxbow lakes), evidence contributing to the impression of naturalness and visual complexity of landscape elements (i.e. non-geometric patterns) and effects possibly restricted to a single season. Such effects may contribute to positive impressions of landscapes, based on the theory of ecological models that landscape quality is related to naturalness or ecosystem integrity (Daniel & Vining, 1983).

1.4.2 Scenarios and Landscape Change

Several international, European and national initiatives or studies have developed high-level socio-economic scenarios, some being combined with biophysical aspects (e.g. climate change through emissions factors). Examples include those developed for the IPCC, MEA, EEA, UK Foresight, UK NEA and ESPON. Most of these are spatially explicit, using contextual biophysical and/or socio-economic information of the area in question. The European Commission Standing Committee on Agricultural Research Foresight Exercises regularly conducts foresighting exercises including how Agricultural Knowledge and Innovation Systems (AKIS) may need to evolve to inform policy in the agricultural and food sectors (European Commission, 2015).

European Union projects which have used scenario approaches in regard to land use and landscape change, either exploiting existing frameworks or developing new ones, include ALARM, CLUE-S (Agarwal et al., 2000), PRELUDE (EEA, 2007), Dyna-CLUE (Verburg & Overmars, 2009), IMAGES (Verburg et al., 2010), LN-LCN (Schroter et al., 2004), ITE^{2}M (Waldhardt et al., 2010), PLUREL, VOLANTE (Paterson et al., 2012), MOLAND (Shahumyan et al., 2011), EURURALIS and VisuLands (e.g. Miller & Morrice, 2006). The driving force for the development of these scenarios has often been to understand the impact of policies on landscape functionality in order to support decision-making.

Case Studies 1.1 and 1.2 present two approaches for how scenarios could be integrated with visualisation tools to support the development of NBS in different contexts.

1.5 SOCIO-ECONOMIC DRIVERS OF CHANGE

The Millennium Ecosystem Assessment (MEA) sets out one exploration of alternative futures through the use of scenarios and the IPCC SRES (Nakicenovic & Swart, 2000) provides an overarching framework to contextualise future socio-economic change for scenarios of land use. This framework categorises scenarios based upon two axes that define major uncertainties in future global development: global versus regional governance,

CASE STUDY 1.1 **Community Development of a Green-space Plan**

Participatory techniques were used to identify current uses of a green space in Dundee, UK, with community stakeholders, and to develop insight to links between use and human well-being and how and why people engage with green spaces.

Interactive virtual reality tools were used in discussions with residents and park users to capture information on the different uses of the park; factors which might deter the use, such as lack of facilities, antisocial behaviour, footpath quality; means of physical access; and landscape views (Figure 1.5a).

Audiences prioritised topics (e.g. woodland, access, facilities, transport, lighting, etc.) and selected types of feature to locate in the park. Discussions within the group identified options for park management, layout or content which might increase use or other benefits (e.g. personal health, biodiversity, water quality in the burn, social space for different age groups). Based upon the findings, maps of the potential multiple uses of the green space were developed with the local community, and identification of the implementation of different forms of NBS.

Findings identified the importance of the multiple services provided by green spaces. Common uses of the green space for adults and children were for peace and quiet outdoors, and avoidance of disturbance such as noise, argument, music or television. It is a place for meeting with friends, taking physical exercise, and for fresh air. The green space used for dog walking was most often small in size, the closest to home, and frequently used in the early morning or late evening, at regular times daily, or weekly.

Figure 1.5b shows a framework for targeting investment in resources to improve the park space, including the enhancement of an environment offering benefits of well-being.

CASE STUDY 1.1 **(cont.)**

FIGURE 1.5 (a) Features added by local residents to the 3D model of Finlathen Park, Dundee, UK. (b) Example spatial plan for park and adjacent area derived from engagement events. (Source: Authors, James Hutton Institute.) (A black and white version of this figure will appear in some formats. For the colour version, please refer to the plate section.)

CASE STUDY 1.2 **Climate Change and Landscape: Project Aim – Exploration, Timescale Short**

One threat to landscapes in general and cultural and historical landscapes in particular is that of climate change, which may influence people's perceptions of an area's history and the cultural services it supports (Fyrhi et al., 2009). The impacts of climate change on ecosystems and in the redefinition of biotopes, an effect already observed in geotope change, also affects more forested landscapes and rural communities.

Testing public reactions to alternative futures under climate change has been undertaken in several studies. One, by the University of British Columbia, Canada, explored public perceptions of future landscapes in the rural community of the city of Kimberley. The community has a desire to plan for a range of climate change–related issues and impacts, including rising snowlines, and changing hydrological regimes, forest pest infestations and increasing lengths of the fire season. Thematic layers were used to represent current and future vulnerabilities under climate change, together with scenarios of adaptation to climate change. This approach was used to support communications with local stakeholders of their perspectives of potential future land uses, over a short-term time frame.

Schroth et al. (2015) presents the modelling workflow used in a GIS to combine aerial photographs, development proposals, future snowpack modelling, flood risk, mountain pine beetle susceptibility and fire model and later presented in a virtual globe model. This enabled a dialogue with local stakeholders in which NBS could be considered as approaches to reducing risks and mitigating effects of climate change. During an open day for the community different forms of presentation were used for the visualisation in order to test the effectiveness of engagement (Schroth et al., 2015). The study demonstrated the effectiveness of visualisations of long-term change, and to facilitate understanding and increased awareness of participants at the open house event.

CASE STUDY 1.2 **(cont.)**

FIGURE 1.6 An example of the potential impacts of climate change for the rural community of the city of Kimberley, Canada. From Schroth et al. (2015). (A black and white version of this figure will appear in some formats. For the colour version, please refer to the plate section.)

and market-oriented versus environmental values. Figure 1.7 shows four scenarios of development pathways based upon the UK Climate Impacts Programme (UKCP; Berkhout et al., 2002) version of the IPCC SRES, with specific emphasis on aspects of land-use change (Brown & Castellazzi, 2014).

Brown and Castellazzi (2014) show how scenarios, storylines and policy objectives can be translated into spatially explicit realisations at the level of the land parcel or field, using LandSFACTS software and the Integrated Agriculture and Control System (IACS) data in a stochastic process to create allocations of agricultural and forest land uses that meet set constraints (e.g. proportion of increased woodland across a catchment). Such an approach can be equally used with any spatial unit (e.g. land use or cover polygon, population ward, or water catchment) to explore alternative options for land uses.

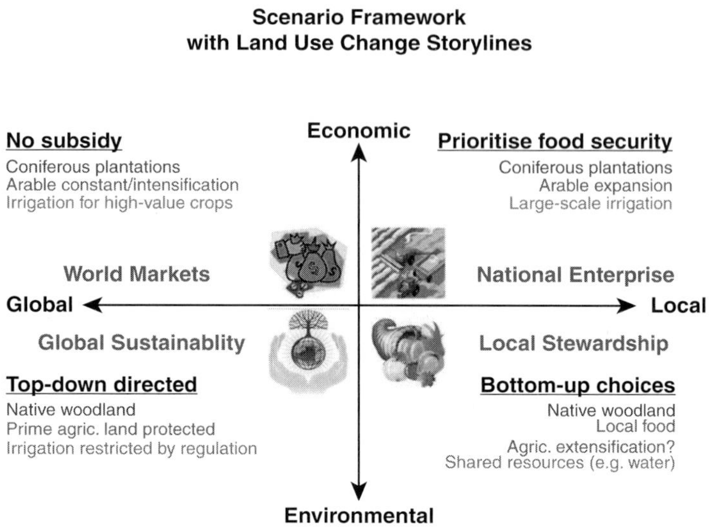

FIGURE 1.7 Scenarios of development pathways, based on the UK National Ecosystem Assessment. (Source: UK NEA, 2011.) (A black and white version of this figure will appear in some formats. For the colour version, please refer to the plate section.)

Figure 1.8 shows the spatial distribution of land cover and use based on three scenarios calculated for 2050: World Markets, National Enterprise and Global Sustainability, at two scales of the river catchment (River Dee, NE Scotland), and the subcatchment (Tarland).

The outputs from spatial rule–based models developed for sectoral strategies, such as woodland expansion, wind energy, urban development, can be used as inputs to developing scenarios in case-study areas, and outputs interpreted with respect to landscape character and special qualities to assess potential impacts on cultural landscapes and their visual representation. Stakeholder-based elaboration of scenarios enables assessments of options for managing or adapting to environmental and socio-economic change under scenario conditions. The spatial models shown in Figure 1.10 were used as the basis for visualisation of changes in the current landscape (2012), as influenced by each of the three scenarios and an additional locally defined scenario (Local Stewardship). The 3D model was then used in

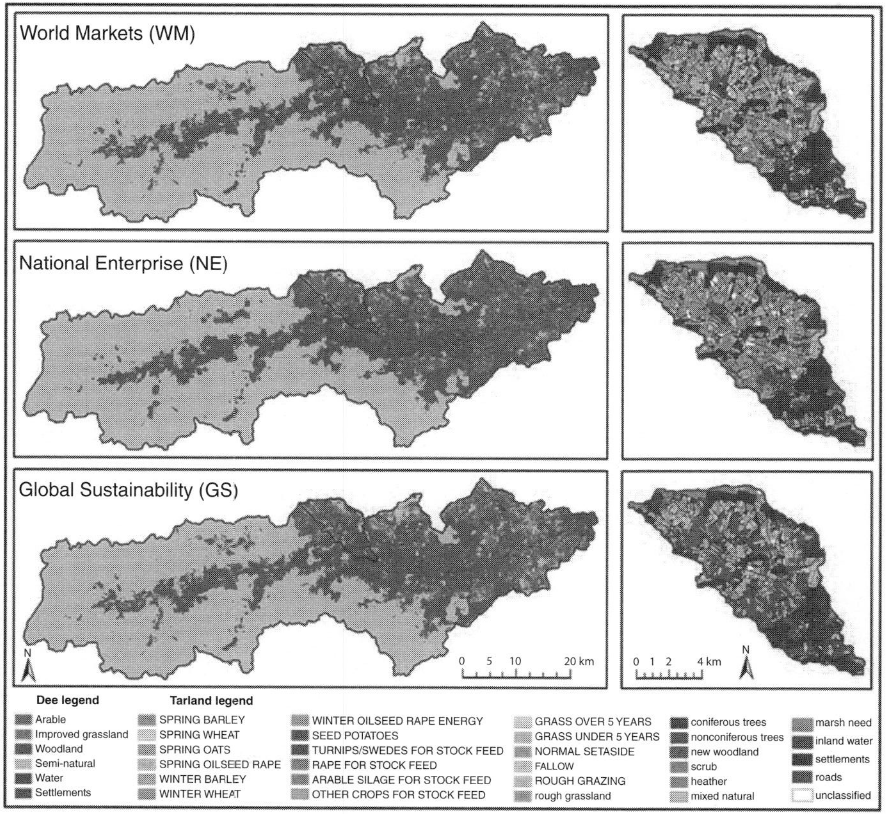

FIGURE 1.8 Spatial representation of scenarios for 2050 for the Dee catchment and Tarland subcatchment, NE Scotland. (Source: Brown & Castellazzi, 2014.) (A black and white version of this figure will appear in some formats. For the colour version, please refer to the plate section.)

FIGURE 1.9 Eliciting public opinions on alternative future land uses in the Virtual Landscape Theatre with audiences from: (a) Birmingham, (b) Ballater, north-east Scotland. (Photographs courtesy of David Riley, James Hutton Institute.)

a mobile virtual reality environment (Virtual Landscape Theatre, www.hutton.ac.uk/learning/exhibits/vlt) (Wang et al., 2016). This theatre was then used in venues in different places in the United Kingdom to elicit audience preferences for the prospective landscapes (Figure 1.9) and to produce audience-prepared Local Stewardship scenarios in which participants selected and located features in the virtual reality model and environment (Ball et al., 2008).

Findings on landscape preference were interpreted with respect to the VisuLands framework of landscape concepts. In summary, audiences were positive towards landscapes with a visible mix of land uses, sound stewardship, elements of perceived naturalness and visual diversity. Of the representations of pre-prepared scenarios, Global Sustainability was preferred. Once developed, the landscape representing the Local Stewardship scenario then ranked highest among local participants, which was influenced by the bottom-up nature of its development.

Comparing between the consultation events, there was commonality between audiences in a desire for amenity woodland in fields adjacent to the village, quality recreation areas in the village, conservation interests and recognition of risks to water quality with increased agricultural activity. Audiences local and non-local to the study area were positive towards small-scale wind turbines associated with farming or communities.

FIGURE 1.10 Overview of land use and landscape features developed from an audience local to the case study area. (Source: Chapter authors, James Hutton Institute, SLU.)

However, significant differences between audiences arose with respect to the siting of medium-sized windfarms on hills in the north of the area. Those unfamiliar with the area (i.e. in Birmingham and some in Edinburgh) argued that renewable energy was a priority and highlighted open hilltops as opportunities for maximising energy return. Those familiar with the area, even if not resident, were conscious of its local significance and previous rejections of proposals for such developments.

Figure 1.10 shows a refined Local Stewardship scenario produced from one of the workshop sessions using the virtual reality environment with audiences local to the case study area. This highlights the recognition of risks to the existing community (e.g. flooding), mitigation measures, increased provision of local energy and amenities and a desire to protect local resources (e.g. water quality and woodlands). The opportunities for interventions within a Local Stewardship scenario included the identification of those offering multiple benefits (e.g. riparian planting) which are consistent with NBS in support of biodiversity, water quality protection and recreational resources.

The same approach to developing a 'Local Stewardship' scenario by audiences which are not local to the site did not identify the importance of mitigation of risk, or to the protection of certain local resources. The non-local audience focused on the provision of new resources (e.g. housing and renewable energy), but in different places in the local landscape.

The differences between the scenarios of Local Stewardship can be interpreted with respect to the recognition and experience of threats to landscapes and resources and attitudes and identification of opportunities. It also raises an overall question of governance in terms of who has the right of decision-making, and therefore the legitimacy of the development of scenarios, both top-down and bottom-up, to different parts of the community. It may lead to distinctions being made between the content of scenarios developed by communities of place and community of interest.

1.6 DISCUSSION

The evolution in use of methods for developing and using scenario tools has contributed to their uptake in relation to assessing consequences of drivers of change at different geographic scales. However, there are certain requirements for the operationalisation of such tools. These include their role in the process of scenario development (e.g. participatory approaches), or assessment of implications (e.g. assessments of landscapes).

The engagement of stakeholders in the development of scenarios of alternative futures, and the associated evolution of landscapes, contributes to the aspirations and requirements of the Aarhus Declaration on access to information and public participation in decision-making (UNECE, 1998). The General Provisions of the Declaration note that governments should take legislative and regulatory steps to 'promote environmental education and environmental

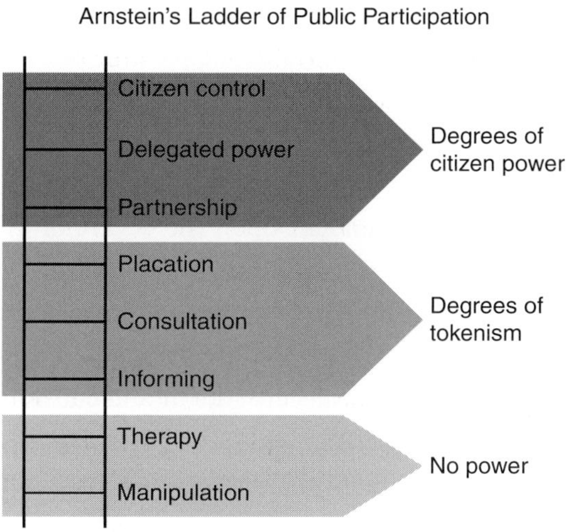

FIGURE 1.11 Arnstein's ladder of participation (developed based on Arnstein, 1969).

awareness among the public, especially on how to obtain access to information, to participate in decision-making and to obtain access to justice in environmental matters'. The importance of engaging the public in environmental issues is included in a Specific Provision of the European Landscape Convention.

The delegation of responsibility for developing these scenarios, and the authority they then carry, can be considered with respect to Arnstein's ladder of participation (Arnstein, 1969; Figure 1.11). This seminal work defined a multi-level participatory classification, comprising eight levels of involvement, clustered under three main categories: non-participation, tokenism and citizen power. Non-participation embraces levels where citizens' involvement is largely at an educational level, meaning they are informed and educated on a subject, but where only one-way communication exists (i.e. Mode 1). Tokenism involves active participation from citizens, but with their opinions not significantly influencing final decisions. Under 'citizen power' there is, to different degrees, direct influence of citizens on the decision-making process.

In circumstances where the governance structure of the engagement confers authority to the process such that the scenarios evolve into plans, the position on Arnstein's ladder is one of the higher 'degrees of citizen power'.

The degree of impact of public participation on decision-making processes is dependent upon the degree of involvement of the public which, in practice, falls into three main levels: (1) *information*, dissemination or directive participation (where information is communicated primarily in one direction to the public); (2) *consultation*, where public opinions are sought and considered in expert or managerial decision-making; and (3) *collaboration*, where representatives of the public are involved actively in developing solutions and directly influencing decisions to a greater or lesser degree (Sheppard, 2005). The involvement of local people through truly collaborative processes of co-planning, co-design and co-management is a key component of the NBS concept through its potential to ensure long-term viability and necessary site adaptation of different solutions. This could be enhanced through the integration of different scenario and impact modelling techniques (Figure 1.12).

In addressing environmental issues with long-term consequences, decisions extend beyond the scientific context and interact with their social and political contexts. Decisions about how to deal with the inherent uncertainties, what risks to take and what contingencies to plan for (Brown, 2018) are informed by science, but ultimately they are an expression of human ethics and preferences and of the socio-political context in which they are made (Kay et al., 1999).

These types of problems are designated by several authors as social decision problems (see, for example, Healy, 1999; Cortner, 2000; Papamichail & Robertson, 2003) and represent situations in which scientists cannot provide any useful input without interacting with the rest of the society, and where it is difficult for the rest of the society to perform sound decision-making without interacting with scientists (Munda, 2004). Authors such as Kay et al. (1999), Mayumi

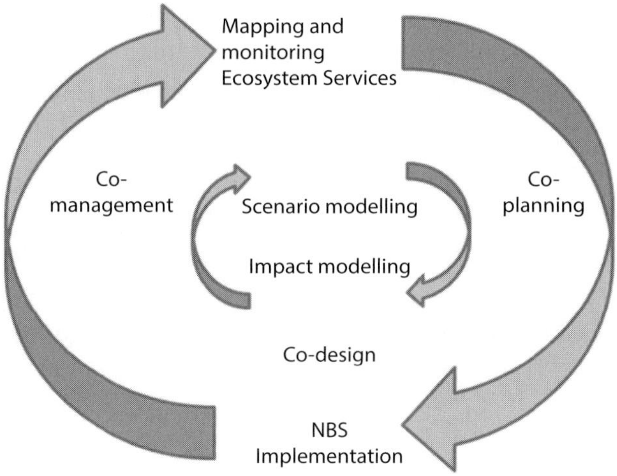

FIGURE 1.12 Integration of different scenario and impact modelling techniques within the co-planning, co-design and co-management process could support the long-term viability and necessary site adaptation of different solutions.

and Giampietro (2006), Luks (1999), Haag and Kaupenjohann (2001), Ravetz (2004) and Funtowicz and Ravetz (1994) argue that public opinion is a crucial aspect in legitimising policy-making for science and technology, requiring effective two-way communication pathways, trust-building, citizen participation and learning processes.

As discussed earlier, scenarios provide means of considering options and assessing a range of alternative outcomes. The development of scenarios and their assessment can be considered with respect to questions of governance and authority. High-level global scenarios can be used to provide an overall context for considering continental, national and large area regional change. Such scenarios are likely to have been developed with expert panels supported by analysis of trends (e.g. MEA). Such high-level scenarios provide a context, or bounds, for the development of those used at regional and local levels. These are most likely to be considered to be 'informing' or 'consultation', particularly in the development of scenarios of 'Local Stewardship' as per the UK NEA.

Landscapes can withstand disturbance and change. However, Ahern (1999) notes that they are vulnerable to irrevocable disturbance, or permanent change. To support discussion and assessment of actions and development pathways within the context of alternative futures there is a requirement for comparisons to be made of the impacts and implications on natural and cultural heritage features, such as water quality, habitats and their connectivity, and landscapes. These should be of a form which can be readily interpreted and meaningful for the task in hand, and designed with the target audience in mind, whether domain expert, policy officer, land manager or member of the public.

Information and Communication Technology (ICT) tools, and visualisation in particular, have been used increasingly as part of information, consultation and collaboration in relation to issues of global significance. For example, the representation of landscapes of the future including 3D imagery (e.g. Dockerty et al., 2006; Donaldson-Selby et al., 2012), sketches or imagery (e.g. Palomo et al., 2011) enable the interpretation of change in relation to landscapes. Visualisation tools have been used for helping communities to plan for adaptation against impacts and effects of climate change as demonstrated by the research team at the Collaborative for Advanced Landscape Planning, at the University of British Columbia, Canada (Sheppard et al., 2013). They have developed the use of virtual and augmented reality and GIS, with tools such as Community Viz (Placeways, 2013), and provide a video game which they describe as empowering lifelong learners to creatively construct their own futures.

Stock et al. (2005) describe the use of visualisation tools linked to GIS to support discussion with land managers with respect to future land uses and indicators of change in landscape features (e.g. water). The system developed is the 'Spatial Information Exploration and Visualisation Environment' (SIEVE). The tool uses a gaming engine and a GIS, with visualisation tools to help communities envisage scenarios of landscape change as described by Chen et al. (2008). The translation of such change into impacts on the character of landscapes is described by Ode et al. (2009) and Ode and Miller (2011).

Sets of indicators can also be used through the application of models to representations of outputs under different scenarios. For example, Waldhart et al. (2010) use the model network ITE^{2}M, which comprises other models such as ATOMIS, SWAT, ProF, GEPARD, ProLand and CHOICE for the provision of indicators. The outputs provided for stakeholders are combinations of numerical summaries, charts and maps. Such outputs enable discussions by stakeholder on trade-offs through multiple scenarios (Palomo et al., 2011).

To help decision makers focus on the key implications, Steinitz et al. (2003) present summaries of the impacts of 10 alternative futures, by percentage change relative to a baseline condition and by percent ranking within the range of futures. Brown and Castellazzi (2014) use assessments by ecosystem service, presenting the results in the form of spider diagrams and maps, both by scenario and by geographic scale.

The defined geographic area of interest needs to be consistent with the nature and content of the scenarios (e.g. relevance of the drivers of change; constraints on change). The work presented in the examples above are both geographically defined by water catchments (Wetter, Germany: Waldhart et al., 2010; Dee, Scotland: Brown & Castellazzi, 2014). These provide discrete geographic units for assessing and comparing the implications on the provision of ecosystem services, between scenarios.

The increasing popularity of citizen science offers the prospect of greater levels of data capture, with online tools providing mechanisms for such data to be geospecific. The uptake of mobile technologies provides new opportunities for the capture and presentation of information about the environment. This includes the representation of landscapes augmented with information on attributes which may not be visible, such as soil erosion risk or pollutant flows.

1.7 FUTURE DEVELOPMENT

The development of tools should take account of the following factors which are of increasing importance.

(1) **Geographic area and scale.** The application of scenarios and the calculation or interpretation of potential impacts on the landscape are generally within a defined spatial unit (e.g. water catchment), with representations using eye-level imagery from set viewpoints. This enables a structured approach to the design of scenarios, the assessment of landscape impacts and analysis which takes account of boundary issues (e.g. including views of landscapes outwith the area defined but visible from within it). However, this is somewhat inflexible.

There may be no clear biophysically or politically defined boundary of an area of interest. Stakeholders may not always restrict the assessment of impacts to within an area, perhaps wishing to include the approaches to an area when considering its setting, potential cumulative impacts of developments, or the experiences of travel to and from an area.

Therefore, when designing a scenario development exercise, and the evaluation of potential impacts on landscapes, greater account should be taken of the availability and usability of data in areas surrounding that of primary interest. This will enable consideration of flows of ecosystem services across what may have been considered to be a boundary, a geographic context for evaluating impacts on landscapes, and flexibility for participants to evaluate impacts.

Similarly, the stakeholder or participant should be able to view the landscapes from locations of their choice, and not restricted to eye-level views. To support this, information associated with spatial data should enable changeable 'levels of detail', to generate a model of the landscape with generalisation and simplification of representation.

(2) **Pathways of change.** Scenarios of alternative futures, with impacts on landscapes, rarely present a sequence of change for each scenario (i.e. a *transient scenario*), such as progressive changes in vegetation cover, or the timing of events (e.g. earlier crop harvests, year on year). When designing NBS to, for example, mitigate or adapt to climate change, the significance of changes in the timing of growth cycles should be considered. This should recognise the changes that could arise within

an NBS as well as in the characteristics of the challenge it is intended to address.

The narratives or storylines of a scenario could include information on the pathways of change. For example, a long-term goal of improved habitat quality could include the thinning or removal of commercial woodland with a short-term adverse impact on the visual landscape, such as increase in visual disturbance, with a longer-term increase in perceived naturalness and reduced incoherence in a landscape view.

Communicating the impacts of a scenario should include information about the interim stages through which a landscape may go, including the adverse impacts. This will aid:

(a) credibility of the exercise and others which may follow;
(b) understanding of the potential complexity of the issues being discussed;
(c) relevance to participants, with steps along each pathway of change over meaningful timescales rather than only over the long term.

This creates challenges for the modelling and representation of landscape change, with likely increases in the temporal resolution of information (e.g. annual rather than decadal or more), indicators which are sensitive to the nature of changes and technical demands of the creation of the spatial representation of scenarios of change and the evaluation of change through time. These data should support the development and evaluation of the narratives of each scenario, with the capability for the stakeholders or participants to query the state of an area at any point in time. In the case of landscapes, such queries should be reported with respect to the landscape concepts to enable explanations of the assessments as landscapes evolve, and used together with quantitative indicators to interpret changes in benefits through time.

The types of tools currently available and envisaged, for scenario development or evaluation, can be made available for use by the communities of interest, practice and place which have a stake in the nature of change in landscapes. The mechanisms of access may be online for use on a desktop computer, or for use in the field via mobile devices or mixed-reality headsets and motion controllers which enable the augmentation of a scene with visual representation of features, and associated graphical or numerical information, and user interaction with the virtual environment.

Such tools would need to support the capture and sharing of information, not just receiving and viewing, and be within an understood system of governance. Therefore, the authority with which participants could contribute (i.e. place on the Arnstein ladder of participation) should be clear to all parties. Such an evolution of the social structures, tools and data would be in line with the aspirations of both the Aarhus Convention and the European Landscape Convention, which underpin many current public policies across Europe and more broadly.

1.8 SUMMARY

- Engaging stakeholders in developing scenarios of alternative futures and landscape change contributes to public policies linked to the Aarhus Declaration on access to information and public participation in decision-making.
- The use of scenarios enables consideration of options and assessing alternative outcomes and futures. However, narratives and storylines should consider the pathways of change, which could include adverse short-term impacts on landscapes before realising longer-term benefits.
- 3D visualisation tools, linked to spatially expressed scenarios and modelling, provide effective means of communicating, but need to be easily interpreted and designed with the target audience in mind, whether domain expert, policy officer, land manager or member of the public.
- The increasing popularity of citizen science has the potential for capturing data on stakeholder's opinions on landscapes and potential impacts of pressures for change, using 3D tools which enable geospecific representations of alternative futures.

ACKNOWLEDGEMENTS

This chapter draws on the findings of the GreenHealth project, funded by Scottish Government Project No. MLU/ECA/UGW/847/08 (www.hutton.ac.uk/research/projects/green-health) and the Scottish Government Strategic Research Programme (2011–2016). Thanks are also due to Jane Morrice, Sue Morris, Paula Horne and David Riley for the work using the Virtual Landscape Theatre and the photographs. Finally, thanks to the participants in the research project events and for their permission to be included in photographs of those events.

REFERENCES

Agarwal, C., Green, G. L., Grove, M., Evans, T. & Schweik, C. 2000. *A Review and Assessment of Land Use Change Models Dynamics of Space, Time and Human Choice*. Bloomington, IN: Indiana University Press.

Ahern, J. 1999. Spatial concepts, planning strategies, and future scenarios: a framework method for integrating landscape ecology and landscape planning. *In*: *Landscape Ecological Analysis*, pp. 175–201. New York, NY: Springer.

Alcamo, J., Van Vuuren, D. & Cramer, W. 2006. Changes in ecosystem services and their drivers across the scenarios. *In*: Carpenter, S. R. (ed.) *Ecosystems and Human Well-being: Findings of the Scenarios Working Group*. Washington, DC: Island Press.

Aldred, O. & Fairclough, G. 2003. *Historic Landscape Characterization: Taking Stock of the Methods – the National HLC Method Review 2002 Carried out by English Heritage for Somerset County Council*. London: English Heritage.

Antrop, M. 2004. Rural–urban conflicts and opportunities. *In*: Jogman, R. H. G. (ed.) *The New Dimensions of the European Landscape*. Dordrecht: Springer.

Antrop, M. 2005. Why landscapes of the past are important for the future. *Landscape and Urban Planning*, 70, 21–34.

Arnstein, S. 1969. A ladder of citizen participation. *Journal of the American Institute of Planners*, 35, 216–224.

Ball, J., Capanni, N. & Watt, S. 2008. Virtual reality for mutual understanding in landscape planning. *International Journal of Social Sciences*, 2(2), 78–88.

Berkhout, F., Hertin, J. & Jordan, A. 2002. Socio-economic futures in climate change impact assessment: using scenarios as 'learning machines'. *Global Environmental Change: Human and Policy Dimensions*, 12, 13.

Brown, I. 2018. Assessing climate change risks to the natural environment to facilitate cross-sectoral adaptation policy. *Philosophical Transactions of the Royal Society A*, 376(2121). https://doi.org/10.1098/rsta.2017.0297

Brown, I. & Castellazzi, M. 2014. Scenario analysis for regional decision-making on sustainable multifunctional land uses. *Regional Environmental Change*, 14, 15.

Clark, J., Darlington, J. & Fairclough, G. 2004. *Using Historic Landscape Characterisation*. London: English Heritage Publications.

Cortner, H. J. 2000. Making science relevant to environmental policy. *Environmental Science & Policy*, 3, 21–30.

Couclelis, H. 2005. 'Where has the future gone?' Rethinking the role of integrated land-use models in spatial planning. *Environment and Planning A*, 37, 1353–1371.

Council of Europe. 2000. European Landscape Convention: Committee of Ministers of the Council of Europe. Florence.

Daniel, T. C., Muhar, A., Arnberger, A., Aznar, O., Boyd, J. W., Chan, K. M. A., et al. 2012. Contributions of cultural services to the ecosystem services agenda. *Proceedings of the National Academy of Sciences of the United States of America*, 109, 8.

Daniel, T. C. & Vining, J. 1983. Methodological issues in the assessment of landscape quality. *In*: Altman, I. & Wohlwill, J. F. (eds.) *Behaviour and the Natural Environment*. New York, NY: Plenum Press.

De Groot, R., Wilson, M. A. & Boumans, R. M. J. 2002. A typology for the classification, description and valuation of ecosystem functions, goods and services. *Ecological Economics*, 41, 16.

Dickinson, D. C. & Hobbs, R.J. 2017. Cultural ecosystem services: characteristics, challenges and lessons for urban green space research. *Ecosystem Services*, 25, 179–194.

Dockerty, T., Lovett, A., Appleton, K., Bone, A. & Sunnenberg, G. 2006. Developing scenarios and visualisations to illustrate potential policy and climatic influences on future agricultural landscapes. *Agriculture, Ecosystems and Environment*, 114, 18.

Donaldson-Selby, G., Wang, C., Miller, D., Horne, P., Castellazzi, M., Brown, I., et al. 2012. Testing public preferences for future land uses and landscape. *In*: *Proceedings of GIS Research UK*, 11–13 April 2012, University of Lancaster.

EEA. 2007. *Land-use Scenarios for Europe: Qualitative and Quantitative Analysis on a European Scale*. Copenhagen: European Environment Agency.

EEA. 2009. *Water Resources across Europe – Confronting Water Scarcity and Drought*. Copenhagen: European Environment Agency.

European Commission. 2015. Sustainable Agriculture, Forestry and Fisheries in the Bioeconomy: A Challenge for Europe. 4th SCAR Foresight Exercise. European Commission. http://ec.europa.eu/research/scar/pdf//ki-01-15-295-enn.pdf #view=fit&pagemode=none

Fairclough, G. & Macinnes, L. 2002. *Understanding Historic Landscape Character, A Paper Exploring the Relationship between Landscape Character Assessment and Historic Landscape Characterisation/Historic Land-use Assessment,*

Topic Paper 5. Scottish Natural Heritage, The Countryside Agency, Historic Scotland and English Heritage.

Fjellstad, W. J. & Dramstad, W. E. 1999. Patterns of changes in two contrasting Norwegian agricultural landscapes. *Landscape and Urban Planning*, 45, 177–191.

Foresight Land Use Futures Project. 2010. Final project report. London: Government Office for Science.

Forman, R. 1995. *Landscape Ecology*. New York, NY: Wiley.

Fry, G., Tveit, M., Ode, A. & Velarde, M. 2009. The ecology of visual landscapes: exploring the conceptual common ground of visual and ecological landscape indicators. *Ecological Indicators*, 9, 933–947.

Funtowicz, S. O. & Ravetz, J. R. 1994. The worth of a songbird: economics as a post-normal science. *Ecological Economics*, 10, 197–207.

Fyrhi, A., Jacobsen, J. & Tommervik, H. 2009. Tourists' landscape perceptions and preferences in a Scandinavian coastal region. *Landscape and Urban Planning*, 91, 10.

Gallopin, G., Hammond, A., Raskin, P. & Swart, R. 1997. *Branch Points: Global Scenarios and Human Choice*. Stockholm: Stockholm Environment Institute.

Green, B. and Vos, W. 2001. *Threatened Landscapes: Conserving Cultural Environments*. London: Spon.

Gupta, R. & Gregg, M. 2012. Climate change adaptations. *In*: Smith, S., Elsinga, M., Mahony, L., Eng, O., Wachter, S. & Lovell, H. (eds.) *International Encyclopaedia of Housing and Home*. Oxford: Elsevier.

Haag, D. & Kaupenjohann, M. 2001. Parameters, prediction, post-normal science and the precautionary principle – a roadmap for modelling decision-making. *Ecological Modelling*, 144, 45–60.

Halfacree, K. 2006. From dropping out to leading on? British counter-cultural back-to-the-land in a changing rurality. *Progress in Human Geography*, 30, 309–336.

Healy, S. 1999. Extended peer communities and the ascendance of post-normal politics. *Futures*, 31, 655–669.

Kahane, A. 1998. Imaging South Africa's future: how scenarios helped discover common ground. *In*: Fahey, L. & Randall, R. (eds.) *Learning from the Future: Competitive Foresight Scenarios*. New York, NY: Wiley & Sons.

Kay, J. J., Regier, H. A., Boyle, M. & Francis, G. 1999. An ecosystem approach for sustainability: addressing the challenge of complexity. *Futures*, 31, 721–742.

Luks, F. 1999. Post-normal science and the rhetoric of inquiry: deconstructing normal science. *Futures*, 31, 705–719.

Mayumi, K. & Giampietro, M. 2006. The epistemological challenge of self-modifying systems: governance and sustainability in the post-normal science era. *Ecological Economics*, 57, 382–399.

MEA. 2005. *Millennium Ecosystem Assessment (MEA): Ecosystems and Human Well-being: Synthesis*. Washington, DC, Island Press.

Miller, D., Kruse, A. & Roth. M. 2018. Adaptive management strategies for renewable energy landscapes. *In*: Roth, M., Eiter, S., Rohner, S., Kruse, A., Schmitz, S., Frantal, B., et al. (eds.) *Renewable Energy and Landscape Quality*, Chapter 5.2, pp. 226–235. Berlin: Jovis.

Miller, D. & Morrice, J. 2006. *Visualisation Tools for Public Participation in the Management of Landscape Change*. Aberdeen: The Macaulay Land Use Research Institute.

Munda, G. 2004. Social multi-criteria evaluation: methodological foundations and operational consequences. *European Journal of Operational Research*, 158, 662–677.

Nakicenovic, N. & Swart, R. 2000. *Emissions Scenarios 2000 – Special Report of the Intergovernmental Panel on Climate Change*. Cambridge: Cambridge University Press.

Nassauer, J. I. 1995. Messy ecosystems, orderly frames. *Landscape Journal*, 14, 161–170.

Naveh, Z. 2007. *Transdisciplinary Challenges in Landscape Ecology and Restoration Ecology: An Anthology*. Dordrecht: Springer.

Nord, J. 2009. Changing landscapes and persistent places: an exploration of the Bjare peninsula. PhD thesis, University of Lund, Sweden.

Ode, Å., Fry, G., Tveit, M. S., Messager, P. & Miller, D. 2009. Indicators of perceived naturalness as drivers of landscape preference. *Journal of Environmental Management*, 90, 375–383.

Ode, Å. & Miller, D. 2011. Analysing the relationship between indicators of landscape complexity and preference. *Environment and Planning B*, 38, 17.

Ode, Å., Tveit, M. & Fry, G. 2008. Capturing landscape visual character using indicators – touching base with landscape aesthetic theory. *Landscape Research*, 33, 89–117.

OECD. 2001. *Environmental Indicators for Agriculture: Methods and Results*. Paris: OECD.

Palomo, I., Martín-López, B., López-Santiago, C. & Montes, C. 2011. Participatory scenario planning for protected areas management under the ecosystem services framework: the Doñana social ecological system in Southwestern Spain. *Ecology and Society*, 16(1), 23.

Papamichail, K. N. & Robertson, I. 2003. Supporting societal decision making: a process perspective. *Journal of Multicriteria Decision Analysis*, 12, 203–212.

Parry, M. L., Fischer, C., Livermore, M., Rosenzweig, C. & Iglesias, A. 1999. Climate change and world food security: a new assessment. *Global Environmental Change*, 9, 17.

Paterson, J., Metzger, M. and Walz, A. 2012. The VOLANTE scenarios: framework, storylines and drivers. EU VOLANTE project, Deliverable 9.1 report.

Pauleit, S., Hansen, R., Lorance Rall, E., Zölch, T., Andersson, E., Catarina Luz, A., et al. 2017. Urban landscapes and green infrastructure. *In*: *Environment and Human Health, Management and Planning*. Oxford Research Encyclopedia of Environmental Science. DOI:10.1093/acrefore/9780199389414.013.23

Pilgrim, S. & Pretty, J. 2010. *Nature and Culture: Rebuilding Lost Connections*. London: Earthscan.

Placeways. 2013. *Community Viz* [Online]. http://placeways.com/communityviz/

Potting, J. & Bakkes, J. (eds.) 2004. *The GEO-3 Scenarios 2002–2032 Quantification and Analysis of Environmental Impacts*. Nairobi: UNEP and Bilthoven: RIVM.

Ravetz, J. 2004. The post-normal science of precaution. *Futures*, 36, 347–357.

Ringland, G. 1998. *Scenario Planning*. Chichester: John Wiley & Sons.

Rothman, D. 2008. A survey of environmental scenarios. *In*: Alcamo, J. (ed.) *Environmental Futures: The Practice of Environmental Scenario Analysis*. Amsterdam: Elsevier.

Schroter, D., Metzger, M., Cramer, W. & Leemans, R. 2004. Vulnerability assessment – analysing the human–environment system in the face of global environmental change. *Environmental Science Section Bulletin*, 2, 7.

Schroth, O., Pond, E., & Sheppard, S. R. 2015. Evaluating presentation formats of local climate change in community planning with regard to process and outcomes. *Landscape and Urban Planning*, 142, 147–158.

Shahumyan, H., White, R., Petrov, L., Williams, B., Convery, S. & Brennan, M. 2011. Urban development scenarios and probability mapping for Greater Dublin Region: the MOLAND model applications. *In*: *International Conference on Computational Science and Its Applications*, pp. 119–134. Berlin: Springer.

Sheppard, S. 2005. Participatory decision support for sustainable forest management: a framework for planning with local communities at the landscape level. *Canadian Journal of Forest Research*, 33, 1515–1526.

Sheppard, S. R. J., Shaw, A., Flanders, D., Burch, S. & Schroth, O. 2013. Bringing climate change science to the landscape level: Canadian experiences in using landscape visualisation within participatory processes for community planning. *In*: Fu, B. & Jones, K. B. (eds.) *Landscape Ecology for Sustainable Environment and Culture*. Dordrecht: Springer Netherlands.

Stanners, D. & Bourdeau, P. 1995. *Europe's Environment: The Dobois Assessment*. Copenhagen: European Environment Agency.

Steinitz, C., Arias, H., Bassett, S., Flaxman, M., Goode, T., Maddock, T., et al. 2003. *Alternative Futures for Changing Landscapes. The Upper San Pedro River Basin in Arizona and Sonora*. Washington, DC: Island Press.

Stock, C. & Bishop, I. 2005. Helping rural communities envision their future. *In*: Bishop, I. & Lange, E. (eds.) *Visualization in Landscape and Environmental Planning: Technology and Applications*, pp.145–151. London: Taylor & Francis.

Turner, R. K., Georgiou, S., Gren, I.-M., Wulff, F., Barrett, S., Söderqvist, T., et al. 1999. Managing nutrient fluxes and pollution in the Baltic: an interdisciplinary simulation study. *Ecological Economics*, 30, 333–352.

Tveit, M. & Ode-Sang, Å. 2014. Landscape assessment in metropolitan areas – developing a visual indicator-based approach. *SPOOL*, 1(1).

Tveit, M., Ode, Å. & Fry, G. 2006. Key visual concepts in a framework for analyzing visual landscape character. *Landscape Research*, 31, 229–255.

UK NEA. 2011. *UK National Ecosystem Assessment. Understanding Nature's Value to Society. Synthesis of the Key Findings*. Cambridge: UNEP-WCMC.

UNECE. 1998. *Convention on Access to Information, Public Participation in Decision-making and Access to Justice in Environmental Matters*. Århus: UNECE.

UNESCO World Heritage Convention. 1992. *Operational Guidelines for the Implementation of the World Heritage Convention*. Paris: UNESCO.

Unwin, K. I. 1975. The relationship of observer and landscape in landscape evaluation. *Transactions of the Institute of British Geographers*, 66, 130–133.

Van Der Heijden, K. 1966. *Scenarios: The Art of Strategic Conversation*. Chichester: John Wiley & Sons.

Van Der Heijden, K., Bradfield, R., Burt, G., Cairns, G. & Wright, G. 2002. *The Sixth Sense: Accelerating Organizational Learning with Scenarios*. Chichester: John Wiley & Sons.

Van Notten, P. W. F., Rotmans, J., Van Asselt, M. B. A. & Rothman, D. 2003. An updated scenario typology. *Futures*, 35, 21.

Verburg, P. & Overmars, K. P. 2009. Combining top-down and bottom-up dynamics in land use modeling: exploring the future of abandoned farmlands in Europe with the Dyna-CLUE model. *Landscape Ecology*, 24, 15.

Verburg, P. H., van Berkel, D. B., van Doorn, A. M., van Eupen, M. & van den Heiligenberg, H. 2010. Trajectories of land use change in Europe: a model-based exploration of rural futures. *Landscape Ecology*, 25, 217–232.

Von Reibnitz, U. H. 1988. *Scenario Techniques*: Hamburg: McGraw Hill.

Vos, W. & Klijn, J. 2000. Trends in European landscape development: prospects for a sustainable future. *In*: Klijn, J. & Vos, W. (eds.) *From Landscape Ecology to Landscape Science*. Wageningen: Kluwer Academic Publishers.

Wack, P. 1985. Scenarios: shooting the rapids. *Harvard Business Review*, November.

Waldhardt, R., Bach, M., Borresch, R., Breuer, L., Diekotter, T., Frede, H.-G., et al. 2010. Evaluating today's landscape multifunctionality and providing an alterbnative future: a normative scenario approach. *Ecology & Society*, 15(3), 30.

Wang, C. Miller, D.R., Brown, I., Jiang, Y. & Castellazzi, M. 2016. Visualisation techniques to support public interpretation of future climate change and land use choices: a case study from N-E Scotland. *International Journal of Digital Earth*, 9, 586–605. http://dx.doi.org/10.1080/17538947.2015.1111949

2 Agent-based Models of Coupled Social and Natural Systems

Jiaqi Ge and Gary Polhill

2.1 INTRODUCTION

Agent-based models are dynamic computer simulations that explicitly represent the interactions of heterogeneous individuals. Interest in such models stems from a number of disciplines. Some economists see agent-based models as enabling them to escape the restrictive assumptions of human rationality needed for tractable mathematical analysis under the classical paradigm, among other reasons (Axtell, 2000). Indeed, the broad affiliation of disciplines interested in a 'complex systems' perspective, in which systems of multiple interacting heterogeneous elements generate 'emergent' structure and order at the aggregate scale, offers a new metaphor for understanding economic systems. Arthur, Durlauf and Lane's (1997) introduction to *The Economy as a Complex Evolving System*, for example, cites various features of real economic systems that are challenging to classical analysis, but entirely natural from a complex systems perspective: e.g. out-of-equilibrium dynamics, dispersed interaction and the lack of a global mediator. Agent-based models are closely aligned conceptually to a complex systems view of the world. Broader interest in agent-based modelling in the social sciences is derived from its perceived potential as a 'third way' between the quantitative and qualitative camps (Moss, 1999). The conceptual chasm between these two is often overemphasised, with most pragmatic social scientists willing to adopt mixed-methods approaches to case studies, but if seen as a formal environment in which to explore the dynamic outcomes of more assumptions than the human mind can reason with logically, agent-based models offer qualitative social scientists new tools to explore their findings, which can potentially be fitted to data gathered and analysed by quantitative social scientists. Geographers are interested in agent-based models because they can be used to represent space explicitly.

Agent-based models (ABMs) are used to study coupled human and natural systems (CHANS) because of their capability to represent spatially embedded complex adaptive systems, and their ability to model interactions within and between the natural and human subsystems. Hare and Deadman (2004) see ABM as a suitable tool for modelling coupled social and environmental systems for several reasons. First, agent-based modelling is capable of spatially explicit representation of the environment, which enables capturing the effects of spatially mediated interactions that would otherwise be ignored despite having a potentially significant effect on the dynamics of the system (Filatova et al., 2013). Second, ABMs can represent the feedback loops within and between human–natural systems (Parker et al., 2008; Filatova et al., 2013). Finally, ABMs allow multiple complex subsystems to co-evolve. In particular, they allow individual agents to react to a dynamic and responsive environment and to learn according to some decision models. Decision models in ABMs are not restricted to assumptions of rationality or bounded rationality as in most standard economics models. Other behavioural models such as rule-based, heuristic or adaptive algorithms can also be used.

2.2 PRACTICAL ISSUES

Boero and Squazzoni (2005) offer one perspective on the spectrum of approaches to agent-based modelling, ranging from abstract, conceptual models to fitted case studies. Agent-based modelling's transition from more stylised models to empirically calibrated models is documented in Janssen and Ostrom's (2006) introduction to a special issue of *Ecology & Society* on the subject.

Except for the purely theoretical papers, most studies included in this review have used empirical evidence to initialise and calibrate their ABMs. Model initialisation and calibration draw on various sources of data: primary data collected by the researcher through interviews, surveys and/or social network analysis, secondary data sets (especially census and cadastral data), as well as information in the form of theories and conclusions drawn from observations in previous research. The data can be qualitative or quantitative as discussed above, and in models of CHANS, ecological/geographic data may complement social, psychological and demographic data. Smajgl et al. (2011) review the various ways empirical models can be and have been used in the agent-based model development cycle. Model calibration using available data and other empirical evidence have become common practice in the development of ABMs, especially when the research goal is to study real-world systems and concrete policy implications. Indeed, the data demands of empirical ABMs can be significant, and rely on the integration of diverse sources (see e.g. Gotts et al., 2014).

Perhaps as a consequence of the data demands, the area of out-of-sample model validation remains largely open. Not many agent-based modellers of coupled human and natural systems use out-of-sample data to validate their models, although some do. The ones that do out-of-sample validation do it in a less rigorous way (e.g. at an aggregate level, or using a small sample size), partly due to data limitations. Adding to the difficulty is that agent-based modelling of CHANS often has a high-dimensional parameter space and a large output set, due to the complexity of the model (as understood by the number of phenomena and entities it represents). ABMs may require different data and techniques to perform model validation than equation-based models, not least because fitting the data well is only part of the story – agent-based modellers are also concerned with the representation or ontology by which the fit has been achieved (Polhill & Gotts, 2009).

Increased computational cost is another issue in the use of agent-based modelling to model CHANS. Including multiple coupled systems in the model has significantly increased the degree of complexity and thus the computational cost of the model. Bithell and Brasington (2009) modelled land-use change in a 4.1-km^2 catchment area with three coupled systems: hydrology, ecology and human. The authors encountered challenges from the significant increase in complexities and non-linearity in the coupling of multiple systems even in a small confined area. They concluded that modelling coupled complex systems is very different from modelling each complex system individually. The degree of complexity increases exponentially by including multiple systems in the model, requiring larger computational capacity to accommodate it.

There is a long tradition of stakeholder participation in the research community in modelling CHANS, using agent-based approaches and otherwise. Voinov and Bousquet (2010) reviewed different types of stakeholder modelling exercises, how they are carried out and any issues with them. Involving local stakeholders in the modelling process can be beneficial in many ways: it will encourage mutual learning and facilitate better decision-making; it will also help avoid potential conflicts between stakeholders and researchers, and among different types of stakeholders, especially when the stakeholders from different groups compete for scarce resources and have conflicting interests. It is especially important if policy recommendations arising from research will eventually be implemented in the local community. Researchers developing ABMs of coupled social and natural systems have included stakeholders in model development and validation process.

Although numbers of research teams have been using participatory model development exercises for some time, they have yet to become a widespread practice in developing agent-based models, partly because such exercises can be resource-intensive, and in any case need a community of stakeholders willing to engage with the process and can see a benefit from doing so. The 'companion modelling' community (referred to as the 'French school' by Moss (2008) because the membership of the community is chiefly from French research establishments) typically undertakes work in situations of conflict over environmental resources among the stakeholders. Bommel et al. (2014) developed visualisation tools such as using

Unified Modelling Language (UML) diagrams to assist stakeholder participation. They did a case study of rangeland management and drought phenomena in Uruguay with local livestock farmers who were heavily involved in the model development process. This participation entailed several participatory workshops where ABMs were presented and explained to local livestock farmers using various visualisation tools, including UML diagrams. The feedback from local farmers was then incorporated in redesigning the model.

2.3 THEORETICAL ISSUES

One of the earliest questions in the agent-based modelling community was, 'What is an agent?' Much of the debate focuses on what are necessary and sufficient conditions for an entity to be considered as an agent, but consideration is also given as to whether an implementation of a model of an agent meets these criteria. The diverse disciplinary backgrounds of the researchers engaged in agent-based modelling means that there is not a consensus. In the Artificial Intelligence/Sociology literature, an agent is often an autonomous entity with rich cognitive models implementing decision-making and behaviour (Arifovic, 1994; Chen & Yeh, 2001); in the Economics literature, an agent is often an individual human or organisation with objectives and goals (Janssen et al., 2000; Zellner et al., 2009). Among geographers and in the GIS literature an agent may simply be a patch of land (Torrens & O'Sullivan, 2001; Torrens & Nara, 2007), particularly where there are links with the cellular automata community. In the Complex Systems/Econophysics literature there tends to be greater interest in generating complex emergent behaviour from simple interacting agents, and behavioural models can be (metaphorically) based on such things as fields of magnetic particles, or more generally, simple heuristic algorithms (Flentge et al., 2001; Farmer et al., 2005).

One way to draw these viewpoints together is to see agency as a narrative concept in much the same way as Dennett treats intentionality in his famous Intentional Stance (Dennett, 1989). Just as Dennett argues that an entity may be seen as intentional if its behaviour can be explained by reasoning about beliefs, desires and intentions ascribed to it by a third party, agency can be seen as something ascribed to an entity by an observer. To some extent, agency can be seen as a narrative concept – i.e. real-world entities are not objectively agents (at least from a modelling perspective), but the model is being used to tell a story, and in the manifestation of that story it may make sense to represent as agents things (such as patches of land) that might not be seen as having agency under traditional conceptualisations of the term.

In CHANS literature, an agent can be an environmental entity such as a patch of land or a social entity such as a household. Agents in the CHANS studies in this review include individuals and households (farmers, households, managers and policy makers), formal and informal social organiaations (juridical regions, irrigation and canal systems, and social networks) as well natural entities (crops, land patches, forests and rivers).

Although the stated goals of ABMs are to model individual decision-making and interactions explicitly, it should not be assumed that methods and algorithms for either are settled or standardised. In the case of decision-making, this issue is derived from the various disciplinary backgrounds of those applying ABMs, discussed earlier. An (2012) categorised decision models used by agent-based models on coupled human and natural systems into nine groups based on the approach and the underpinning theory: (1) microeconomic models, (2) space theory–based models, (3) psychosocial and cognitive models, (4) institution-based models, (5) experience or preference-based decision models, (6) participatory agent–based modelling, (7) empirical or heuristic rules, (8) evolutionary programming, and finally (9) assumption and/or calibration-based rules. We will briefly talk about each decision model in the following paragraph.

Microeconomic models refer to agents making decisions to maximise revenue or profit. Space theory–based models assume agents' decision-making is a function of their distance to the closest physical and social features. Psychosocial and cognitive models implement agents that make decisions based on their beliefs or intentions, aspirations, reputation of other agents and social norms. Institution-based models postulate that agents in the same environment will copy each other. Experience or preference-based decision models are simple, straightforward and often self-evident real-world strategies based on observations or ethnographic histories. Participatory agent–based modelling involves real people directly telling the modeller what they would do under certain conditions. Empirical or heuristic rules are assigned decision rules derived from empirical data or observations without a strong theoretical basis or other guidelines. In evolutionary programming literature, decision rules emerge from processes similar to those in natural selection theory with the ability to copy, cross-breed and mutate. Finally, assumption and/or calibration-based rules are used in places where inadequate data or theory exists such as daily activity routines and social contact structure in public health or epidemiology fields.

One dimension of decision models is the degree to which individual agents optimise. Heuristic decision rules such as rule of thumb, imitation, following and flocking have a low degree of optimisation. Heuristic decision rules are more in line with the early guideline (often based on a more complex systems theory perspective) that decision rules in agent-based models should be simple, the so-called 'keep it simple, stupid' (KISS) principle (Axelrod, 1997). By contrast, individuals with optimisation decision algorithms do have objectives or goals in mind when they are making decisions. They attempt to achieve certain goals or to maximise a certain objective function, under possible constraints of information and mental/computing power available to them. A mixture of heuristics and optimisation rules can also be used. For example, individuals can use heuristics rules until a certain threshold has been reached, after which they switch to optimisation rules. Another dimension of decision models is how consistent they are with major psychological theory. Here, the emphasis is on attempting to represent in the simulation the ways in which real people make decisions. An example is Aamodt and Plaza's (1994) Case-Based

Reasoning algorithm, which is intended as a model of the way in which real-world experts make decisions by looking for similarities between the case in hand and their earlier experiences of similar situations.

Research has shown that different decision models implemented at an individual level will lead to different aggregate results. Jager et al. (2000) compare an artificial ecological–economic system in which agents have to choose between working in a fishery, which acts as a common pool resource, or in a mine; one implementation dominated by *Homo economicus* agents using optimisation rules, the other by *Homo psychologicus* agents using heuristics. They found that in the latter case, the transition from a fishing to a mining society is more complete than in the former case. Moreover, when individuals are heterogeneous in working ability, *Homo economicus* agents on average decrease their time spent working, whereas *Homo psychologicus* agents increase their time spent working. They also showed that macro-level indicators of sustainability are strongly affected by behavioural assumptions at an individual level; for example, fish stocks are depleted less in the *Homo psychologicus* implementation. In related work, Boschetti (2007) compared results when individuals act on selfish, unselfish (social) and collective intelligence goals. He found that when individuals act on collective intelligence, meaning they consider the impact of their behaviour on the community and maximise their profit, each individual and the community as a whole can achieve optimal results altogether.

In Figure 2.1 we summarise the nine decision rules in An (2012) along the two dimensions: degree of optimisation and psychological basis.

Voinov and Shugart (2013) discussed issues associated with coupling social and physical system models together. Lack of consistency and compatibility problems arise when individual models developed under different domains for different purpose with different spatial and temporal scales are coupled as submodels in a larger model – especially where the outputs of one model are fed in to the inputs of another. Using metaphors such as the 'blivet' optical illusion (Figure 2.2), the authors warned that 'integronsters' (statistically valid, but ugly and

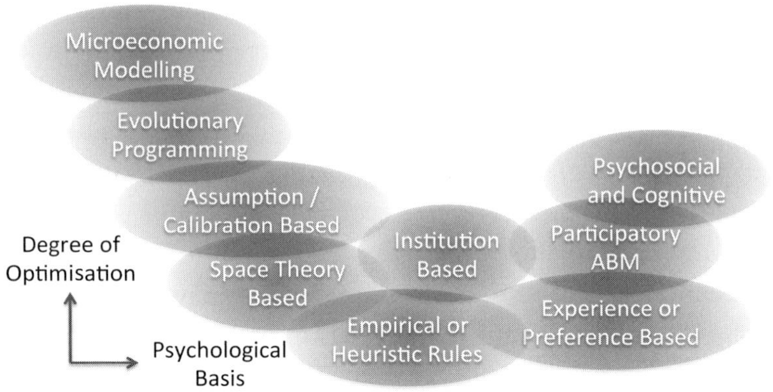

FIGURE 2.1 Rough ordering of various approaches to modelling decision-making in agent-based models with respect to the degree to which they attempt to optimise the outcome and their basis in psychology.

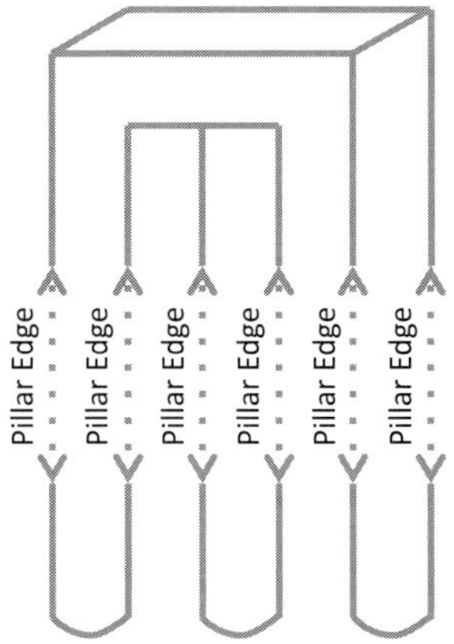

FIGURE 2.2 The 'blivet' optical illusion as a metaphor for issues with connecting submodels with semantically labelled inputs and outputs together. Image taken from Polhill et al. (2012).

useless models) may be produced as a result of connecting submodels together. These problems can be seen in more general terms as arising from issues of semantic heterogeneity. Bellatreche et al. (2006) list common problems that come under the heading of semantic heterogeneity: *naming conflicts* (where the same name is used for different entities, or different names for the same entity), *scaling conflicts* (where concepts are represented at different spatial or temporal scales), *confounding conflicts* (where concepts appear to have the same meaning, but don't) and *representation concepts* (where concepts are represented in different ways). Although typically applied to data integration across multiple heterogeneous databases, integration of models is no less susceptible. Indeed, Polhill and Gotts (2011) have argued that model integration has additional challenges for semantic heterogeneity through *algorithmic conflicts*, where submodels may represent the same subprocess using different algorithms to model the dynamics.

2.4 CASE STUDIES OF APPLICATION

Applications of agent-based modelling have been made in areas of land-use change, urban development and management of natural resources such as farmland, forestry and water resources. There have been a number of recent reviews on the subject. Filatova et al. (2013) reviewed and identified four key challenges agent-based modelling faces when modelling CHANS, including (1) design and parameterising of agent decision models, (2) verification, validation and sensitivity analysis, (3) integration of socio-demographic, ecological, and (4) biophysical models and issue of spatial representation. Heckbert et al. (2010) reviewed contributions of agent-based modelling in ecological economics in areas such as natural resource management and land-use change, urban systems modelling, market dynamics, changes in consumer attitudes, innovation, and diffusion of technology and management practices, commons dilemmas and self-governance, and psychological aspects to human decision-making and behaviour change. Matthews et al. (2007) reviewed applications of agent-based land-use models and discussed the models' usefulness as research tools to provide new insights into complex natural resource systems. Parker et al. (2008) did cross-site comparisons of four important case studies of agent-based land-use models and proposed a general framework for model comparisons and generalisation. Finally, as previously stated, An (2012) reviewed various decision models used in agent-based modelling of CHANS dynamics, and discussed their strengths and weaknesses.

CASE STUDY 2.1 The Amudarya River Basin in Central Asia – Schlüter and Pahl-Wostl (2007)

The Amudarya is a major river in Central Asia (see Figure 2.3). Shared by Afghanistan, Uzbekistan, Turkmenistan and Tajikistan, the irrigation systems in the Amudarya River basin are among the most highly developed and complex in the world. More than 90% of the surface water resources are currently used for irrigation. The massive expansion of irrigated agriculture has caused severe degradation of riverine ecosystems and impacted the economic and health situation of the local human population. Schlüter and Pahl-Wostl (2007) develop an agent-based model of the socio-ecological system in the Amudarya River basin to study the impact of different water management regimes.

The bottom-up modelling approach explicitly addressed the two-way interactions between the human agents represented by their resource allocation decision-making and the environmental system in a river basin including both water resources and aquatic ecosystems.

FIGURE 2.3 Aerial photograph of the Amudarya River basin landscape. (Photo © Maja Schlüter and used with permission.) (A black and white version of this figure will appear in some formats. For the colour version, please refer to the plate section.)

CASE STUDY 2.1 **(cont.)**

The social–ecological system in the delta area is represented by three subsystems: the social system, the irrigation system and the aquatic ecosystem. The available water resources support both the irrigation system and the aquatic ecosystem. The authors compare the impact of centralised and decentralised water management regimes and find that while the centralised regime has access to information of total water flows into the region, and takes allocation decisions that aim to optimise return at the global level using global financial resources, the decentralised regime has information on flows received at a certain location along the river, and takes allocation decisions that aim to increase individual returns using the available individual financial resources.

CASE STUDY 2.2 **Communal Livestock Producers in South Africa**

Rasch et al.'s (2016) study of rangeland grazing coupled an ABM of 162 households in the South African village of Sediba with a biophysical model of grass biomass production and livestock grazing in the 2500-ha rangeland used by the villagers. In the case study area, maintenance of the grazing quality of the rangeland – in particular, avoidance of overgrazing – is achieved through social norms among households rather than formal institutions. The situation in the case study is a case of a social dilemma with respect to a common environmental resource (see Gotts et al., 2003). The coupled model was built with the purpose of exploring whether endogenously evolving social norms can avoid collapse of the rangeland grazing system. The model was based on a survey of 350 households in Sediba and three other villages in the local area (Thaba Nchu). The household agents' decision-making algorithm is boundedly rational, using adaptive heuristics to simulate the agents not having full information or the computational capacity to make fully rational planning decisions. These heuristics were based on evidence gathered from real households during the survey and checked with the field researcher, similarly to the approach taken by

CASE STUDY 2.2 **(cont.)**

FIGURE 2.4 Rangeland landscape in Thaba Nchu area. (Photo © Sebastian Rasch and used with permission.) (A black and white version of this figure will appear in some formats. For the colour version, please refer to the plate section.)

Polhill et al. (2010) when incorporating qualitative evidence into their model. They use a Design of Experiments approach to compute the likelihood of cooperation over a wide range of driving parameter values. Their results show how heuristic norm-guided behaviour constitutes an effective, cognitively cheap means for self-governance of ecosystems.

2.4.1 *National Scale*

Caillault et al. (2013) implemented a simple theoretical model to look at multi-scale incentive networks and how they affect farmer decision and landscape changes. The three incentive scales being modelled are a global 'policy' network promoting specific land uses, an intermediate 'social' network with shared knowledge and collective promotion of land-use practices and a local 'neighbourhood' network where neighbours influence each other's land-use practices. The model is abstract and has not been implemented in a real-world setting.

The fact that we can hardly find any ABMs of CHANS implemented at the national or international scale in a real-world context reveals the difficulty of the task. The level of complexity and data requirements make it extremely challenging for ABMs of CHANS to go beyond regional/local scale. A further issue is computational capacity. As previously stated, as we include multiple systems and interactions between the systems, complexity in the model increases exponentially even considering a small area (Bithell & Brasington, 2009). Current computational capacity may not be able to support models at a national or international scale. The other problem is data availability. Empirical ABMs usually require individual-level data and detailed geographic and ecological data to be calibrated and validated. Such data at a national or international level are hard to acquire. Finally, there is the problem of model accessibility. A model too complex and at too large a scale could become hard to understand and thus less useful. For these reasons, researchers so far have chosen to apply agent-based modelling of CHANS in a regional/local context.

2.4.2 *Regional/Local Scale*

Most ABMs are done at the regional or local scale, perhaps due to limitations on available data and computing capacity as previously stated. An issue with developing ABMs of CHANS at the local or regional scale for specific purposes is that it makes the models hard to generalise. Parker et al. (2008) note that these models are developed to specific research questions as they apply in a particular research site. They also require data sets tailored to the study site in order to be calibrated. As a result, the models cannot be easily applied to other research sites or be generalised to answer higher-level research questions, thus running the risk of being relegated to the status of a scientific curiosity. The authors then proposed that all land change models take certain processes in a general framework. The question of generalisation from one case study to another, however, runs deeper in the social sciences than in the application of modelling. Indeed, to some extent, it is a reflection of the ability of agent-based modelling to bridge the gap between the qualitative and quantitative social sciences that it offers a context in which to discuss the issue. The following are examples of agent-based modelling applied in regional or local CHANS.

Gaube and Remesch (2013) modelled land-use and energy consumption in the urban setting of Vienna. Modelling around 770,000 households living in 59 neighbourhoods within 23 administrative districts in Vienna, the authors analyse the effect of residential location decisions of households on the spatial pattern of energy consumption. The model is carefully calibrated using both demographic data and data on spatial landscape. For example, model initialisation is drawn from a data set of 1651 Vienna households (3402 persons). The categorisation of households is based on an empirical study, which uses data from interviews with 8300 persons in Vienna. Population growth, rental income and landscape features in the simulation are derived from data and empirical study as well.

Valbuena et al. (2010) developed an agent-based model and performed a case study in the eastern part of the Netherlands of size about 600 km^2 with around 2700 agricultural holdings. They used a detailed survey of 333 farmers to build agent typology and to initialise individual farmer characteristics. Five agent types are defined by their likelihood to participate in certain processes such as stop farming, increase/decrease production and diversification.

Another example is that of Smajgl and Bohensky (2013), in which the authors developed an agent-based model to study the effect of poverty-alleviation policies such as fuel subsidies on poverty and deforestation patterns in East Kalimantan, Indonesia. The research features deep involvement and two-way communications with local communities and stakeholders. For example, to derive household typologies for the local households, a survey was carried out by a local research team of around 3000 households. After the survey, a three-day workshop with local experts was held to validate and put into context the survey results, and the process went on for several rounds.

2.5 USE OF AGENT-BASED MODELS IN POLICY-RELEVANT AND DECISION-MAKING SCENARIOS

Agent-based modelling is often used in policy-relevant and decision-making scenarios. It is a strength of agent-based modelling to simulate scenarios of major policy changes, to look at out-of-equilibrium dynamics the policy changes bring about, and the adaptation and evolving of the systems in the long run triggered by policy changes. The following are examples of agent-based modelling of CHANS applied in policy-relevant scenarios.

One of the earliest examples of agent-based modelling being used in a policy-relevant scenario is the work of Lansing and Kremer (1993) on Balinese water temple networks in the context of the Green Revolution programme in Bali, Indonesia. In this case study, rice farming households (*subaks*) in Balinese river basins had to coordinate over irrigation and rice planting synchrony to manage the supply of water and to control pests. Water temples featured in the landscape, and their role in the coordination of rice planting was not immediately apparent because the practices were embedded in a religion with a history of several hundred years. Using a simulation model calibrated with observations and data from field studies, the authors found that the structure of water temple networks could have developed through a process of spontaneous self-organisation, rather than deliberate planning by royal engineers or other planners. Moreover, contrary to international development agencies' assessment that an end to the productive role of water temples was an almost inevitable result of technical progress, the authors found that self-organising temple networks are intrinsically capable of a better job of water management than either individual autonomous *subaks* or centralised hierarchical control.

Becu et al. (2003) modelled a catchment area in northern Thailand to analyse local conflicts over the use of water and other natural resources. In particular, they developed simulation models to analyse local conflict between upstream irrigation management and downstream agricultural viability, which has both biophysical and social origins. Their model features an interface called 'viewpoint', which allows stakeholders to interactively select their chosen behaviour in the model. By showing people these 'viewpoints' explicitly, the stakeholders are able to see choices made by others, and hence to come to understand each other's point of view. They argued that, as multiple rural stakeholders are involved, appropriate solutions should only emerge from negotiation. This is an example of Companion Modelling, a branch of agent-based modelling typically applied in situations of conflict over environmental resources. Companion modelling adopts a radically constructivist perspective in order to engage the stakeholders in the modelling activity. This means the model attempts to match the way the stakeholders *say* the system works rather than necessarily the way scientists say it works. (Although some companion modelling exercises do draw on scientific models.) This is important in allowing the stakeholders to trust the model. In these exercises, the model acts as a tool to facilitate negotiation and mutual understanding; as such, it is an output of the process, and to some extent is secondary to the desired outcome of facilitating peaceful interactions among diverse stakeholders in managing environmental resources.

Happe et al. (2008) describe an agent-based spatial model to simulate the impact of agricultural policy change on different farm structure. They look at the policy impact on two very different farm business types: one characterised by small-scale, family-operated farms, the other by large-scale agribusiness farms. They then carry out a series of policy experiments with different payment structures, such as guaranteed prices and decoupled payments proposed in the 2003 reform of the EU's Common Agricultural Policy. The results show that the two different farm business types respond differently to policy regimes, which should be taken into account when designing policies.

Janssen et al. (2000) built an agent-based model to capture the interactions between grass, shrubs, sheep, pastoralists and the policy environment. In particular, they studied the co-evolution of pastoralists' management styles and governmental policies. They found that each policy has different and often unexpected economic and ecological consequences.

Polhill et al. (2013) studied the relationship between agri-environmental incentive schemes and environmental benefit using a coupled ABM of land-use change and species meta-community model. They tested four kinds of policy and found non-linearity in the relationships between the amount of incentive and environmental benefit resulting from them. The study highlighted the importance of context in determining the success of agri-environmental incentive schemes and suggested that policies have a localised component.

Zellner et al. (2009) looked at the impact of zoning restrictions on land-use patterns, and the emergence of a variety of zoning policy games played between neighbouring jurisdictions. Smajgl et al. (2009) assess impacts of fuel subsidy on poverty and fish catch in central Java, Indonesia.

Cellular automata as models of socio-ecosystems are spatially explicit models in which behaviour is located in cells (discrete spatial regions). Each cell can exist in a defined set of states, which depends on its own state and those of its spatial neighbours. The transition rules, the set of states and the rules defining which cells are neighbours of which other cells are the same for all cells. The long-run (macro) behaviour of cellular automata can sometimes be analysed mathematically. There is an intersection between ABMs and cellular automata models where behaviour is located in spatial cells, and the state of those cells is of significant interest. In cellular ABMs, however, the strict rules of cellular automata are often relaxed – e.g. cells may have different neighbourhoods, or different transition rules. In some cases, agents may interact with a cellular biophysical model; the state of the biophysical cell depending on the behaviour of the spatially embedded agents as well as the state of its neighbouring cells.

Millington et al. (2009) developed a Cellular Automaton (CA) model of forest fire spread. A spatially explicit Landscape Fire-Succession Model (LFSM) was developed to represent Mediterranean

Basin landscapes and human activity. Perry and Millington (2008) reviewed and discussed wildfire models including ABMs such as LFSM. The authors consider the two motivations of wildfire models, prediction and exploration, to be complementary rather than competing. Hu and Sun (2007) developed an ABM of wildfire suppression on a discrete cellular space. They then used the experiment results to demonstrate strategies used by firefighting agents in different fire suppression scenarios. Bousquet et al. (2002) developed an ABM of virtual forests and used role-play games to study forest management with two groups of agents, forest and herdsmen, who have potential conflicts but are subject to the same fire hazards. Walsh et al. (2008) developed a CA model of CHANS in the Northern Ecuadorian Amazon to understand linkage between people and the forestry environment, and the evolving nature of human–environment interactions over time and space in response to exogenous shocks such as changes in policy and regulation.

2.6 SUMMARY

- Agent-based models are dynamic computer simulations that explicitly represent the interactions of heterogeneous individuals. They are typically (but not always) spatially explicit, especially when simulating coupled social and natural systems.
- ABMs are well suited to studying human–environment interactions at the local/regional scale and for exploring policy-relevant questions, with or without participatory involvement of stakeholders.
- It is the strength of agent-based modelling to simulate scenarios of major policy changes, to look at out-of-equilibrium dynamics the policy changes bring about, and the adaptation and evolving of the systems in the long run triggered by policy changes.
- Applications of agent-based modelling in coupled human–natural systems have been made in areas of agricultural land-use change, urban land-use and planning, and natural resource management such as farmland, forestry and water resources.
- In empirical applied contexts, agent-based models can be data-intensive, but they can also be used to explore more conceptual questions. Calibration

and validation of empirical ABMs is still an open research issue, as it is for complex open systems more generally (Oreskes et al., 1994).

NBS are concerned with various aspects of coupled human and natural systems. Because of the interconnected nature of these systems, each environmental objective should not be treated as separate and independent: policy promoting one of the environmental objectives might end up 'unintentionally' affecting other systems as well. Without a holistic approach to coupled human and natural systems, there is a risk of missing important 'water-bed' effects arising from the interactions among different parts of the coupled systems.

The cited examples of ABMs of CHANS cover a wide range of issues in rural and urban land use as well as water management. Systems modelled include water networks, farmland, rangeland, watershed and forestry with consideration to social systems such as irrigation management, urban systems, social and management structure and labour and commodity markets. Various decision rules have been used to replicate human behaviour from simple heuristics to utility maximisation. Agent-based modelling of CHANS therefore provides a promising way to model multiple connected systems and examine the system-wide impact of environmental policies.

Due to the complex and dynamic nature of CHANS, agent-based modelling could be a suitable research tool for policy analysis in CHANS. For example, ABMs can be used to test policy sustainability, to screen out unintended consequences, to test system resilience under extreme circumstances such as a natural disaster and social unrest, and to analyse the comprehensive, long-run impact of a policy. Moreover, due to their flexibility, ABMs can be developed in such a general way that they serve as templates or test beds to be used by different research teams as policy analysis tools. Templates such as AgriPoliS and SimPaSi have already been developed to assess agricultural policies.

However, modelling CHANS (with or without agents) is no easy task. Even a confined area with relatively simple natural and social structures could pose modelling challenges when multiple coupled systems are included. Empirical modelling with agents is data-intensive, and requires effort to integrate the diverse data sources and prepare them for use in the model.

One thing we can learn from the examples is the interconnectedness of ecological and social systems. Policy makers should not only consider the impact of a policy on the system directly affected by the policy, they should also consider the indirect effect of the policy on other related systems. A locally implemented policy can trigger strategic responses from neighbouring areas and lead to unintended consequences in the neighbouring areas and the area itself (Zellner et al., 2009).

Another thing we can learn is the relevance of local context in policy making. The same policy tools may create different and sometimes even have opposite effects on local systems with different institutional and cultural contexts (Happe et al., 2008; Caillault et al., 2013; Polhill et al., 2013). A further complication is that local institutional structures and cultural factors could also adapt to and evolve with policy changes (Janssen et al., 2000). The relevance of local context calls for more local stakeholder involvement both during model development and later during model validation.

Interest in agent-based modelling of coupled human and natural systems has been growing exponentially since the turn of the millennium, at least in terms of crude metrics such as number of publications (Polhill et al., 2011). Although there are unsettled questions pertaining to the representation of human behaviour and interactions in these models, and when applied in empirical contexts, to their calibration and validation, they are useful for exploring the logical consequences of concatenations of assumptions with dynamic implications that are beyond the capacity for human reasoning or tractable mathematical analysis.

ACKNOWLEDGEMENTS

Agent-based modelling work at the James Hutton Institute has been supported by the Scottish Government Environment, Agriculture and

Food Strategic Research Portfolio (2005–2010, 2011–2016, 2016–2021), the European Commission (Grant Agreement Nos. 12186, 225383, 265155, 613420), the Macaulay Development Trust (Fellowship E000677), the Economic and Social Research Council (grant reference RES-149–25-1075) and the Norwegian Research Council (Biosmart, project No. 244608; Newpath, project No. 235670).

REFERENCES

Aamodt, A. & Plaza, E. 1994. Case-based reasoning: foundational issues, methodological variations, and system approaches. *AI Communications*, 7(1), 39–59.

An, L. 2012. Modeling human decisions in coupled human and natural systems: review of agent-based models. *Ecological Modelling*, 229, 25–36.

Arifovic, J. 1994. Genetic algorithm learning and the cobweb model. *Journal of Economic Dynamics and Control*, 18(1), 3–28.

Arthur, W. B., Durlauf, S. N. & Lane, D. A. (eds.) 1997. *Economy as a Complex Evolving System II*. Boca Raton, FL: CRC Press.

Axelrod, R. M. 1997. *The Complexity of Cooperation: Agent-based Models of Competition and Collaboration*. Princeton, NJ: Princeton University Press.

Axtell, R. 2000. Why agents? On the varied motivations for agent computing in the social sciences. Center on Social and Economy Dynamics Working Paper No. 17. www.brookings.edu/research/why-agents-on-the-varied-motivations-for-agent-computing-in-the-social-sciences/

Becu, N., Perez, P., Walker, A., Barreteau, O. & Le Page, C. 2003. Agent based simulation of a small catchment water management in northern Thailand: description of the CATCHSCAPE model. *Ecological Modelling*, 170(2), 319–331.

Bellatreche, L., Dung, N. X., Pierra, G. & Hondjack, D. 2006. Contribution of ontology-based data modeling to automatic integration of electronic catalogues within engineering databases. *Computers in Industry*, 57(8–9), 711–724.

Bithell, M. & Brasington, J. 2009. Coupling agent-based models of subsistence farming with individual-based forest models and dynamic models of water distribution. *Environmental Modelling & Software*, 24(2), 173–190.

Boero, R. & Squazzoni, F. 2005. Does empirical embeddedness matter? Methodological issues on agent-based models for analytical social science. *Journal of Artificial Societies and Social Simulation*, 8(4), 6. http://jasss.soc.surrey.ac.uk/8/4/6.html

Bommel, P., Dieguez, F., Bartaburu, D., Duarte, E., Montes, E., Machín, M. P., et al. 2014. A further step towards participatory modelling: fostering stakeholder involvement in designing models by using executable UML. *Journal of Artificial Societies and Social Simulation*, 17(1), 6. http://jasss.soc.surrey.ac.uk/17/1/6.html

Boschetti, F. 2007. Improving resource exploitation via collective intelligence by assessing agents' impact on the community outcome. *Ecological Economics*, 63(2), 553–562.

Bousquet, F., Barreteau, O., d'Aquino, P., Etienne, M., Boissau, S., Aubert, S., et al. 2002. Multi-agent systems and role games: collective learning processes for ecosystem management. *In*: Janssen, M. A. (ed.) *Complexity and Ecosystem Management. The Theory and Practice of Multi-agent Systems*, pp. 248–286. Cheltenham, UK: Edward Elgar.

Caillault, S., Miahle, F., Vannier, C., Delmotte, S., Kedowide, C., Amblard, F., et al. 2013. Influence of incentive networks on landscape changes: a simple agent-based simulation approach. *Environmental Modelling & Software*, 45, 64–73.

Chen, S.-H. & Yeh, C.-H. 2001. Evolving traders and the business school with genetic programming: a new architecture of the agent-based artificial stock market. *Journal of Economic Dynamics and Control*, 25(3), 363–393.

Dennett, D. C. 1989. *The Intentional Stance*. Cambridge, MA: MIT Press.

Farmer, J. D., Patelli, P. & Zovko, I. I. 2005. The predictive power of zero intelligence in financial markets. *Proceedings of the National Academy of Sciences of the United States of America*, 102(6), 2254–2259.

Filatova, T., Verburg, P. H., Parker, D. C. & Stannard, C. A. 2013. Spatial agent-based models for socio-ecological systems: challenges and prospects. *Environmental Modelling & Software*, 45: 1–7.

Flentge, F., Polani, D. & Uthmann, T. 2001. Modelling the emergence of possession norms using memes. *Journal of Artificial Societies and Social Simulation*, 4(4), 3. http://jasss.soc.surrey.ac.uk/4/4/3.html

Gaube, V. & Remesch, A. 2013. Impact of urban planning on household's residential decisions: an agent-based simulation model for Vienna. *Environmental Modelling & Software*, 45, 92–103.

Gotts, N. M., Polhill, G., Craig, T. & Galan-Diaz, C. 2014. Combining diverse data sources for CEDSS, an agent-based model of domestic energy demand. *Structure and Dynamics: eJournal of Anthropological and Related Sciences*, 7(1). http://eprints.gla.ac.uk/143757/1/143757.pdf

Gotts, N. M., Polhill, J. G. & Law, A. N. R. 2003. Agent-based simulation in the study of social dilemmas. *Artificial Intelligence Review*, 19, 3–92.

Happe, K., Bahmann, A., Kellermann, K. & Sahrbacher, C. 2008. Does structure matter? The impact of switching the agricultural policy regime on farm structures. *Journal of Economic Behavior & Organization*, 67(2), 431–444.

Hare, M. & Deadman, P. 2004. Further towards a taxonomy of agent-based simulation models in environmental management. *Mathematics and Computers in Simulation*, 64(1), 25–40.

Heckbert, S., Baynes, T. & Reeson, A. 2010. Agent-based modeling in ecological economics. *Annals of the New York Academy of Sciences*, 1185(1), 39–53.

Hu, X. & Sun,Y. 2007. Agent-based modeling and simulation of wildland fire suppression. Presented at the 2007 Winter Simulation Conference, IEEE. https://ieeexplore.ieee.org/document/4419732

Jager, W., Janssen, M. A., De Vries, H. J. M., De Greef, J. & Vlek, C. A. J. 2000. Behaviour in commons dilemmas: *Homo economicus* and *Homo psychologicus* in an ecological–economic model. *Ecological Economics*, 35(3), 357–379.

Janssen, M. A. & Ostrom, E. 2006. Empirically based, agent-based models. *Ecology and Society*, 11(2), 37.

Janssen, M. A., Walker, B. A., Langridge, J. & Abel, N. 2000. An adaptive agent model for analysing co-evolution of management and policies in a complex rangeland system. *Ecological Modelling*, 131(2), 249–268.

Lansing, J. S. & Kremer, J. N. 1993. Emergent properties of Balinese water temple networks: coadaptation on a rugged fitness landscape. *American Anthropologist*, 95(1), 97–114.

Matthews, R. B., Gilbert, N. G., Roach, A., Polhill, J. G. & Gotts, N. M. 2007. Agent-based land-use models: a review of applications. *Landscape Ecology*, 22(10), 1447–1459.

Millington, J. D. A., Wainwright, J., Perry, G. L. W., Romero-Calcerrada, R. & Malamud, B. D. 2009. Modelling Mediterranean landscape succession-disturbance dynamics: a landscape fire-succession model. *Environmental Modelling & Software*, 24(10), 1196–1208.

Moss, S. 1999. Relevance, realism and rigour: a third way for social and economic research. CPM Report No. 99–56. http://cfpm.org/cpmrep56.html

Moss, S. 2008. Alternative approaches to the empirical validation of agent-based models. *Journal of Artificial Societies and Social Simulation*, 11(1), 5. http://jasss.soc.surrey.ac.uk/11/1/5.html

Oreskes, N., Shrader-Frechette, K. & Belitz, K. 1994. Verification, validation, and confirmation of numerical models in the Earth Sciences. *Science*, 263(5147), 641–646.

Parker, D. C., Entwisle, B., Rindfuss, R. R., Vanwey, L. K., Manson, S. M., Moran, E., et al. 2008. Case studies, cross-site comparisons, and the challenge of generalization: comparing agent-based models of land-use change in frontier regions. *Journal of Land Use Science*, 3(1), 41–72.

Perry, G. L. W. & Millington, J. D. A. 2008. Spatial modelling of succession-disturbance dynamics in forest ecosystems: concepts and examples. *Perspectives in Plant Ecology, Evolution and Systematics*, 9(3–4), 191–210.

Polhill, G. & Gotts, N. 2011. Semantic model integration: an application for OWL. Presented at the European Social Simulation Association Conference (ESSA 2011), Montpellier, France.

Polhill, G., Gotts, N., Sánchez-Maroño, N., Pignotti, E., Fontenia-Romero, Ó., Rodríguez-García, M., et al. 2012. An ontology-based design for modelling case studies of everyday pro-environmental behaviour in the workplace. *In*: Seppelt, R., Voinov, A. A., Lange, S. & Bankamp, D. (eds.) *International Environmental Modelling and Software Society (iEMSS) 2012 International Congress on Environmental Modelling and Software*. Leipzig: IEMSS.

Polhill, J. G., Gimona, A. & Aspinall, R. J. 2011. Agent-based modelling of land use effects on ecosystem processes and services. *Journal of Land Use Science*, 6(2–3), 75–81.

Polhill, J. G., Gimona, A. & Gotts, N. M. 2013. Nonlinearities in biodiversity incentive schemes: a study using an integrated agent-based and metacommunity model. *Environmental Modelling & Software*, 45, 74–91.

Polhill, J. G. & Gotts, N. M. 2009. Ontologies for transparent integrated human-natural system modelling. *Landscape Ecology*, 24(9), 1255–1267.

Polhill, J. G., Sutherland, L.-A. & Gotts, N. M. 2010. Using qualitative evidence to enhance an agent-based modelling system for studying land use change. *Journal of Artificial Societies and Social Simulation*, 13(2), 10. http://jasss.soc.surrey.ac.uk/13/2/10.html

Rasch, S., Heckelei, T., Oomen, R. & Naumann, C. 2016. Cooperation and collapse in a communal livestockproduction SES model – a case from South Africa. *Environmental Modelling & Software*, 75, 402–413.

Schlüter, M. & Pahl-Wostl, C. 2007. Mechanisms of resilience in common-pool resource management systems: an agent-based model of water use in a river basin. *Ecology and Society*, 12(2), 4. www.ecologyandsociety.org/vol12/iss2/art4/

Smajgl, A. & Bohensky, E. 2013. Behaviour and space in agent-based modelling: poverty patterns in East Kalimantan, Indonesia. *Environmental Modelling & Software*, 45, 8–14.

Smajgl, A., Brown, D. G., Valbuena, D. & Huigen, M. G. A. 2011. Empirical characterisation of agent behaviours in socio-ecological systems. *Environmental Modelling & Software*, 26(7), 837–844.

Smajgl, A., Carlin, G., Pambudhi, F., Bohensky, E., House, A., Butler, J., et al. 2009. Assessing impacts of fuel subsidy decisions on poverty and fish catch in Central Java, Indonesia: an agent-based analysis. Analysing Pathways to Sustainability in Indonesia Discussion Paper. CSIRO Sustainable Ecosystems, Townsville. https://publications.csiro.au/rpr/pub?list=BRO&pid=changeme:525

Torrens, P. M. & Nara, A. 2007. Modeling gentrification dynamics: a hybrid approach. *Computers, Environment and Urban Systems*, 31(3), 337–361.

Torrens, P. M. & O'Sullivan, D. 2001. Cellular automata and urban simulation: where do we go from here? *Environment and Planning B: Planning and Design*, 28(2), 163–168.

Valbuena, D., Verburg, P. H., Bregt, A. K. & Ligtenberg, A. 2010. An agent-based approach to model land-use change at a regional scale. *Landscape Ecology*, 25(2), 185–199.

Voinov, A. & Bousquet, F. 2010. Modelling with stakeholders. *Environmental Modelling & Software*, 25(11), 1268–1281.

Voinov, A. & Shugart, H. H. 2013. 'Integronsters', integral and integrated modeling. *Environmental Modelling & Software*, 39, 149–158.

Walsh, S. J., Messina, J. P., Mena, C. F., Malanson, G. P. & Page, P. H. 2008. Complexity theory, spatial simulation models, and land use dynamics in the Northern Ecuadorian Amazon. *Geoforum*, 39(2), 867–878.

Zellner, M. L., Page, S. E., Rand, W., Brown, D. G., Robinson, D. T., Nassauer, J., et al. 2009. The emergence of zoning policy games in exurban jurisdictions: informing collective action theory. *Land Use Policy*, 26(2), 356–367.

3 Modelling Nature-based Solutions from Soil Ecosystem Services

Matthew Aitkenhead

3.1 INTRODUCTION

In this chapter, a review of soil models is carried out. The number of models within the literature is too high to cover every example in depth, so a selection has been made based on age, stage of development and specificity to soil modelling. In addition, several existing soil model reviews have been investigated, to determine the depth of information already available. The best examples for further reading that have been found are those by Molina and Smith (1998), Manzoni and Porporato (2009), Kinnell (2010) and Sheng (2011). Models have also been evaluated for their potential in exploring nature-based solutions, and several recent studies have been highlighted in this area that are relevant for soil modelling.

In addition to the large number of soil model reviews that have been published in the literature, there are several internet fora that are relevant. The one considered most prominent and likely to provide useful information is at https://soil-modeling.org.[1]

3.2 METHODS

A total of over 200 soil-related models were identified from the literature. A brief examination of each was carried out to determine whether it should be included in this report. Criteria for selection included the following.

1 For further information see: https://wiki.csiro.au/display/SoilModelling/Home; http://www.soilerosion.net/; http://opensees.berkeley.edu/community/viewforum.php?f=8; http://eusoils.jrc.ec.europa.eu/.

- Age: how old was the model, and therefore how likely was it to have been made redundant by advances since its development? Some models have been incorporated into other, more sophisticated ones over time and so their effectiveness is reduced, while others may have been developed over 20 years ago and are still relevant. Whether a model was discarded based on age was not simply dependent on a threshold of years, but also on relevance within the subject area.
- Development: some models have been described in the literature, but either not formally coded or if coded have seen little use since beyond a preliminary implementation. As such, it would be necessary either to develop their computer code from a sole, often opaque literature source or to track down the original authors and ask if their code was still available. If the effort required to have an executable soil model was considered greater than the benefit of having it, then the model was not included at this stage.
- Specificity: several models were discovered that included a soil component but that had a much stronger leaning towards ecological, hydrological or atmospheric processes. In cases where the soil component was sufficiently sophisticated to be considered as a model in its own right, then it was included at this stage. If the soil component of the model was overly simplistic or considered unlikely to add any new information, then it was discarded.

A total of 51 soil or soil-related models were retained. A structure by which to evaluate them was required, and it was decided to use one similar to that of Manzoni and Porporato (2009). The focus of the selected models was those including carbon and nitrogen cycling. This was principally due to the central importance of these cycles in environmental sustainability, but it also allowed a better comparison to be made between the models. These criteria have been added to with the inclusion of additional model classes, and each soil model is now described in a single table with common characteristics as described in Tables 3.1 and 3.2. A general summary of the strengths and weaknesses of soil modelling for several NBS is given in Table 3.3.

3.3 MODELS FOR SOIL-DEPENDENT NBS

Keesstra et al. (2018) demonstrated a series of case studies involving different NBS strategies in Spain, Slovenia, Iceland, Ethiopia and

Table 3.1 *Model classification code legend*

Model class	
M	Soil microbiology, soil aggregate and rhizosphere models
L	Litter decomposition models
S	Soil models with no dynamic vegetation components
E	Coupled soil–plant dynamic models
G	Coupled soil–plant–atmosphere models for global application
H	Soil hydrology/catchment dynamics models
I	Model integration frameworks
Spatial scale	
1	$<10^2$ m
2	10^2–10 m
3	10–10^2 m
4	10^2–10^4 m
5	$> 10^4$ m
Temporal scale	
1	$<$ 10 days
2	10–10^1 days
3	$10^{1-}10^2$ days
4	10^2–10^3 days
5	$> 10^3$ days

Sweden. They made the distinction between soil-based and landscape-based solutions. For the soil-based solutions, the importance of identifying the specific ecosystem services to be restored are vital, as are the soil properties and functions that will be affected by the solution. Therefore, for a model to provide useful information in different situations, it must be sufficiently generally applicable that the costs of parameterisation do not outweigh the benefits of actually using the model.

This discussion focuses on those models considered most relevant, representative of their topics and most likely to be of use in future work. The intention here is not to discard the rest of the 51

Table 3.2 *Model formulation code legend*

Respiration models	
GRW	Growth respiration
MNT	Maintenance respiration
G&M	Both growth and maintenance respiration
CO	Respiration defined to compensate stoichiometric imbalances
Decomposition models	
CONS	Constant rate
LIN	Linear model with respect to C_S
LINB	Linear model with respect to C_B
MULT	Multiplicative model
MM	Michaelis–Menten model
NL	Other non-linear or mixed formulations
Mineralisation scheme	
DIR	Direct hypothesis
MIT	Mineralisation–immobilisation–turnover
PAR	Parallel hypothesis
MIX	Other schemes with simultaneous mineralisation and immobilisation
SIMP	Simplified model or regression equation (no microbial stoichiometry)
N-limitation model	
CM	C-only (or dry weight–only) models neglecting N dynamics
IND	No N-limitation
INH	Inhibition factors
CO	Carbon overflow
CN	N-limitation effects on microbial or substrate C/N
MIX	Multiple N-limitation effects are considered

models that have been considered, but to highlight those that are most easily available and implemented, commonly and successfully used and that cover the range of topics within soil modelling. The models evaluated in this review fall into five main types, as listed

Table 3.3 *Strengths and limitations of soil modelling for understanding NBS*

Nature-based solution	Advantages of soil modelling	Limitations of soil modelling
Reduced climate impact	Good choice of soil carbon and nitrogen models available; existing frameworks for integration of soil models within global circulation models	Models appropriate for climate modelling are at the simple end of the scale, and do not incorporate some important processes very well (soil hydrology in particular)
Ensuring quality groundwater	Catchment-scale soil models incorporate multiple processes relating to erosion and chemical transport; the models are flexible and relatively accurate, and operate at small spatial and temporal resolution	Models relevant for this objective do not include all possible chemicals of concern (although they do cover a wide range); soil hydrology models generally lack implementations of snow and ice
Ensuring biodiversity in wetlands	Soil models designed to simulate peat soils specifically have been developed	The peatland condition is difficult to assess for baseline data of these models, which has a strong bearing on the accuracy of the results
Sustainable food production in a varied landscape	Crop growth models exist that can be used for scenario modelling and multiple crop types	These models often require a great deal of parameterisation, are complex and the results require careful interpretation

below. A subset of the 51 models has been identified that satisfy criteria of availability, accuracy, flexibility and sophistication for each of the five types. Each of these models is briefly discussed, along with its relevance for NBS.

3.3.1 NBS: Soil Erosion and Catchment Dynamics

Integrated water resource management can often include aspects of NBS. As these solutions often influence water and biodiversity in several different ways, the outcomes of any solution applied can be difficult to predict. Boelee et al. (2017) argue that using integrated water resource management frameworks can help understand and guide the implementation of NBS. Wild et al. (2017) discuss the complexities involved when attempting to understand the impacts of NBS activities on water within an urban context and demonstrate the need for further work (including modelling work that incorporates biophysical aspects of the system). Useful models in this area therefore need to include multiple biological and physical processes in order to accurately represent the catchment of interest. Five key models of relevance here are are follows.

CREAMS (Chemicals, Run-off and Erosion from Agricultural Management Systems) (Silburn and Loch, 1989) – this model provided the basis for several later versions of relevance within the subject, each of which is available for download. The general nature of the model framework has made it relevant for a wide range of catchment-based research in agricultural land, particularly looking at the impacts of land management options on erosion and nutrient run-off. As such, it is suitable for exploring NBS options as to their impacts on soil erosion. The number of processes and input data types required mean that this is not an easy model to run in the first instance, but it does provide a level of sophistication and integration that is high in comparison to many other models in this area.

EUROSEM (European Soil Erosion Model) (Morgan et al., 1998) – more relevant for the modelling of extreme rainfall events and their impact on soil erosion under different land management types, this model is freely available but comes with health warnings; no support is available in order to implement the model so if difficulties are encountered, a programming solution will have to be sought. This model is suitable for exploring flood mitigation/avoidance NBS options.

INCA (Integrated Catchment Model) (Wade et al., 2002) – this model focuses on transport and fate of nutrients and pollutants within soil and catchments and is available as an executable file. There are several different versions that look at different chemicals and nutrients, but the underlying model integrates soil, hydrology and vegetative processes. As such, it requires a significant amount of input data to run and produces output data of high complexity. It does not include erosion as a process, and so is less relevant for extreme weather event scenarios or for NBS work aimed to reduce soil erosion. However, it would be useful for evaluating NBS options aimed at reducing pollution transport as it specifically incorporates pollution concentrations.

SWAT (Soil and Water Assessment Tool) (Arnold et al., 1993) – designed to facilitate decision-making in large, managed catchments, recent versions of this model can be used to simulate aspects of hydrology, erosion and sediment transport, nutrient and pollutant transport and fate. It is relatively complex and sophisticated, but comes with a user interface to make implementation easier. SWAT can be used to simulate a wide range of management options and climate/weather scenarios, and so is potentially very useful for exploring NBS options if used with sufficient expertise (as demonstrated in Case Study 3.1).

WATEM (Water and Tillage Erosion Model) (Van Oost et al., 2000) – this now exists as WaTEM/SEDEM, an integration of two models of sediment transport and erosion under different land management options. The model is designed to operate within a GIS environment and is freely downloadable. It uses a version of the RUSLE soil loss equation to calculate erosion rates and links this to run-off patterns calculated from topography and land-cover parameters. As this model does not contain many vegetation classes, its application for NBS is probably limited.

3.3.2 NBS Soil Carbon and Nitrogen Cycling

The modelling of soil carbon and nitrogen involves numerous biological, chemical and physical processes and, as such, models that can

CASE STUDY 3.1 **Soil Modelling and Nature-based Solutions for Resilience to Wildfire**

Fire is a common occurrence in Mediterranean forests, and results in increased run-off and soil erosion. Nunes et al. (2018) used the SWAT (Soil and Water Assessment Tool) model to assess the impacts of fires on several ecosystem services provided by forests in the Macieira de Alcôba catchment in north-western Portugal.

The catchment has an area of 94 ha and is a mixture of forest plantation and agriculture, with a history of forest fires. The effects of a fire in 2011 were used as the basis for the modelling work, which assessed the impacts over a 10-year period on streamflow, soil erosion and sediment output using several different land management scenarios. The SWAT model enabled this to be carried out as it incorporates relevant hydrological, erosive and vegetation processes on a daily time step. Previous work in the study catchment enabled the model to be conceptualised and parameterised.

Validation of the model against observed streamflow and sediment values showed that the model worked well and matched the effects of the fire. In comparison to the agricultural areas where most erosion occurred during the wet season, burnt areas of forest saw erosion during all rainfall events and produced the majority of erosion and sediments during the post-fire vegetation disturbance period. In brief the paper concludes:

- fires had a strong effect on soil erosion and a moderate effect on water quality (sediment);
- fires in forested areas resulted in greater soil erosion than in agricultural or shrubland areas;
- reduced post-fire management resulted in lower erosion and sediment release;
- replacing eucalyptus species with pines or native species also reduced the effects of fire;

CASE STUDY 3.1 **(cont.)**

FIGURE 3.1 Burning shrubland (image CC: Antonio Jordán). (A black and white version of this figure will appear in some formats. For the colour version, please refer to the plate section.)

- different management scenarios produced greatly different erosion and sediment levels. Scenarios with fire resulted in high-erosion burnt areas and increased sediment yield, with the only exception being the scenario that instead replaced forestry with shrubland, clearly demonstrating the value of this option as an NBS for sediment retention.

Overall, the use of the SWAT model was successful for investigating management options for fire-prone catchments, shows promise for assessing future NBS options in this area and others and is flexible enough to allow other climatic, soil and vegetation options to be considered.

achieve this accurately must be relatively complex. Exploring methods of retaining or increasing soil carbon has become increasingly prioritised in recent years (e.g. the '4 per mil' initiative (www.4p1000.org/)) and so models that allow successful NBS to be explored are vital. Five key models of relevance here are as follows.

CarboSOIL (Munoz-Rojas et al., 2013, 2015) – this model operates as an application within ArcGIS 10.0, and is particularly appropriate for exploring the impacts of land use on soil carbon in Europe as it incorporates characterisations of the land-cover classes within CORINE. It does require a lot of input data in order to run, however, and only contains a few land-cover classes so will not allow specific vegetation species to be explored.

CENTURY (Parton et al., 1988) – the first version of this model has now been superseded and expanded into multiple versions appropriate for different land-cover types. It can be used to explore relationships between land management, climate, soil carbon, nitrogen, phosphorus and sulphur. The model requires a lot of information to set up and run but is considered 'industry standard' among some researchers in this subject area. As such, it is commonly used, and results can be compared with those of other researchers quite readily. While there are still some limitations on vegetative type and parameterisation, this model is flexible enough to allow many NBS scenarios to be explored.

DAYCENT (Del Grosso et al., 2002) – this version of CENTURY runs on a daily time step, and as such incorporates more detailed and sophisticated submodels of soil, water and temperature, as well as several rapid processes taking place within the soil. It is therefore more relevant than CENTURY for modelling the effects of specific, time-dependent land management and crop growth activities on soil carbon and nitrogen dynamics. Whether this makes it more useful for NBS work is unclear because while it represents relevant functions, this may be on too fine a spatio-temporal scale.

DNDC (Denitrification–Decomposition) (Li et al., 1992) – another commonly used model of carbon and nitrogen dynamics in agricultural systems, DNDC can be used to simulate crop yield, carbon sequestration, nitrogen leaching and several other processes of social, environmental and political importance within agriculture. It does not incorporate the effects of short-term extreme weather events, so soil erosion and run-off are not included. This and the fact that DNDC is restricted to agricultural systems limits its potential for NBS other than in a longer-term, strategic context.

Roth-C (Farina et al., 2013) – a soil carbon turnover model with a long and distinguished pedigree, this relatively simple model of carbon dynamics in mineral soils has been incorporated into several other soil models and has been refined and adapted over the years into its current version. There are currently other models that are more sophisticated and accurate in describing carbon dynamics, but Roth-C is very useful for initiating carbon pool sizes in soil process models, something that is often challenging and that has large impacts on eventual model accuracy. The user can define soil and vegetation characteristics with a fair degree of freedom, giving flexibility in which scenarios can be explored, but from an NBS perspective it is more likely to be a precursor to parameterise other models.

3.3.3 NBS: Crop Productivity

Crop intensification through short-duration crop types does not work everywhere and can cause issues with soil damage. In some areas around the world (particularly where social or biophysical factors limit crop productivity) it may be more effective to plant perennial grain crops that require lower maintenance and are more sustainable. These less intensive methods also provide a nature-based solution on a range of dimensions such as fostering biodiversity and reducing eutrophication. Identification of locations where this cropping strategy is better than using short-duration crops requires an understanding of the underlying biophysical and socio-economic factors (Peter et al., 2017). It could also benefit from appropriate soil modelling, which would enable the interactions of different crops and soil conditions to be explored. A critical condition here for modelling to support NBS work is model flexibility in defining vegetation characteristics, to allow different plant species to be explored. From this perspective two models stand out.

DSSAT (Decision Support System for Agrotechnology Transfer) (Jones et al., 2003; Dzotsi et al., 2010) – this is less of a model than a system for implementing crop simulation models, and for integrating soil databases, climate data, experimental results and other data into these models. It is commonly used for land management decision support under different climatic conditions and can be used to explore the impacts of different management options on crop yield and condition. It is restricted to specific crop types so is possibly only of limited use for NBS in certain regions.

MONICA (Model for Nitrogen and Carbon in Agroecosystems) (Nendel et al., 2011) – this relatively new model could also be included under the 'carbon and nitrogen cycling' heading, but has much more of a focus than those models on crop management, yield and condition, while still retaining useful submodels on carbon and nitrogen cycling and related hydrological processes. It is relevant across a very wide range of environmental conditions and is relatively simple to set up and run. It does not include soil erosion and is focused on crop yield, so will not allow exploration of a full range of NBS activities.

3.3.4 NBS: Energy Balance

SCOPE (Soil, Canopy Observation, Photochemistry and Energy fluxes) (van der Tol et al., 2009) – this model links vegetation photosynthesis with incoming spectral radiance and fluxes of water, heat and carbon dioxide in the plant/soil system. The main bias of the model is towards vegetation radiative transfer, but it also incorporates soil and atmosphere components, and so can be considered to be fully integrative. The model is not fully available to download, but may be available from the authors upon request. The requirement for energy balance models to NBS is likely to be dependent on the specific situation, but if and when this does occur, SCOPE would appear to satisfy most if not all requirements.

3.3.5 *Ecosystem/Biosphere Modelling*

Paraphrasing one of the conclusions of Nesshover et al. (2017), due to its integrative nature the NBS concept has broad application to drive transdisciplinary research within a coherent framework. One of the key requirements to understanding individual NBS approaches within this framework is adequate modelling of all components, including socio-economic and biophysical, to allow candidate NBS to be explored prior to implementation. If understood well, NBS provide an opportunity to transform economies away from the current contest between economic growth and environmental sustainability (Maes & Jacobs, 2017). If implemented appropriately, Maes and Jacobs (2017) also argue that NBS provide a means to accomplish this while avoiding the political arguments that paralyse progression towards a healthy, strong and sustainable economy. Three models in particular seek to better support modelling of soil within this wider perspective by building in, or linking with, models of landscape systems such as hydrology and atmospheric processes.

DRAINMOD-DSSAT (Negm et al., 2014) – developed as a model for describing hydrology of poorly drained soils, DRAINMOD incorporates climate, soil and vegetation characteristics into its implementation. DRAINMOD has been integrated into the framework of DSSAT (above) to provide a model that includes not just the hydrology of the soils considered but also water quality and crop yield. It is considered still 'under development' in some areas that will improve its flexibility for different crop types and environmental conditions, but another version (DRAINMOD-FOREST) also exists for forestry. Calibration is required against existing site data for the model to run accurately, but overall it appears much more flexible and appropriate for NBS applications than DSSAT.

IBIS (Integrated Biosphere Simulation) (Kucharik et al., 2000) – the latest version of this model, IBIS-2, does what its acronym suggests: it is an Integrated Biosphere Simulator. As such it is used for linking soil and vegetation processes within a single framework, and modelling the dynamics of water, carbon and vegetation growth all together. It is relatively complex as would be expected and includes a very large number of processes and parameters. The input data required to run are also quite demanding, but the model is very flexible and can be used for several different scenario modelling questions. For NBS work, this is potentially very useful, although it would require significant effort to develop baseline data for any scenarios.

MBL-GEM (Marine Biological Laboratory General Ecosystem Model) (Rastetter et al., 1991; Le Dizes et al., 2003) – simulates plant growth and development, allocation of C and N throughout the plant/soil system, soil C decomposition and sequestration. This model very much considers the plants and soil as a single system and has been designed with this concept in mind. As it operates on a point-by-point basis, it does not incorporate matter or energy flow between grid cells and so cannot be used for hydrological dynamics. Depending on the NBS scenarios being investigated, this could either render it unusable or make no difference at all.

3.4 SUMMARY

Several models have been evaluated that have relevance for land management decision-making and NBS scenario modelling. The spatial and temporal scales over which these models operate vary considerably, as do the parameters that are output. For soil erosion and nutrient loss modelling, the models commonly operate at the catchment scale or smaller and over a relatively short time step. Producing regional-scale, long-term scenario predictions would require a lot of computational and data resources but is less likely to be a requirement for NBS work, which tends to take place at smaller scales.

For models of soil carbon and nitrogen cycling, the spatial and temporal scales vary considerably, as does the complexity of the models applied, meaning that scenarios can be explored at scales from local to national, and daily to multi-annual. The data complexity of the models also varies, with those that are applicable at larger scales being less complex and easier to implement. It is therefore easier to identify a model that is more relevant for the scale in question for soil carbon/nitrogen models than it is for soil erosion models. This is due in part to the fact that soil erosion models incorporate hydrological processes that operate over a range of spatial scales. As NBS scenario modelling can focus on either erosion or carbon/nitrogen or both, this means that model selection remains problematic.

Crop productivity models can generally be applied at the spatial scales desired, but require significant data resources to implement and operate on short time steps. They also often require specific information about the crops of interest and are unlikely to be much use for NBS unless the focus is on native crops. More generally applicable ecosystem/biosphere models have similarities to crop productivity models in that they incorporate information on soils, vegetation, climate and topography/hydrology, but these often take the form of frameworks rather than specific models and can accommodate different types of submodels within their operation. They are complex and require a lot of data to initialise, often in the form of field measurements of the ecosystem being simulated. They are therefore less relevant to decision-making over regional scales than crop productivity models. Table 3.3 summarises the implications of this with respect to the spatial and temporal scale to which models may inform key Environmental Objectives.

In addition to the biophysical aspects of NBS work, there are socio-economic impacts that should be explored. Human mental well-being is a societal challenge that can in some cases be directly addressed by NBS activities. One example is visiting urban green spaces as a nature-based solution to well-being issues related to increased air temperatures in the urban heat island (Panno et al., 2017). The NBS in this case would be the creation, protection and management of urban green spaces. These green spaces can also include community urban gardens (allotments) that increase urban and social resilience. The success of community urban garden projects is influenced by several factors which imply that a bottom-up approach works best (van der Jagt et al., 2017). The use of soil modelling in an NBS capacity could arguably provide a surprising amount of useful knowledge in this area, provided that such initiatives have access to the relevant expertise.

Faivre et al. (2017) argue that NBS are an opportunity for innovation and improved competitiveness and describe how the European Commission has been seeking to define, integrate and make recommendations for NBS particularly in urban areas. Calls for project proposals to develop an evidence base for implementation of NBS have been increasing in frequency, and the development of best practice for solutions is an important component of this. While large-scale experimental projects can provide important information, they cannot provide information on the full range of scenarios and situations and soil modelling will be vital for developing information about how plant–soil–atmosphere interactions will influence the success of NBS implementations.

REFERENCES

Arnold, J. G., Allen, P. M. & Bernhardt, G. 1993. A comprehensive surface-groundwater flow model. *Journal of Hydrology*, 142, 47–69.

Boelee, E., Janse, J., Le Gal, A., Kok, M., Alkemade, R. & Ligtvoet, W. 2017. Overcoming water challenges through nature-based solutions. *Water Policy*, 19(5), 820–836.

Del Grosso, S., Ojima, D., Parton, W., Mosier, A., Peterson, G. & Schimel, D. 2002. Simulated effects of dryland cropping intensification on soil organic matter and greenhouse gas exchanges using the DAYCENT ecosystem model. *Environmental Pollution*, 116, S75–S83.

Dzotsi, K. A., Jones, J. W., Adiku, S. G. K., Naab, J. B., Singh, U., Porter, C. H., et al. 2010. Modeling soil and plant phosphorus within DSSAT. *Ecological Modelling*, 221, 2839–2849.

Faivre, N., Fritz, M., Freitas, T., De Boissezon, B. & Vandewoestijne, S. 2017. Nature-based solutions in the EU: innovating with nature to address social, economic and environmental challenges. *Environmental Research*, 159, 509–518.

Farina, R., Coleman, K. & Whitmore, A. P. 2013. Modification of the RothC model for simulations of soil organic C dynamics in dryland regions. *Geoderma*, 200, 18–30.

Jones, J. W., Hoogenboom, G., Porter, C. H., Boote, K. J., Batchelor, W. D., Hunt, L. A., et al. 2003. The DSSAT cropping system model. *European Journal of Agronomy*, 18, 235–265.

Keesstra, S., Nunes, J., Novara, A., Finger, D., Avelar, D., Kalantari, Z., et al. 2018. The superior effect of nature based solutions in land management for enhancing ecosystem services. *Science of the Total Environment*, 610, 997–1009.

Kinnell, P. I. A. 2010. Event soil loss, runoff and the Universal Soil Loss Equation family of models: a review. *Journal of Hydrology*, 385, 384–397.

Kucharik, C. J., Foley, J. A., Delire, C., Fisher, V. A., Coe, M. T., Lenters, J. D., et al. 2000. Testing the performance of a Dynamic Global Ecosystem Model: water balance, carbon balance, and vegetation structure. *Global Biogeochemical Cycles*, 14, 795–825.

Le Dizes, S., Kwiatkowski, B. L., Rastetter, E. B., Hope, A., Hobbie, J. E., Stow, D., et al. 2003. Modeling biogeochemical responses of tundra ecosystems to temporal and spatial variations in climate in the Kuparuk River Basin (Alaska). *Journal of Geophysical Research – Atmospheres*, 108(D2), Alt6-1–Alt6-20.

Li, C. S., Frolking, S. & Frolking, T. A. 1992. A model of nitrous-oxide evolution from soil driven by rainfall events. 1. Model structure and sensitivity. *Journal of Geophysical Research – Atmospheres*, 97, 9759–9776.

Maes, J. & Jacobs, S. 2017. Nature-based solutions for Europe's sustainable development. *Conservation Letters*, 10(1), 121–124.

Manzoni, S. & Porporato, A. 2009. Soil carbon and nitrogen mineralization: theory and models across scales. *Soil Biology & Biochemistry*, 41, 1355–1379.

Molina, J. A. E. & Smith, P. 1998. Modeling carbon and nitrogen processes in soils. *Advances in Agronomy*, 62, 253–298.

Morgan, R. P. C., Quinton, J. N., Smith, R. E., Govers, G., Poesen, J. W. A., Auerswald, K., et al. 1998. The European Soil Erosion Model (EUROSEM): a dynamic approach for redirecting sediment transport from fields and small catchments. *Earth Surface Processes and Landforms*, 23, 527–544.

Munoz-Rojas, M., Jordan, A., Zavala, L. M., De La Rosa, D., Abd-Elmabod, S. K. & Anaya-Romero, M. 2015. Impact of land use and land cover changes on organic carbon stocks in Mediterranean soils (1956–2007). *Land Degradation & Development*, 26, 168–179.

Munoz-Rojas, M., Jordan, A., Zavala, L. M., Gonzalez-Penaloza, F. A., De La Rosa, D., Pino-Mejias, R., et al. 2013. Modelling soil organic carbon stocks in global change scenarios: a CarboSOIL application. *Biogeosciences*, 10, 8253–8268.

Negm, L. M., Youssef, M. A., Skaggs, R. W., Chescheir, G. M. & Jones, J. 2014. DRAINMOD-DSSAT model for simulating hydrology, soil carbon and nitrogen dynamics, and crop growth for drained crop land. *Agricultural Water Management*, 137, 30–45.

Nendel, C., Berg, M., Kersebaum, K. C., Mirschel, W., Specka, X., Wegehenkel, M., et al. 2011. The MONICA model: testing predictability for crop growth, soil moisture and nitrogen dynamics. *Ecological Modelling*, 222, 1614–1625.

Nesshover, C., Assmuth, T., Irvine, K. N., Rusch, G. M., Waylen, K. A., Delbaere, B., et al. 2017. The science, policy and practice of nature-based solutions: an interdisciplinary perspective. *Science of the Total Environment*, 579, 1215–1227.

Nunes, J. P., Quintanilla, P. N., Santos, J. M., Serpa, D., Carvalho-Santos, C., Rocha, J., et al. 2018. Afforestation, subsequent forest fires and provision of hydrological services: a model-based analysis for a Mediterranean mountainous catchment. *Land Degradation & Development*, 28, 776–788.

Panno, A., Carrus, G., Lafortezza, R., Mariani, L. & Sanesi, G. 2017. Nature-based solutions to promote human resilience and wellbeing in cities during increasingly hot summers. *Environmental Research*, 159, 249–256.

Parton, W. J., Stewart, J. W. B. & Cole, C. V. 1988. Dynamics of C, N, P and S in grassland soils – a model. *Biogeochemistry*, 5, 109–131.

Peter, B. G., Mungai, L. M., Messina, J. P. & Snapp, S. S. 2017. Nature-based agricultural solutions: scaling perennial grains across Africa. *Environmental Research*, 159, 283–290.

Rastetter, E. B., Ryan, M. G., Shaver, G. R., Melillo, J. M., Nadelhoffer, K. J., Hobbie, J. E., et al.1991. A general biogeochemical model describing the responses of the C-cycle and N-cycle in terrestrial ecosystems to changes in CO2, climate, and N-deposition. *Tree Physiology*, 9, 101–126.

Sheng, D. C. 2011. Review of fundamental principles in modelling unsaturated soil behaviour. *Computers and Geotechnics*, 38, 757–776.

Silburn, D. M. & Loch, R. J. 1989. Evaluation of the Creams Model. 1. Sensitivity analysis of the soil-erosion sedimentation component for aggregated clay soils. *Australian Journal of Soil Research*, 27, 545–561.

van der Jagt, A. P. N., Szaraz, L. R., Delshammar, T., Cvejic, R., Santos, A., Goodness, J., et al. 2017. Cultivating nature-based solutions: the governance of communal urban gardens in the European Union. *Environmental Research*, 159, 264–275.

Van Der Tol, C., Verhoef, W., Timmermans, J., Verhoef, A. & Su, Z. 2009. An integrated model of soil-canopy spectral radiances, photosynthesis, fluorescence, temperature and energy balance. *Biogeosciences*, 6, 3109–3129.

Van Oost, K., Govers, G. & Desmet, P. 2000. Evaluating the effects of changes in landscape structure on soil erosion by water and tillage. *Landscape Ecology*, 15, 577–589.

Wade, A. J., Whitehead, P. G. & Butterfield, D. 2002. The Integrated Catchments model of Phosphorus dynamics (INCA-P), a new approach for multiple source assessment in heterogeneous river systems: model structure and equations. *Hydrology and Earth System Sciences*, 6, 583–606.

Wild, T. C., Henneberry, J. & Gill, L. 2017. Comprehending the multiple 'values' of green infrastructure – valuing nature-based solutions for urban water management from multiple perspectives. *Environmental Research*, 158, 179–187.

4 Modelling Water Resources for Nature-based Solutions

Sarah Dunn

4.1 INTRODUCTION

This chapter first summarises different approaches to hydrological and hydrochemical modelling of freshwater, and then goes on to provide an overview of how models are being used in practice to address typical policy and environmental issues, with a special focus on nature-based solutions (NBS). For a broader overview of hydrologic and water quality models the reader is referred to review articles such as Singh and Woolhiser (2002), Borah and Bera (2003), Cox (2003), Kampf and Burges (2007), Schoumans et al. (2009a, 2009b), Arthington et al. (2010), Ampadu et al. (2013), Kelly et al (2013), Li and Heap (2014). Several categories of NBS approaches, as defined by Cohen-Schacham et al. (2016) relate to the water environment. These include: climate adaptation services (e.g. modification of water use through changed agricultural practice), natural/green infrastructure (e.g. natural flood retention ponds), integrated water resources management to meet the needs of multiple stakeholders, and area-based conservation (e.g. protection of wetland areas). These approaches are not specifically new, but can be clustered as part of the overarching NBS concept and contribute to the development of an operational framework for NBS. This chapter considers the role of modelling in evaluating and designing NBS for water.

4.2 MODELLING APPROACHES

4.2.1 Model Types

Jajarmizadeh et al. (2012) undertook a review of different model classifications that are commonly applied within hydrological and water quality studies. Although the precise terminology has differed, there are three main model typologies that can be defined as empirical, conceptual and physically based (also sometimes termed deterministic or mechanistic). There are a further two additional approaches that have been receiving increased interest and attention in recent years: data-based mechanistic modelling (Young & Beven, 1994), which exploits the power of recursive estimation to help identify relevant model structures to characterise linear and non-linear processes, and Bayesian network approaches (Reckhow, 1999; Borsuk et al., 2004) that attempt to structure complex behaviour into a probabilistic explanatory network. The latter have proven to be of particular benefit for application to address complex interdisciplinary problems and to aid communication with stakeholders and end-users. An overview of these five modelling approaches is given in Table 4.1, together with a simple summary of some of the pros and cons of each.

4.2.2 Spatial and Temporal Scale

Many models have a degree of flexibility with regard to the spatial and temporal scales at which they can be implemented, but identification of relevant scales is important in selecting the most appropriate modelling approach. The purpose of the modelling is likely to be a key factor in this decision; Kelly et al. (2013) identified types of purpose as prediction, forecasting, management and decision-making under uncertainty, social learning and developing system understanding/experimentation. In the context of modelling NBS to manage water resources, a high level of spatial detail may be required.

In terms of spatial delineation, models are commonly classified either as lumped, semi-distributed or distributed. A lumped model represents the catchment or study area as a single unit with homogeneous properties, whereas a distributed model attempts to characterise the full range of heterogeneity in physical, topographic and climatic properties across the study area, using some form of gridded network (e.g. Abbott et al., 1986). A semi-distributed model lies somewhere in between, representing the study area as some

Table 4.1 *Pros and cons of commonly adopted approaches to hydrology and water quality modelling*

Pros	Cons
Physically based models	
Capture key processes and interrelationships and feedbacks between them	Commonly a mismatch between scales of implementation and scale of heterogeneity in properties
Represent heterogeneity in systems	Many parameters and, in practice, most still require calibration
Parameters should be related to measurable properties	Equifinality issues (Beven, 1993)
More robust for extrapolation to different conditions (e.g. climate/ land-use change)	Underpinning physical representations are not always appropriate at relevant scales of application (Christiaens & Feyen, 2001)
	Long processing times
Examples	
SHE: Abbott et al., 1986; MIKE SHE: Refsgaard and Storm, 1995; HYDRUS: Simunek et al., 2008; PSYCHIC: Davison et al., 2008; Stroemqvist et al., 2008.	
Conceptual models	
Usually less computationally demanding than physically based approaches	Likely to be restricted in suitable range of applications depending on processes included
Fewer parameters to calibrate (especially if spatially lumped)	Can still have many parameters
Uncertainty analysis easier with fewer parameters	Parameters need calibration
	Equifinality is still an issue
	Extrapolation to changed conditions is only appropriate where relevant affected processes are included in the model structure

Table 4.1 (*cont.*)

Pros	Cons
Examples	
TOPMODEL: Beven et al., 1984; Quinn et al., 1991; MAGIC: Wright et al., 1986; Cosby et al., 2001; SWAT: Arnold et al., 1998; Arnold and Fohrer, 2005; Gassman et al., 2007; HSPF: Bicknell, 1997; AGNPS: Young et al., 1989; Bosch et al., 1998; INCA: Wade et al., 2002a, 2002b; SWIM: Krysanova et al., 1998.	
Empirical models	
Simple to apply and short simulation times	Restricted in geographic range of applicability
Transparent and easy to interpret outputs	Not applicable to simulate responses to changed conditions
Suitable for application at large scales	Non dynamic (temporally lumped)
Input data based on measurable system properties (e.g. area of land use, topography, etc.)	
Examples	
Export coefficient: Johnes, 1996; Phosphorus Index: Gburek et al., 2000; Phosphorus indicators tool: Heathwaite, 2003; SCIMAP: Reaney et al., 2011; Artificial Neural Network models: Maier and Dandy, 2000, 2001; Zhang and Govindaraju, 2000.	
Data-based mechanistic models	
No prior assumptions about key processes in catchment	Dependent on good-quality observational data
Efficient simulation avoiding over-parameterisation	May be limited in transferability to changed conditions if relevant processes not characterised by initial model structure
Less data-intensive than physically based models	
Examples	
Young, 1992; Young and Beven, 1994; Chappell et al., 1999; Romanowicz et al., 2008.	

Table 4.1 (*cont.*)

Pros	Cons
Bayesian network models	
Allow a complex causal chain to be articulated	Generally non-spatial and non-temporal
Incorporate uncertainty directly using probability distribution functions	Model assessment of structural uncertainty is often neglected
Can integrate different types and sources of information	Often require discretisation of continuous variables
Suitable for communication of model results to end-users	
Examples	
Reckhow, 1999; Borsuk et al., 2004; Dorner et al., 2006; Castelletti and Soncini-Sessa, 2007; McDowell et al., 2009; Stewart-Koster et al., 2010.	

form of hydrological or chemical response units (Kouwen et al., 1993; Bende, 1997) defined on the basis of a range of common characteristics.

Due to their high data demands, physically based distributed modelling approaches are most likely to be applied at the smallest scales with simpler, more empirical approaches more appropriate at larger scales. Conceptual modelling is commonly used in catchment and river basin–scale studies. Different data sources will be more suited to different spatial scales of application and different modelling objectives will require assessment at different scales. For example, in order to consider how siting of manure stores might impact on losses of pollutants from fields to water courses, a model that can be applied at the scale of a field or farm is likely to be considered appropriate (Davison et al., 2008), whereas a model aimed at identification of regional hotspots of pollution would likely involve different data sources and scale of application (Dunn et al., 2004a, 2004b). One common issue in modelling studies is that a mismatch between measurement and modelling scales can lead to a need for estimation of 'effective' parameters (Pachepsky et al., 2004). The adoption of a nested hierarchical approach of scale-appropriate modelling (Quinn, 2004) has become increasingly popular (Volk et al., 2010).

The temporal scale of a model needs to be linked to the temporal scale of the processes that require interpretation. In some cases this can be challenging where linked subsystems may operate at different spatial and temporal scales. For example, groundwater is an important component of the water balance in some areas, but its response times (which may be years to decades) are likely to be very different from surface waters. Some models are non-temporal, for example where key attributes of a system, such as hydrological connectivity, might be modelled under different land-use or management scenarios, and others refer to a lumped output, for example aggregated over an annual timescale. In other situations the temporal dynamics of weather patterns and biogeochemical cycling are important influences on responses and in these cases models are commonly run at daily resolution. For responses strongly influenced by extreme events, such as high flows, it may be necessary to run models at subhourly resolution. Temporal scale is also linked to spatial scale in the sense that smaller systems will generally respond more rapidly and therefore may need a shorter model time step to capture the dynamics of the system.

4.2.3 Model Evaluation

Model evaluation is a critical step in any model application and includes procedures such as model sensitivity analysis, calibration, validation and uncertainty analysis. Protocols for implementing suitable procedures have been proposed (Beven & Freer, 2001; Jakeman et al., 2006; Refsgaard et al., 2007) and some variations on these approaches form the basis of current accepted modelling practice. A detailed discussion of these protocols is beyond the remit of this chapter, but it is vital in all modelling activities that users understand the constraints of the tools that they are applying.

4.2.4 *Stakeholder Participation*

For a number of reasons the application of hydrology and water quality models to aid practical river basin management and decision support has lagged behind their use in research contexts. Models which have been developed by scientists for scientific purposes are often not suitable for practical management due to their often (too) high complexity, low user-friendliness, and lack of problem/solution orientation (Borowski & Hare, 2007). NBS may involve quite complex system manipulation that is difficult to characterise and may necessitate application of some of these more complex process-based models (Bouraoui & Grizzetti, 2014). Good communication between the modeller and stakeholders is therefore important. The implementation needs of the EU Water Framework Directive (WFD) proved to be a key turning point in making models more accessible and relevant to end-user needs. Saloranta et al. (2003) developed a set of benchmark criteria to help water managers and other users in selecting appropriate models to address their needs. Many decision support tools have been developed to facilitate practical implementation of models, but it has been found in practice that these are not always adopted as widely as expected (Junier & Mostert, 2014). Participation is considered a key concept in bridging this gap between modellers and stakeholders (Barthel et al., 2016). Participatory modelling has emerged as a powerful tool that can (a) enhance the stakeholders' knowledge and understanding of a system and (b) identify and clarify the impacts of solutions to a given problem, usually related to supporting decision-making, policy, regulation or management (Voinov & Busquet, 2010). Voinov and Busquet (2010) discuss the various different approaches to stakeholder involvement and the situations in which each may be appropriate. They found that stakeholder participation helps to relate models to real needs, and can be beneficial in terms of providing new data and ideas. Kelly et al. (2013) explored approaches for facilitating stakeholder engagement in the modelling process through using models that could accommodate multiple issues, values, scales and uncertainty considerations. NBS may involve important trade-offs and a participatory process becomes critical, and can be especially pertinent, when their aim is to better connect people with their local natural resources (Nesshöver et al., 2017).

4.3 NATURE-BASED SOLUTIONS AND MODELLING OF COMMON WATER ISSUES

There is a wide range of water issues that may require addressing in order to meet legislative needs in different regions across the world. Modelling tools have the potential to address many of these issues, but there has been mixed success in terms of how well this has been achieved. Collins and McGonigle (2008) outlined a number of common and important diffuse pollution issues that needed to be addressed to meet the requirements of the EU WFD. This included: coupling of pollutant loadings to ecological impacts; multiple pollutants and the risk of pollution swapping; appropriate spatial targeting of mitigation methods; the important role of sediment; and delays in water quality responses resulting from mitigation of diffuse pollution. Other aspects of hydrology and water quality are associated with different sets of issues such as: reliability of water supply quantity and quality; flood risk assessment; and future-proofing of water resources against potential changes in climate and land use. For each of these challenges there may be NBS which could be considered as part of an intervention programme. However, their integration in a modelling framework can add yet more complexity to the detail required by the modelling process. The following sections of this review consider some typical practical situations in which hydrological and water quality models could be – and have proven to be – of value. It examines how models can contribute and which tools have been used. Several case studies are included to illustrate some examples of how NBS may be explored using modelling tools in different water modelling contexts.

4.3.1 NBS: Integrated River Basin Management

In Europe, the WFD introduced a number of mandatory river basin management procedures that regulatory authorities were required to undertake. Many of these processes can be assisted by model applications. In the early stages of WFD implementation models were used to assist with the task of river basin characterisation, e.g. to support gaps in evidence from monitoring data (Hojberg et al., 2007) or for delineation of groundwater bodies (Cools et al., 2006).

Modelling tools are also used to assist with prioritisation of river basin management, for example through carrying out source apportionment to identify pollution hotspots. Panagopoulos et al. (2011) applied the SWAT model (Arnold et al., 1998) to help identify high-risk areas of pollution from sediment, nitrogen (N) and phosphorous (P) in a typical Greek catchment with limited available monitoring data (provided by national-level monitoring). The study found that even in data-limited situations the model could be usefully applied to target diffuse pollution abatement actions. In the UK the SAGIS (source apportionment GIS) model (www.ukwir.org/tool s/sagis), which builds on the earlier SIMCAT (simulation catchment) model, has been adopted by both the Environment Agency of England and Wales (EA) and the Scottish Environmental Protection Agency (SEPA). Models commonly used by the EA such as SIMCAT rarely appear in the literature because they are not generally used for regulation outside of the UK. This is probably due to their stochastic component as well as a lack of commercial exposure (Cox, 2003), but their wide usage by the regulatory authorities highlights the benefits of simplicity in models for practical decision-making.

Parry et al. (1999) outline the regulatory and non-regulatory programmes developed by the US Environmental Protection Agency (USEPA) to implement its legal mandate to control water pollution. Following implementation of the basic laws, states are required to identify and list waters that are not meeting standards, to prioritise them and to develop Total Maximum Daily Loads (TMDLs) for the pollutants of concern. Models are used to support the development of TMDLs and a review of the various options has been undertaken by Borah et al. (2006). Radcliffe et al. (2009) compared modelling procedures for phosphorus in the USA, based around the TMDL concept, with those more commonly applied in Europe to address similar issues. They found that the European approaches were more likely to take into account leaching of phosphorus and the identification of critical source areas, but that scaling up of these models to the watershed scale was an issue, as a result of over-parameterisation. A need for more parsimonious models and better monitoring data (to take advantage of the technological improvements that allow nearly continuous sampling for P and sediment) was identified. The TMDL developed for Chesapeake Bay is an excellent example of how the hugely complex issues of managing a large area (166,000 km^2) can be tackled by breaking the problem down into much smaller jurisdiction/river basin management plans where local solutions can be identified to tackle sources of pollution, thus integrating NBS (Case Study 4.1).

Klauer et al. (2012) present a decision support tool (BASINFORM) for river basin planning. The tool comprises (i) a procedure for framing the specific problems in the water bodies, including quantification of the need for action; (ii) modelling tools for quantifying the impacts of management measures; and (iii) a method for selecting cost-effective combinations of measures. One innovative feature of BASINFORM is that it structures the complex decision problems appropriately for practical use and provides a framework for integrating scientific and practical knowledge. BASINFORM has been used for practical implementation of the WFD in the German Federal State of Thuringia. A similar set of objectives was addressed by Barton et al. (2008) by developing a Bayesian network approach to manage a river basin in Norway. This tool was used to evaluate eutrophication mitigation costs relative to benefits, as part of the economic analysis under the WFD.

Participatory approaches have become increasingly common for addressing river basin management and many of these are framed around the use of Bayesian network (BN) models. Castelletti and Soncini-Sessa (2007) present one such example. The pros and cons of such an approach were discussed by framing their use within the context of a participatory and integrated planning procedure, and

CASE STUDY 4.1 **Chesapeake Bay Total Maximum Daily Load**

The Chesapeake Bay watershed covers approximately 166,000 km^2 of the eastern USA. Most of the Chesapeake Bay and its tidal waters are listed as impaired due to excess nitrogen, phosphorus and sediment. The high levels of pollutants enter the water from agricultural operations, urban and suburban storm water run-off, wastewater facilities, air pollution and other sources (USEPA, 2010a). A doubling of the population in the 50 years up to 2000 has contributed to an impaired bay ecosystem, including habitat loss and water quantity/quality degradation (Phillips, 2006).

ROLE OF NBS

In line with the US regulatory programme, states are required to develop Total Maximum Daily Loads (TMDLs) for the pollutants of concern in waterbodies that do not meet standards. Implementation of a TMDL at the scale of Chesapeake Bay is problematic due to the vast heterogeneity in land use and management across the area as a whole. Therefore, the Bay TMDL (the largest ever developed) was constructed from a combination of 92 smaller TMDLs for individual basin segments in order to assign variable target loads according to the natural and human-influenced characteristics of each area. This allowed high-risk areas to be set more stringent targets, resulting in more efficient implementation. The approach also involved a highly transparent and engaging process of public participation. In so doing, the process has embraced many of the traits of NBS and has significant co-benefits for multiple waterbodies and their associated ecosystem services (USEPA, 2010a).

MODELLING APPROACHES USED

The SPARROW (SPAtially Referenced Regression On Watershed Attributes) model integrates monitoring data with landscape information and uses statistical methods to relate water quality

CASE STUDY 4.1 **(cont.)**

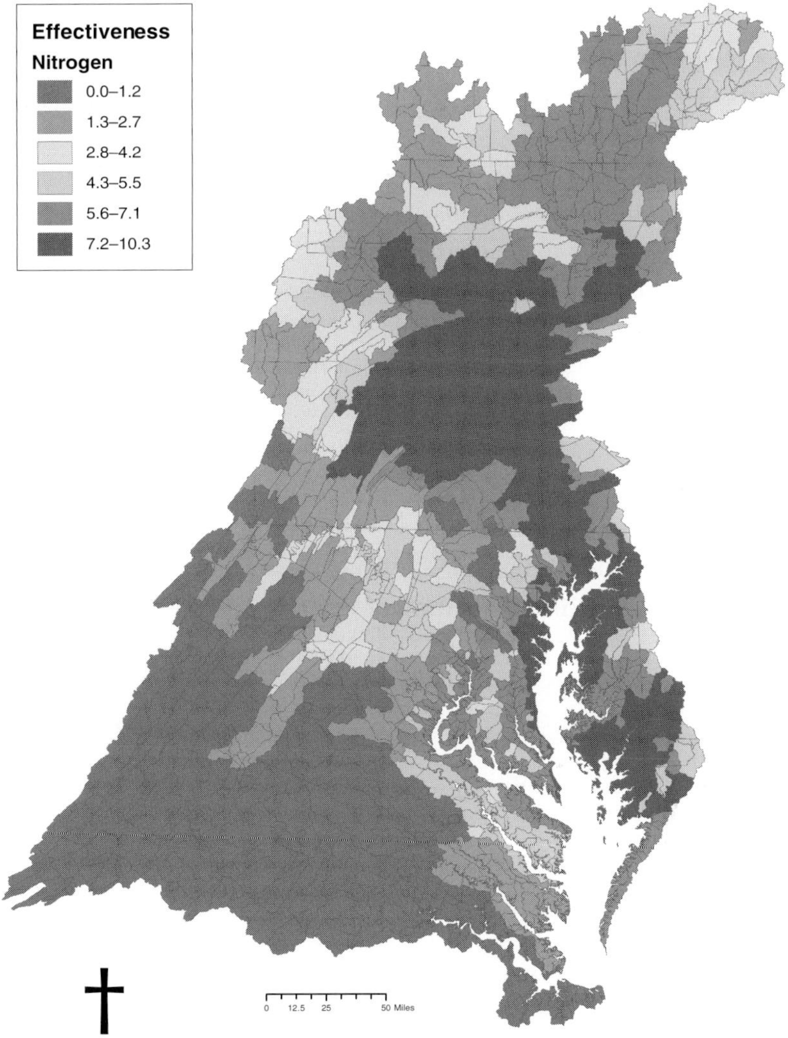

FIGURE 4.1 Subbasins across the Chesapeake Bay watershed with the highest (red) to lowest (blue) nitrogen loading effect on bay water quality. (A black and white version of this figure will appear in some formats. For the colour version, please refer to the plate section.)

monitoring data to upstream sources and watershed characteristics (e.g. soil characteristics, precipitation and land cover; Preston et al.,

CASE STUDY 4.1 **(cont.)**

2009). The model can be used to quantify the incremental yield of total N, P or sediment generated in each reach independent of the upstream load, highlighting those areas most important for targeting.

Applications of the Hydrologic Simulation Program-Fortran (HSPF) model (Bicknell et al., 2005) to the Chesapeake basin have evolved over time to create the Phase 5.3 Watershed Model (Shenk & Linker, 2013). This complex, process-based model simulates hydrochemical functioning in the soil and water bodies and outputs time-series predictions of flow, nutrient and sediment loads for any segment on the stream network or integrated effect on bay water quality (Figure 4.1). The model can be used in scenario mode to explore the effectiveness of Watershed Implementation Plans or best management practices (BMPs) (e.g. forest/grass buffers, wetland conversion, livestock exclusion, use of cover crops), thus enabling evaluation of the success of various NBS in achieving target TMDLs.

exploring how they could be integrated with other types of models. Xue et al. (2017a) present a BN framework for coupling ecosystem services with integrated water resource management. An approach of this type is consistent with many of the objectives of NBS and is presented in Case Study 4.2.

Stithou et al. (2012) describe the implementation of an alternative participatory modelling approach to support integrated catchment management planning in Ireland. This involved a Choice Experiment method of valuation to capture a number of different components of ecological status beyond chemical and biological determinands to include the value that the targeted population of the catchment place on the non-market economic benefits of ecology. The value of participatory modelling approaches was also examined in

CASE STUDY 4.2 **Coupling Ecosystem Services with Water Resource Management in North-west China**

The Qira River catchment of north-west China is characterised by extremely low precipitation (39 mm year^{-1}), strong evaporation (2700 mm year^{-1}) and highly vulnerable ecosystems (Bruelheide et al., 2003). Farmland expansion in the upper reaches of the river has led to increased abstraction of river water and resulted in frequent drying up of the river. The agricultural ecosystem is essential for food production and human welfare, while at the same time the downstream natural ecosystem provides crucial services for human survival and settlement, such as desert vegetation acting as a natural barrier to maintain biodiversity, prevent farmland erosion and to combat desertification and sandstorms (Xue et al., 2017a) (Figure 4.2). Consequently, the area is facing severe water competition between the demands of human activities and natural ecosystems. To achieve consensus on management among the stakeholders, a participatory approach is beneficial to explore the trade-offs and synergies of water use.

ROLE OF NBS

An NBS to management of a catchment of this type requires consensus among the various stakeholders to resolve the conflicts. A participatory approach was proposed that involved four participant groups: stakeholders from various agricultural and environmental bureaus, together with the village head; the water manager; water management experts; and researchers. The expectation was that stakeholder participation would make the solution more straightforward and improve mutual understanding.

MODELLING APPROACHES USED

An approach was developed to couple ecosystem services (ES) into Integrated Water Resource Management (IWRM) through use of a participatory BN model (Xue et al., 2017b). The ES-based IWRM framework includes three steps: identifying water-related services

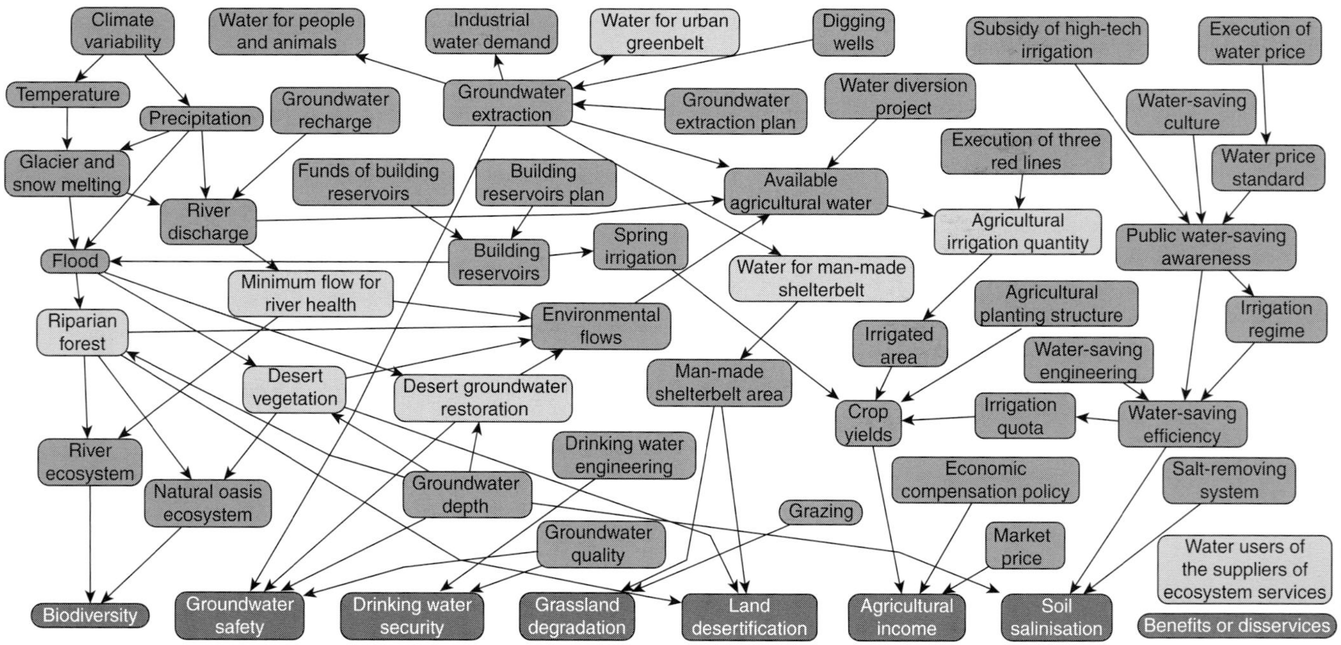

FIGURE 4.2 Participatory BN model for ecosystem services-based IWRM.

CASE STUDY 4.2 **(cont.)**

of ecosystems; analysis of the trade-off and synergy among users of water; and ES-based IWRM implementation using the participatory BN model. Participants first identified the relevant issues before designing the logic of the BN to reflect the cause–effect relationships between variables. Once it had been constructed and evaluated the BN model could be used to analyse different management scenarios and simulate the relative likelihood of changes in target variables associated with the management actions. In the case of the Qiri catchment it was found that acceptable management intervention scenarios would be unable to sustain the ecosystem health in water-related ES. Greater cooperation among the stakeholders is necessary for dealing with such water conflicts. The BN modelling approach was, however, found to be an appropriate method for attempting to resolve the competition for water between human activities and ecosystems.

a study in south-eastern Sweden (Jonsson et al., 2011). This compared three approaches to formulating objectives to address eutrophication via model-assisted dialogue and found that local stakeholder participation was a valuable approach for formulating goals at the local level.

4.3.2 NBS: Water Supply and Drinking Water Quality

Understanding of the resilience of water supplies and drinking water quality is of great importance and is a topic that can be improved and supported by the use of models. NBS in support of drinking water quality will involve management options that target reduction in both point and diffuse sources of pollution. The latter are discussed in more detail in Section 4.3.4.

Several countries have developed national water resources models to support planning. Denmark established a national model in 2003 in order to assess their exploitable groundwater resources

(Henriksen et al., 2008). The model is set up in the MIKE SHE/MIKE 11 modelling system (Abbott et al., 1986; Graham & Butts, 2006) to generate a physically based and fully distributed description of the entire land phase of the hydrologic cycle. The Danish model has been widely utilised for national- and regional-scale assessments. For example, Henriksen et al. (2008) present an application to examine the use of different resource indicators relating abstraction limits to groundwater recharge and their implications for exploitable resources. The reliability and uncertainty within the original version of the model has been subject to ongoing debate and, consequently, it has recently been enhanced and updated (Hojberg et al., 2013).

In the Netherlands, a national hydrological model, the National Hydrological Instrument (NHI) (www.nhi.nu), has also been developed (de Lange et al., 2014), which is an integral water management model focused on water shortage and on the very detailed surface water distribution system in the country. The NHI consists of various physical models at appropriate temporal and spatial scales for all parts of the water system.

On a global scale, pathogenic contamination of drinking water poses the most significant health risk to humans, although significant risks to human health may also result from exposure to non-pathogenic toxic contaminants that are often globally ubiquitous in waters from which drinking water is derived (Ritter et al., 2002). Modelling of pathogen contamination has proved notoriously difficult due to difficulties in forecasting the highly variable sources of pathogens both in time and space and understanding of the precise mechanisms of pathogen transport (Ferguson et al., 2003). Bradford et al. (2013) summarise the many challenges in understanding and modelling these processes and summarise current conceptual and quantitative models for pathogen transport and fate in agricultural settings over a wide range of spatial and temporal scales. Greatest success in this area has been where pathogenic monitoring data have been combined with modelled discharge, for example from Combined Sewer Overflows (Mahajan et al., 2013). The SWAT model, although coded to model bacteria fate and transport, has rarely been used in this context and a review of the model processes is considered necessary to enhance its capability (Baffaut & Sadeghi, 2010). In a novel approach focused on identification of source hotspots, Sokolova et al. (2012) applied a microbial source tracking methodology linked to fate and transport modelling to provide information on the contribution from different contamination sources to the pathogen concentrations at the intake of a drinking water treatment plant.

Pesticides are another key contaminant of concern in relation to drinking water quality. Modelling of pesticides has also proved somewhat problematic, but gradual progress has been made in this regard. One of the earlier tools applied to model pesticide fate and transport was the Root Zone Water Quality Model (RZWQM). A review of applications of RZWQM found that three key processes in achieving good pesticide simulation were: accurate parameterisation of soil permeability at different depths; simulation of pesticide sorption kinetics; and calibration of the pesticide half-life (Malone et al., 2004). Köhne et al. (2009) reviewed progress in pesticide models incorporating preferential flow and found that the principal difficulty relates to appropriate parameterisation of the preferential flow and pesticide processes. Payraudeau and Gregoire (2012) also reviewed a large number of pesticide modelling studies and found that while indicators inferred from conceptual or physically based models are useful as operational tools, only physically based models are capable of capturing all the processes and feedbacks that may be important.

Nitrate may cause health problems if present in high concentrations in public or private water supplies. The US EPA applies a maximum contaminant level goal of 10 mg/l nitrate-N while in Europe the EC Nitrates Directive (1991) sets a maximum concentration of 50 mg/l nitrate (equivalent to 11.3 mg/l nitrate-N) for all groundwaters and surface waters used for drinking water abstraction. In Europe this has led to the designation of Nitrate Vulnerable Zones (NVZs) where action programmes must be implemented to reduce losses of N from agricultural land. Modelling approaches have been used to support both the designation of NVZs and also to assess the effectiveness of measures to reduce nitrate pollution. Lake et al. (2003) used a GIS modelling approach to collate data on root zone leaching, soil and geological attributes to make recommendations for an enhanced set of groundwater NVZs in England and Wales. Sample and Dunn (2014) undertook a national-scale modelling exercise to predict average concentrations of nitrate leaching from agricultural land. This was linked to national monitoring data and groundwater body definitions in order to support decisions for the 2013 review of NVZ boundaries. Many modelling studies have also been undertaken to examine the effectiveness of NVZ action programmes on reducing nitrate concentrations in drinking water. These are discussed in Section 4.3.4.

Sediment is also important for drinking water quality. Modelling of sediment at catchment scales has proved quite problematic due to the high heterogeneity in sources and transport processes, and the importance of deposition and remobilisation. De Vente et al. (2013) undertook a critical evaluation of a range of models. They identified that modelling of soil erosion and sediment yield strongly depends on the spatial and temporal scales considered. In large catchments, non-linear regression models were found to be the most useful, whereas in medium-sized catchments the best results were obtained by factorial scoring models like PSIAC, FSM and SSY Index (De Vente et al., 2005). Most of the conceptual and process-based models were found to represent only a selection of erosion and sediment transport processes and therefore can only provide reliable results where the considered processes are indeed dominant.

4.3.3 NBS: In-stream Chemistry, Eutrophication and Ecology

Eutrophication of rivers and lakes arises from an oversupply of nutrients which can lead to detrimental impacts such as an increase in the biomass of algae and especially increases in cyanobacterial dominance of phytoplankton (Smith, 2003). The EU WFD has recognised the importance of the ecological integrity of freshwaters through setting targets for surface water status in terms of ecological quality. This has altered the emphasis of water quality studies from previous hydrochemical-based assessment. However, modelling of freshwater ecology has proved extremely challenging, not least because of the apparently large variability in the importance of different factors in different geographic and climatic settings. Consequently, implementation of the EU WFD has continued to rely heavily on monitoring and prediction of chemical status (especially N and P) as key factors in determining overall ecological quality.

The SWAT (Soil and Water Assessment Tool) model (Arnold et al., 1998) has been extensively applied globally and is referred to by more than 1700 literature citations. This success is primarily down to accessibility rather than performance per se. SWAT includes equations to simulate hydrology, N, P, pesticides, bacteria, carbon, sediment, biological oxygen demand and dissolved oxygen in rivers (Neitsch et al., 2011). It also includes an extremely comprehensive set of management options for exploration of varying agricultural practices and implementation of NBS. The disadvantage of this is that there are a vast number of parameters that need to be identified and very often, where local information is lacking, default values for these are selected by the user. The danger in this is that the end-user believes that the model can do more than is genuinely true as the underpinning data and information are inadequate (Silgram et al., 2009; Daggupati et al., 2011). Conan et al. (2003) coupled the SWAT model with a groundwater model, MODFLOW, and its companion contaminant and solute transport model, MT3DMS (Prommer et al., 2003), to assess the benefits of decreasing manure application from 210 to 170 kg N ha^{-1} as required by the EC Nitrates Directive.

The AnnAGNPS (Annualized Agricultural Nonpoint-Source Pollution) model (Bosch et al., 1998) has also received widespread use to predict non–point-source pollutant loadings from agricultural watersheds especially to compare the effects of implementing various NBS within a watershed. It has been most commonly used in studies of run-off and sediment losses and their relationship to land-use planning (Sarangi et al., 2007).

In Europe, the Integrated Nitrogen in Catchments model (INCA) (Whitehead et al., 1998; Wade et al., 2002a) has also been widely used. INCA simulates nitrogen export from different land-use types within a river system, together with the resulting in-stream nitrate and ammonium concentrations at catchment scales. The primary objective of the model is to provide a tool which aids the understanding of nitrogen dynamics and which thereby can be used to help support river basin management and policy-making (Wade et al., 2002b). The structure of the INCA nitrogen model has also been used to develop separate models for sediment and phosphorus (Wade et al., 2002c), dissolved organic carbon (Futter et al., 2007) and mercury (Futter et al., 2012). Examples of recent applications of INCA models include: better understanding of controls on inorganic nitrogen leaching in Finland (Rankinen et al., 2013); to determine the key factors controlling run-off, sediment and phosphorus losses in Norway (Farkas et al., 2013); and to improve understanding of dissolved organic carbon dynamics in the context of drinking water supply in Sweden (Ledesma et al., 2012). Although INCA has been found to give good simulations of many aspects of the relevant biogeochemical cycles, it also suffers from issues of difficulties in parameter identification (McIntyre et al., 2005; Dean et al., 2009) and some questions remain regarding the representation of certain processes of the phosphorus cycle (Farkas et al., 2013).

Problems in modelling phosphorus at catchment scales are quite widespread and are underpinned by a poor knowledge base regarding the extrapolation of understanding from small-scale mechanistic studies on the sources and mobilisation of P (Haygarth et al., 2005). In general, models have been found to give an acceptable estimate of P loadings at annual timescales, but simulations of daily, or even monthly, variability in concentrations and loads are much poorer (Chu et al., 2004; Silgram et al., 2009). It is notable that the majority of performance metrics cited for P simulation are in relation to estimates of loads rather than concentrations, with a good hydrological simulation being a key factor in determining the former.

In the context of predicting the ecological impacts of N and P on primary production in surface waters, Keck and Lepori (2012) used data from a large number of experiments to develop regression models to examine the relationships between N, P and microphytobenthos biomass, but found that without information on factors such as light and disturbance, the predictive ability of the models was limited. This highlighted the importance of considering factors beyond nutrient concentrations in developing models of ecological response. Zhang and Rao (2012) applied the Water Analysis Simulation Program (WASP: James et al., 1997) to simulate eutrophication of lake water. As well as including two nutrient cycles (N and P) and three functional phytoplankton groups, this lake model also considers distinct features of the morphological, hydrological and climate conditions. Inputs of N and P for lake models of this type could potentially be generated by catchment models such as SWAT or INCA to enable the effects of different N : P loading ratios on the lake ecosystem to be assessed in terms of simulated phytoplankton biomass.

4.3.4 Effectiveness of Pollution Mitigation Measures

The EU WFD requires member states to adopt cost-effective mitigation measures to achieve good status for all waters and with agriculture considered as a primary source of rural diffuse pollution, many of the potential mitigation methods are targeted at management of agricultural systems. Many of the mitigation methods can also be classified as NBS as they involve simple manipulation of nutrient cycles and/or runoff to reduce the amount of pollutant reaching a water body.

The difficulty in monitoring sources of diffuse pollution has raised important questions about how to evaluate the effectiveness of individual actions and there is a clear role for numerical models to assist with this. Shepherd et al. (2011) evaluated a range of published models for their capability to simulate agricultural production systems and their associated environmental system losses under a changing climate, as well as the ability of the models to handle adaptation and mitigation methods. This study identified three models, DAYCENT (del Grosso et al., 2002), PASIM (Riedo et al., 1998) and SPACSYS (Wu et al., 2007), which accommodate most of the features required to assess the effects of farm mitigation and adaptation on environmental losses under a changing climate. These three models all include process-based representation of agricultural systems including full C and N cycles, water and energy. While models such as these enable improved understanding of effectiveness at a field scale, they do not address the challenge of integration to the spatial scales to meet the requirements of the WFD objectives (Iho, 2005); although measures are implemented at farm level, the ecological targets are set at the subcatchment or catchment scales (Bouraoui & Grizzetti, 2014). Temporal issues also need to be taken into account, as achievement of good ecological status over short timescales appears problematic due to lags in water quality responses (Meals et al., 2010).

Various approaches (Cherry et al., 2008; Collins et al., 2014) have been used to assess the effectiveness of a broad suite of potential mitigation options (Newell Price et al., 2011; Schoumans et al., 2014) at other scales. These approaches have included the use of literature data and expert judgement (Newell Price et al., 2011), application of generalised farm-scale models (Gooday et al., 2014) and the application of catchment models ranging in complexity from simple empirical loss coefficient approaches to complex process-based models (Bouraoui & Grizzetti, 2014). The capabilities of models depend essentially on the purpose for which they were developed (Schoumans et al., 2009a). The FARMSCOPER tool (Gooday et al., 2014) has been designed in collaboration with the UK Department for Environment Food and Rural Affairs (Defra) as a decision support tool to assess diffuse agricultural pollutant loads on a farm and quantify the impacts of farm mitigation methods on these pollutants. The farm systems within the tool can be customised to reflect management and environmental conditions representative of farming across England and Wales and over 100 mitigation methods are incorporated, including many of those in the latest Defra Mitigation Method User Guide. Models such as FARMSCOPER provide invaluable management tools to support farm advisors, although their application at catchment scales (Zhang et al., 2012) has been found to have some limitations. Case Study 4.3 demonstrates how the approach has been used to support implementation of NBS as part of the Countryside Stewardship Scheme in England.

More complex catchment-scale process-based models operate at the scale used to assess effectiveness and are better at handling important temporal and spatial aspects. However, they suffer from other issues, including difficulties in data provision and model parameterisation, leading to high uncertainty in model predictions. Also, many catchment models lack characterisation of key farm-scale management activities that can have a strong influence on simulated diffuse pollution (Dunn et al., 2013). The INCA suite of models is very good at combining both point and diffuse sources of pollution together with in-stream processing, but is very limited in the range of agricultural management options that it can represent. Whitehead et al. (2013) demonstrated how the model could be used to examine the effectiveness of measures for phosphorus mitigation in the Thames catchment in England, where point sources from sewage effluent are a major source. As a result of the broad range of management options integrated in the SWAT model it has been widely used to assess the effectiveness of measures (see e.g. Holvoet et al., 2007; Panagopoulos et al., 2011; Lescot et al., 2013). Barlund et al. (2007) assessed the utility of the model in this context for a catchment in Finland and found that the SWAT descriptions of the management options required some modifications in order to describe correctly the reduction efficiency for local conditions. This highlights the significant uncertainty that can be associated with modelling approaches of this type and it is important that this aspect is not neglected. Vagstad et al. (2009) compared results from different models and found big differences in the predicted effect of the management scenarios, leading to different management practices being identified as most effective for reducing nutrient losses.

The results of some modelling assessments have highlighted that delivery of WFD water quality objectives for some systems could be extremely challenging. Volk et al. (2008, 2009) used a spatial decision support system to integrate ecological and socio-economic assessment methods, scale-specific and GIS-based data and knowledge modelling and visualisation techniques. They explored various land-use and management strategies by applying the SWAT model to a river basin in north-western Germany and found that substantial, expensive, water and land management changes at different scales would be necessary to achieve the WFD water quality targets. Similarly, Glavan et al. (2012) undertook a study of the Axe catchment in south-west England and examined the effect of three different mitigation scenarios by applying the SWAT model. The results of the model analysis suggested that there may be a fundamental incompatibility between the delivery of WFD targets and the maintenance of viable agricultural systems in this region.

Zhang et al. (2017) explored the potential impact of mitigation scenarios associated with the Countryside Stewardship (CS) scheme by constructing theoretical scenarios to model processes across different stages of the water pollutant transfer continuum (from the soil to river and catchment scales) and integrated this into a national-scale modelling framework (Collins et al., 2016). The FARMSCOPER modelling framework (Zhang et al., 2012; Gooday et al., 2014) was used to explore 98 different measures assigned to three mutually exclusive groups targeting the different stages of transfer: source control measures, mobilisation control measures and delivery control measures. A fourth scenario included a combination of all three of these as a means of assessing maximum potential impacts of combined measures. Details of the various measures are listed in Zhang et al. (2017). The modelling results suggested that source control measures (Figure 4.3) will deliver more impact on pollutant emissions than either mobilisation control or delivery control options, but these may be harder to implement as they frequently require fundamental change to farming systems and involve higher capital outlays.

CASE STUDY 4.3 **Countryside Stewardship Scheme**

Agricultural diffuse sources of pollution are recognised as the principal polluters of many rivers and lakes worldwide. There are several policy approaches in England for controlling agricultural pollution including regulatory, incentivised and voluntary codes of good practice (Zhang et al., 2017). The Countryside Stewardship (CS) scheme aims to 'protect and enhance the natural environment, in particular the diversity of wildlife (biodiversity) and water quality' (Countryside Stewardship, 2015) through providing financial incentives for land managers to look after their environment.

ROLE OF NBS

The CS scheme is one which particularly promotes the use of NBS for managing agricultural activities with objectives which include: conserving and restoring wildlife habitats, flood risk management and reducing diffuse water pollution from agriculture. The CS scheme has identified areas for prioritisation of on-farm mitigation as research has shown spatial targeting, to address critical source areas, to be the most cost-effective approach (Doody et al., 2012). Many measures for controlling diffuse pollution (e.g. nutrient management planning, cover crops, buffer strips) use natural processes to manipulate or control nutrient cycles in order to minimise losses from the system, and many of these can also help protect natural resources and support a range of ecosystem services (Boatman et al., 2008).

MODELLING APPROACHES USED

Extensive research has assessed the costs and effectiveness of individual control measures for diffuse pollution in specific settings (Cherry et al., 2008; Schoumans et al., 2014). However, extrapolation to coarser (e.g. water body) scales, for sets of combined pollution control measures, is required to help better understand the role that the various methods can play.

CASE STUDY 4.3 **(cont.)**

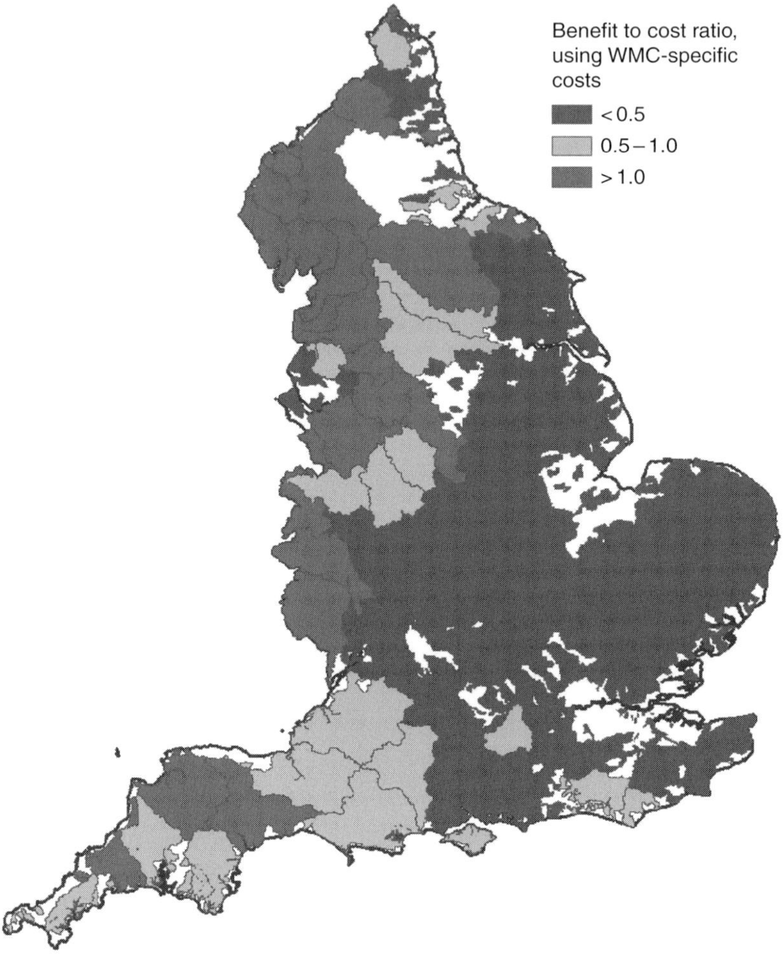

FIGURE 4.3 Estimated ratio of environment benefit to on-farm implementation costs for source control scenario within CS priority areas. (A black and white version of this figure will appear in some formats. For the colour version, please refer to the plate section.)

Another important issue in the context of the effectiveness of mitigation measures is the expected timescales of recovery. Meals et al. (2010) summarised the important processes influencing lag time as hydrology, vegetation growth, transport rate and path, hydraulic residence time, pollutant sorption properties and ecosystem linkages. The magnitude of lag time is highly site- and pollutant-specific, and may range from years to decades for excessive P levels in agricultural soils, and decades or more for sediment accumulated in river systems. Groundwater travel time is also an important contributor to lag time and may introduce a lag of decades between changes in agricultural practices and improvement in water quality. Thus, evaluation of effectiveness through monitoring alone is very challenging and process-based modelling can be a valuable tool to aid understanding. Some studies have used atmospheric tracers to support inverse modelling of groundwater residence times, particularly in the context of predicting recovery from nitrate pollution (Osenbrück et al., 2006; Dunn et al., 2012b). Recovery from P pollution is less well understood and MacDonald et al. (2012) highlighted a need for an improved ability to predict the dynamics of recovery after termination of agricultural use.

4.3.5 Scenario Assessment

Future climate and land-use changes will have implications for water quantity and quality and could make attainment of targets, such as those set by the EU Water Framework Directive, harder to achieve. High uncertainty in how climate and land use will change, coupled with the extreme complexities of modelling multi-pollutant water quality on larger scales, means that it is difficult to factor future changes into policy decisions. Scenario-based planning is commonly adopted as a means of articulating mental models about the future and can help support managers in making better decisions (Dong et al., 2013). Hydrology and water quality models can play an extremely valuable role in demonstrating how future scenarios might be expected to impact on surface and groundwater systems. Stakeholder interaction is an important aspect of scenario-based assessments, and Jessel and Jacobs (2005) described the benefits of stakeholder input at two different stages of the process, both as a means of establishing relevant scenarios prior to model application and then subsequently in interpreting the results of hydrological and water quality modelling to establish management priorities. A similar participatory approach was adopted by Andersson et al. (2008), who used model outputs to guide stakeholders in reaching agreement on environmental goals and then to develop suitable mitigation plans for achieving these.

Wilby et al. (2006) explored an integrated approach to climate change impact assessment by linking established models of regional climate (SDSM), water resources (CATCHMOD) and water quality (INCA) within a single framework. The results confirmed large uncertainty in the impacts on freshwater resulting from climate change uncertainty, as characterised here by the choice of general circulation model, but showed that delivery of EU WFD objectives under climate change could be evaluated using the same framework. In the UK, the 2009 UK Climate Projections (UKCP09) delivered a more robust base for climate change assessments than previous scenarios because they provided future data based upon a more systematic characterisation of uncertainty across several climate models (Murphy et al., 2009; Street et al., 2009).

As well as the hydrological drivers of climate change on pollutant losses, changes in the bioavailability of pollutants may also be important, with changes in biogeochemical cycling triggered by changes in temperature and soil moisture. While increases in temperature from climate change might be expected to increase the rates of some chemical processes, such as mineralisation of soil organic matter, this may be offset against the effects of modified water availability. A detailed study of the effect of wetting and drying cycles on nitrogen mineralisation concluded that increasing summer droughts would most likely reduce the mineralisation and fluxes of N (Beier et al., 2008; Borken & Matzner, 2009). Other processes such as plant uptake or gaseous emissions could also be enhanced by temperature increases and would tend to counteract any increases in mineralisation. Increased denitrification in aquatic systems may also be offset by increased N fixation (Jarvie et al., 2012). Projections made at the European level for winter wheat for the 2071–2100 time-slice showed large spatial variations in N-leaching due to the many interactions between changes in crop uptake, fertilisation, nitrogen mineralisation and soil water balance (Olesen et al., 2007). Current models may be quite limited in how well all of these key processes are characterised and this should be an important consideration in their selection and application to climate change studies.

Many recent watershed modelling studies have examined the impacts of climate change and land-use change on a range of hydrological and water quality determinands including: stream temperature (e.g. Luo et al., 2013), sediment (e.g. Zabaleta et al., 2014), nitrogen (e.g. Salmon-Monviola et al., 2013) and phosphorus (Woodbury & Shoemaker, 2013). Steffens et al. (2014) summarised the relative importance of parameter uncertainty in modelling pesticide leaching versus the uncertainty in future climate scenarios. While the SWAT model is most commonly cited in relation to these types of scenario assessment, other models have also been found useful. Yang and Wang (2010) evaluated the utility of the HSPF model (Bicknell, 1997) for predicting responses to climate and land-use change scenarios in the context of river basin planning and the future delivery of WFD targets. Novotna et al. (2014) applied the WaSim model to an agricultural catchment in Quebec to assess the impacts of climate change on suspended sediment and nutrient loadings. Couture et al. (2014) applied the INCA model chained with the MyLake model to examine the potential impacts of climate and land-use change on lake phosphorus loadings and chlorophyll concentrations.

In some circumstances, climate change adaptation may be necessary where impacts are such that present ecosystem functioning and services can no longer be maintained. Modelling approaches can be used to explore what forms of adaptation could be most successful to meet the needs of various stakeholders. Case Study 4.4 outlines how alternative water policies for the Murray–Darling basin in Australia are being examined, to adapt agricultural systems in a manner that will also allow for maintenance of environmental flows in the river. Similarly, in the Mediterranean region, Brouziyne et al. (2018) have used the SWAT model to evaluate climate change adaptation strategies to improve crop water productivity while preserving hydrologic resources. This explored NBS including no tillage and changes in crop sowing dates.

At larger (e.g. national) scales, there is a demand for scenario assessment to inform implementation of the EU WFD and other policies. Dunn et al. (2012a) examined the relative importance of potential changes in climate versus potential changes in land use in terms of runoff and nitrate leaching by applying a conceptual national-scale water balance and nitrogen budgeting model. Van Roosmalen et al. (2007) undertook a regional impact study of the effects of climate change on groundwater recharge in Denmark using a physically based modelling approach. However, at large scales, implementation of complex multi-pollutant modelling tools may be an impractical option, and simpler approaches may be more appropriate for development of horizon scanning policy. Heathwaite (2003) applied very simple pollutant export models based on expert knowledge and these approaches have been further developed more recently; for example, by integrating fuzzy logic with simple export coefficient models (Islam et al., 2013) or by using literature reviews and expert opinion to develop rule-based models (Zhang et al., 2013). A key attribute of simpler modelling approaches is that their objectives need to be quite tightly defined and limitations in model structures can be problematic when they are extrapolated to differing environmental conditions (Refsgaard et al., 2006). It is the scale and direction of change in water quality that is of primary interest in relation to horizon scanning policy, and a simple qualitative methodology focused on this was found to provide SEPA with appropriate understanding to inform their future evaluation of Significant Water Management Issues for the WFD (Towers et al., 2012). Macleod et al. (2012) also found expert knowledge on the key drivers of pollutant loss to be helpful for rapid evaluation of the direction and sensitivity of water quality responses to future climate and land-use scenarios. An important aspect of an approach presented by Volk et al. (2008) was found to be a visualisation tool that enabled simple explanation of complex system interrelationships in communicating with stakeholders. Integration of this type of relative-risk modelling approach with spatial data on environmental characteristics can create a powerful tool while retaining advantages of simplicity in terms of tracking of errors and immediate visualisation of results (Pistocchi et al., 2010). Tools of this type may be less applicable to developing NBS for water management.

4.4 KEY GAPS, LIMITATIONS AND FUTURE APPROACHES

The preceding review has outlined the current state of the art with regard to modelling of hydrology and freshwater quality and illustrated its applicability in relation to NBS for water management. Limitations of the current suite of modelling tools and methods have been highlighted where relevant, but in summarising it is worth reiterating some of these issues.

There are still fundamental gaps in scientific understanding that limit the capability of models to address important questions. This is especially true of the relationships between chemical composition and ecological status. Noges et al. (2009) outlined some of the remaining challenges in assessing ecological status and despite scientific progress since then, many of these remain true today. Another challenge that is only starting to be considered is that of multi-pollutant impacts and pollutant swapping (Collins & McGonigle, 2008). Van Groenigen et al. (2008) developed a national-scale model and used it to quantify the effects on GHG emissions of environmental policies aimed at reducing NO_3^- leaching and NH_3 volatilisation in Europe, but there appear to be few other modelling studies that have considered management in the context of multiple pollutants.

Although modelling tools are available to simulate a broad range of water quality variables, there are still many uncertainties not just in relation to model parameterisation but also the model

CASE STUDY 4.4 **Climate Adaptation in the Murray–Darling River Basin**

In certain regions of the world, climate change projections are for hotter, drier conditions and floods are expected to be less frequent. Existing floodplains may persist with modified structure and function, or else transform to terrestrial (flood-independent) ecosystems (Colloff et al., 2016) (Figure 4.4). Traditional agricultural production systems may no longer support sustainable water use or allow for adequate environmental flows. Many currently valued ecosystem services will reduce in supply or become unavailable, but these may be replaced by different services.

The Murray–Darling river basin in Australia is an area where major changes to floodplain ecosystems are being predicted. In addition, over-allocation of irrigation water compounded by predicted reductions in rainfall have highlighted a need for reassessment of effective government policies for water allocation (Ejaz Qureshi et al., 2013). Interventions are required which deliver effective solutions to these challenges.

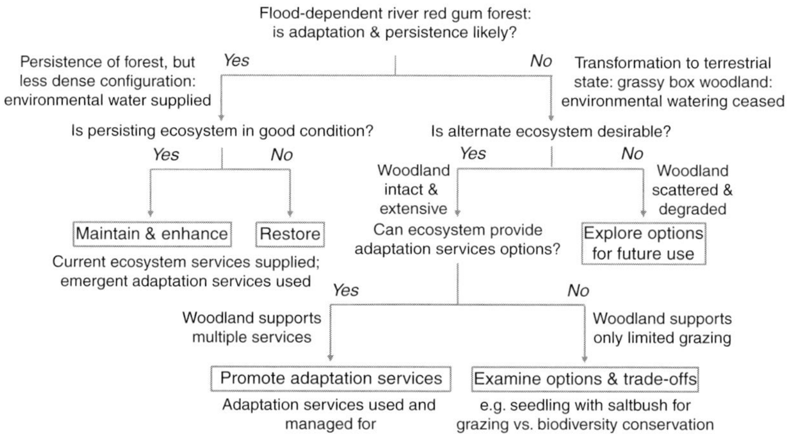

FIGURE 4.4 Decision tree for management for adaptation services under climate change in the Murray–Darling river basin.

CASE STUDY 4.4 **(cont.)**

ROLE OF NBS

Nature-based approaches to climate change adaptation seek to prepare ecosystems for climate change so that they can continue to provide humans with required services, as well as buffering the negative impacts of climate change (Neumann et al., 2014). They often embrace 'no-regret' options (Rizvi et al., 2014), meaning that the measures are useful even if the effects of climate change do not materialise as predicted. In the Murray–Darling basin, adaptations such as the substitution of irrigated agriculture with dryland cropping and floodplain grazing or increasing recreational opportunities from fewer, smaller wetlands that can be maintained with reduced environmental flows may be appropriate.

MODELLING APPROACHES USED

Ejaz Qureshi et al. (2013) demonstrated a Positive Mathematical Programming approach (Howitt, 1995) combining biophysical assessment with an economic analysis to explore climate scenarios and alternative water policies in the Murray–Darling basin. The modelling approach included all the major climate-related impacts, including impact on water allocations, crop effective rainfall, crop evapotranspiration, crop water requirement and impact on irrigation water quality, all of which can have important influences on ecosystem services. The model was run for four climate scenarios with four different states of nature (linked to water salinity) and three policies. The results showed that on-farm adaptation options and water markets could only mitigate against some of the economic losses resulting from changes in agricultural production. The agricultural economics need to be considered alongside management options for persistence or adaptation of key ecosystems (Colloff et al., 2016) in order to successfully implement optimal NBS for the river basin.

structures and their inherent assumptions. Models developed in specific regions are likely to have limitations when applied in different geographic and climatic zones due to the importance of different processes that may be inadequately characterised by the model structure. Another key limitation is the availability of data at appropriate spatial and temporal resolutions to parameterise and calibrate/validate models.

Ensemble modelling is increasingly recognised as a suitable approach to address issues of structural uncertainty in models (Refsgaard et al., 2006). This procedure involves the application of multiple models to simulate the same determinand followed by intercomparison of the results to derive uncertainty bounds. Kronvang et al. (2009) applied eight models for N and five models for P and found coefficients of variation between the model simulations of 67% for gross P loss and 40% for gross N loss. Exbrayat et al. (2013) explored the utility of the approach for simulating N responses to simple fertiliser management changes. The results showed that although each of four models gave good calibration statistics, one of the models simulated a very different response to management changes. The authors proposed an adaptation of the reliability ensemble averaging philosophy to weight the outputs in a situation of this type.

The increasing interest in participatory modelling approaches (Voinov & Busquet, 2010) reflects a growing recognition that models can serve as extremely valuable platforms for assisting stakeholders in understanding current conditions and the causes behind these conditions (Andersson et al., 2008). Kelly et al. (2013) have developed a framework to assist modellers and model users to select an appropriate participatory modelling approach according to the purpose of the model application. Approaches of this type are considered likely to increase in popularity in the future and represent a partial solution to the current limitations because they generally demand less precise, but more flexible, approaches to explore solutions while bringing together a range of expertise.

ACKNOWLEDGEMENTS

This chapter is based on research undertaken while the author was employed at the James Hutton Institute working with a team of interdisciplinary environmental and social scientists. Many people have contributed to the breadth of understanding in modelling water resources for nature-based solutions.

REFERENCES

Abbott, M. B., Bathurst, J. C., Cunge, J. A., O'Connell, P. E. & Rasmussen, J. 1986. An introduction to the European Hydrological System – Systeme Hydrologique Europeen, SHE. 1. History and philosophy of a physically-based, distributed modeling system. *Journal of Hydrology*, 87, 45–59.

Ampadu, B., Chappell, N. A. & Kasei, R. A. 2013. Rainfall–riverflow modelling approaches: making a choice of data-based mechanistic modelling approach for data limited catchments: a review. *Canadian Journal of Pure & Applied Sciences*, 7, 2571–2580.

Andersson, L., Olsson, J. A., Arheimer, B. & Jonsson, A. 2008. Use of participatory scenario modelling as platforms in stakeholder dialogues. *Water SA*, 34, 439–447.

Arnold, J. G. & Fohrer, N. 2005. SWAT2000: current capabilities and research opportunities in applied watershed modelling. *Hydrological Processes*, 19, 563–572.

Arnold, J. G., Srinivasan, R., Muttiah, R. S. & Williams, J. R. 1998. Large area hydrologic modeling and assessment – Part 1: Model development. *Journal of the American Water Resources Association*, 34, 73–89.

Arthington, A. H., Naiman, R. J., McClain, M. E. & Nilsson, C. 2010. Preserving the biodiversity and ecological services of rivers: new challenges and research opportunities. *Freshwater Biology*, 55, 1–16.

Baffaut, C. & Sadeghi, A. 2010. Bacteria modeling with SWAT for assessment and remediation studies: a review. *Transactions of the ASABE*, 53, 1585–1594.

Barlund, I., Kirkkala, T., Malve, O. & Kamari, J. 2007. Assessing SWAT model performance in the evaluation of management actions for the implementation of the Water Framework Directive in a Finnish catchment. *Environmental Modelling & Software*, 22, 719–724.

Barthel, R., Seidl, R., Nickel, D. & Buttner, H. 2016. Global change impacts on the Upper Danube Catchment (Central Europe): a study of participatory modelling. *Regional Environmental Change*, 16, 1595–1611.

Barton, D. N., Saloranta, T., Moe, S. J., Eggestad, H. O. & Kuikka, S. 2008. Bayesian belief networks as a meta-modelling tool in integrated river basin management – pros and cons in evaluating nutrient abatement decisions under uncertainty in a Norwegian river basin. *Ecological Economics*, 66, 91–104.

Beier, C., Emmett, B. A., Penuelas, J., Schmidt, I. K., Tietema, A., Estiarte, M., et al. 2008. Carbon and nitrogen cycles in European ecosystems respond differently to global warming. *Science of the Total Environment*, 407, 692–697.

Bende, U. 1997. Regional hydrochemical modelling by delineation of chemical hydrological response units (CHRUs) within a GIS: an approach of observing man-made impacts in the Broel River catchment (Germany). *Mathematics and Computers in Simulation*, 43, 305–312.

Beven, K. 1993. Prophecy, reality and uncertainty in distributed hydrological modeling. *Advances in Water Resources*, 16, 41–51.

Beven, K. & Freer, J. 2001. Equifinality, data assimilation, and uncertainty estimation in mechanistic modelling of complex environmental systems using the GLUE methodology. *Journal of Hydrology*, 249, 11–29.

Beven, K. J., Kirkby, M. J., Schofield, N. & Tagg, A. F. 1984. Testing a physically-based flood forecasting-model (TOPMODEL) for 3 UK catchments. *Journal of Hydrology*, 69, 119–143.

Bicknell, B. R. 1997. *Hydrological Simulation Program – Fortran. User's Manual for Version 11.* Imhoff, J. C., Kittle, J. L. Jr, Donigian, A. S. Jr & Johanson, R. C. (eds.). Athens, GA: US Environmental Protection Agency, National Exposure Research Laboratory, EPA/600/R-97/080.

Bicknell, B. R., Imhoff, J. C., Kittle, J. L., Jobes, T. H. & Donigian, A. S. 2005. *Hydrological Simulation Program – FORTRAN. User's Manual for Release 12.2.* Athens, GA: US Environmental Protection Agency, Ecosystem Research Division, and Reston, VA: US Geological Survey, Office of Surface Water.

Boatman, N., Ramwell, C., Parry, H., Jones, N., Bishop, J., Gaskell, P., et al. 2008. *A Review of Environmental Benefits Supplied by Agri-environment Schemes.* Peterborough: Land Use Policy Group (FST20/79/041).

Borah, D. K. & Bera, M. 2003. Watershed-scale hydrologic and nonpoint-source pollution models: review of mathematical bases. *Transactions of the ASABE*, 46, 1553–1566.

Borah, D. K., Yagow, G., Saleh, A., Barnes, P. L., Rosenthal, W., Krug, E. C., et al. 2006. Sediment and nutrient modeling for TMDL development and implementation. *Transactions of the ASABE*, 49, 967–986.

Borken, W. & Matzner, E. 2009. Reappraisal of drying and wetting effects on C and N mineralization and fluxes in soils. *Global Change Biology*, 15, 808–824.

Borowski, I. & Hare, M. 2007. Exploring the gap between water managers and researchers: difficulties of model-based tools to support practical water management. *Water Resources Management*, 21, 1049–1074.

Borsuk, M. E., Stow, C. A. & Reckhow, K. H. 2004. A Bayesian network of eutrophication models for synthesis, prediction, and uncertainty analysis. *Ecological Modelling*, 173, 219–239.

Bosch, D. D., Bingner, R. L., Theurer, F. D., Felton, G. & Chaubey, I. 1998. Evaluation of the AnnAGNPS water quality model. Presented at the ASAE Annual International Meeting, Orlando, Florida, USA, 12–16 July 1998.

Bouraoui, F. & Grizzetti, B. 2014. Modelling mitigation options to reduce diffuse nitrogen water pollution from agriculture. *Science of the Total Environment*, 468, 1267–1277.

Bradford, S. A., Morales, V. L., Zhang, W., Harvey, R. W., Packman, A. I., Mohanram, A., et al. 2013. Transport and fate of microbial pathogens in agricultural settings. *Critical Reviews in Environmental Science and Technology*, 43, 775–893.

Brouziyne, Y., Abouabdillah, A., Hirich, A., Bouabid, R., Zaaboul, R. & Benaabidate, L. 2018. Modeling sustainable adaptation strategies toward a climate-smart agriculture in a Mediterranean watershed under projected climate change scenarios. *Agricultural Systems*, 162, 154–163.

Bruelheide, H., Jandt, U., Gries, D., Thomas, F. M., Foetzki, A., Buerkert, A., et al. 2003. Vegetation changes in a river oasis on the southern rim of the Taklamakan Desert in China between 1956 and 2000. *Phytocoenologia*, 33, 801–818.

Castelletti, A. & Soncini-Sessa, R. 2007. Bayesian networks and participatory modelling in water resource management. *Environmental Modelling & Software*, 22, 1075–1088.

Chappell, N. A., McKenna, P., Bidin, K., Douglas, I. & Walsh, R. P. D. 1999. Parsimonious modelling of water and suspended sediment flux from nested catchments affected by selective tropical forestry. *Philosophical Transactions of the Royal Society B – Biological Sciences*, 354, 1831–1846.

Cherry, K. A., Shepherd, M., Withers, P. J. A. & Mooney, S. J. 2008. Assessing the effectiveness of actions to mitigate nutrient loss from agriculture: a review of methods. *Science of the Total Environment*, 406, 1–23.

Christiaens, K. & Feyen, J. 2001. Analysis of uncertainties associated with different methods to determine soil hydraulic properties and their propagation in the distributed hydrological MIKE SHE model. *Journal of Hydrology*, 246, 63–81.

Chu, T. W., Shirmohammadi, A., Montas, H. & Sadeghi, A. 2004. Evaluation of the SWAT model's sediment and nutrient components in the piedmont physiographic region of Maryland. *Transactions of the ASABE*, 47, 1523–1538.

Cohen-Shacham, E., Janzen, C., Maginnis, S. & Walters, G. 2016. *Nature-based Solutions to Address Global Societal Challenges*. Gland: IUCN. DOI:https://doi.org/10.2305/IUCN.CH.2016.13.en

Collins, A. L. & McGonigle, D. F. 2008. Monitoring and modelling diffuse pollution from agriculture for policy support: UK and European experience. *Environmental Science & Policy*, 11, 97–101.

Collins, A. L., Stutter, M. & Kronvang, B. 2014. Mitigating diffuse pollution from agriculture: international approaches and experience. *Science of the Total Environment*, 468, 1173–1177.

Collins, A. L., Zhang, Y. S., Winter, M., Inman, A., Jones, J. I., Johnes, P. J., et al. 2016. Tackling agricultural diffuse pollution: what might uptake of farmer-preferred measures deliver for emissions to water and air? *Science of the Total Environment*, 547, 261–289.

Colloff, M. J., Lavorel, S., Wise, R. M., Dunlop, M., Overton, I. C. & Williams, K. J. 2016. Adaptation services of floodplains and wetlands under transformational climate change. *Ecological Applications*, 26, 1003–1017.

Conan, C., Bouraoui, F., Turpin, N., De Marsily, G. & Bidoglio, G. 2003. Modeling flow and nitrate fate at catchment scale in Brittany (France). *Journal of Environmental Quality*, 32, 2026–2032.

Cools, J., Meyus, Y., Woldeamlak, S. T., Batelaan, O. & De Smedt, F. 2006. Large-scale GIS-based hydrogeological modeling of Flanders: a tool for groundwater management. *Environmental Geology*, 50, 1201–1209.

Cosby, B. J., Ferrier, R. C., Jenkins, A. & Wright, R. F. 2001. Modelling the effects of acid deposition: refinements, adjustments and inclusion of nitrogen dynamics in the MAGIC model. *Hydrology and Earth System Sciences*, 5, 499–517.

Countryside Stewardship. 2015. www.gov.uk/guidance/countryside-stewardship manual/1-scheme-overview

Couture, R.-M., Tominaga, K., Starrfelt, J., Moe, S. J., Kaste, O. & Wright, R. F. 2014. Modelling phosphorus loading and algal blooms in a Nordic agricultural catchment–lake system under changing land-use and climate. *Environmental Science-Processes & Impacts*, 16, 1588–1599.

Cox, B. A. 2003. A review of currently available in-stream water-quality models and their applicability for simulating dissolved oxygen in lowland rivers. *Science of the Total Environment*, 314, 335–377.

Daggupati, P., Douglas-Mankin, K. R., Sheshukov, A. Y., Barnes, P. L. & Devlin, D. L. 2011. Field-level targeting using SWAT: mapping output from HRUs to fields and assessing limitations of GIS input data. *Transactions of the ASABE*, 54, 501–514.

Davison, P. S., Withers, P. J. A., Lord, E. I., Betson, M. J. & Stroemqvist, J. 2008. PSYCHIC – a process-based model of phosphorus and sediment mobilisation and delivery within agricultural catchments. Part 1: model description and parameterisation. *Journal of Hydrology*, 350, 290–302.

De Lange, W. J., Prinsen, G. F., Hoogewoud, J. C., Veldhuizen, A. A., Verkaik, J., Essink, G. H. P. O., et al. 2014. An operational, multi-scale, multi-model system for consensus-based, integrated water management and policy analysis: the Netherlands Hydrological Instrument. *Environmental Modelling & Software*, 59, 98–108.

De Vente, J., Poesen, J. & Verstraeten, G. 2005. The application of semi-quantitative methods and reservoir sedimentation rates for the prediction of basin sediment yield in Spain. *Journal of Hydrology*, 305, 63–86.

De Vente, J., Poesen, J., Verstraeten, G., Govers, G., Vanmaercke, M., Van Rompaey, A., et al. 2013. Predicting soil erosion and sediment yield at regional scales: where do we stand? *Earth-Science Reviews*, 127, 16–29.

Dean, S., Freer, J., Beven, K., Wade, A. J. & Butterfield, D. 2009. Uncertainty assessment of a process-based integrated catchment model of phosphorus. *Stochastic Environmental Research and Risk Assessment*, 23, 991–1010.

Del Grosso, S., Ojima, D., Parton, W., Mosier, A., Peterson, G. & Schimel, D. 2002. Simulated effects of dryland cropping intensification on soil organic matter and greenhouse gas exchanges using the DAYCENT ecosystem model. *Environmental Pollution*, 116, S75–S83.

Dong, C., Schoups, G. & Van De Giesen, N. 2013. Scenario development for water resource planning and management: a review. *Technological Forecasting and Social Change*, 80, 749–761.

Doody, D.G., Archbold, M., Foy, R. H. & Flynn R. 2012. Approaches to the implementation of the Water Framework Directive: targeting mitigation measures at critical source areas of diffuse phosphorus in Irish catchments. *Journal of Environmental Management*, 93, 225–234.

Dorner, S. M., Anderson, W. B., Slawson, R. M., Kouwen, N. & Huck, P. M. 2006. Hydrologic modeling of pathogen fate and transport. *Environmental Science & Technology*, 40, 4746–4753.

Dunn, S. M., Brown, I., Sample, J. & Post, H. 2012a. Relationships between climate, water resources, land use and diffuse pollution and the significance of uncertainty in climate change. *Journal of Hydrology*, 434, 19–35.

Dunn, S. M., Darling, W. G., Birkel, C. & Bacon, J. R. 2012b. The role of groundwater characteristics in catchment recovery from nitrate pollution. *Hydrology Research*, 43, 560–575.

Dunn, S. M., Johnston, L., Taylor, C., Watson, H., Cook, Y. & Langan, S. J. 2013. Capability and limitations of a simple grid-based model for simulating land use influences on stream nitrate concentrations. *Journal of Hydrology*, 507, 110–123.

Dunn, S. M., Lilly, A., Degroote, J. & Vinten, A. A. 2004a. Nitrogen risk assessment model for Scotland: II. Hydrological transport and model testing. *Hydrology and Earth System Sciences*, 8, 205–219.

Dunn, S. M., Vinten, A. J. A., Lilly, A., Degroote, J., Sutton, M. A. & Mcgechan, M. 2004b. Nitrogen risk assessment model for Scotland: I. Nitrogen leaching. *Hydrology and Earth System Sciences*, 8, 191–204.

Ejaz Qureshi, M., Whitten, S. M., Mainuddin, M., Marvanek, S. & Elmahdi, A. 2013. A biophysical and economic model of agriculture and water in the Murray–Darling Basin, Australia. *Environmental Modelling & Software*, 41, 98–106.

Exbrayat, J. F., Viney, N. R., Frede, H. G. & Breuer, L. 2013. Using multi-model averaging to improve the reliability of catchment scale nitrogen predictions. *Geoscientific Model Development*, 6, 117–125.

Farkas, C., Beldring, S., Bechmann, M. & Deelstra, J. 2013. Soil erosion and phosphorus losses under variable land use as simulated by the INCA-P model. *Soil Use and Management*, 29, 124–137.

Ferguson, C., Husman, A. M. D., Altavilla, N., Deere, D. & Ashbolt, N. 2003. Fate and transport of surface water pathogens in watersheds. *Critical Reviews in Environmental Science and Technology*, 3, 299–361.

Futter, M. N., Butterfield, D., Cosby, B. J., Dillon, P. J., Wade, A. J. & Whitehead, P. G. 2007. Modeling the mechanisms that control in-stream dissolved organic carbon dynamics in upland and forested catchments. *Water Resources Research*, 43(2).

Futter, M. N., Poste, A. E., Butterfield, D., Dillon, P. J., Whitehead, P. G., Dastoor, A. P., et al. 2012. Using the INCA-Hg model of mercury cycling to simulate total and methyl mercury concentrations in forest streams and catchments. *Science of the Total Environment*, 424, 219–231.

Gassman, P. W., Reyes, M. R., Green, C. H. & Arnold, J. G. 2007. The soil and water assessment tool: historical development, applications, and future research directions. *Transactions of the ASABE*, 50, 1211–1250.

Gburek, W. J., Sharpley, A. N., Heathwaite, L. & Folmar, G. J. 2000. Phosphorus management at the watershed scale: a modification of the phosphorus index. *Journal of Environmental Quality*, 29, 130–144.

Glavan, M., White, S. M. & Holman, I. P. 2012. Water quality targets and maintenance of valued landscape character – experience in the Axe catchment, UK. *Journal of Environmental Management*, 103, 142–153.

Gooday, R. D., Anthony, S. G., Chadwick, D. R., Newell-Price, P., Harris, D., Duethmann, D., et al. 2014. Modelling the cost-effectiveness of mitigation methods for multiple pollutants at farm scale. *Science of the Total Environment*, 468, 1198–1209.

Graham, D. & Butts, M. 2005. Flexible integrated watershed modeling with MIKE SHE. *In*: Singh, V. P. & Frevert, D. K. (eds.) *Watershed Modelling*, pp. 245–272. Boca Raton, FL: CRC Press.

Haygarth, P. M., Condron, L. M., Heathwaite, A. L., Turner, B. L. & Harris, G. P. 2005. The phosphorus transfer continuum: linking source to impact with an interdisciplinary and multi-scaled approach. *Science of the Total Environment*, 344, 5–14.

Heathwaite, A. L. 2003. Making process-based knowledge useable at the operational level: a framework for modelling diffuse pollution from agricultural land. *Environmental Modelling & Software*, 18, 753–760.

Henriksen, H. J., Troldborg, L., Hojberg, A. L. & Refsgaard, J. C. 2008. Assessment of exploitable groundwater resources of Denmark by use of ensemble resource indicators and a numerical groundwater-surface water model. *Journal of Hydrology*, 348, 224–240.

Hojberg, A. L., Refsgaard, J. C., Van Geer, F., Jorgensen, L. F. & Zsuffa, I. 2007. Use of models to support the monitoring requirements in the Water Framework Directive. *Water Resources Management*, 21, 1649–1672.

Hojberg, A. L., Troldborg, L., Stisen, S., Christensen, B. B. S. & Henriksen, H. J. 2013. Stakeholder driven update and improvement of a national water resources model. *Environmental Modelling & Software*, 40, 202–213.

Holvoet, K., Gevaert, V., Van Griensven, A., Seuntjens, P. & Vanrolleghem, P. A. 2007. Modelling the effectiveness of agricultural measures to reduce the amount of pesticides entering surface waters. *Water Resources Management*, 21, 2027–2035.

Howitt, R. E. 1995. Positive mathematical-programming. *American Journal of Agricultural Economics*, 77, 329–342.

Iho, A. 2005. Does scale matter? Cost-effectiveness of agricultural nutrient abatement when target level varies. *Agricultural and Food Science*, 14, 277–292.

Islam, N., Sadiq, R., Rodriguez, M. J. & Francisque, A. 2013. Evaluation of source water protection strategies: a fuzzy-based model. *Journal of Environmental Management*, 121, 191–201.

Jajarmizadeh, M., Harun, S. & Salarpour, M. 2012. A review on theoretical consideration and types of models in hydrology. *Journal of Environmental Science and Technology*, 5, 249–261.

Jakeman, A. J., Letcher, R. A. & Norton, J. P. 2006. Ten iterative steps in development and evaluation of environmental models. *Environmental Modelling & Software*, 21, 602–614.

James, R. T., Martin, J., Wool, T. & Wang, P. F. 1997. A sediment resuspension and water quality model of Lake Okeechobee. *Journal of the American Water Resources Association*, 33, 661–680.

Jarvie, H. P., Jickells, T. D., Skeffington, R. A. & Withers, P. J. A. 2012. Climate change and coupling of macronutrient cycles along the atmospheric, terrestrial, freshwater and estuarine continuum. *Science of the Total Environment*, 434, 252–258.

Jessel, B. & Jacobs, J. 2005. Land use scenario development and stakeholder involvement as tools for watershed management within the Havel River Basin. *Limnologica*, 35, 220–233.

Johnes, P. J. 1996. Evaluation and management of the impact of land use change on the nitrogen and phosphorus load delivered to surface waters: the export coefficient modelling approach. *Journal of Hydrology*, 183, 323–349.

Jonsson, A. C., Andersson, L., Olsson, J. A. & Johansson, M. 2011. Defining goals in participatory water management: merging local visions and expert judgements. *Journal of Environmental Planning and Management*, 54, 909–935.

Junier, S. & Mostert, E. 2014. A decision support system for the implementation of the Water Framework Directive in the Netherlands: process, validity and useful information. *Environmental Science & Policy*, 40, 49–56.

Kampf, S. K. & Burges, S. J. 2007. A framework for classifying and comparing distributed hillslope and catchment hydrologic models. *Water Resources Research*, 43(5).

Keck, F. & Lepori, F. 2012. Can we predict nutrient limitation in streams and rivers? *Freshwater Biology*, 57, 1410–1421.

Kelly, R. A., Jakeman, A. J., Barreteau, O., Borsuk, M. E., Elsawah, S., Hamilton, S. H., et al. 2013. Selecting among five common modelling approaches for integrated environmental assessment and management. *Environmental Modelling & Software*, 47, 159–181.

Klauer, B., Rode, M., Schiller, J., Franko, U. & Mewes, M. 2012. Decision support for the selection of measures according to the requirements of the EU Water Framework Directive. *Water Resources Management*, 26, 775–798.

Köhne, J. M., Köhne, S. H. & Simunek, J. 2009. A review of model applications for structured soils: b) Pesticide transport. *Journal of Contaminant Hydrology*, 104, 36–60. DOI:10.1016/j.jconhyd.2008.10.003

Kouwen, N., Soulis, E. D., Pietroniro, A., Donald, J. & Harrington, R. A. 1993. Grouped response units for distributed hydrologic modeling. *Journal of Water Resources Planning and Management – ASCE*, 119, 289–305.

Kronvang, B., Behrendt, H., Andersen, H. E., Arheimer, B., Barr, A., Borgvang, S. A., et al. 2009. Ensemble modelling of nutrient loads and nutrient load partitioning in 17 European catchments. *Journal of Environmental Monitoring*, 11, 572–583.

Krysanova, V., Muller-Wohlfeil, D. I. & Becker, A. 1998. Development and test of a spatially distributed hydrological water quality model for mesoscale watersheds. *Ecological Modelling*, 106, 261–289.

Lake, I. R., Lovett, A. A., Hiscock, K. M., Betson, M., Foley, A., Sunnenberg, G., et al. 2003. Evaluating factors influencing groundwater vulnerability to nitrate pollution: developing the potential of GIS. *Journal of Environmental Management*, 68, 315–328.

Ledesma, J. L. J., Kohler, S. J. & Futter, M. N. 2012. Long-term dynamics of dissolved organic carbon: implications for drinking water supply. *Science of the Total Environment*, 432, 1–11.

Lescot, J.-M., Bordenave, P., Petit, K. & Leccia, O. 2013. A spatially-distributed cost-effectiveness analysis framework for controlling water pollution. *Environmental Modelling & Software*, 41, 107–122.

Li, J. & Heap, A. D. 2014. Spatial interpolation methods applied in the environmental sciences: a review. *Environmental Modelling & Software*, 53, 173–189.

Luo, Y., Ficklin, D. L., Liu, X. & Zhang, M. 2013. Assessment of climate change impacts on hydrology and water quality with a watershed modeling approach. *Science of the Total Environment*, 450, 72–82.

MacDonald, G. K., Bennett, E. M. & Taranu, Z. E. 2012. The influence of time, soil characteristics, and land-use history on soil phosphorus legacies: a global meta-analysis. *Global Change Biology*, 18, 1904–1917.

Macleod, C. J. A., Falloon, P. D., Evans, R. & Haygarth, P. M. 2012. The effects of climate change on the mobilization of diffuse substances from agricultural systems. *In*: Sparks, D. L. (ed.) *Advances in Agronomy*, Vol. 115, pp. 41–77. Oxford: Elsevier.

Mahajan, R., Uber, J. G. & Eisenberg, J. N. S. 2013. A dynamic model to quantify pathogen loadings from Combined Sewer Overflows suitable for river basin scale exposure assessments. *Water Quality, Exposure and Health*, 5, 163–172.

Maier, H. R. & Dandy, G. C. 2000. Neural networks for the prediction and forecasting of water resources variables: a review of modelling issues and applications. *Environmental Modelling & Software*, 15, 101–124.

Maier, H. R. & Dandy, G. C. 2001. Neural network based modelling of environmental variables: a systematic approach. *Mathematical and Computer Modelling*, 33, 669–682.

Malone, R. W., Ahuja, L. R., Ma, L. W., Wauchope, R. D., Ma, Q. L. & Rojas, K. W. 2004. Application of the Root Zone Water Quality Model (RZWQM) to pesticide fate and transport: an overview. *Pest Management Science*, 60, 205–221.

McDowell, R. W., Nash, D., George, A., Wang, Q. J. & Duncan, R. 2009. Approaches for quantifying and managing diffuse phosphorus exports at the farm/small catchment scale. *Journal of Environmental Quality*, 38, 1968–1980.

McIntyre, N., Jackson, B., Wade, A. J., Butterfield, D. & Wheater, H. S. 2005. Sensitivity analysis of a catchment-scale nitrogen model. *Journal of Hydrology*, 315, 71–92.

Meals, D. W., Dressing, S. A. & Davenport, T. E. 2010. Lag time in water quality response to best management practices: a review. *Journal of Environmental Quality*, 39, 85–96.

Murphy, J. M., Sexton, D. M. H., Jenkins, G. J., Booth, B. B. B., Brown, C. C., Clark, R. T., et al. 2009. *UK Climate Projections Science Report: Climate Change Projections*. Exeter: Met Office Hadley Centre.

Neitsch, S. L., Arnold, J. G., Kiniry, J. R. & Williams, J. R. 2011. *Soil and Water Assessment Tool Theoretical Documentation Version 2009*. College Station, TX: Texas Water Resources Institute.

Nesshöver, C., Assmuth, T., Irvine, K. N., Rusch, G. M., Waylen, K. A., Delbaere, B., et al. 2017. The science, policy and practice of nature-based solutions: an interdisciplinary perspective. *Science of the Total Environment*, 579, 1215–1227.

Neumann, S., Kaphengst, T., McFarland, K. & Stadler, J. 2014. *Nature-based Approaches for Climate Change Mitigation and Adaptation*. Bonn: German Federal Agency for Nature Conservation.

Newell Price, J. P., Harris, D., Taylor, M., Williams, J. R., Anthony, S. G., Duethmann, D., et al. 2011. *An Inventory of Mitigation Methods and Guide to their Effects on Diffuse Water Pollution, Greenhouse Gas Emissions and Ammonia Emissions from Agriculture*. Abingdon: ADAS.

Noges, P., Van De Bund, W., Cardoso, A. C., Solimini, A. G. & Heiskanen, A.-S. 2009. Assessment of the ecological status of European surface waters: a work in progress. *Hydrobiologia*, 633, 197–211.

Novotna, B., Van Bochove, E. & Theriault, G. 2014. Potential ecological impact of climate change on the water quality of an intensively managed agricultural watershed in Quebec, Canada. *Journal of Water and Climate Change*, 5, 81–99.

Olesen, J. E., Carter, T. R., Diaz-Ambrona, C. H., Fronzek, S., Heidmann, T., Hickler, T., et al. 2007. Uncertainties in projected impacts of climate change on European agriculture and terrestrial ecosystems based on scenarios from regional climate models. *Climatic Change*, 81, 123–143.

Osenbrück, K., Fiedler, S., Knöller, K., Weise, S. M., Sültenfuß, J., Oster, H., et al. 2006. Timescales and development of groundwater pollution by nitrate in drinking water wells of the Jahna-Aue, Saxonia, Germany. *Water Resources Research*, 42(12). https://doi.org/10.1029/2006WR004977

Pachepsky, Y. A., Smettem, K. R. J., Vanderborght, J., Herbst, M., Vereecken, H. & Wosten, J. H. M. 2004. *Reality and Fiction of Models and Data in Soil Hydrology*. Dordrecht: Springer.

Panagopoulos, Y., Makropoulos, C., Baltas, E. & Mimikou, M. 2011. SWAT parameterization for the identification of critical diffuse pollution source areas under data limitations. *Ecological Modelling*, 222, 3500–3512.

Parry, M. L., Fischer, C., Livermore, M., Rosenzweig, C., Iglesias, A. 1999. Climate change and world food security: a new assessment. *Global Environmental Change*, 9, 17.

Payraudeau, S. & Gregoire, C. 2012. Modelling pesticides transfer to surface water at the catchment scale: a multi-criteria analysis. *Agronomy for Sustainable Development*, 32, 479–500.

Phillips, S. W. 2006. *US Geological Survey Chesapeake Bay Studies: Scientific Solutions for a Healthy Bay and Watershed*. Reston, VA: US Department of the Interior, US Geological Survey.

Pistocchi, A., Sarigiannis, D. A. & Vizcaino, P. 2010. Spatially explicit multimedia fate models for pollutants in Europe: state of the art and perspectives. *Science of the Total Environment*, 408, 3817–3830.

Preston, S. D., Alexander, R. B., Woodside, M. D. & Hamilton, P. A. 2009. *Sparrow Modeling – Enhancing Understanding of the Nation's Water Quality*. Reston, VA: US Geological Survey, Fact Sheet 2009–3019.

Prommer, H., Barry, D. A. & Zheng, C. 2003. MODFLOW/MT3DMS-based reactive multicomponent transport modeling. *Ground Water*, 41, 247–257.

Quinn, P. 2004. Scale appropriate modelling: representing cause-and-effect relationships in nitrate pollution at the catchment scale for the purpose of catchment scale planning. *Journal of Hydrology*, 291, 197–217.

Quinn, P., Beven, K., Chevallier, P. & Planchon, O. 1991. The prediction of hillslope flow paths for distributed hydrological modeling using digital terrain models. *Hydrological Processes*, 5, 59–79.

Radcliffe, D. E., Freer, J. & Schoumans, O. 2009. Diffuse phosphorus models in the United States and Europe: their usages, scales, and uncertainties. *Journal of Environmental Quality*, 38, 1956–1967.

Rankinen, K., Granlund, K., Futter, M. N., Butterfield, D., Wade, A. J., Skeffington, R., et al. 2013. Controls on inorganic nitrogen leaching from Finnish catchments assessed using a sensitivity and uncertainty analysis of the INCA-N model. *Boreal Environment Research*, 18, 373–386.

Reaney, S. M., Lane, S. N., Heathwaite, A. L. & Dugdale, L. J. 2011. Risk-based modelling of diffuse land use impacts from rural landscapes upon salmonid fry abundance. *Ecological Modelling*, 222, 1016–1029.

Reckhow, K. H. 1999. Water quality prediction and probability network models. *Canadian Journal of Fisheries and Aquatic Sciences*, 56, 1150–1158.

Refsgaard, J. C. & Storm, B. 1995. MIKE SHE. *In*: Singh, V. P. (ed.) *Computer Models of Watershed Hydrology*, pp. 809–846. Lone Tree, CO: Water Resource Publications.

Refsgaard, J. C., Van Der Sluijs, J. P., Brown, J. & Van Der Keur, P. 2006. A framework for dealing with uncertainty due to model structure error. *Advances in Water Resources*, 29, 1586–1597.

Refsgaard, J. C., Van Der Sluijs, J. P., Hojberg, A. L. & Vanrolleghem, P. A. 2007. Uncertainty in the environmental modelling process – a framework and guidance. *Environmental Modelling & Software*, 22, 1543–1556.

Riedo, M., Grub, A., Rosset, M. & Fuhrer, J. 1998. A pasture simulation model for dry matter production, and fluxes of carbon, nitrogen, water and energy. *Ecological Modelling*, 105, 141–183.

Ritter, L., Solomon, K., Sibley, P., Hall, K., Keen, P., Mattu, G., et al. 2002. Sources, pathways, and relative risks of contaminants in surface water and groundwater: a perspective prepared for the Walkerton inquiry. *Journal of Toxicology and Environmental Health Part A Current Issues*, 65, 1–142.

Rizvi, A. R., Barrow, E., Zapata, F., Cordero, D., Podvin, K., Kutegeka, S., et al. 2014. *Ecosystem-based Adaptation: Building on No Regret Adaptation Measures*. Gland: International Union for Conservation of Nature, Technical Paper.

Romanowicz, R. J., Young, P. C., Beven, K. J. & Pappenberger, F. 2008. A data based mechanistic approach to nonlinear flood routing and adaptive flood level forecasting. *Advances in Water Resources*, 31, 1048–1056.

Salmon-Monviola, J., Moreau, P., Benhamou, C., Durand, P., Merot, P., Oehler, F., et al. 2013. Effect of climate change and increased atmospheric CO2 on hydrological and nitrogen cycling in an intensive agricultural headwater catchment in western France. *Climatic Change*, 120, 433–447.

Saloranta, T. M., Kamari, J., Rekolainen, S. & Malve, O. 2003. Benchmark criteria: a tool for selecting appropriate models in the field of water management. *Environmental Management*, 32, 322–333.

Sample, J. & Dunn, S. M. 2014. *Spatially Distributed Modelling in Support of the 2013 Review of the Nitrates Directive.* Aberdeen: Scotland's Centre of Expertise for Waters.

Sarangi, A., Cox, C. A. & Madramootoo, C. A. 2007. Evaluation of the AnnAGNPS model for prediction of runoff and sediment yields in St Lucia watersheds. *Biosystems Engineering*, 97, 241–256.

Schoumans, O. F., Chardon, W. J., Bechmann, M. E., Gascuel-Odoux, C., Hofman, G., Kronvang, B., et al. 2014. Mitigation options to reduce phosphorus losses from the agricultural sector and improve surface water quality: a review. *Science of the Total Environment*, 468, 1255–1266.

Schoumans, O. F., Silgram, M., Groenendijk, P., Bouraoui, F., Andersen, H. E., Kronvang, B., et al. 2009a. Description of nine nutrient loss models: capabilities and suitability based on their characteristics. *Journal of Environmental Monitoring*, 11, 506–514.

Schoumans, O. F., Silgram, M., Walvoort, D. J. J., Groenendijk, P., Bouraoui, F., Andersen, H. E., et al. 2009b. Evaluation of the difference of eight model applications to assess diffuse annual nutrient losses from agricultural land. *Journal of Environmental Monitoring*, 11, 540–553.

Shenk, G. W. & Linker, L .C. 2013. Development and application of the 2010 Chesapeake Bay Watershed total maximum daily load model. *Journal of the American Water Resources Association*, 49, 1042–1056.

Shepherd, A., Wu, L. H., Chadwick, D. & Bol, R. 2011. A review of quantitative tools for assessing the diffuse pollution response to farmer adaptations and mitigation methods under climate change. *In*: Sparks, D. L. (ed.) *Advances in Agronomy*, Vol. 112. Oxford: Elsevier.

Silgram, M., Schoumans, O. F., Walvoort, D. J. J., Anthony, S. G., Groenendijk, P., Stromqvist, J., et al. 2009. Subannual models for catchment management: evaluating model performance on three European catchments. *Journal of Environmental Monitoring*, 11, 526–539.

Simunek, J., Van Genuchten, M. T. & SEJNA, M. 2008. Development and applications of the HYDRUS and STANMOD software packages and related codes. *Vadose Zone Journal*, 7, 587–600.

Singh, V. P. & Woolhiser, D. A. 2002. Mathematical modeling of watershed hydrology. *Journal of Hydrologic Engineering*, 7, 270–292.

Smith, V. H. 2003. Eutrophication of freshwater and coastal marine ecosystems – a global problem. *Environmental Science and Pollution Research*, 10, 126–139.

Sokolova, E., Astrom, J., Pettersson, T. J. R., Bergstedt, O. & Hermansson, M. 2012. Estimation of pathogen concentrations in a drinking water source using hydrodynamic modelling and microbial source tracking. *Journal of Water and Health*, 10, 358–370.

Steffens, K., Larsbo, M., Moeys, J., Kjellstrom, E., Jarvis, N. & Lewan, E. 2014. Modelling pesticide leaching under climate change: parameter vs. climate input uncertainty. *Hydrology and Earth System Sciences*, 18, 479–491.

Stewart-Koster, B., Bunn, S. E., Mackay, S. J., Poff, N. L., Naiman, R. J. & Lake, P. S. 2010. The use of Bayesian networks to guide investments in flow and catchment restoration for impaired river ecosystems. *Freshwater Biology*, 55, 243–260.

Stithou, M., Hynes, S., Hanley, N. & Campbell, D. 2012. Estimating the value of achieving 'good ecological status' in the Boyne River catchment in Ireland using choice experiments. *Economic and Social Review*, 43, 397–422.

Street, R. B., Steynor, A., Bowyer, P. & Humphrey, K. 2009. Delivering and using the UK climate projections 2009. *Weather*, 64, 227–231.

Stroemqvist, J., Collins, A. L., Davison, P. S. & Lord, E. I. 2008. PSYCHIC – a process-based model of phosphorus and sediment transfers within agricultural catchments. Part 2. A preliminary evaluation. *Journal of Hydrology*, 350, 303–316.

Towers, W., Dunn, S. M., Sample, J. & Dawson, J. 2012. *The Potential Risks to Water Quality from Diffuse Pollution Driven by Future Land Use and Climate Change*. Aberdeen: CREW.

USEPA (US Environmental Protection Agency). 2010a. *Chesapeake Bay Total Maximum Daily Load for Nitrogen, Phosphorus and Sediment*. Washington, DC: USEPA.

USEPA (US Environmental Protection Agency). 2010b. *Chesapeake Bay Phase 5.3 Community Watershed Model*. EPA 903S10002 – CBP/TRS-303–10. Annapolis, MD: USEPA, Chesapeake Bay Program Office.

Vagstad, N., French, H. K., Andersen, H. E., Behrendt, H., Grizzetti, B., Groenendijk, P., et al. 2009. Comparative study of model prediction of diffuse nutrient losses in response to changes in agricultural practices. *Journal of Environmental Monitoring*, 11, 594–601.

Van Groenigen, J. W., Schils, R. L. M., Velthof, G. L., Kuikman, P. J., Oudendag, D. A. & Oenema, O. 2008. Mitigation strategies for greenhouse gas emissions from animal production systems: synergy between measuring and modelling at different scales. *Australian Journal of Experimental Agriculture*, 48, 46–53.

Van Roosmalen, L., Christensen, B. S. B. & Sonnenborg, T. O. 2007. Regional differences in climate change impacts on groundwater and stream discharge in Denmark. *Vadose Zone Journal*, 6, 554–571.

Voinov, A. & Bousquet, F. 2010. Modelling with stakeholders. *Environmental Modelling & Software*, 25, 1268–1281.

Volk, M., Hirschfeld, J., Dehnhardt, A., Schmidt, G., Bohn, C., Liersch, S. & Gassman, P. W. 2008. Integrated ecological–economic modelling of water pollution abatement management options in the Upper Ems River Basin. *Ecological Economics*, 66, 66–76.

Volk, M., Liersch, S. & Schmidt, G. 2009. Towards the implementation of the European Water Framework Directive? Lessons learned from water quality simulations in an agricultural watershed. *Land Use Policy*, 26, 580–588.

Volk, M., Moeller, M. & Wurbs, D. 2010. A pragmatic approach for soil erosion risk assessment within policy hierarchies. *Land Use Policy*, 27, 997–1009.

Wade, A. J., Durand, P., Beaujouan, V., Wessel, W. W., Raat, K. J., Whitehead, P. G., et al. 2002a. A nitrogen model for European catchments: INCA, new model structure and equations. *Hydrology and Earth System Sciences*, 6, 559–582.

Wade, A. J., Whitehead, P. G. & Butterfield, D. 2002b. The Integrated Catchments model of Phosphorus dynamics (INCA-P), a new approach for multiple source assessment in heterogeneous river systems: model structure and equations. *Hydrology and Earth System Sciences*, 6, 583–606.

Wade, A. J., Whitehead, P. G. & O'Shea, L. C. M. 2002c. The prediction and management of aquatic nitrogen pollution across Europe: an introduction to the Integrated Nitrogen in European Catchments project (INCA). *Hydrology and Earth System Sciences*, 6, 299–313.

Whitehead, P. G., Crossman, J., Balana, B. B., Futter, M. N., Comber, S., Jin, L., et al. 2013. A cost-effectiveness analysis of water security and water quality: impacts of climate and land-use change on the River Thames system. *Philosophical Transactions of the Royal Society A – Mathematical Physical and Engineering Sciences*, 371(2002).

Whitehead, P. G., Wilson, E. J. & Butterfield, D. 1998. A semi-distributed Integrated Nitrogen model for multiple source assessment in Catchments (INCA): Part I – model structure and process equations. *Science of the Total Environment*, 210, 547–558.

Wilby, R. L., Orr, H. G., Hedger, M., Forrow, D. & Blackmore, M. 2006. Risks posed by climate change to the delivery of Water Framework Directive objectives in the UK. *Environment International*, 32, 1043–1055.

Woodbury, J. & Shoemaker, C. A. 2013. Stochastic assessment of long-term impacts of phosphorus management options on sustainability with and without climate change. *Journal of Water Resources Planning and Management*, 139, 512–519.

Wright, R. F., Cosby, B. J., Hornberger, G. M. & Galloway, J. N. 1986. Comparison of paleolimnological with magic model reconstructions of water acidification. *Water, Air and Soil Pollution*, 30, 367–380.

Wu, L., McGechan, M. B., McRoberts, N., Baddeley, J. A. & Watson, C. A. 2007. SPACSYS: integration of a 3D root architecture component to carbon, nitrogen and water cycling-model description. *Ecological Modelling*, 200, 343–359.

Xue, J., Gui, D. W., Lei, J. Q., Sun, H. W., Zeng, F. J. & Feng, X. L. 2017a. A hybrid Bayesian network approach for trade-offs between environmental flows and agricultural water using dynamic discretization. *Advances in Water Resources*, 110, 445–458.

Xue, J., Gui, D., Lei, J., Zeng, F., Mao, D. & Zhang, Z. 2017b. Model development of a participatory Bayesian network for coupling ecosystem services into integrated water resources management. *Journal of Hydrology*, 554, 50–65.

Yang, Y. S. & Wang, L. 2010. A review of modelling tools for implementation of the EU Water Framework Directive in handling diffuse water pollution. *Water Resources Management*, 24, 1819–1843.

Young, P. C. 1992. Parallel processes in hydrology and water-quality – a unified time-series approach. *Journal of the Institution of Water and Environmental Management*, 6, 598–612.

Young, P. C. & Beven, K. J. 1994. Data-based mechanistic modeling and the rainfall-flow nonlinearity. *Environmetrics*, 5, 335–363.

Young, R. A., Onstad, C. A., Bosch, D. D. & Anderson, W. P. 1989. AGNPS – a nonpoint-source pollution model for evaluating agricultural watersheds. *Journal of Soil and Water Conservation*, 44, 168–173.

Zabaleta, A., Meaurio, M., Ruiz, E. & Antigueedad, I. 2014. Simulation climate change impact on runoff and sediment yield in a small watershed in the Basque Country, Northern Spain. *Journal of Environmental Quality*, 43, 235–245.

Zhang, B. & Govindaraju, R. S. 2000. Prediction of watershed runoff using Bayesian concepts and modular neural networks. *Water Resources Research*, 36, 753–762.

Zhang, T., Page, T., Heathwaite, L., Beven, K., Oliver, D. M. & Haygarth, P. M. 2013. Estimating phosphorus delivery with its mitigation measures from soil to stream using fuzzy rules. *Soil Use and Management*, 29, 187–198.

Zhang, W. & Rao, Y. R. 2012. Application of a eutrophication model for assessing water quality in Lake Winnipeg. *Journal of Great Lakes Research*, 38, 158–173.

Zhang, Y., Collins, A. L. & Gooday, R. D. 2012. Application of the FARMSCOPER tool for assessing agricultural diffuse pollution mitigation methods across the Hampshire Avon Demonstration Test Catchment, UK. *Environmental Science & Policy*, 24, 120–131.

Zhang, Y., Collins, A. L., Jones, J. I., Johnes, P. J., Inman, A. & Freer, J. E. 2017. The potential benefits of on-farm mitigation scenarios for reducing multiple pollutant loadings in prioritised agri-environment areas across England. *Environmental Science & Policy*, 73, 100–114.

5 Models at the Service of Marine Nature-based Solutions

Ioanna Akoumianaki and Arthur Capet

5.1 INTRODUCTION

A broad marine management goal is to maintain healthy *marine social–ecological systems* that sustain desirable marine ecosystem services (MES) and have the capacity to adapt to change. Models, as representations of how systems work, are promising tools for understanding marine *ecosystem and socio-economic processes* (Addison et al., 2017; Zedler, 2017). Marine models can translate alternative scenarios exploring the projected consequences on marine ecosystem function of possible futures for drivers of change such as greenhouse gas (GhG) emissions, coastal development, and market, political and socio-cultural forces on seafood consumption (Millennium Ecosystem Assessment (MEA), 2005; Inniss et al., 2016; Intergovernmental Science-Policy Platform on Biodiversity and Ecosystem Services (IPBES), 2016; Katona et al., 2017). They can also help decision-makers to evaluate national or local scenarios examining the effectiveness of alternative past or future policy interventions influencing society's demand for specific MES and their delivery to society (Guerry et al., 2012; IPBES, 2016; Arkema et al., 2017).

Marine nature-based solutions (NBS) are increasingly incorporated in approaches towards sustainable and adaptive management of marine social–ecological systems (Herr & Landis, 2016; IUCN, 2017; Schueler, 2017; UN-Water, 2018). Here, we present modelling approaches applied in marine NBS applications. We reviewed assessment reports and peer-reviewed literature mentioning the term marine NBS or ecosystem-based adaptation in the context of marine social–ecological systems or coupled human–nature systems. Based on our findings, we evaluated models with respect to their complexity and the decision-making context and identified challenges for marine NBS modelling.

5.2 SCOPE OF MARINE NBS AND THEIR MODELLING

5.2.1 Marine Ecosystems and Their Services and Benefits

Marine ecosystems include all types of ecosystems below the low-water mark: saltmarshes, estuaries, mangroves, seagrass beds, coral reefs, oyster and rocky reefs, the continental shelf, the open sea and the deep sea. Their function refers to the ecological, biogeochemical, hydrodynamic and other abiotic processes that control the fluxes of energy, genes, nutrients and organic matter through the marine environment (de Groot et al., 2010; Cardinale et al., 2012; Hattam et al., 2015; Alexander et al., 2016). These processes underpin MES, which are classified into: provisioning (e.g. seafood or pharmaceutical substances provision); regulating (e.g. carbon storage and coastal protection); habitat (e.g. biodiversity); and cultural services (e.g. recreation, sense of place, research and education) (de Groot et al., 2010; Böhnke-Henrichs et al., 2013).

Ecosystem services (ES) are contributions of ecosystems to human well-being (de Groot et al., 2010). The term well-being encompasses access to basic materials for a good life, good health, good social relations, and to a variety of options for decision-making (McMichael et al., 2005). Ecosystem benefits refer to the 'exports' from the ecosystems to society (Banzhaf & Boyd, 2012) and they can be determined using monetary and non-monetary valuation. Monetary metrics may include: income generation from commercial or recreational fisheries and tourism supported by marine ecosystems, cost avoided by preventing damage to property through natural coastal defences and cost avoided by slowing down global warming through restoring blue carbon ecosystems (Herr & Landis, 2016; Morris et al., 2018). Examples of non-monetary valuation metrics include valuing biodiversity for its own sake or its socio-cultural value, and biophysical values, e.g. erosion reduction and good water quality (Ruckelshaus et al., 2015).

5.2.2 *Marine NBS*

NBS applications combine disaster risk management, climate change mitigation and adaptation, biodiversity conservation and sustainable resources management and provide low-cost options for climate change mitigation and adaptation actions (Cohen-Shacham et al., 2016; Albert et al., 2017; Rockström & Tyrell, 2017). As an umbrella concept, marine NBS cover a wide range of marine ecosystem-based mitigation and adaptation approaches and initiatives towards enhancing adaptation capacity and ensuring ocean sustainability, including nature-based coastal protection and blue carbon sequestration and storage (Spalding et al., 2014; Cohen-Shacham et al., 2016; Herr & Landis, 2016; Nesshöver et al., 2017; Morris et al., 2018). Here, adaptation capacity relates to societies' ability and willingness to cope with the impacts of climate change (Rizvi & Van Riel, 2013).

Marine NBS is a key component of the United Nations (UN) 2030 Agenda for sustainable development (United Nations, 2015), which aims to end poverty and increase prosperity while mitigating climate change and protecting all ecosystems from degradation. Marine NBS is also at the heart of blue economy (World Bank & UNDESA, 2017), a concept comprising the range of economic sectors and related policies that together determine whether the use of oceanic resources is sustainable. Further, marine NBS are included in the adaptation strategies of 59 countries as part of their National Determined Contributions (NDCs) towards achieving the global warming limit necessary to combat climate change under the UN Framework Convention on Climate Change and the Paris Agreement, i.e. a global average increase well below 2°C and pursuing efforts to limit the temperature increase to 1.5°C above pre-industrial levels (UNFCCC, 2015).

Regardless of specific application and purpose, a key feature of marine NBS is the delivery of additional ES (or co-benefits) compared with stand-alone hard infrastructure for coastal protection (Pontee et al., 2016) or policy interventions to reduce GhG emissions from human activity (Bridges et al., 2015; European Commission, 2015; Sutton-Grier et al., 2015; Bilkovic et al., 2016; Nesshöver et al., 2017; Roberts et al., 2017; Schueler, 2017; Morris et al., 2018). For example, ecosystems that are protected, restored or created to act as natural coastal defences or blue carbon sinks also contribute in varying degrees to biodiversity maintenance, commercial or recreational fish-stock recovery, waste assimilation, as well as to sustaining local livelihoods and local economies and supporting social resilience (Guerry et al., 2012). Conversely, decisions for implementing marine NBS for a specific purpose may also lead to disadvantages (aka dis-benefits) compared to pre-NBS ecosystem function and services (Levin & Lubchenco, 2008). For instance, planting mangroves for coastal defence may be inimical for existing degraded saltmarsh habitats because mangroves are invasive (Chapman & Underwood, 2011).

5.2.2.1 NBS: Nature-based Coastal Protection

Marine NBS for coastal protection is critical for supporting disaster risk management and resilience to coastal hazards (e.g. sea-level rise, storm surges, flooding, erosion and tsunami). Coastal protection ES refer to protection, restoration or creation of habitats generating and supporting processes, such as wave attenuation, sediment retention, seabed stabilisation, near-bottom turbulence and wave energy dissipation (Borsje et al., 2011; Chapman & Underwood, 2011; Temmerman et al., 2013; Bouma et al., 2014; Spalding et al., 2014; Bridges et al., 2015; Ruckelshaus et al., 2015; Brandon et al., 2016; Gittman et al., 2016; Narayan et al., 2016, 2017; O'Donnell, 2016; Pontee et al., 2016; Reddy et al., 2016; Stark et al., 2016; Arkema et al., 2017; Moosavi, 2017; Nowacki et al., 2017; Thorslund et al., 2017; Ysebaert et al., 2017; Morris et al., 2018).

Nature-based coastal protection includes the following approaches.

- Designation of marine protected areas (MPA), whereby human activity is prohibited or controlled to protect habitats such as mangroves, saltmarshes, seagrass beds and coral reefs.

- Restoration of habitats, such as oyster reefs, saltmarshes, seagrass beds and mangroves.
- Ecological engineering involving stand-alone natural or hybrid (combinations of natural and man-made) applications, such as establishing habitats of:
  - Ecosystem engineering species (e.g. oysters).
  - Benthic communities on hard substrates (e.g. rock sills, or anchored wood).
  - Oyster reefs or seagrass beds in front of artificial man-made structures (aka hard engineering or grey infrastructure), such as seawalls, dykes and breakwaters, in order to prevent their overtopping or damage during extreme events.
  - Saltmarshes through sand nourishment or artificial channels to encourage sediment deposition and retreat in response to rising sea levels (managed realignment).

5.2.2.2 *NBS: Blue Carbon Sequestration and Storage*

Much less studies refer to NBS using coastal ecosystems for blue carbon sequestration/storage and climate change mitigation and adaptation (e.g. Pendleton et al., 2012; Herr & Landis, 2016; Griscom et al., 2017; UN-Water, 2018). Major blue carbon sinks at local and global scales refer to coastal wetlands, i.e. mangroves, saltmarshes, seagrass beds and constructed wetlands for wastewater treatment (MEA, 2005; Pendleton et al., 2012; Inniss et al., 2016). Climate change and adaptation strategies incorporating blue carbon ecosystems to achieve national and global targets under the UNFCCC and the Paris Agreement are as follows (Herr & Landis, 2016; Wilson & Forsyth, 2018).

- Climate change mitigation strategies involving 'protection of carbon sinks'.
- Climate change adaptation strategies, which may involve three different approaches:
  - Designation of MPA to sustain fisheries and biodiversity.
  - Marine spatial planning, i.e. a process for the management of the coast that considers all aspects of the coastal zone, including geographical and political boundaries, to achieve sustainability.

  - Adaptation in the fisheries sector by prioritising job-generating sectors using coastal and marine resources (e.g. fisheries and mangrove forestry) and promoting blue economy.

- Strategies encouraging management of coastal ecosystems as examples of synergies between climate change mitigation and adaptation, e.g. MPA are associated with natural carbon removal, and thus have direct climate change mitigation benefits.

5.3 DATA REQUIREMENTS FOR MODELLING MARINE NBS

Integrating the different components of marine social–ecological systems into models requires a great diversity of types of data. Quantitative data may refer to biophysical measurements collected through regulatory monitoring, research sampling, long-term deployed probes, autonomous systems, satellite imagery and versatile data collection tools supported by mobile phone apps capturing daily, seasonal, annual and event-based variability (Edgar et al., 2016; Addison et al., 2017). Databases may also include data from expert judgement, traditional knowledge, model output and citizen initiatives as well as monetary valuation metrics (Gimenez et al., 2014; Vitolo et al., 2015; Addison et al., 2017).

Hattam et al. (2015) suggested that data for developing indicators and models for MES (and by extension marine NBS) must be:

- measurable, i.e. in the form of quantitative variables describing the state of an environmental characteristic or a component of the social–ecological system, or the rate of a process;
- sensitive to MES change over time;
- specific for the purpose of a management intervention or policy;
- scalable, i.e. valid to describe the delivery of MES at different spatial scales; and
- transferable, i.e. useful for more than one location or study.

5.4 MODEL ATTRIBUTES FOR MARINE NBS

This wide scope of marine NBS applications and implications for ecosystems and society requires modelling approaches that can integrate the environmental, social and economic dimensions of marine social–ecological systems and consider their connections, interdependencies and conflicts (Arkema et al., 2017). There is plenty of guidance and model selection criteria for decision-making in ecosystem-based adaptation (Fulton et al., 2003; Plagányi, 2007; Bagstad et al., 2013; Beck & Lange, 2016; Christin et al., 2016; IPBES, 2016; Bullock & Ding, 2018; Harrison et al., 2018). Most of this guidance refers to models operated in terrestrial contexts or for fisheries management. However, we consider that, in principle, it is relevant to marine NBS modelling approaches.

For example, based on discussions with both stakeholders and scientists, Bagstad et al. (2013) determined key criteria for the evaluation of (terrestrial mainly) ES models preferred by decision-makers, which are: model output data; time to run a model; model software availability in the public domain; model validation; documentation of methods, assumptions and algorithms; applicability in terms of spatial scale and context; and value-added by using the model. Bullock and Ding (2018) highlighted the importance of model complexity in the decision-making process. Simple models can focus on individual decisions; for example, exploring whether ecosystem change influences the delivery of a service such as fisheries, recreation, coastal protection or climate change mitigation. However, decisions about where and when to restore an ecosystem to deliver desired benefits in the short and long run require more complex modelling approaches, skills and resources. Fulton et al. (2003) described the factors influencing the structural complexity of a model: the number of parameters it includes; the number of ecosystem components and processes it simulates; the temporal scale; the non-linearities, log effects, thresholds and cumulative effects incorporated in those processes; and whether it includes features such as spatial dynamics or stochasticity.

In marine modelling, complexity increases from simple conceptual models to statistical through to process-based models (Addison et al., 2017): conceptual models can help display our understanding of how systems work using qualitative information;

statistical models can help interpret existing monitoring data, and quantify spatial or temporal patterns in data; and process-based models can mathematically represent the variability of the system, inform variable selection for monitoring and extrapolate monitoring data over larger scales with accompanying estimates of uncertainty in model predictions. Accuracy of model predictions improves with model complexity because complex models use a range of variables (descriptors) which better represent the processes underpinning ES. However, accuracy is known only with model output validation against measured data.

It must also be noted that marine models rarely fall in clear-cut complexity and accuracy categories as those suggested by Addison et al. (2017), but rather tend to fall along a continuum, depending on available data, assumptions and purpose of modelling. For example, conceptual models inform statistical models and the calibration and evaluation of process-based models. Further, statistical models can be integrated into parameter estimation of process-based models, so that model parameter values are not fixed to one value but rather sampled from probability distributions representing uncertainty. Finally, integrating models of different types, complexity and scope to a toolbox (or ensemble) has the potential to address uncertainty due to model structure by comparing outcomes from different modelling approaches (Gregr & Chan, 2014; Addison et al., 2017). However, toolbox approaches are often the most complex (Addison et al., 2017).

5.5 MES ASESSMENT FRAMEWORK

Assessing a marine ecosystem and its services in an integrated manner before applying NBS is difficult because social–ecological systems are too large and complex to permit holistic assessments (Katona et al., 2017). The MES assessment (MESA) framework (Arkema et al., 2017) is an effective approach consistent with the complexity of marine social–ecological systems. It effectively relates change in ecosystem resulting from a policy or management action to change in the benefits that matter to people (Daily et al., 2009; Arkema et al., 2015). Ruckelshaus et al. (2015) argued that the MESA framework is the most effective approach in leading to policy change as part of an iterative science-policy process that enables scientific knowledge to reach real-world decision-making. The MESA framework is increasingly used in the context of marine NBS (Arkema et al., 2017). It includes three steps (Arkema et al., 2017). Step one identifies the problem and what marine NBS application is relevant. Step two quantifies links between the biophysical processes supporting MES and benefits to society before and after the NBS implementation (aka ecological production function, see section referring to the Marine Integrated Valuation of ES and Trade-offs (INVEST) model). Step three characterises MES demand with regards to the proximity and composition of affected populations, the preferences and information available to those individuals, the types of facilities affected by coastal hazards and the structure of related markets. When sufficient data and expertise are available, incorporating process-based models in steps one and two can quantify the magnitude of changes in MES (e.g. Guerry et al., 2012; Bridges et al., 2015; Storlazzi et al., 2017) and expected damages (Guerry et al., 2012; Arkema et al., 2015; Barbier, 2015; Reddy et al., 2017; Storlazzi et al., 2017).

5.6 MODELS APPLIED IN MARINE NBS

Harrison et al. (2018) reviewed and categorised modelling methods and tools that have been developed under the MESA framework in specific situations into three groups: (i) broadly *biophysical methods*; (ii) broadly *socio-cultural methods*; and (iii) broadly *monetary techniques*. This categorisation is used here to facilitate the description of marine models operated within the MESA framework and that have been applied in marine NBS.

5.7 (BROADLY) BIOPHYSICAL MODELS

The group of broadly biophysical models includes (Harrison et al., 2018) the following.

- Biophysical models assessing the processes underpinning ES. In the marine context, these processes refer to physical process (e.g. ocean circulation, hydrodynamics, wind–wave interactions and particle transport), biogeochemical processes, species distribution and population dynamics, and ecological/food web dynamics.
- ES models assessing the supply (and sometimes the demand) of multiple ES usually in a specialised GIS-like software environment.
- Agent-based models (ABMs) simulating the human decision-making process involved in ES management or policy.
- Simple GIS mapping of ES using GIS software if spatially explicit data are directly available for a service (e.g. food production or wave attenuation).

5.7.1 Ocean and Coastal Hydrodynamics and Wind–Wave Models

A great variety of marine models have been developed to project ocean circulation, hydrodynamics and wind–wave interactions. A complete analysis of all the many characteristics, challenges and applications of physical models is beyond the scope of this review. Here we focus on process-based models with the potential to allow better understanding and quantification of the physical processes underpinning MES. Readers further interested in the characteristics of marine physical models are referred to: Bedri et al. (2013); Dyke (2001); Legrand et al. (2006); Stock et al. (2011); The WAMDI Group (1988); Beck and Lange (2016) and Plagányi (2007).

5.7.1.1 Ocean General Circulation Models (O-GCM)

O-GCM represent ocean state at a coarse resolution (5–50 km) in real time and provide boundary conditions for coastal and regional models as well as oceanic boundary conditions for a global coupled atmosphere–ocean general circulation models (AOGCM) prediction model. O-GCM are essential for ecosystem modelling. An example is the HYbrid Coordinate Ocean Model (HYCOM) (Bleck, 2002), a primitive equation general circulation model which is isopycnal in the open, stratified ocean, but uses the layered continuity equation to make a dynamically smooth transition to a terrain following coordinates in shallow coastal regions, and to *z*-level coordinates in the mixed layer and/or unstratified seas. HYCOM was developed to overcome design limitations of the existing operational global ocean prediction systems as well as limitations in vertical and horizontal resolution. Thus, it has improved performance in shallow water areas and in handling the transition from deep to shallow water. The model is available upon account request. The output of HYCOM has been used to construct a null model of passive larval dispersal at the MPA network of the Island of Hawaii, to simulate ocean flows and track virtual larvae ('drifters') during the pelagic larval duration for evaluating the resilience of fragmented coral reef habitats (Christie et al., 2010). It can also be coupled with the ecosystem model Atlantis (Link et al., 2010, 2011; Fay et al., 2017); see also Section 5.6.1.

For HYCOM, there are detailed user's guide, user's manual and software design documentation describing usage (e.g. it is domain-independent); the running environment (e.g. it is portable among all UNIX-based systems); directory structure (e.g. all of the pre- and post-processing programs are compiled only once and a second directory contains the data files and scripts needed to run a simulation for a specific domain); input/ouput file formats; and the steps for setting up HYCOM for a new domain and running a simulation (Bleck et al., 2002; Wallcraft et al., 2003, 2009). For setting up bathymetry, HYCOM uses data sets from Earth Topography 2 (ETOPO2), Global Earth Topography from the National Geophysical Data Center (NGDC). The HYCOM user has control over setting up the model domain, generating the forcing fields and ingesting either the climatology or output fields from other model simulations to use for boundary and interior relaxation. Output includes 2D and 3D temperature and salinity, currents, sea-surface elevation and turbulence nowcasts and forecasts.

It must be noted that coupled AOGCM simulations prepared by modelling groups around the world for the Intergovernmental Panel on Climate Change (IPCC) AR4 are state-of-the-art tools for studying current and future climate; however, these models are not further reviewed here. For extensive information on coupled AOGCM readers are referred to Randall et al. (2007).

5.7.1.2 *Coastal Hydrodynamic Models*

These are spatially explicit models, based on understanding of fluid mechanics. They describe water motion and associated descriptors: temperature and salinity, currents, vertical turbulences and sea-surface elevation. They require gridded information on the domain bathymetry and dynamic external forcing, i.e. atmospheric conditions (humidity, winds, air temperature, pressure, solar irradiation and precipitation) and freshwater run-off. To resolve circulation dynamics at regional scales, high-resolution implementations of hydrodynamical models are considered which require the provision of hydrodynamic descriptors on the open boundaries (i.e. typically offshore). Nested subdomains with increasing resolution may be considered in this effect (Mason et al., 2010). Alternatively, using unstructured grid domains (i.e. meshes with varying size) focuses the computational effort on fine-scale coastline features and/or areas of particular interest such as straits, estuaries and harbours, whereby the domain bathymetry is required at a corresponding spatial resolution. Three notable examples of hydrodynamic models applied in marine NBS are reviewed below.

TELEMAC 2D. A widely used hydrodynamic modelling system, which is part of the TELEMAC-MASCARET modelling suite and contains the relevant physical processes with respect to tidal wave propagation in estuaries (Hervouet, 2007). Detailed descriptions of its modules are given in the website of the model (TELEMAC-MASCARET, n.d.), from where the model can be downloaded free of charge. Space is discretised into an unstructured 2D grid of triangular elements, so that the calculation grid can be refined locally in areas of interest. Output includes plots of current flow direction and wave direction and amplitude. TELEMAC 2D can also simulate the transport of dissolved tracers. Stark et al. (2016) used TELEMAC 2D to study the capacity of a 3000-ha intertidal saltmarsh (SW Netherlands) to locally attenuate peak water levels during storm. Model simulations were used to assess the effect of marsh size (i.e. storage area) and whether it is a limiting factor for storm surge attenuation in case of surge events larger than the observed range. The model was calibrated on tidal water levels by implementing zones with different Manning's bottom friction coefficients. Model performance was validated by a comparison between modelled and observed tidal water–level series at measurement locations. Model results indicated that peak water level reduction largely varies between individual flooding events and between different locations in the marsh. Scenarios with variable dyke positions showed that attenuation rates can be minimised by blockage and set up of water levels against dykes or other structures confining the marsh size.

ADvanced CIRCulation Model (ADCIRC). This is a finite-element, time-dependent, long-wave, hydrodynamic circulation model for the simulation of water level and current over an unstructured gridded domain (Luettich et al., 1992; Westerinck et al., 2008). It conducts short- and long-term simulations of tide and storm surge elevations and velocities in deep-ocean, continental shelves, coastal seas and small-scale estuarine systems. It was developed by experts in hydrodynamic engineering at the US Army Corps of Engineers Coastal and Hydraulics Laboratory (USACE-CHL) to predict storm surge water level and help control the impact of storm damage. ADCIRC maintains both accuracy and robustness when applied to the wide range of scales of motion and wide range of hydrodynamic balances that exist when computing deep-ocean flows that transition to flows in inlets and land. ADCIRC runs as a 2D depth-integrated model or as a 3D model to solve time-dependent free surface circulation and transport problems. The use of an unstructured grid allows for high localised grid resolution where solution gradients are large and low grid resolution where solution gradients are small, minimising both local and global error norms for a given computational cost. Output includes plots of salinity, temperature, density, turbulence, sea level and inundation. The model is well developed and documented (http://adcirc.org/) and available upon request for research and education purposes. ADCIRC coupled with the wave model Simulating Waves Nearshore (SWAN) helped to quantify storm tides and significant wave heights (e.g. after Hurricane Sandy) in the presence and absence of oyster beds (e.g. Brandon et al., 2016).

General Estuarine Transport Model (GETM). This is a 3D finite-difference hydrodynamic model (Burchard & Bolding, 2002). It simulates hydrodynamics and sediment transport at the land–coastal sea interface based on mass conservation, momentum advection, a k-ε turbulence closure model, using the general z vertical coordinate system with possible flooding/drying of coastal grid cells. It requires 12 hours to simulate one year in the North-German Supercomputing Alliance (HLRN). It is open-access, well developed and well documented (GETM, n.d.). It is commonly coupled with biogeochemical models, e.g. the European Regional Seas Ecosystem Model (ERSEM) (see Section 5.7.2.1).

5.7.1.3 Wind–Wave Models

These models represent the growth, dissipation and transport of sea surface waves to provide quantitative information to ocean users, mainly in the coastal zone. Open boundary conditions can be obtained from the WaveWatch III global service (Tolman, 2009). Required accuracy may be compromised by uncertain bathymetry, variations in vegetation coverage and other unmeasured hydrodynamic forces. Required resolution and accuracy of surface wind forcing are additional crucial limitations. Second-generation wave models have started using an unstructured mesh to enable an accurate representation of coastlines and islands, especially where a finer resolution is key (e.g. heterogeneous coastal landscapes), and reduce singularities associated with the poles in geographic coordinates (Gourgue et al., 2013; Elskens et al., 2014). Third-generation models parameterise explicitly wave built-up processes, non-linear transfer of energy and dissipation (WAMDI Group, 1988). Validation against observations is essential to characterise deficiencies and identify areas for improvement. In-situ observations are obtained from buoys, ships and oil platforms. Altimetry data from satellites, such as GEOSAT and TOPEX, can also be used to infer the characteristics of wind waves. Hindcasts of wave models during extreme conditions also serve as a useful test-bed for the models (Cardone et al., 1996).

Simulating Waves Nearshore (SWAN). SWAN is an open-access, third-generation wave model for obtaining realistic estimates of wave parameters in coastal areas, lakes and estuaries from given wind, bottom and current conditions (Booij et al., 1999). It is based on the wave action balance equation with sources and sinks and accounts for wave generation by wind, dissipation due to aquatic vegetation (e.g. seagrass, saltmarsh, mangroves) and other structures (e.g. biogenic reefs), turbulent flow and viscous fluid mud. Output includes, *inter alia,* significant wave height and wave periods, dissipation and wave-induced force. SWAN can be used on any scale relevant for wind-generated surface gravity waves. It is well developed and well documented (SWAN, n.d.). SWAN has been used to evaluate the wave dissipation efficiency of vegetated habitats (e.g. Guannel et al., 2015; Reddy et al., 2016; Vuik et al., 2016; Mendoza et al., 2017; van Wesenbeeck et al., 2017); oyster reefs (e.g. Brandon et al., 2016); and coral reefs (Storlazzi et al., 2017; Osorio-Cano et al., 2019). A case study of the use of SWAN as part of the MESA framework to assess coral reef protection priority sites in Hawaii is presented in Case Study 5.1.

XBEACH. This process-based model was developed by USACE to provide a tool with which nearshore hydrodynamics and morphological effects (e.g. shoreline erosion, overwash and scour around buildings) due to hurricanes can be simulated and measures can be evaluated (McCall et al., 2010; Roelvink et al., 2010). The model can simulate the 2D horizontal nearshore hydrodynamics of waves on the timescale of wave-groups, including surfbeat (long waves, infragravity waves) and wave-induced currents in combination with non-cohesive sediment transports, avalanching of dune fronts and morphological change on the timescale of storm events. The output includes wave height and wave period. The model is well developed and documented (XBEACH, n.d.) and has many applications. For example, Smallegan et al. (2017) used XBEACH to evaluate the effectiveness of several adaptation strategies, including combinations of (nature-based) raised beach and dunes and hard structures (e.g. seawalls) under future sea-level scenarios. Karanci et al. (2017) use XBEACH as part of an agent-based model. Storlazzi et al. (2017) projected wave propagation over coral reefs using XBEACH (Case Study 5.1).

5.7.2 *Biogeochemical and Ecosystem Models*

Many models focus on simple or complex representations of marine biogeochemical and ecosystem processes. Data availability along with the improvement of computational skills have led to the development of conceptual and statistical models as well as sophisticated process-based approaches. Even so, in many cases key ecosystem processes are still simplistically represented, frequently lacking clear mechanistic basis with questionable assumptions and respect to the mass conservation principle (the verification problem). Model descriptions are also compromised by poor consistency between modelled output and observations (the validation problem). This is because of our limited understanding of key processes (e.g. mineralisation); the functional role of groups of species (e.g. marine microbes); and of specific ecosystem compartments (e.g. benthic recycling). In addition, fitting the small spatio-temporal scales of biogeochemical processes to the large scale of whole ecosystem and physical processes, i.e. from hours to decades and from kilometres to global, creates the so-called 'multi-scale problem' in ecosystem modelling.

Readers interested in model names and broad characteristics per biogeochemical and ecosystem model type are referred to Piroddi et al. (2015). Here, we focus on examples of biogeochemical and ecosystem models applied for marine NBS.

5.7.2.1 *Marine Biogeochemical Models (BGCM)*

Marine BGCM describe the evolution of dissolved or particulate substances that are transported and dispersed by currents or sink to the sea bottom upon a fixed spatial grid framework, while these undergo chemical and biological transformations. Variables may include: dissolved nutrients (nitrate, phosphate, silicate, iron, dissolved inorganic carbon); pH and alkalinity; phyto- and zooplankton; and particulate and dissolved detrital (organic) matter. Empirical marine BGCM apply only under restricted conditions set by the range of the calibrated data set. Dynamic mass-balance model BGCM are difficult and costly to calibrate, validate and run, and tend to accumulate uncertainty in the prediction. Process-based BGCM include representations of singular (e.g. carbon-C, nitrogen-N) or multiple element cycles (e.g. C, N, phosphorus-P, oxygen-O, silicon-Si) through dissolved/particulate, organic/inorganic forms; discretisation of plankton groups into size-based classes (Moloney & Field, 1991); a spatial dimension along with depth (e.g. Dadou et al., 2001); coupling of BGCM with hydrodynamic models in three dimensions (3D) (e.g. Koné et al., 2005; Dippner, 2006); and coupling of plankton BGCM with High Trophic Level (HTL) models, also known as ecosystem models (Fennel et al., 2001). BGCM validation relies on dissolved oxygen, chlorophyll and particle content based on satellite imaging or optical measurements, autonomous devices (e.g. Argo, gliders, towed moorings) and routine monitoring. Observations in ocean carbon chemistry remain a challenge limiting validation of these models (Mongin et al., 2016).

CASE STUDY 5.1 Assessing Services and Benefits of the Coral Reef Habitat off Maui, Hawaii, USA (Storlazzi et al., 2017, and literature cited therein)

The problem: The population of reef-lined islands resides in low-lying areas within a few metres of the coast. These areas are vulnerable to coastal flooding during storm surges.

The Nature-based Solution: Coral reefs attenuate waves, thus helping to narrow the extent of flooding.

The Approach: Applying the three steps of the MESA framework to provide a quantitative valuation of the coastal protection benefits of coral reefs under numerous current and future storm intensity levels in Maui, Hawaii, as an initial test case before applying the method in all coral reef-lined coasts of Hawaii, Florida, Guam, American Samoa, the US Virgin Islands and the Northern Mariana Islands.

STEP ONE: SPECIFYING THE COASTAL HAZARD (FIGURE 5.1A)

Sixty-one years of validated hourly hindcast wave data were extracted from the Global Ocean Wave database for the Hawaiian Islands and subsequently synthesised into 500 combinations of sea states (wave height, wave periods and wave direction) that best represented the range of wave conditions in the area. A series of three dynamically downscaled nested grids were used to provide spatially varying boundary conditions for finer SWAN grids, which were generated using grid cell averaging of the NOAA Tsunami Inundation Digital Elevation Model. The finest SWAN grids were extracted at 100-m intervals along the coastline and then were reconstructed as shallow-water wave data using multidimensional interpolation.

CASE STUDY 5.1 **(cont.)**

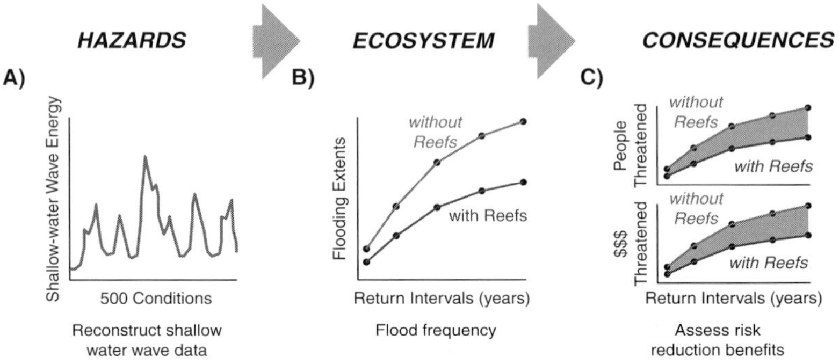

FIGURE 5.1 Schematic of methodology used to evaluate role of coral reefs in coastal hazard risk reduction off Maui, Hawaii. (Source: Storlazzi et al., 2017.) (A black and white version of this figure will appear in some formats. For the colour version, please refer to the plate section.)

STEP 2: LINKING PROCESS-BASED MODEL WITH COASTAL PROTECTION SERVICES WITH/WITHOUT REEFS (FIGURE 5.1B)

A seamless bathymetric/topographic and coral coverage data map was extracted from ArcGIS layers of benthic habitat maps defining coral reef spatial extent and percent coral cover and coastline maps, using transects crossing the –30-m and +20-m elevation contours. The wave energies associated with the 5-, 10-, 25-, 50-, 100- and 250-year return period (six water-level profiles) were obtained by the 500 synthesised nearshore wave conditions to a General Extreme Value Distribution. XBEACH for coral reefs was used to project total water-level variations and coastal flooding extent. The friction induced by corals was parameterised based on the spatially varying coral coverage data map and wave-breaking studies over various reef configurations and friction coefficients. The wave heights and water levels were also propagated to account for the loss of the coral reef and to quantify the wave-driven flooding along the six water-level profiles with and without reefs.

CASE STUDY 5.1 **(cont.)**

STEP 3: DEFINING DEMAND FOR COASTAL PROTECTION SERVICE (FIGURE 5.1C)

The flooding extent was used for creating a flood mask layer in ArcGIS, and people and associated social characteristics (e.g. ethnic origin, income) and built infrastructure impacted by wave-driven flooding within it were computed. The value of coral reefs in terms of coastal hazard risk reduction was then determined as the difference in people and infrastructure impacted by wave-driven flooding in the simulations including coral reefs compared to those without coral reefs.

Links to management: This output will inform: (i) government efforts on where coral reef conservation, restoration and management is socially and economically important; and (ii) financing for reef management from new funding sources interested in investing in reef conservation and management (e.g. defence, transportation and climate change management agencies).

Potential future scenarios: The entire process-based model can be rerun to evaluate: (i) climate scenarios, e.g. 1 m of sea-level rise to determine changes in the effectiveness of the reef in response to sea-level rise; (ii) population and economic growth scenarios, e.g. to show how the importance of the reef as coastal defence to people will be influenced by demographic change; (iii) ecosystem scenarios, e.g. increase in coral cover and thus frictional effects, e.g. to provide guidance as to where coral reef restoration will be more effective for providing coastal protection services and benefits.

European Regional Seas Ecosystem Model – Biogeochemical Flux Model (ERSEM-BFM). This is a notable example of an open-access (upon registration code) process-based, spatially explicit BGCM, which describes the dynamics of the biogeochemical fluxes within the pelagic and benthic environment (Baretta et al., 1995; Baretta-Bekker et al., 1997; Blackford et al., 2004; Ruardij et al., 2005; Vichi et al., 2007; Hyder et al., 2015; Butenschön et al., 2016). It is used for shelf seas water quality monitoring and climate impact assessment and is also run operationally by the UK Met Office. ERSEM-BFM represents many key biogeochemical processes of temperate shelf systems (e.g. carbon cycle and carbonate chemistry, nutrient uptake by phytoplankton and cycling of labile/semi-labile organic matter in water column and benthos; temperature dependence of mineralisation and physiological rates; the microbial loop; and plankton functional types). It consists of an interlinked set of boxes representing lower and higher trophic levels and the cycling of carbon and macronutrients (nitrogen, phosphorus, silicon) and oxygen in the water column, stratified or mixed, and the benthic system. The biological components are organised into functional groups, in the pelagic and benthic submodels. For example, the pelagic module includes: (i) parameterisation for diatoms for spring growth; (ii) transparent extracellular polysaccharides (TEPs) excretion by diatoms under nutrient stress; (iii) formation of TEP–diatom macro-aggregates to represent food supply to benthos; (iv) a *Phaeocystis* functional group to simulate primary production in coastal areas; and (v) suspended particulate matter (SPM) resuspension. It also includes a three-layer benthic module to resolve benthic processes and benthic–pelagic coupling (Radach & Moll, 2006). The model simulates multiple ecosystem states. This increases uncertainty because the validation of plankton functional types, and especially bacteria, as well as other processes is problematic due to limited evidence. ERSEM-BFM is one of the computationally expensive and underperforming models, due to its using a large number of state variables (>40) (Kwiatkowski et al., 2014).

Aldridge et al. (2012) fitted GETM-ERSEM-BFM coupled with a nutrient sink to simulate the effects of macroalgae farming on the marine biogeochemical environment of Scottish coastal waters in the North Sea and assess trade-offs/interactions associated with it versus protecting, conserving and enhancing biodiversity. The model predicted that nitrogen removal associated with seaweed farming will benefit areas subject to anthropogenic nutrient inputs but may lead to decreased energy fluxes to the benthic community, potentially altering its structure.

5.7.2.2 *Habitat Suitability Models (HSMs)*

HSMs (sometimes called species distribution modelling) are increasingly being used to predict distribution patterns of a species, or a group of species, based on their observed relationship with environmental conditions, with a focus on supporting decision-making for delineating MPA for fisheries objectives (Hirzel et al., 2006; Elith & Leathwick, 2009). For example, the successive steps of the general and most widespread fish habitat mapping approach include: (i) selecting the fish species accounted for; (ii) fitting and evaluating habitat suitability models that relate fish species or stage-specific distribution to environmental descriptors; (iii) using habitat suitability indices from model outputs to create predicted fish distribution maps within GIS; and (iv) combining these maps to help decision-making for delineating MPA (Le Pape et al., 2014). To effectively use HSMs as decision-making tools involves using abundance data (as opposed to relying only on presence-absence data), validation against fine-resolution measured data, ensemble modelling and estimates of model uncertainty (Rooper et al., 2014; Anderson et al., 2016). High-resolution multi-beam data and seafloor images are promising techniques for validating HSM for benthic and reef systems (e.g. Howell et al., 2011).

A notable example of HSMs for marine NBS is presented by Zhou et al. (2016), who used a GIS-based habitat suitability index (HSI) model to identify suitable areas for eelgrass (*Zostera marina* L.) restoration in the subtidal zone of Xiaoheishan Island, China. The environmental descriptors in the model, in order of importance, were: Secchi depth (i.e. water transparency), sediment composition, water temperature, salinity, current velocity, water depth and nutrient quality. The inverse distance weighted (IDW) interpolation tool was used to produce eelgrass maps in the region. Similar approaches have been used by Vaudrey et al. (2013) and Novak and Short (2012.)

5.7.2.3 *Population Dynamics Models*

Population dynamics models (aka multi-species models) consider the direct predator–prey or indirect competitive relationships across a complex trophic network of multiple species, multiple life stages and/or size-classes within populations (Hollowed et al., 2000; Shin & Cury, 2001; Christensen & Walters, 2004; Fung et al., 2015). They are used in determining trophic interactions in ecosystems with commercial fisheries (e.g. for stock assessments) and in evaluating ecosystem effects of different fishing policies.

A public-domain software suite with widespread use is Ecopath with Ecosim (EwE) (Pauly et al., 2000; Falk-Petersen, 2004; Plaganyi & Butterworth, 2004; Christensen et al., 2005; del Monte-Luna et al., 2007; Essington, 2007; Espinosa-Romero et al., 2011; Heymans et al., 2012). It comprises: (i) a mass-balance food web model representing an ecosystem at a steady state by a network of quantified flows between ecosystem compartments principally designed to answer ecological questions and evaluate fishing impacts (Ecopath); (ii) a time-dynamic simulation module for scenario exploration (Ecosim); and (iii) a spatial and temporal dynamic module designed for exploring impact and placement of MPA (Ecospace). Repeating Ecosim simulations allows for the fitting of predicted biomasses to time-series data. Predation pressure on a particular prey population is determined by a vulnerability constant, which represents prey mortality relative to predator biomass. Ecosim also contains a routine to allow a 'forcing function', which may represent environmental conditions and fishing pressure, to influence these trophic interactions.

EwE for Marine NBS. Weijerman et al. (2018) used EwE to evaluate the effects of alternative management and climate scenarios at Puakō, Hawaii, on three coral reef MES, i.e. ecosystem resilience, recreation and food. Reef species were aggregated into 27 functional groups: 15 fish, one sea turtle, six invertebrate, four primary producer and one detritus. Local pressures were fishing (net-, spear- and line fishing) and untreated sewage. The model was validated by verifying that a 100-year run with no perturbations produced stable trajectories, and calibrated by fitting biomass, catches and vulnerability parameters to historical survey data from unpublished coral reef data sets using EwE's least-square fitting criterion. In addition to 'Current Management', there were also simulated three alternative fishery management scenarios, a no-take MPA scenario and one pollution management scenario. ES were evaluated by equally weighting their performance indicators under future high and low severity (in terms of coral bleaching events) climate scenarios. Only line fishing improved resilience and recreation under low and high severity climate scenarios compared to 'Current Management' at the cost of the fishery service. EwE alone could not account for differences in compliance and feasibility of enforcement for the various scenarios and changes in fishing effort. However, it provided insights on trade-offs among competing management strategies within a consistent decision-making context.

5.7.2.4 End-to-end Approaches

These approaches were developed to account for the dynamic forcing effect of climate effects (e.g. ocean acidification) and other man-made effects such as fisheries on multiple trophic levels (e.g. Fulton, 2010; Fay et al., 2017). This is the most complex type of ecosystem model as it accounts for multi-species or multifunctional groups and their direct and indirect interactions with the abiotic environment from nutrient to fish in a variety of spatio-temporal scales. As a result, end-to-end models are subject to verification, validation and multi-scale problems.

The model Atlantis (e.g. Fulton et al., 2011) has been used to explore fishery management options in an ecosystem context as well as to assess the effects of acidification on fishery yield and ecosystem structure (e.g. Fay et al., 2017). This is a spatially explicit box model that links the output from a process-based hydrodynamic model to a biophysical model of the food web to economic models describing human uses. Atlantis is suitable for conducting ecosystem-level management strategy evaluation, and has been used to rank alternative policy scenarios and quantitatively evaluate fisheries and ecosystem management strategies (e.g. Fulton et al., 2011; Kaplan et al., 2012). Atlantis is time- and data-intensive to apply and is used by a small community of practice (IPBES, 2016).

Atlantis NEUS. This version of the Atlantis model covers the area from Cape Hatteras to the Gulf of Maine (Link et al., 2010, 2011). It contains 22 dynamic spatial boxes stratified by depth. The model uses output from (i) HYCOM; (ii) an ecological model, which comprises a food web of 45 functional benthic and pelagic groups; and (iii) a human model consisting of 18 fishing fleets, each specific for a unique group of species and parameterised to mimic the general historical pattern of species dynamics and fishing history for the years 1963–2004. Fay et al. (2017) used Atlantis-NEUS to explore acidification effects scenarios (from zero acidification effects to increased mortality or decreased growth) on eight calcifying benthic invertebrate groups, phytoplankton and zooplankton. A set of indicators was also determined to assess scenario performance (i.e. group-specific biomass and catch, trophic level of catch, ratio of system biomass to total primary production and ratio of demersal species biomass to total primary production). The model predicted variable and inconsistent acidification effects among species groups under constant fishing pressure, demonstrating that Atlantis-NEUS can help the understanding of trade-offs that emerge from different pressures, and thus it is a promising tool for decision-making for climate change adaptation.

5.7.3 *ES Models*

ES models examine how changes in marine processes flow to people and highlight trade-off among objectives of multiple management sectors such as fisheries, tourism, recreation and coastal infrastructure (e.g. Guerry et al., 2012; Reddy et al., 2016; Arkema et al., 2017). A notable example of modelling a single ES is the modelling of fisheries, which has provided a wealth of information on the interactions between humans and marine ecosystems, although with a narrow focus on food provision and its economic and ecological implications (Plagányi, 2007). In the context of marine NBS, modelling for multiple MES is required for more informed decision-making accounting of the multitude of connections and trade-offs among the human and ecosystem components of social–ecological systems. The tools and approaches to explore multiple MES and change in their delivery under different management or climate scenarios are briefly summarised below.

5.7.3.1 *Conceptual Ecosystem Models (CEMs)*

These outline qualitative components of social–ecological systems to help stakeholders and decision-makers discover, integrate and communicate relationships that exist among ecosystems and humans (Kelble et al., 2013; Ingram et al., 2018). They are ideal for the first step of the MESA framework and for scoping next steps within it (Levin et al., 2009). CEMs can help to understand the dynamics of a marine social–ecological system (e.g. a local seagrass bed and the community generating income and food through the fisheries supported by healthy seagrass) and the effects of different governance on ES (e.g. fish biomass and landings) and social outcomes (e.g. equity) (Ostrom, 2009; Cullen-Unsworth et al., 2014). Another CEM application refers to presenting interrelations and mutual influences of institutions and governance and ecosystems within MPA in Vietnam as a cause–effect relationship diagram (Ho et al., 2014). Further, Ingram et al. (2018) developed a participatory CEM approach outlining which activities affect the nearshore marine ecosystem along the west coast of Hawaii Island. The approach was based on local stakeholder perceptions of drivers and pressures influencing coral reefs, fisheries and water quality before and after provision of scientific facts and expert opinion.

5.7.3.2 *Tools with Limited Application in Marine Contexts*

There are several ES tools that have limited application in the marine NBS context. For example:

- Artificial Intelligence for Ecosystem Services (ARIES) offers a suite of applications such as probabilistic Bayesian models, machine learning and pattern recognition to assess the provision, use and flow of ES, without exploring biophysical relationships or providing an economic valuation of ES (Beck & Lange, 2016). ARIES includes generalised models, so it can be used in data-poor contexts (Villa et al., 2014). It does not require special programming skills, but a good understanding of Bayesian statistics will aid interpretation. It is an open-source, standalone modelling platform still in development. It has been used to assess subsistence fisheries and coastal protection in Madagascar (Bagstad et al., 2011).
- Tools such as Marxan with zones and MarineMap are web-based decision support toolkits without mapping ES. They have been applied only in the USA to support marine spatial planning efforts through online and interactive maps of appropriate information (Guerry et al., 2013).
- Multi-scale Integrated Models for ES (MIMES) is a toolbox of models simulating ecosystem and socio-economic systems and the interactions between them using monetary valuation methods. It has mainly been used in terrestrial contexts, it is not spatially explicit, and it is very complex to develop and use (Bagstad et al., 2013). It is place-specific, and a long lead time is required for first runs in new locations, because a highly technical user or a consultant needs to program it (Bagstad et al., 2013). However, the Massachusetts Ocean Partnership used MIMES to evaluate trade-offs to inform marine spatial planning (White et al., 2012).

5.7.3.3 *Coastal Resilience Tool*

This open-source decision support tool in GIS aims to assess the social and economic risks associated with storms and sea-level rise and identify natural and nature-based solutions to help reduce these risks (Beck & Lange, 2016, and literature cited therein). The tool runs globally and at regional and local scales; all codes are available on GitHub. Coastal Resilience enables visualisation of ecological, social and economic information alongside sea-level rise and storm surge scenarios. It also includes module configurations which allow specific geographical areas to have apps and display alternative scenarios to stakeholders. For example, Future Habitat app was applied in Old Saybrook, Connecticut, where it helped visualise how and where saltmarsh habitats may migrate landwards under different sea-level rise scenarios, and identify adaptive solutions to improve community resilience (Nature Conservancy, 2018).

5.7.3.4 *Risk and Vulnerability Assessment Methodology Development Project (RiVAMP)*

RiVAMP is a coastal risk assessment framework in GIS. It uses a range of process-based and spatially explicit models and expertise to highlight how sea-level rise and storm surges could affect beach erosion, coastal populations and infrastructure (Chatenoux et al., 2012a). It also considers important social factors such as local livelihoods and environmental governance. Input data may refer to tides, sea-level rise projections, storm surges, wave characteristics for beach erosion, wave propagation inland as well as maps of habitats and distributions of human population and assets for the location of interest. RiVAMP is a rather complex model: it does not provide a user-friendly interface; requires a digital elevation model for the given location; relies on maps, which may not be available; and biophysical input data require user parameterisation. RiVAMP was piloted in Jamaica to assess the role of coral reefs and seagrasses in coastal hazard risk reduction (Chatenoux et al., 2012b).

5.7.3.5 *Marine Integrated Valuation of ES and Trade-offs (INVEST)*

Marine INVEST is a flexible toolbox of models in ArcGIS using maps as information sources and for producing maps as outputs to assess flows of and changes in different ES including carbon storage, wave energy, recreation, fishery production, erosion control, habitat quality and water quality (Guerry et al., 2012; Arkema et al., 2015, 2017; Verutes et al., 2017). It has a tiered design: lower tiers represent the models with minimal data requirements and higher tiers get increasingly data-intensive. Each MES model uses metrics to quantify the supply (i.e. biophysical processes underpinning an MES), demand (i.e. the delivery of a service) and the monetary value of a service (Tallis et al., 2011; Guerry et al., 2012). The current set includes habitat risk assessment and water quality (which are not considered as MES by the model); provisioning of aesthetic views; recreation; food from fisheries and aquaculture; renewable energy; coastal protection; and carbon sequestration. Users can mix and match models from different tiers to create the best suite of models depending on context.

Marine INVEST builds on the ecological production function approach, which determines how ecosystem benefits vary with ecosystem processes. This allows for a spatially explicit evaluation of the role multiple ecosystem features and processes play within the seascape (Guerry et al., 2012; Arkema et al., 2017; Verutes et al., 2017). A notable strength, compared with stand-alone conceptual, sociocultural or monetary modelling approaches, is that it allows for the comparison of alternative management scenarios based on their actual effects on ecosystems and their services. It also evaluates multiple MES at the same time, as opposed to tools focused on a single service, thus enabling trade-offs among different stakeholders to be evaluated in a balanced way. Additional advantages refer to being: quantifiable, approaching uncertainty through varying inputs; open-access; fully developed; scalable (in terrestrial contexts, presumably also in marine contexts); generalisable but relies on local data for

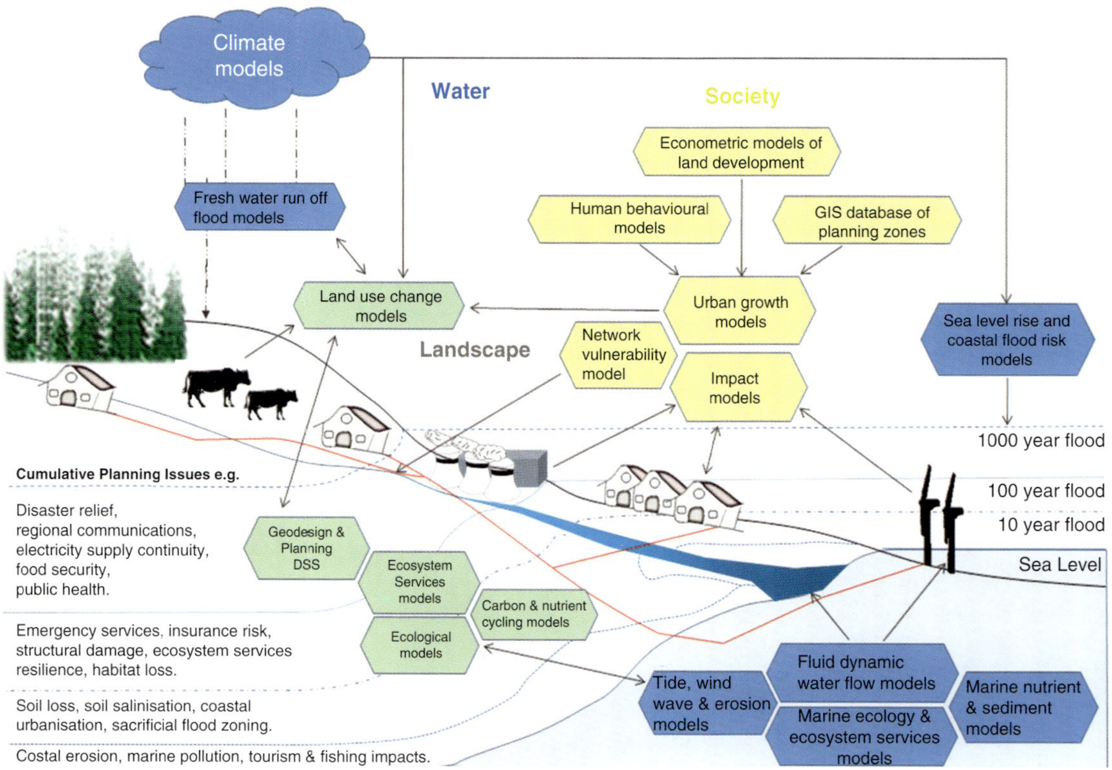

FIGURE 1.1 A coupled socio-environmental system. (A black and white version of this figure will appear in some formats.)

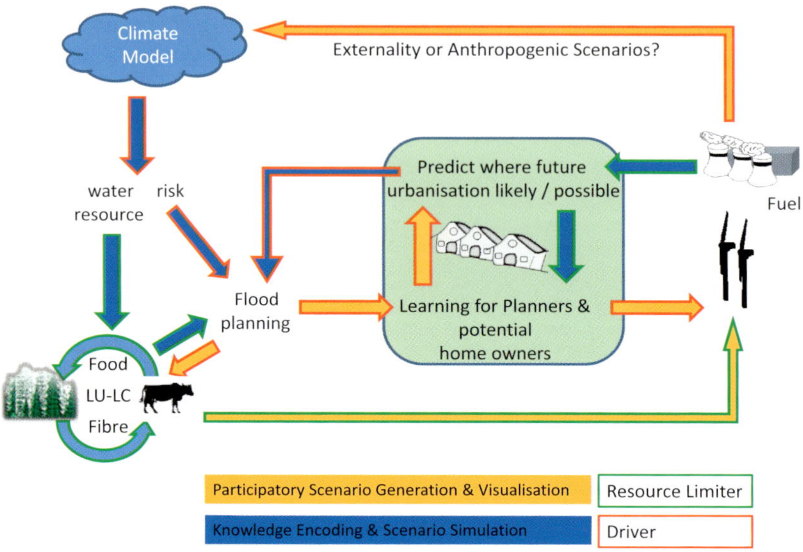

FIGURE I.2 A meta-model of a coupled socio-environmental system. (A black and white version of this figure will appear in some formats.)

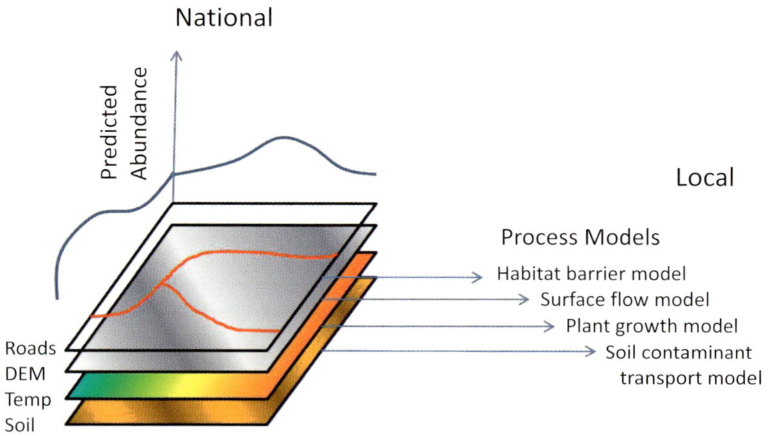

FIGURE I.3 Spatial scale, modelling approach and example applications. DEM, digital elevation model. (A black and white version of this figure will appear in some formats.)

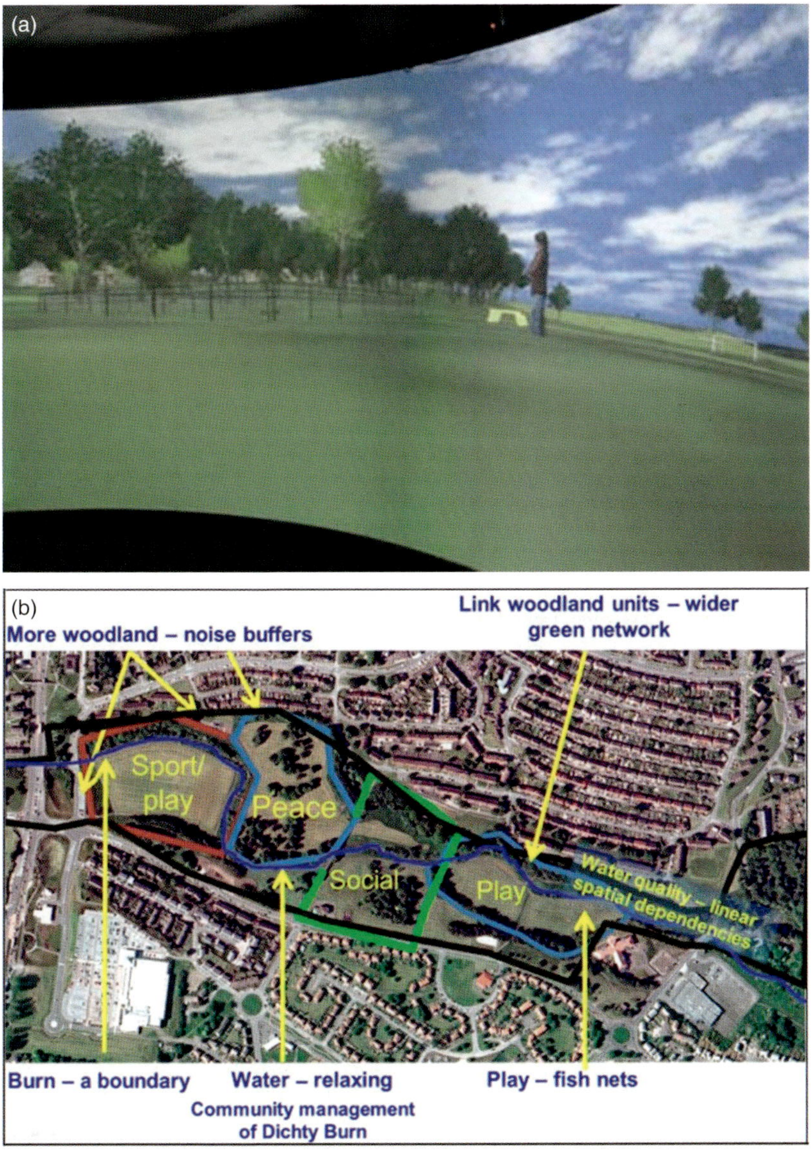

FIGURE 1.5 (a) Features added by local residents to the 3D model of Finlathen Park, Dundee, UK. (b) Example spatial plan for park and adjacent area derived from engagement events. (Source: Authors, James Hutton Institute.) (A black and white version of this figure will appear in some formats.)

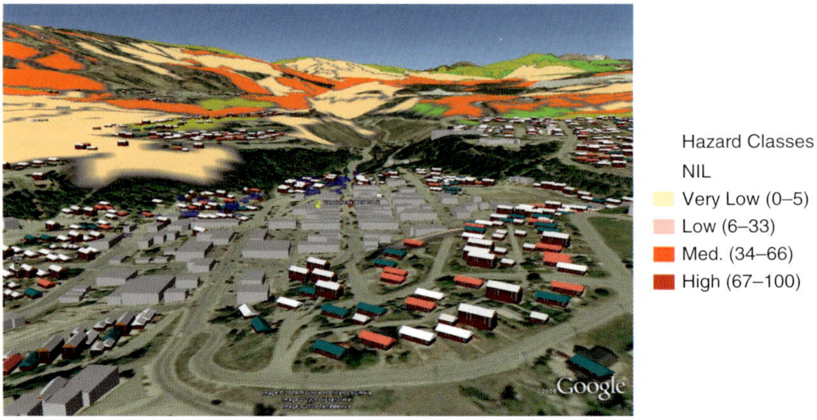

FIGURE 1.6 An example of the potential impacts of climate change for the rural community of the city of Kimberley, Canada. From Schroth et al. (2015). (A black and white version of this figure will appear in some formats.)

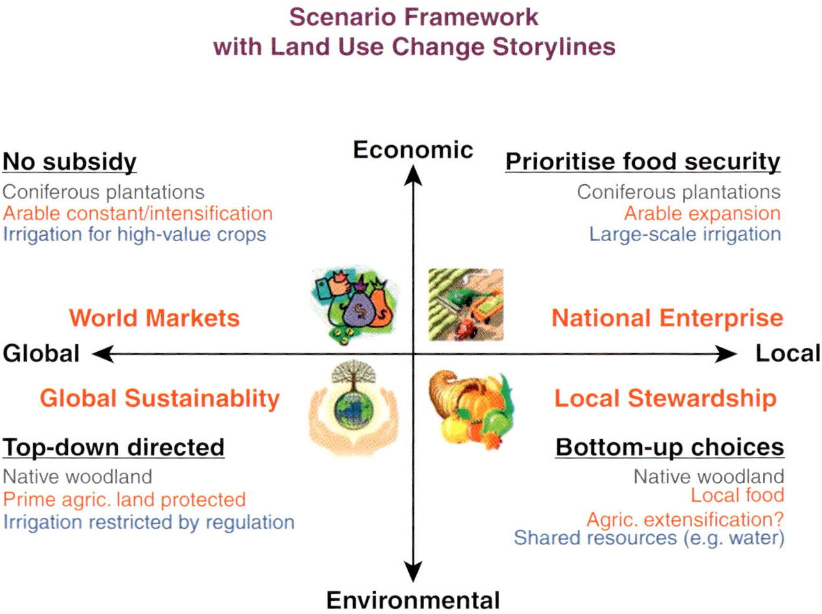

FIGURE 1.7 Scenarios of development pathways, based on the UK National Ecosystem Assessment. (Source: UK NEA, 2011.) (A black and white version of this figure will appear in some formats.)

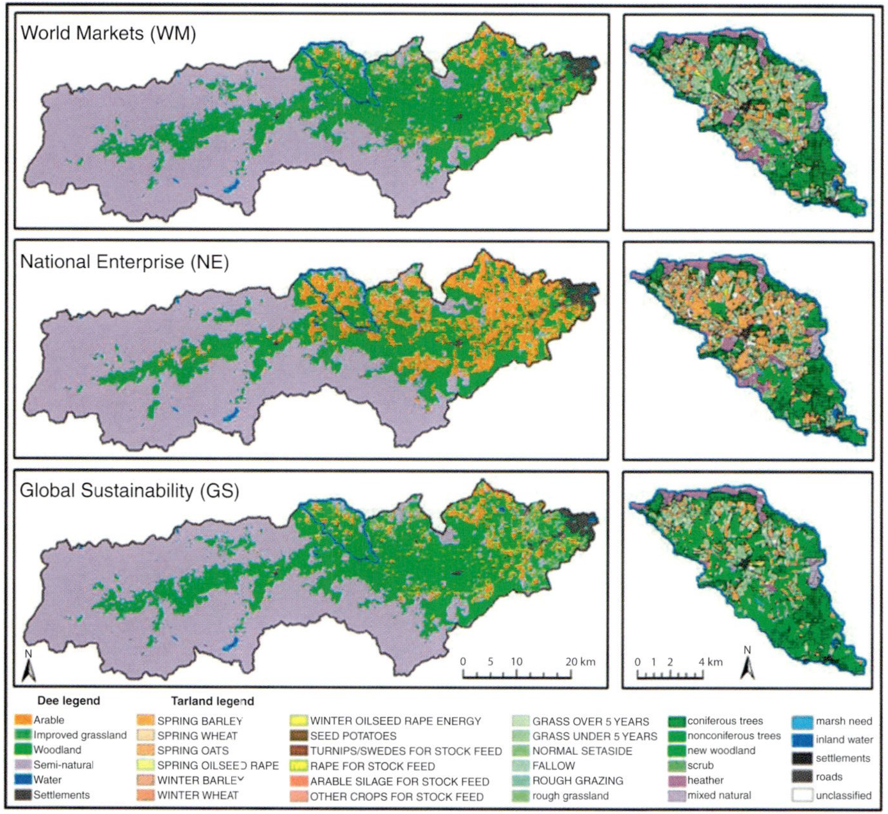

FIGURE 1.8 Spatial representation of scenarios for 2050 for the Dee catchment and Tarland subcatchment, NE Scotland. (Source: Brown & Castellazzi, 2014.) (A black and white version of this figure will appear in some formats.)

FIGURE 2.3 Aerial photograph of the Amudarya River basin landscape. (Photo © Maja Schlüter and used with permission.) (A black and white version of this figure will appear in some formats.)

FIGURE 2.4 Rangeland landscape in Thaba Nchu area. (Photo © Sebastian Rasch and used with permission.) (A black and white version of this figure will appear in some formats.)

FIGURE 3.1 Burning shrubland (image CC: Antonio Jordán). (A black and white version of this figure will appear in some formats.)

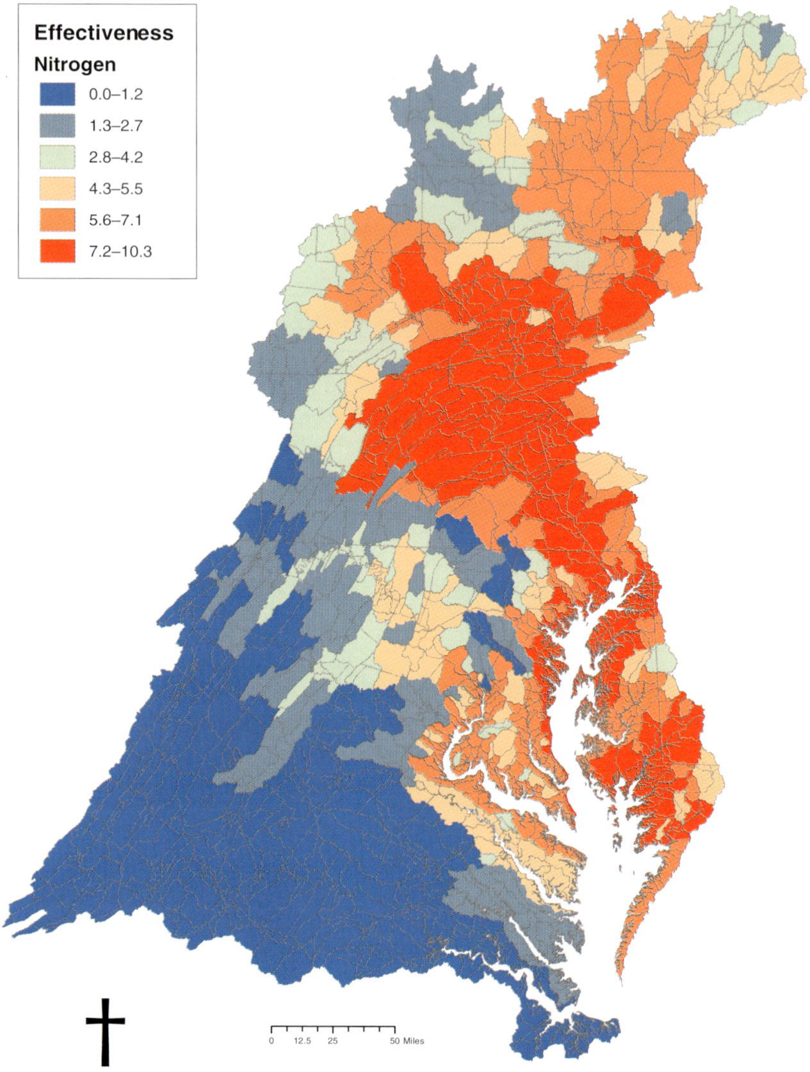

FIGURE 4.1 Subbasins across the Chesapeake Bay watershed with the highest (red) to lowest (blue) nitrogen loading effect on bay water quality. (A black and white version of this figure will appear in some formats.)

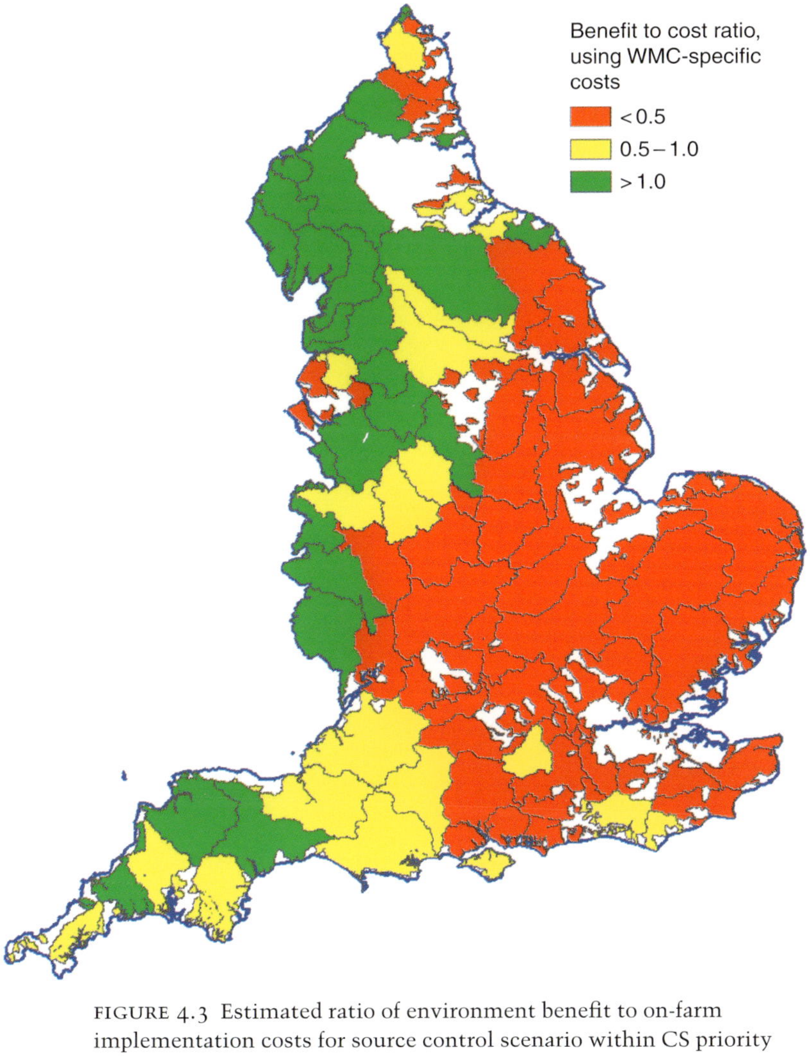

FIGURE 4.3 Estimated ratio of environment benefit to on-farm implementation costs for source control scenario within CS priority areas. (A black and white version of this figure will appear in some formats.)

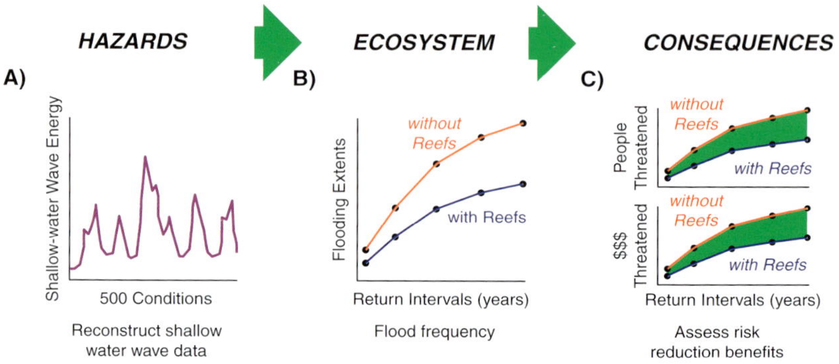

FIGURE 5.1 Schematic of methodology used to evaluate role of coral reefs in coastal hazard risk reduction off Maui, Hawaii. (Source: Storlazzi et al., 2017.) (A black and white version of this figure will appear in some formats.)

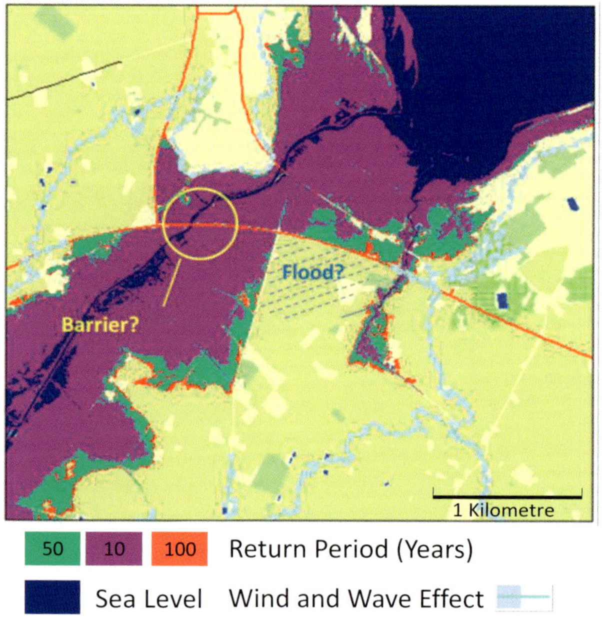

FIGURE 6.1 Flood predictions and the significance of barrier representation. (Source: Flood model in Höganas peninsula, Sweden, from the 'Rising Sea Levels' project, funded by the Swedish Civil Contingencies Agency, MSB.) (A black and white version of this figure will appear in some formats.)

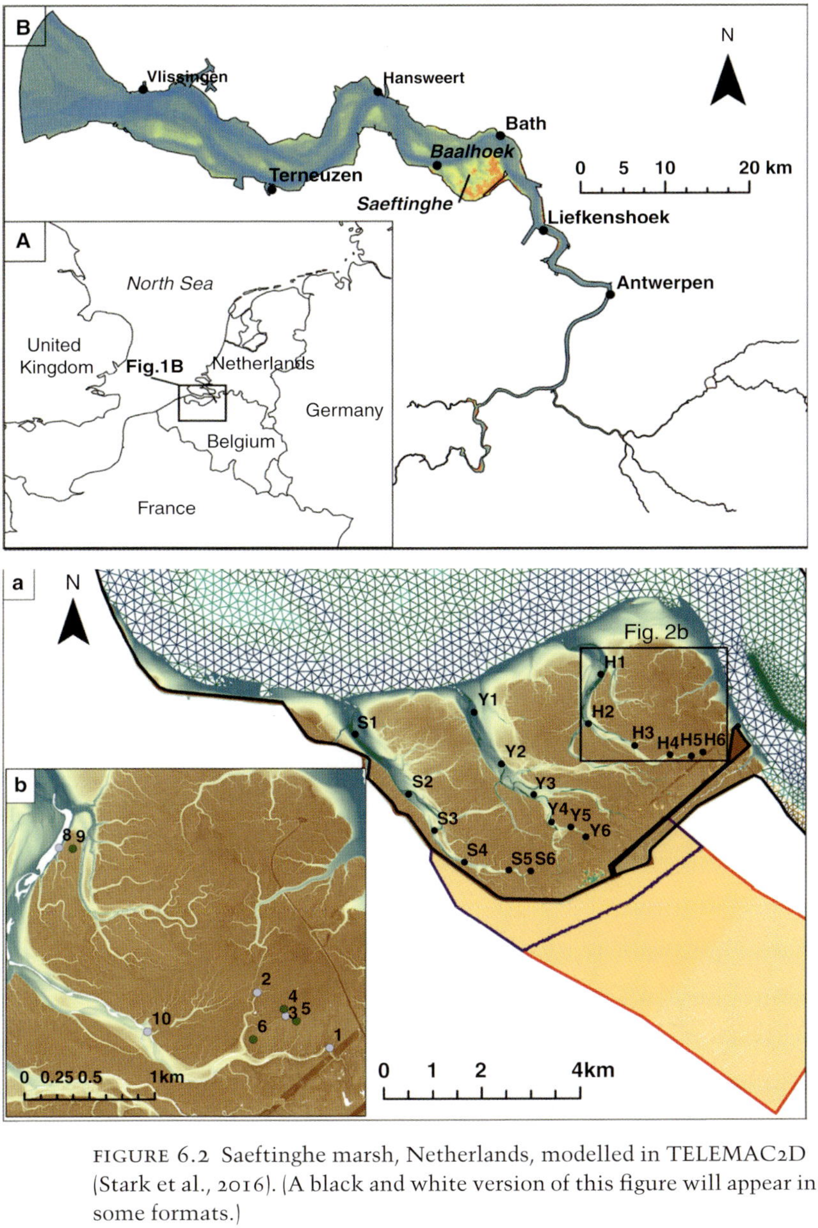

FIGURE 6.2 Saeftinghe marsh, Netherlands, modelled in TELEMAC2D (Stark et al., 2016). (A black and white version of this figure will appear in some formats.)

FIGURE 6.3 Mangrove forests for storm surge defence and as an economic resource (image by kind permission of ICGB-AR). (A black and white version of this figure will appear in some formats.)

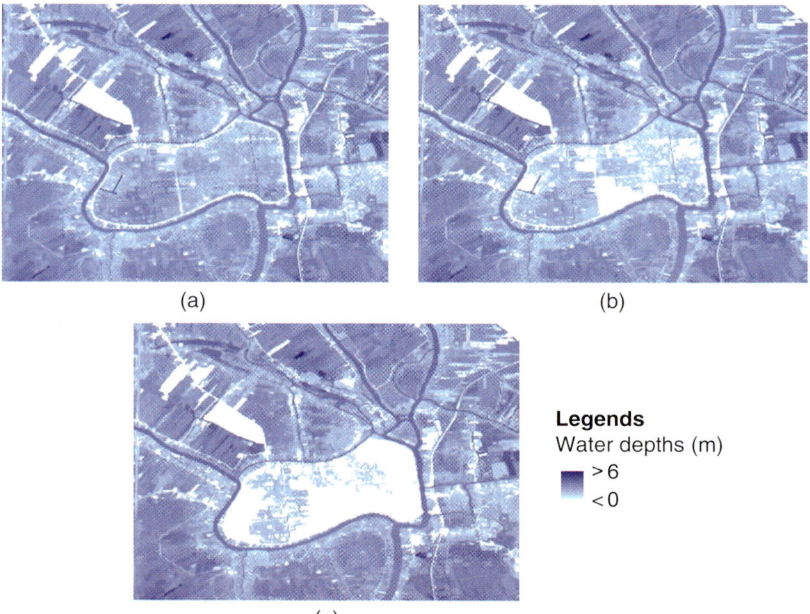

FIGURE 6.4 Simulated flood levels from MIKE based on different scenarios reinstating cultural ecosystem services (Vojinovic et al., 2017). (a) Current situation – Scenario 1, or 'business as usual'; (b) a combination of measures – Scenario 4 (increase of the U-Thong Road dyke height and reinstatement of ancient canals (local measures); and (c) a combination of measures – Scenario 7 Ayutthaya bypass channel + increasing dyke height + ponds + ancient canals (combination of regional and local measures). (A black and white version of this figure will appear in some formats.)

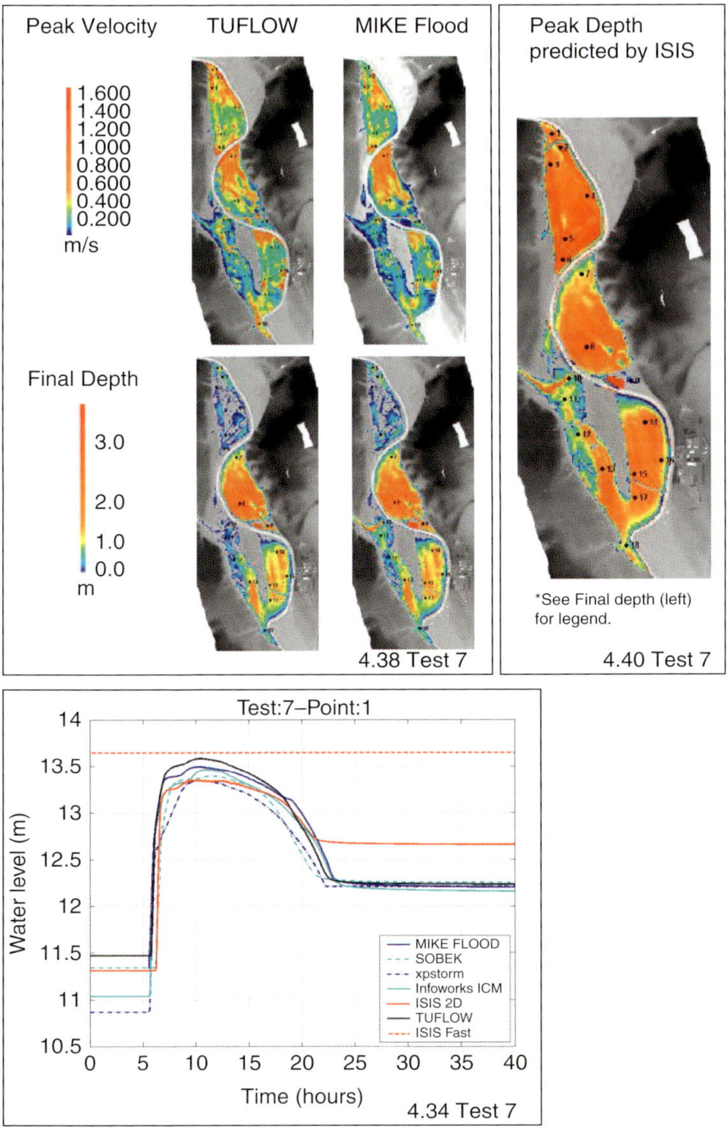

FIGURE 6.5 Comparison of peak flow models (figures combined from Néelz & Pender, 2013 by kind permission of the UK Environment Agency). (A black and white version of this figure will appear in some formats.)

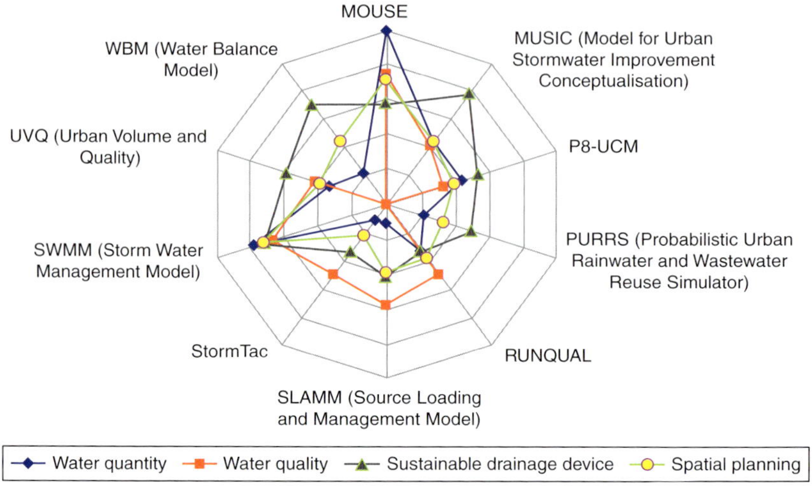

FIGURE 6.7 Potential uses for selected LID models (Zhou, 2014, adapted from Elliot & Trowsdale, 2007). (A black and white version of this figure will appear in some formats.)

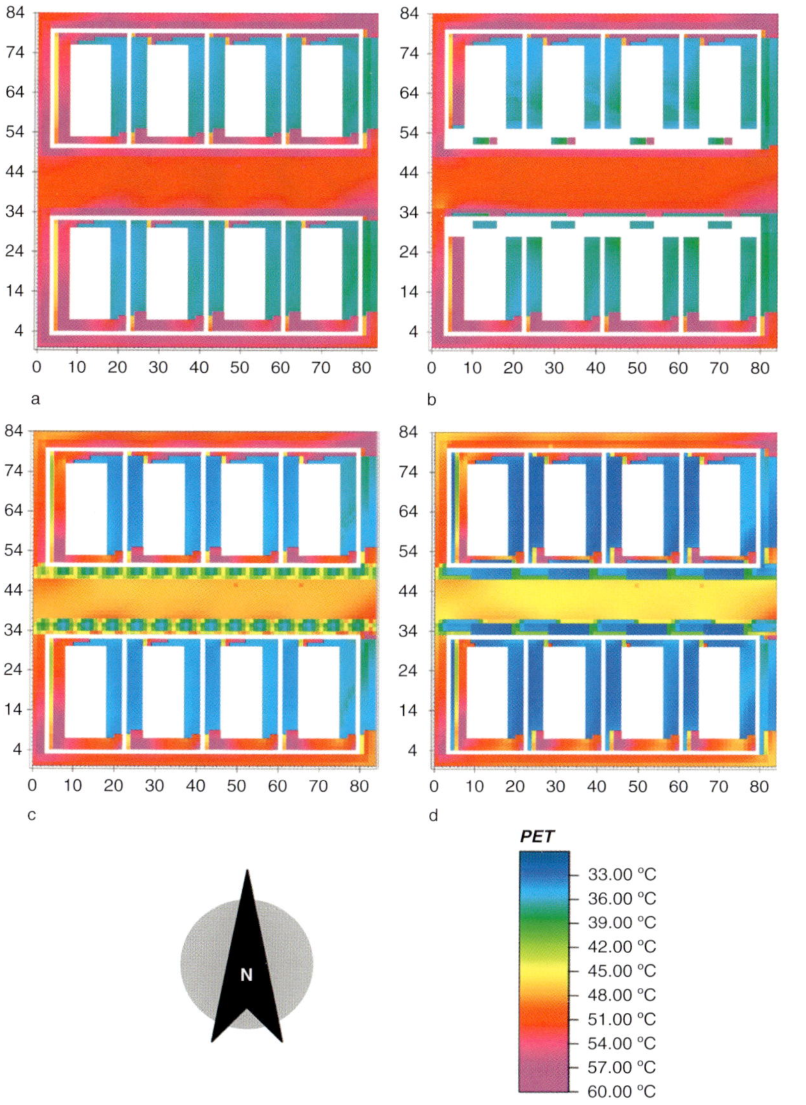

FIGURE 7.2 Calculated maximum PET values (2 pm) for the summer for a street (a) without any shade, (b) changed urban morphology, (c) with street trees and (d) with street trees and horizontal shading devices over the pavements. (A black and white version of this figure will appear in some formats.)

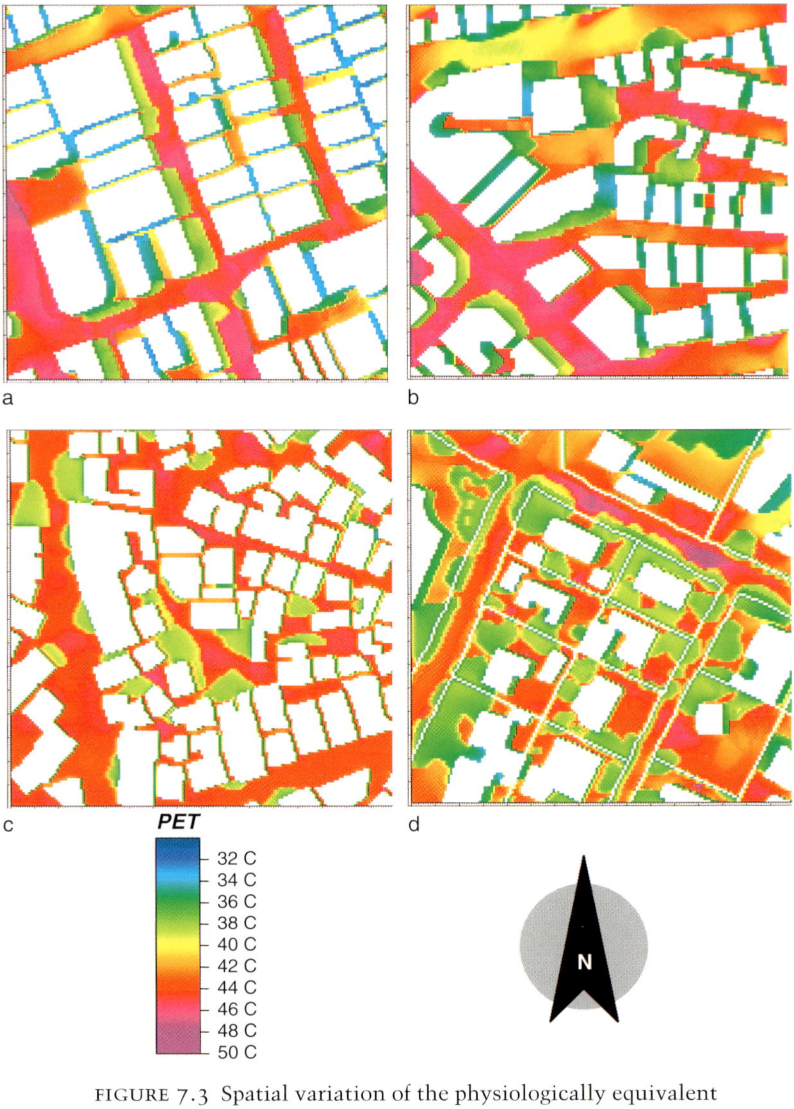

FIGURE 7.3 Spatial variation of the physiologically equivalent temperature for the simulated areas during the hottest time of the day in the hottest month (February at 2 pm) for (a) Kariakoo, (b) city centre, (c) Manzese and (d) Upanga. (A black and white version of this figure will appear in some formats.)

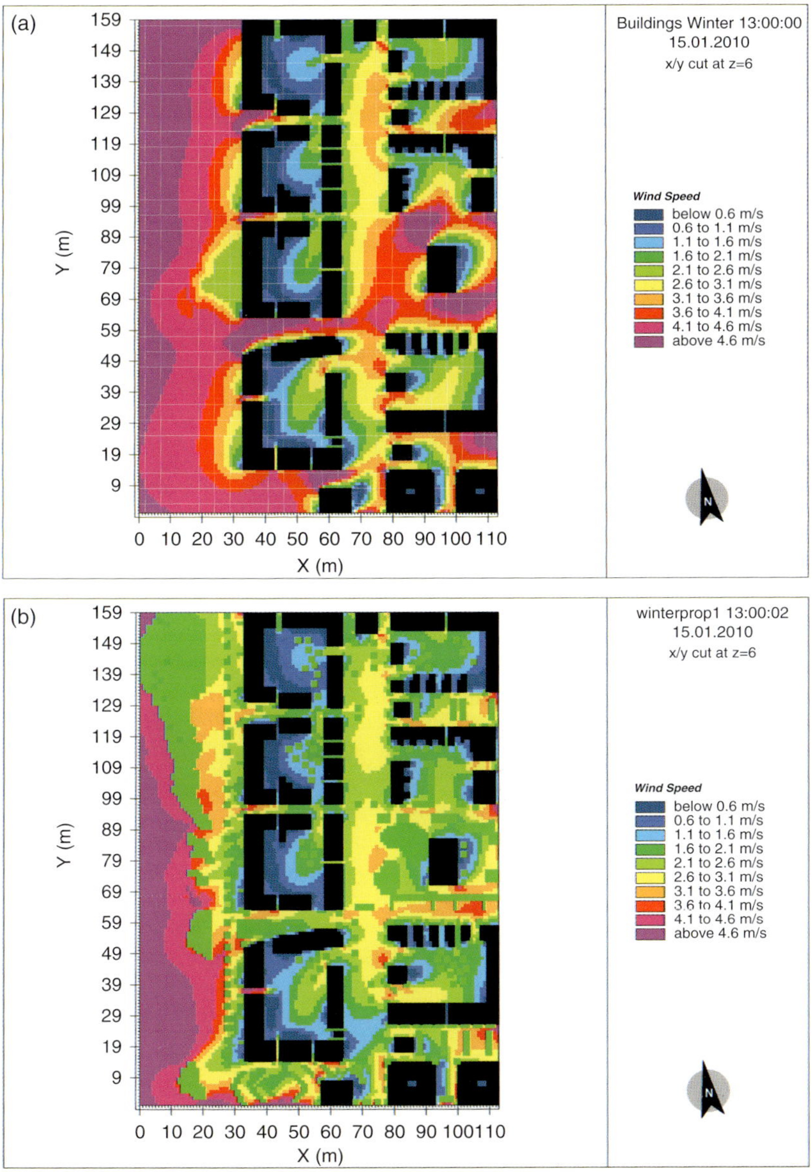

<Left foot> <Right foot>

FIGURE 7.4 Wind speed output from ENVI-met without trees (a, upper) and with trees (b, lower). (A black and white version of this figure will appear in some formats.)

FIGURE 7.6 In temperate climates it is important to consider how different architectural attributes vary among different tree species. An ideal urban tree has low transmissivity in summer when thermal heat stress occurs and high transmissivity in winter when sunshine is limited. Placing trees of high branch area density (e.g. *Carpinus betulus* 'Fastigiata', left) close to south- and west-facing building facades will, for instance, create negative effects on the thermal conditions in and around that building. Low solar azimuth angles and limited hours of solar radiation mean that trees with less branch area density (e.g. *Ginkgo biloba*, right) are better suited in close approximation to buildings or in places where people visit. In situations where the chill effect from wind is of particular concern, trees with a denser makeup of branches can be used strategically to block out wind. This may involve using e.g. columnar hornbeam or oak in strategic places (i.e. street corners) (Deak Sjöman et al., 2016). (A black and white version of this figure will appear in some formats.)

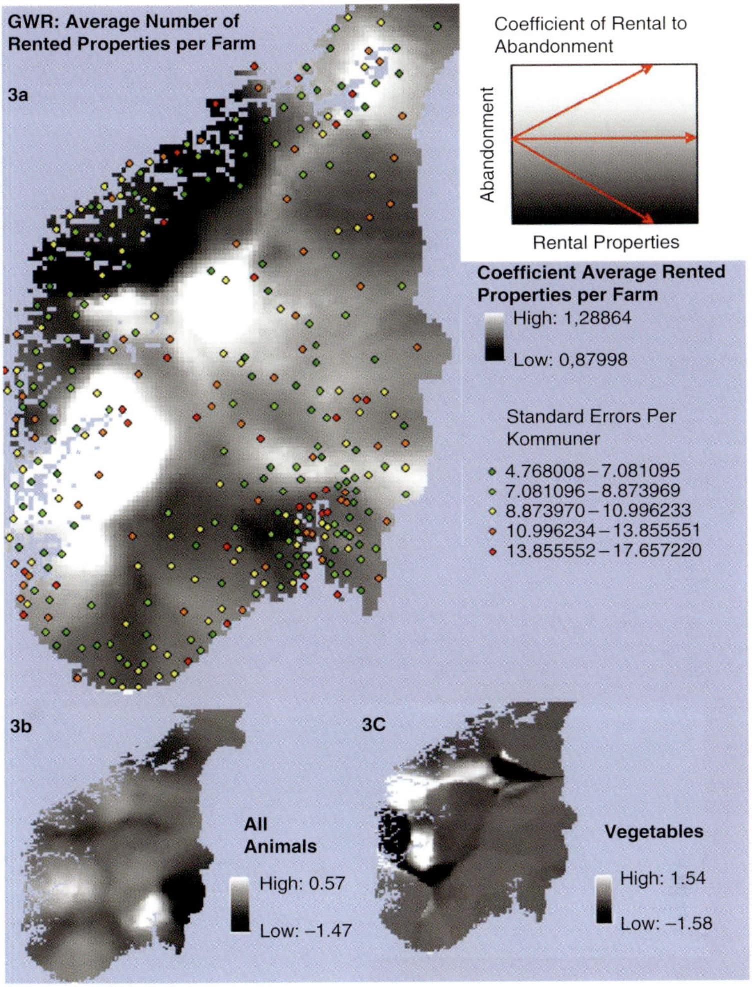

FIGURE 8.1 Geographically weighted regression of farm production data in 2000 against rate of farm abandonment in 2010 (Sang et al., 2014). (A black and white version of this figure will appear in some formats.)

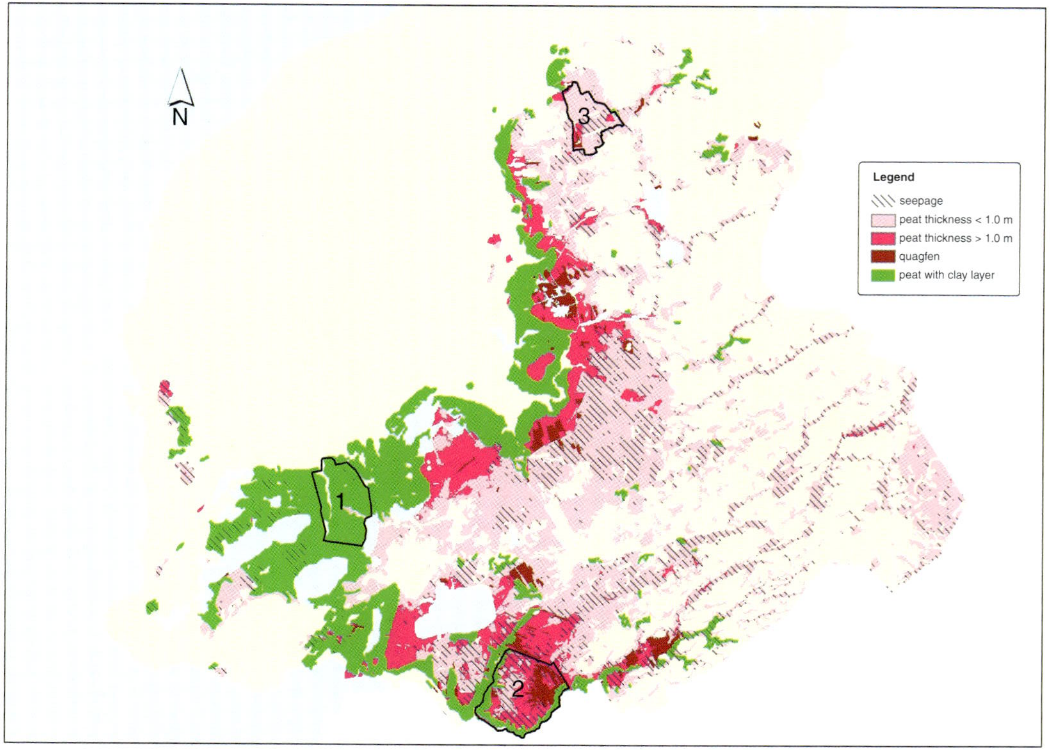

FIGURE 9.2 Map of the province of Friesland (north-west Netherlands) showing the three communes where the workshops took place and different types and densities of peatland (Brouns et al., 2015). (A black and white version of this figure will appear in some formats.)

FIGURE 9.3 Workshop participants around the Touch Table. (A black and white version of this figure will appear in some formats.)

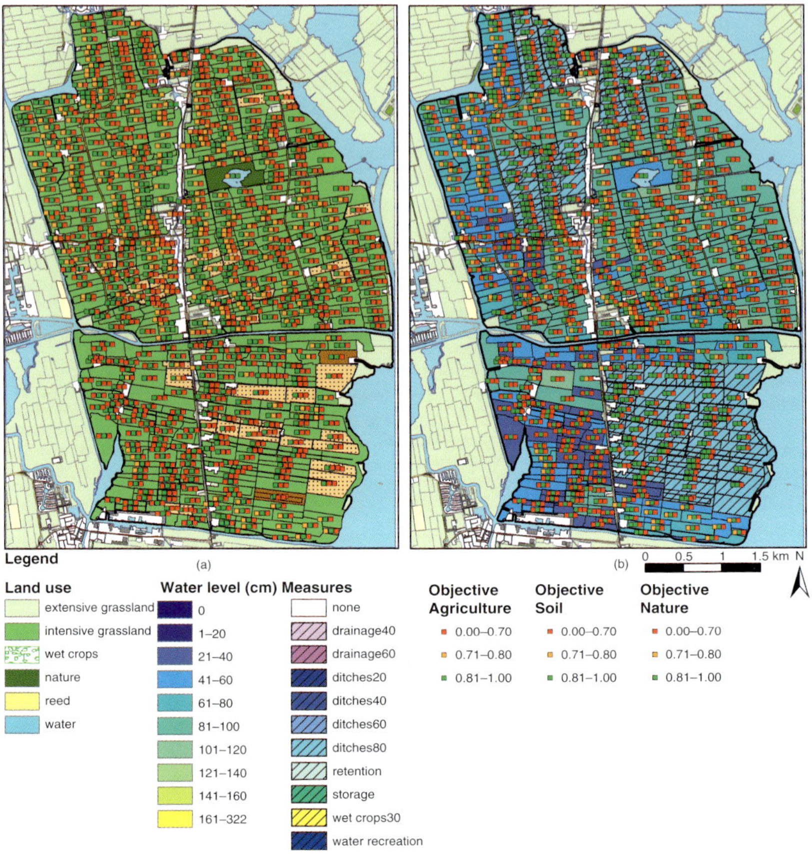

FIGURE 9.4 Use of the design tool for the region 'Hommerts': combined with land use (a) and water levels (b). (A black and white version of this figure will appear in some formats.)

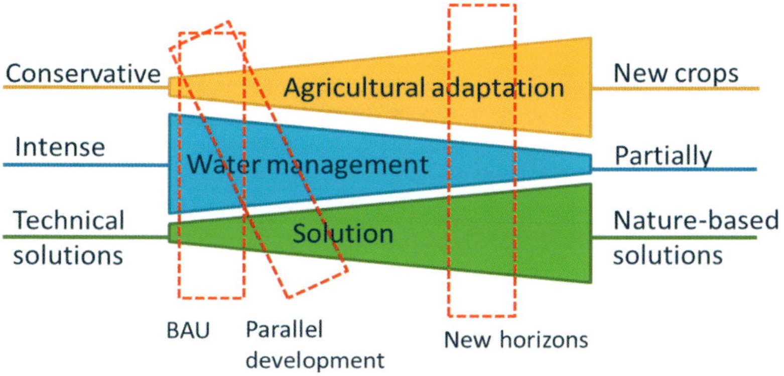

FIGURE 9.5 The share of NBS within the three scenarios. (A black and white version of this figure will appear in some formats.)

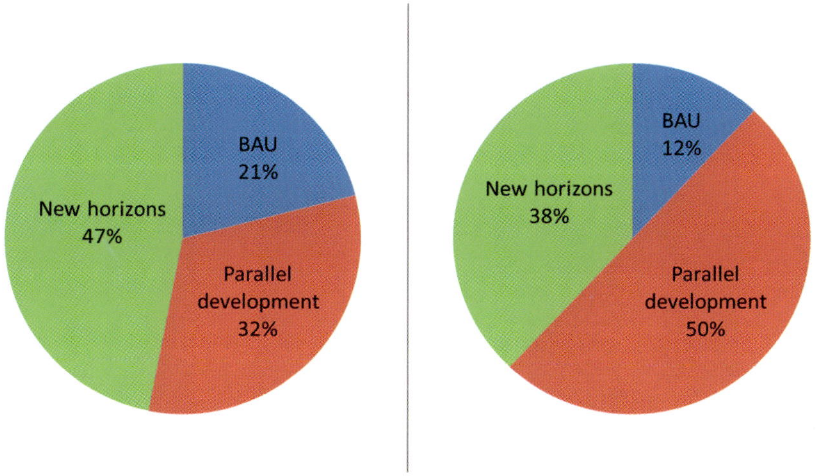

FIGURE 9.6 'What do you consider the most realistic scenario?' – responses before (left) and after (right) the workshop (n = 19). (A black and white version of this figure will appear in some formats.)

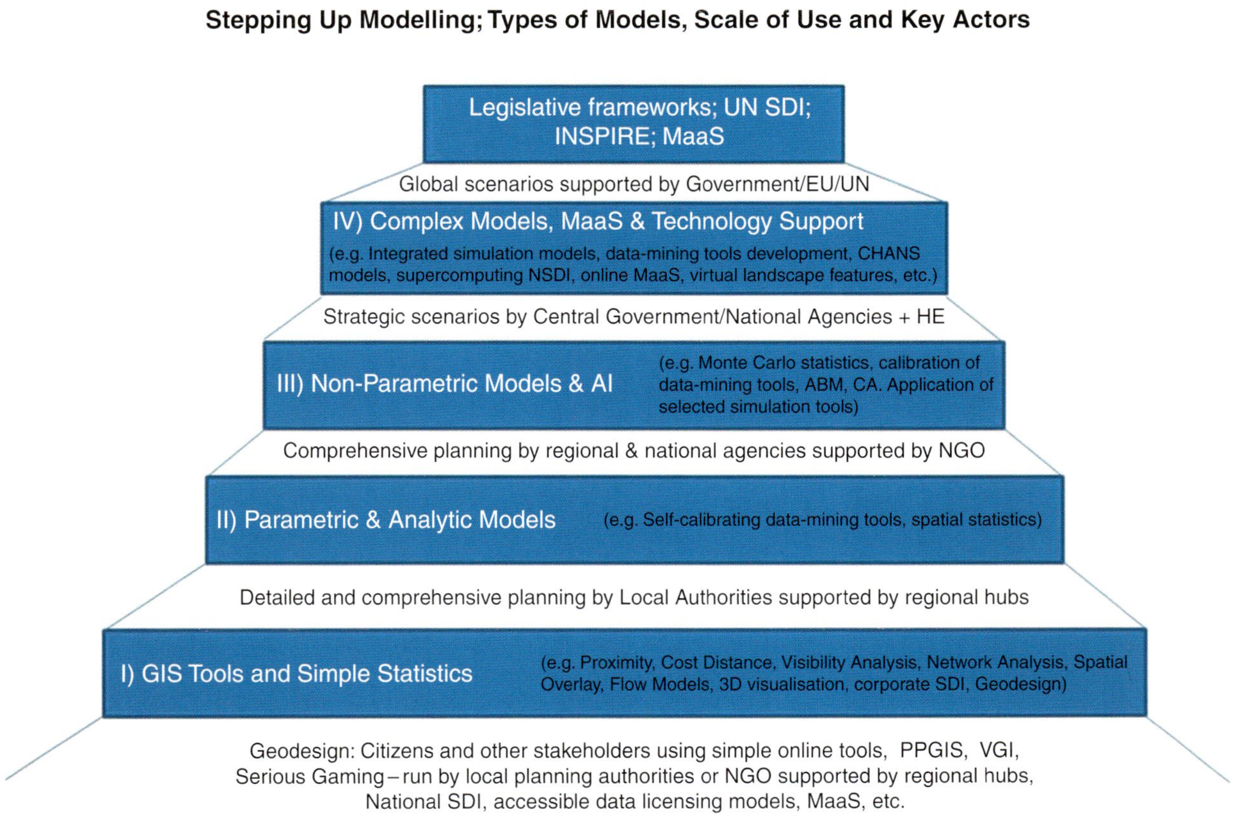

FIGURE 10.1 Types of models, scale of use and key actors. (A black and white version of this figure will appear in some formats.)

calibration and validation; able to provide non-monetary and monetary valuation; and spatially explicit (Bagstad et al., 2013; Bullock & Ding, 2018). However, INVEST applied in terrestrial contexts has been found to be a highly complex model and relatively time-consuming to parameterise and run, especially when applied in new case studies (Bagstad et al., 2013; Bullock & Ding, 2018).

For example, the model was used in Belize to assess risk to coastal marine habitats in the region posed by eight human uses (i.e. coastal development, marine transportation, dredging, fishing, marine recreation, oil exploration, aquaculture and agricultural run-off) (Ruckelshaus et al., 2015; Verutes et al., 2017). Marine INVEST helped to quantify current and future delivery of three MES (i.e. coastal protection, catch and revenue from lobster fishing and tourism) after mapping the current and future uses and formulating scenarios about how coastal development and no-take zones in addition to climate change scenarios would influence these three MES. First, risk to key habitats posed by the eight human activities was mapped and measured with the INVEST habitat risk assessment (HRA) model. Then, the INVEST HRA outputs served as ecosystem inputs for three INVEST models (fisheries production, coastal protection and tourism) to produce spatially explicit values in both biophysical and economic terms to communicate how management decisions made today would influence changes to key benefits in the future. Results were visualised by location, by amount and by MES and supported adaptive coastal zone management in a setting characterised by multiple pressures, conflicting uses, complicated legal and political landscapes, and limited in-country technical capacity.

5.7.4 Agent-based Models

Agent-based modelling (ABM) is an increasingly popular approach to modelling social–ecological systems by representing the behaviour and interactions of organisms, human actors and institutions (Schulze et al., 2017). Typical simulations involve a large number of individuals and evaluate the effects of interactions among individuals and with the environment. ABM is a useful framework for understanding and assessing the role of behavioural differences among individuals in a population, especially in situations dealing with relatively large variability among individuals, thus capturing dynamics not easily captured by other modelling approaches. However, ABM is very complex and computationally demanding. Most of their applications refer to terrestrial contexts (IPBES, 2016; Schulze et al., 2017). Marine ABM is focused on commercial fisheries studies. For example, the model DISPLACE was developed by Bastardie et al. (2016) to support maritime spatial planning and management issues, especially from the perspective of fisheries. The model OSMOSE has been applied to the Benguela upwelling ecosystem (Shin et al., 2004; Travers et al., 2006) to produce simulations of MPA for fisheries objectives (Yemane et al., 2009) and to inform fishing moratoriums (Marzloff et al., 2009).

A few studies have used ABM to simulate effects of human activity, such as coastal housing, tourism, recreational fisheries, shipping, oil and gas production, salt extraction, coastal development, port maintenance as well as commercial fishing and the response of the system to different management regimes. For example:

- North West Shelf (NWS)-INVITRO is the basis for an integrated ecosystem-level management strategy evaluation on the north-west coast of Australia (Gray et al., 2006). Key submodels include: the natural biophysical ecosystem, resource exploitation or modification by each industry sector, monitoring activities and management decision and implementation for each sector. Their combination leads to a highly connected web of interdependent submodels and allows for an analysis of the effectiveness and robustness of various strategies for managing the main human interactions within the NWS of Australia. The approach provides spatially explicit representation of species interactions. Aspects of uncertainty are considered by using 'pessimistic', 'middle-of-the-road' and 'optimistic' parameterisations. An extensive description of the approach is given by Gray et al. (2006).
- Karanci et al. (2017) used ABM to evaluate housing dynamics of coastal communities facing coastal hazards risk. Their model uses storms and sea-level rise as exogenous drivers and simulates (i) the evolution of the beach morphology, using XBEACH (see Section 5.7.1.3; Gray et al., 2006) to

simulate storm impact; (ii) implementation of coastal protection measures such as dune restoration and beach nourishment; and (iii) household's housing decisions based on cadastral properties such as distance to shore, demographics and monetary value and using three types of agents, i.e. homeowners, homebuyers and homesellers. The simulations suggested that increased storm intensity would hinder homeselling and occupancy. The ABM indicated a feedback loop between the natural processes, management decisions and household decisions. Arguably, the output of this approach may inform planning for marine NBS to ensure protection of the coastal community from coastal hazards.

5.8 (BROADLY) SOCIO-CULTURAL MODELS

This group comprises approaches for understanding preferences or social values for ES (Harrison et al., 2018). There is a bias towards approaches referring to terrestrial social–ecological systems and thus it is unclear what types of socio-cultural models are applicable in the context of marine NBS. With this caveat in mind, the deliberative or participatory mapping is a promising tool for informing marine NBS. Participatory mapping refers to a broad group of methods aiming to include stakeholder's local knowledge, values and preferences in creating ES maps. Participatory GIS (PGIS) or Public Participation GIS (PPGIS), in particular, use workshops, face-to-face interviews and/or web-based surveys to integrate perceptions, knowledge (local-based or technical) and values of different stakeholders. For example, Levine and Feinholz (2015) developed a PGIS methodology to gather local knowledge regarding the location and intensity of coastal human activities in Hawaii's priority sites for coral reef management.

5.9 (BROADLY) MONETARY TECHNIQUES

This group includes monetary techniques for estimating economic values for ES (Guerry et al., 2013; Harrison et al., 2018): cost–benefits analysis (CBA); benefit transfer; stated preference methods (e.g. willingness to pay for MES); and revealed preference methods, such as value of ES estimated as market data (e.g. fisheries landings) and hedonic analysis (i.e. ES value based on housing prices).

Guerry et al. (2013) warned that monetary methods for evaluating MES must be used with great care, highlighting that economic valuation is far from the only way to value ES.

An area of increasing interest for ES monetary valuation refers to estimating the value of blue carbon sequestration. One of the most important concepts in economic and policy discussions about global warming is the social cost of carbon (SCC), i.e. the economic cost caused by an additional tonne of carbon emissions. SCC analyses rely on integrated assessment models for empirical estimates of the economics of global warming, such as the Dynamic Integrated model of Climate and the Economy (DICE) (Nordhaus, 2014). DICE views climate change in the framework of economic growth theory. In a standard neoclassical optimal growth model, society invests in capital goods, thereby reducing consumption today in order to increase consumption in the future (Ramsey, 1928 and Koopmans, 1965 cited in Nordhaus, 2014). DICE modifies the Ramsey model to include all elements from economics through climate change to damages, with climate investments being analogous to capital investments in the standard model. The geophysical equations are simplified versions derived from large models or model experiments.

Assigning a monetary value to marine biodiversity and to blue carbon is not currently clearly covered by the UNFCCC and hence is not included in carbon trade (Herr & Landis, 2016; Ganguly et al., 2018; Wilson & Forsyth, 2018). There is also lack of guidance for estimating carbon (as shorthand for carbon dioxide, CO_2) emissions to trade avoided carbon emissions from conservation and restoration of blue carbon ecosystems (Wylie et al., 2016). However, Ganguly et al. (2018) estimated the value of regulatory ES in the form of carbon C sequestration in seagrass beds in India using DICE to consider the sequestration potential of respective ecosystems and the market rate or SCC. First, they estimated the carbon sequestration rates by seagrass beds based on field measurements (including oxygen and CO_2

concentration in water seagrass respiration and sediment organic carbon) and statistical modelling (linear mixed-effects models). Then, they estimated the average SCC using a revised version of the DICE 2016 model (Nordhaus, 2017).

Ganguly et al. (2018) assumed that SCC is proportional to the discounted value of output in each region over the period between 2020 and 2050, discounted at a rate of 5% per year. The following empirical function was used to determine the economic value of blue carbon sequestered:

$$VC_i = SQ_i \times A_i \times SCC$$

where the value of carbon sequestered (VC, in \$ $year^{-1}$) by a particular ecosystem (i) is measured by the product of its rate of carbon sequestration (SQ, as tonnes CO_2 ha^{-1} $year^{-1}$) or carbon storage in the top 1-m sediment per area (A) and the chosen SCC (in \$ per tonnes CO^2 ha^{-1} $year^{-1}$). Accordingly, seagrass sequestration value ranged between \$0.45 million and \$3.89 million, whereas soil sediment storage value ranged between \$109 million and \$146 million. Detailed evaluations of local variables may provide a better monetary estimate of seagrass carbon.

5.10 BAYESIAN BELIEF NETWORKS (BBN)

Most decision contexts involve alternatives, cause-and-effect predictions of expected consequences and, potentially, lack of consensus among experts, providing a natural role for scenarios to characterise alternatives and for models to predict probability of consequences. Modelling tools that can help assess these probabilities include *inter alia* Markov analysis, Monte Carlo simulation and Bayesian belief networks (BBN). BBN have the potential to bridge the gap between qualitative (e.g. expert knowledge) and quantitative (e.g. biophysical data) methods because they can provide an integrated modelling framework to deal with a broad range of ES (Landuyt et al., 2013). Whereas BBN allow for updating and including additional data – which makes them useful for applications with limited data – and explicit treatment of stochastic uncertainty, they are limited by the need for proprietary software, discretisation of the data and the absence of feedback loops (Landuyt et al., 2013). BBN in combination with GIS have been used to assess the consequences of potential marine spatial planning objectives (e.g. Stelzenmüller et al., 2010). However, they have limited application in marine contexts. IPBES (2016) review BBN in the context of terrestrial ES modelling.

5.11 HABITAT MAPPING

Marine habitat mapping is mostly used for delineating MPA for fisheries objectives (Cogan et al., 2009; Lauria et al., 2011; Le Pape et al., 2014). It requires the use of: (i) statistical and GIS methods; (ii) reliable spatial data from observation platforms including satellite imagery, aerial photography, acoustic technology, multi-beam data for bathymetry and seascape analysis; and (iii) other tools (e.g. light availability mapping, modelling of environmental conditions and predictive species distribution maps) to gather maps (layers) of environmental conditions. However, benthic habitats (e.g. seagrass beds, oyster reefs and coral reefs) are not always visible from remote sensing technologies and ground-truthing relies on underwater surveys by divers. For marine habitats managed for other than fisheries provision services there is no comprehensive habitat layer linked to the delivery of one or multiple ES (Maes et al., 2012). Also, habitat mapping alone is inadequate to evaluate trade-offs among provisioning, regulating, supporting and cultural services before planning marine NBS.

Additional challenges with habitat mapping approaches for marine ecosystems include (Guerry et al., 2012; Maes et al., 2012):

(i) Scarcity of geo-referenced data on species distributions, biogeochemical and biophysical processes at high spatial resolution.
(ii) Lack of clear maritime boundaries analogous to land ownership or catchment boundaries in terrestrial systems, which blurs understanding of marine uses for society.
(iii) The 4D structure formed by benthic and pelagic habitats, which is highly dynamic across time and renders mapping prohibitively costly and potentially unrepresentative.

5.12 EVALUATION OF MODELLING APPROACHES FOR MARINE NBS

To provide a baseline for future marine NBS modelling applications, we evaluated the modelling tools reviewed here with respect to complexity (Table 5.1). Complexity can be evaluated against four key criteria: ease of use, input data, output data and cost (Beck & Lange, 2016; IPBES, 2016; Addison et al., 2017; Bullock & Ding, 2018).

1. Ease of use refers to tools that are user-friendly, open-source, easy to program and run, well documented, published and web-based or software-based for application.
2. Input data complexity increases with use of site-, scale- or context-specific (i.e. non-generalisable, non-scalable) data; and requirements for data collection for calibration.
3. Output data complexity increases with
   (i) delivery of biophysical and benefits estimates;
   (ii) number of output variables; and
   (iii) type of output, e.g. from graphical outputs such as maps to numerical outputs.
4. Cost is increased for tools that are not downloadable free of charge and/or require specialised training or an expert to apply and run the tool.

Overall, the review of models showed that the models applied in marine NBS applications have different degrees of complexity, thus posing different intellectual and practical challenges to users and policy makers. More complex models can have a greater range of uses in marine ecosystem-based management approaches, such as providing both biophysical predictions and social or monetary valuation, but they can also be more difficult to develop, use and interpret, e.g. marine INVEST, RiVAMP, INVITRO, DICE. Complex models also require site-specific input data, expertise and rigorous validation, e.g. ERSEM, HSM, EwE and Atlantis. Practically, the selection of a particular tool to apply in a specific case can depend on many factors, including the decision-making context, which determines the purpose of modelling, and the MES at stake as well as aspects of model

Table 5.1 *Description of models and approaches operated within the MESA framework and used to inform marine NBS applications*

Model acronym	Purpose	Ease of use	Input data complexity	Output data complexity	Cost	Marine NBS application: Example Ref.
HYCOM	Predict salinity/temperature vertically and horizontally	Easy	Medium	Low	Medium	Larval dispersal in MPA (Christie et al., 2010)
TELEMAC	Quantify current flow/wave amplitude	Easy	Medium	Low	Medium	Wave attenuation by saltmarsh (Stark et al., 2016)
ADCIRC	Predict storm-surge sea level and control storm damage	Easy	Medium	Medium	Medium	Coastal defence by oyster reef (Brandon et al., 2016)
SWAN	Predict wave propagation	Easy	Medium	Low	Medium	Coastal defence by coral reef (Storlazzi et al., 2017)
XBEACH	Predict wave propagation and morphological changes nearshore during storms	Easy	Medium	Medium	Medium	Evaluation of coastal protection strategies (Smallegan et al., 2017)
ERSEM	Quantify BGC cycles underpinning ES supply	Medium	High	High	Medium	Nutrient removal (Aldridge et al., 2012)
HSM	Predict species distribution and associated ES supply	Medium	Medium	Medium	Medium	Habitat for eelgrass restoration (Zhou et al., 2016)

EwE	Understand how ecological processes influence ES supply	Medium	Medium	Medium	Medium	Coastal resilience (Weijerman et al., 2018)
Atlantis	Understand how food web dynamics in response to drivers of change influence ES supply	Difficult	High	Medium	Medium	Ocean acidification-fishing effects to inform adaptation strategy (Fay et al., 2017)
CEM	Outline qualitative components of social–ecological systems	Easy	Low	Medium	Medium	Participatory evaluation of MES (Ingram et al., 2018)
INVEST	Quantify trade-offs among different ES and among multiple management sectors	Easy	High	High	Medium	Marine spatial planning (Verutes et al., 2017)
ARIES	Assess ES supply and demand in data-poor contexts	Easy	Medium b	Medium	Medium	Fisheries/Coastal protection (Bagstad et al., 2011)
MIMES	Simulate social–ecological systems using monetary valuation	High	High	Medium	High	Marine Spatial planning (White et al., 2012)
Coastal Resilience	Assess and visualise the social and economic risks from storms and sea-level rise	Easy	Medium	Medium	Low	Coastal resilience (Nature Conservancy, 2018)
RiVAMP	Estimate disaster risk under alternative climate scenarios	Difficult	High	Medium	High	Coastal risk reduction (Chatenoux et al., 2012b)
PGIS	Map stakeholders' perception of ES supply and demand	Easy	Low	Low	Medium	MPA siting (Levine & Feinholz, 2015)

Table 5.1 (*cont.*)

Model acronym	Purpose	Ease of use	Input data complexity	Output data complexity	Cost	Marine NBS application	
						Example	Ref.
DICE	Estimate economic values for ES	Difficult	High	High	High	Seagrass monetary value	(Ganguly et al., 2018)
INVITRO	Understand the behaviour and interactions of organisms, human actors and institutions (agent-based model)	Difficult	High	High	High	Management strategy evaluation	(Gray et al., 2006)

complexity. In addition, Case Study 5.1 demonstrated that no model alone can capture the full complexity of marine management issues and predict ecosystem function in response to a suite of drivers, such as sea-level rise or coastal population change. The case study showed that combinations of different models using multiple lines of evidence and operated within the MESA framework can effectively inform policy and support decision-making.

5.13 CHALLENGES IN MARINE NBS MODELLING

The review of models applied for marine NBS revealed a number of challenges facing scientists and decision-makers.

First, modelling marine ecosystem change is difficult. MES around the world are threatened by a multitude of man-made pressures, such as overfishing, pollution, shipping, biological invasions and coastal development, the combinations and intensity of which are site-specific (MEA, 2005; Inniss et al., 2016). Coastal ecosystems and their services are simultaneously vulnerable to climate change-related pressures beyond local control such as ocean acidification, ocean warming, sea-level rise and extreme weather disasters (MEA, 2005; Inniss et al., 2016; Roberts et al., 2017). In addition, change in the processes underpinning MES is non-linear and often unpredictable, especially under increasing pressures (MEA, 2005). Understanding and modelling the thresholds at which these changes will happen to inform sustainable and adaptive management of the marine social–ecological systems is generally difficult, if not impossible (Maes et al., 2012).

Second, quantification of marine ecosystem processes is difficult. MES cannot be directly monitored and quantified because they are underpinned by complex and dynamic ecosystem processes. Indicators, as proxies of complex marine processes, are available for fisheries and habitat services provided by coastal wetlands and coral reefs (Liquete et al., 2013). However, these indicators refer to qualitative variables or monetary values (Seppelt et al., 2011) and 'state of the environment' reporting (e.g. Niemeijer & de Groot, 2008) and not to quantitative variables describing marine processes. Further, monitoring for MES often focuses on only a subset of variables because of (i) insufficient resources to monitor all relevant physical, chemical, biological and human variables and to address multiple, often conflicting, objectives (Heenan et al., 2016); and (ii) poor understanding of the spatial connection between service-providing and service-benefitted areas (Drakou et al., 2017).

Third, there is scarcity of comparisons between 'hard' or 'grey' engineering solutions (e.g. dykes and seawalls) for coastal protection, which are predominantly applied, and NBS for coastal protection (O'Donnell, 2016; Pontee et al., 2016; Morris et al., 2018). As a result, few studies report marine modelling approaches evaluating trade-offs between environmental, economic and social components of marine social–ecological systems pre-NBS and post-NBS implementation (Guerry et al., 2012; Arkema et al., 2017; Weijerman et al., 2018).

Finally, it must be borne in mind that a tool considered as structurally simple for scientists may be practically complex for decision-makers or practitioners; and vice-versa, a tool considered useful by stakeholders may be not be sophisticated from a scientist's point of view (Ruckelhaus et al., 2015). Decision-makers are often best served by relatively simple models, provided they are clearly documented, published and validation tests reveal limitations. Building an effective science–policy interface relies upon simple and transparent tools to explore interactions, trade-offs or scenarios, which can enable stakeholders, including those with limited scientific capacity, to actively engage in a participatory decision-making process (Ruckelshaus et al., 2015).

5.14 CONCLUDING REMARKS

A wealth of marine models has been developed to describe or quantify change in the processes underpinning MES. However, models for marine NBS must help to project whether and where conserving, restoring or creating marine habitats enhances biophysical processes delivering desired MES for addressing site-specific social challenges such as disaster risk management, food insecurity, poverty, pollution and climate change mitigation and adaptation (Guerry et al., 2012;

Spalding et al., 2014; Arkema et al., 2017). Models for marine NBS must operate within the MESA framework, which enables the synthesis of monetary and non-monetary data, and to provide projections about potential future states (Guerry et al., 2012). Furthermore, models for marine NBS must enable exploring the links between change in marine biophysical processes and social well-being as well as the trade-offs that emerge from alternative uses of marine and coastal environments (Guerry et al., 2012; Addison et al., 2017; Arkema et al., 2017).

Despite the potential usefulness of all marine models for marine NBS, there are relatively few published examples of marine models operated within the MESA framework. Each model operated within the MESA framework provided useful insights to stakeholders with regards to policy context. Conceptual and participatory approaches provided useful insights into management options. Empirical models described general relationships among biophysical and/or socio-cultural and monetary variables. More complex approaches, such as process-based models, represented with greater accuracy the variability in the ecosystem processes underpinning MES and their benefits.

Supporting further development of process-based MES models for marine NBS is key to better understanding MES supply and demand. There is also a need to strike a balance between the need for accurate predictions and the higher cost of complex models. Doing so may involve promoting user-friendly and interactive tools, user-training workshops and data-sharing web interfaces. Model validation and communication of uncertainty in model predictions will further enhance the role of models in marine ecosystem-based, adaptive management.

On a final note, adapting to climate change is becoming a pressing priority as suggested by the IPCC Special Report on Global Warming of 1.5°C (aka SR15), which concludes that the impact of global warming is being felt much sooner than expected (IPCC, 2018). As widely recognised, concerted efforts by research institutes, government agencies and multiple national and international organisations have led to significant evidence concerning climate change, vulnerability and adaptation. It is also increasingly acknowledged that climate change adaptation demands an effective science–policy interface for the translation of climate scenarios to adaptation policies. However, the knowledge base from past and ongoing projects exploring marine social–ecological systems is incomplete and biased towards fisheries management. Filling critical knowledge gaps in marine ecosystem-based adaptation depends on the success of the science–policy interface to mainstream approaches towards working with the ocean, in line with the marine NBS concept. Therefore, development and use of tools that explore trade-offs among multiple MES and management options, such as those reviewed here, will be of critical importance.

REFERENCES

Addison, P., Collins, D., Trebilco, R., Howe, S., Bax, N., Hedge, P., et al. 2017. A new wave of marine evidence-based management: emerging challenges and solutions to transform monitoring, evaluating, and reporting. *ICES Journal of Marine Science*, 75(3), 941–952.

Albert, C., Spangenberg, J. H. & Schröter, B. 2017. Nature-based solutions: criteria. *Nature*, 543(7645), 315.

Aldridge, J., Van De Molen, J. & Forster, R. 2012. *Wider Ecological Implications of Macroalgae Cultivation*. The Crown Estate. http://stopptt.com/wp-content/uploads/2018/09/Nitrogen-phosphate-uptake-by-cultivated-seaweed.pdf. Accessed: October 2018.

Alexander, S., Aronson, J., Whaley, O. & Lamb, D. 2016. The relationship between ecological restoration and the ecosystem services concept. *Ecology and Society*, 21(1).

Anderson, O. F., Guinotte, J. M., Rowden, A. A., Clark, M. R., Mormede, S., Davies, A. J., et al. 2016. Field validation of habitat suitability models for vulnerable marine ecosystems in the South Pacific Ocean: implications for the use of broad-scale models in fisheries management. *Ocean & Coastal Management*, 120, 110–126.

Arkema, K. K., Griffin, R., Maldonado, S., Silver, J., Suckale, J. & Guerry, A. D. 2017. Linking social, ecological, and physical science to advance natural and nature-based protection for coastal communities. *Annals of the New York Academy of Sciences*, 1399(1), 5–26.

Arkema, K. K., Verutes, G. M., Wood, S. A., Clarke-Samuels, C., Rosado, S., Canto, M., et al. 2015. Embedding ecosystem services in coastal planning leads to better outcomes for people and nature. *Proceedings of the National Academy of Sciences of the United States of America*, 112, 7390–7395.

Bagstad, K. J., Semmens, D. J., Waage, S. & Winthrop, R. 2013. A comparative assessment of decision-support tools for ecosystem services quantification and valuation. *Ecosystem Services*, 5, 27–39.

Bagstad, K. J., Villa, F., Johnson, G. W. & Voigt, B. 2011. ARIES – Artificial Intelligence for Ecosystem Services: a guide to models and data, version 1.0. ARIES report series n. 1. https://unstats.un.org/unsd/envaccounting/seeaRev/meeting2013/EG13-BG-7.pdf. Accessed: October 2018.

Banzhaf, H. S. & Boyd, J. 2012. The architecture and measurement of an ecosystem services index. *Sustainability*, 4(4), 430–461.

Barbier, E. B. 2015. Valuing the storm protection service of estuarine and coastal ecosystems. *Ecosystem Services*, 11, 32–38.

Baretta, J., Ebenhöh, W. & Ruardij, P. 1995. The European regional seas ecosystem model, a complex marine ecosystem model. *Netherlands Journal of Sea Research*, 33(3), 233–246.

Baretta-Bekker, J., Baretta, J. & Ebenhöh, W. 1997. Microbial dynamics in the marine ecosystem model ERSEM II with decoupled carbon assimilation and nutrient uptake. *Journal of Sea Research*, 38(3), 195–211.

Bastardie, F., Nielsen, J. R. & Miethe, T. 2016. Corrigendum: DISPLACE: a dynamic, individual-based model for spatial fishing planning and effort displacement – integrating underlying fish population models. *Canadian Journal of Fisheries and Aquatic Sciences*, 73(3), 469–469.

Beck, M. & Lange, G. 2016. *Managing Coasts with Natural Solutions: Guidelines for Measuring and Valuing the Coastal Protection Services of Mangroves and Coral Reefs*. Washington, DC: The World Bank.

Bedri, Z., Bruen, M., Dowley, A. & Masterson, B. 2013. Environmental consequences of a power plant shut-down: a three-dimensional water quality model of Dublin Bay. *Marine Pollution Bulletin*, 71(1), 117–128.

Bilkovic, D. M., Mitchell, M., Mason, P. & Duhring, K. 2016. The role of living shorelines as estuarine habitat conservation strategies. *Coastal Management*, 44(3), 161–174.

Blackford, J. C., Allen, J. I. & Gilbert, F. J. 2004. Ecosystem dynamics at six contrasting sites: a generic modelling study. *Journal of Marine Systems*, 52(1–4), 191–215.

Bleck, R. 2002. An oceanic general circulation model framed in hybrid isopycnic-Cartesian coordinates. *Ocean Modelling*, 4(1), 55–88.

Bleck, R., Halliwell, G., Wallcraft, A., Carroll, S., Kelly, K. & Rushing, K. 2002. *HYCOM User's Manual*, 4 March 2002.

Böhnke-Henrichs, A., Baulcomb, C., Koss, R., Hussain, S. S. & De Groot, R. S. 2013. Typology and indicators of ecosystem services for marine spatial planning and management. *Journal of Environmental Management*, 130, 135–145.

Booij, N., Ris, R. C. & Holthuijsen, L. H. 1999. A third-generation wave model for coastal regions: 1. Model description and validation. *Journal of Geophysical Research*, 104(C4), 7649.

Borsje, B. W., Van Wesenbeeck, B. K., Dekker, F., Paalvast, P., Bouma, T. J., Van Katwijk, M. M., et al. 2011. How ecological engineering can serve in coastal protection. *Ecological Engineering*, 37(2), 113–122.

Bouma, T. J., Van Belzen, J., Balke, T., Zhu, Z., Airoldi, L., Blight, A. J., et al. 2014. Identifying knowledge gaps hampering application of intertidal habitats in coastal protection: opportunities & steps to take. *Coastal Engineering*, 87, 147–157.

Brandon, C. M., Woodruff, J. D., Orton, P. M. & Donnelly, J. P. 2016. Evidence for elevated coastal vulnerability following large-scale historical oyster bed harvesting. *Earth Surface Processes and Landforms*, 41(8), 1136–1143.

Bridges, T. S., Burks-Copes, K. A., Bates, M. E., Collier, Z. A., Fischenich, J. C., Piercy, C. D., et al. 2015. *Use of Natural and Nature-based Features (NNBF) for Coastal Resilience*. Washington, DC: US Army Engineer Research and Development Center, Environmental Laboratory, Coastal and Hydraulics Laboratory.

Bullock, J. & Ding, H. 2018. A guide to selecting ecosystem service models for decision-making: lessons from sub-Saharan Africa. www.wri.org/sites/default/files/guide-selecting-ecosystem-service-model-decision-making_0.pdf

Burchard, H. & Bolding, K. 2002. *GETM: A General Estuarine Transport Model; Scientific Documentation*. Luxembourg: European Commission, Joint Research Centre, Institute for Environment and Sustainability.

Butenschön, M., Clark, J., Aldridge, J. N., Allen, J. I., Artioli, Y., Blackford, J., et al. 2016. ERSEM 15.06: a generic model for marine biogeochemistry and the ecosystem dynamics of the lower trophic levels. *Geoscientific Model Development*, 9(4), 1293–1339.

Cardinale, B. J., Duffy, J. E., Gonzalez, A., Hooper, D. U., Perrings, C., Venail, P., et al. 2012. Biodiversity loss and its impact on humanity. *Nature*, 486(7401), 59.

Cardone, V. J., Jensen, R. E., Resio, D. T., Swail, V. R. & Cox, A. T. 1996. Evaluation of contemporary ocean wave models in rare extreme events: the 'Halloween Storm' of October 1991 and the 'Storm of the Century' of March 1993. *Journal of Atmospheric and Oceanic Technology*, 13(1), 198–230.

Chapman, M. & Underwood, A. 2011. Evaluation of ecological engineering of, armoured, shorelines to improve their value as habitat. *Journal of Experimental Marine Biology and Ecology*, 400(1–2), 302–313.

Chatenoux, B., Peduzzi, P. & Velegrakis, A. 2012a. Risk and Vulnerability Assessment Methodology Development Project (RiVAMP): quantifying the role of marine and coastal ecosystems in mitigating beach erosion. https://archive-ouverte.unige.ch/unige:32371. Accessed: October 2018.

Chatenoux, B., Peduzzi, P. & Velegrakis, A. 2012b. *RIVAMP Training on the Role of Coastal and Marine Ecosystems for Mitigating Beach Erosion: The Case of Negril Jamaica*. Geneva: UNEP/GRID-Geneva.

Christensen, V. & Walters, C. J. 2004. Ecopath with Ecosim: methods, capabilities and limitations. *Ecological Modelling*, 172(2–4), 109–139.

Christensen, V., Walters, C. J. & Pauly, D. 2005. *Ecopath with Ecosim: A User's Guide*. Vancouver: Fisheries Centre, University of British Columbia.

Christie, M. R., Tissot, B. N., Albins, M. A., Beets, J. P., Jia, Y., Ortiz, D. M., et al. 2010. Larval connectivity in an effective network of marine protected areas. *PLoS ONE*, 5(12), e15715.

Christin, Z. L., Bagstad, K. J. & Verdone, M. A. 2016. A decision framework for identifying models to estimate forest ecosystem services gains from restoration. *Forest Ecosystems*, 3(1), 3.

Cogan, C. B., Todd, B. J., Lawton, P. & Noji, T. T. 2009. The role of marine habitat mapping in ecosystem-based management. *ICES Journal of Marine Science*, 66(9), 2033–2042.

Cohen-Shacham, E., Walters, G., Janzen, C. & Maginnis, S. 2016. *Nature-based Solutions to Address Global Societal Challenges*. Gland: IUCN.

Cullen-Unsworth, L. C., Nordlund, L. M., Paddock, J., Baker, S., McKenzie, L. J. & Unsworth, R. K. 2014. Seagrass meadows globally as a coupled social–ecological system: implications for human wellbeing. *Marine Pollution Bulletin*, 83(2), 387–397.

Dadou, I., Lamy, F., Rabouille, C., Ruiz-Pino, D., Andersen, V., Bianchi, M., et al. 2001. An integrated biological pump model from the euphotic zone to the sediment: a 1-D application in the Northeast tropical Atlantic. *Deep Sea Research Part II: Topical Studies in Oceanography*, 48(10), 2345–2381.

Daily, G. C., Polasky, S., Goldstein, J., Kareiva, P. M., Mooney, H. A., Pejchar, L., et al. 2009. Ecosystem services in decision making: time to deliver. *Frontiers in Ecology and the Environment*, 7(1), 21–28.

de Groot, R. S., Fisher, B., Christie, M., Aronson, J., Braat, L., Gowdy, J., et al. 2010. Integrating the ecological economic dimensions in biodiversity ecosystem service valuation. *In*: Kumar, P. (ed.) *The Economics of Ecosystems and Biodiversity: Ecological and Economic Foundations*, pp. 9–40. London: Earthscan.

del Monte-Luna, P., Arreguín-Sánchez, F. & Lluch-Belda, D. 2007. Marine ecosystem analyses in the gulf of Ulloa, Mexico: BAC meets Ecopath. *In*: *INCOFISH Ecosystem Models: Transiting from Ecopath to Ecospace*. Vancouver: Fisheries Centre Research Reports, 15(6), 114–133.

Dippner, J. W. 2006. Future aspects in marine ecosystem modelling. *Journal of Marine Systems*, 61(3–4), 246–267. www.sciencedirect.com/science/article/pii/S0924796306000273

Drakou, E. G., Pendleton, L., Effron, M., Ingram, J. C. & Teneva, L. 2017. When ecosystems and their services are not co-located: oceans and coasts. *ICES Journal of Marine Science*, 74(6), 1531–1539.

Dyke, P. P. 2001. *Coastal and Shelf Sea Modelling*. New York, NY: Springer.

Edgar, G. J., Bates, A. E., Bird, T. J., Jones, A. H., Kininmonth, S., Stuart-Smith, R. D., et al. 2016. New approaches to marine conservation through the scaling up of ecological data. *Annual Review of Marine Science*, 8, 435–461.

Elith, J. & Leathwick, J. R. 2009. Species distribution models: ecological explanation and prediction across space and time. *Annual Review of Ecology, Evolution, and Systematics*, 40, 677–697.

Elskens, M., Gourgue, O., Baeyens, W., Chou, L., Deleersnijder, E., Leermakers, M., et al. 2014. Modelling metal speciation in the Scheldt Estuary: combining a flexible-resolution transport model with empirical functions. *Science of the Total Environment*, 476–477, 346–358. www.ncbi.nlm.nih.gov/pubmed/24476975

Espinosa-Romero, M. J., Gregr, E. J., Walters, C., Christensen, V. & Chan, K. 2011. Representing mediating effects and species reintroductions in Ecopath with Ecosim. *Ecological Modelling*, 222(9), 1569–1579.

Essington, T. E. 2007. Evaluating the sensitivity of a trophic mass-balance model (Ecopath) to imprecise data inputs. *Canadian Journal of Fisheries and Aquatic Sciences*, 64(4), 628–637.

European Commission. 2015. *Towards an EU Research and Innovation Policy Agenda for Nature-based Solutions & Re-naturing Cities. Final Report of the Horizon 2020 Group on 'Nature-based Solutions & Re-naturing Cities'*. Brussels: European Commission.

Falk-Petersen, J. 2004. Ecosystem effects of red king crab invasion. A modelling approach using Ecopath with Ecosim. Master's thesis, University of Tromsø.

Fay, G., Link, J. S. & Hare, J. A. 2017. Assessing the effects of ocean acidification in the Northeast US using an end-to-end marine ecosystem model. *Ecological Modelling*, 347, 1–10. www.sciencedirect.com/science/article/pii/S0304380016308237

Fennel, K., Losch, M., Schröter, J. & Wenzel, M. 2001. Testing a marine ecosystem model: sensitivity analysis and parameter optimization. *Journal of Marine Systems*, 28(1–2), 45–63. www.sciencedirect.com/science/article/pii/S092479630000083X

Fulton, E. A. 2010. Approaches to end-to-end ecosystem models. *Journal of Marine Systems*, 81(1–2), 171–183. www.sciencedirect.com/science/article/pii/S0924796309003509

Fulton, E. A., Link, J. S., Kaplan, I. C., Savina-Rolland, M., Johnson, P., Ainsworth, C., et al. 2011. Lessons in modelling and management of marine ecosystems: the Atlantis experience. *Fish and Fisheries*, 12(2), 171–188.

Fulton, E. A., Smith, A. D. & Johnson, C. R. 2003. Effect of complexity on marine ecosystem models. *Marine Ecology Progress Series*, 253, 1–16.

Fung, T., Farnsworth, K. D., Reid, D. G. & Rossberg, A. G. 2015. Impact of biodiversity loss on production in complex marine food webs mitigated by prey-release. *Nature Communications*, 6, 6657.

Ganguly, D., Singh, G., Purvaja, R., Bhatta, R., Selvam, A. P., Banerjee, K., et al. 2018. Valuing the carbon sequestration regulation service by seagrass ecosystems of Palk Bay and Chilika, India. *Ocean & Coastal Management*, 159, 26–33.

GETM. n.d. GETM: a 3D hydrodynamic model for coastal oceans. https://getm.eu/. Accessed: October 2018.

Gimenez, O., Buckland, S. T., Morgan, B. J., Bez, N., Bertrand, S., Choquet, R., et al. 2014. Statistical ecology comes of age. *Biology Letters*, 10(12), 20140698.

Gittman, R. K., Peterson, C. H., Currin, C. A., Fodrie, F. J., Piehler, M. F. & Bruno, J. F. 2016. Living shorelines can enhance the nursery role of threatened estuarine habitats. *Ecological Applications*, 26(1), 249–263.

Gourgue, O., Baeyens, W., Chen, M. S., De Brauwere, A., De Brye, B., Deleersnijder, E., et al. 2013. A depth-averaged two-dimensional sediment transport model for environmental studies in the Scheldt Estuary and tidal river network. *Journal of Marine Systems*, 128, 27–39. www.sciencedirect.com/science/article/pii/S0924796313000833

Gray, R., Fulton, B., Little, R., Scott, R., Hatfield, B., Lyne, V., et al. 2006. North West Shelf Joint Environmental Management Study: Software Description – In Vitro. Canberra: CSIRO Oceans and Atmosphere – Information and Data Centre.

Gregr, E. J. & Chan, K. M. 2014. Leaps of faith: how implicit assumptions compromise the utility of ecosystem models for decision-making. *Bioscience*, 65, 43–54.

Griscom, B. W., Adams, J., Ellis, P. W., Houghton, R. A., Lomax, G., Miteva, D. A., et al. 2017. Natural climate solutions. *Proceedings of the National Academy of Sciences of the United States of America*, 114(44), 11,645–11,650.

Guannel, G., Ruggiero, P., Faries, J., Arkema, K., Pinsky, M., Gelfenbaum, G., et al. 2015. Integrated modeling framework to quantify the coastal protection services supplied by vegetation. *Journal of Geophysical Research: Oceans*, 120(1), 324–345.

Guerry, A. D., Ruckelshaus, M. H., Arkema, K. K., Bernhardt, J. R., Guannel, G., Kim, C.-K., et al. 2012. Modeling benefits from nature: using ecosystem services to inform coastal and marine spatial planning. *International Journal of Biodiversity Science, Ecosystem Services & Management*, 8(1–2), 107–121.

Guerry, A. D., Ruckelshaus, M. H., Plummer, M. L. & Holland, D. 2013. Modeling marine ecosystem services. *In*: Levin, S. A. (ed.) *Encyclopedia of Biodiversity*. 2nd ed., Vol. 5, pp. 329–346. Waltham, MA: Academic Press.

Harrison, P. A., Dunford, R., Barton, D. N., Kelemen, E., Martín-López, B., Norton, L., et al. 2018. Selecting methods for ecosystem service assessment: a decision tree approach. *Ecosystem Services*, 29, 481–498.

Hattam, C., Atkins, J. P., Beaumont, N., Börger, T., Böhnke-Henrichs, A., Burdon, D., et al. 2015. Marine ecosystem services: linking indicators to their classification. *Ecological Indicators*, 49, 61–75.

Heenan, A., Gorospe, K., Williams, I., Levine, A., Maurin, P., Nadon, M., et al. 2016. Ecosystem monitoring for ecosystem-based management: using a polycentric approach to balance information trade-offs. *Journal of Applied Ecology*, 53(3), 699–704.

Herr, D. & Landis, E. 2016. Coastal blue carbon ecosystems. Opportunities for nationally determined contributions. Policy Brief. Gland: IUCN.

Hervouet, J.-M. 2007. *Hydrodynamics of Free Surface Flows: Modelling with the Finite Element Method*. Chichester: John Wiley & Sons.

Heymans, J., Coll, M., Libralato, S. & Christensen, V. 2012. Ecopath theory, modelling and application to coastal ecosystems. *In*: *Treatise on Estuarine and Coastal Science*, pp. 93–113. Oxford: Elsevier.

Hirzel, A. H., Le Lay, G., Helfer, V., Randin, C. & Guisan, A. 2006. Evaluating the ability of habitat suitability models to predict species presences. *Ecological Modelling*, 199(2), 142–152.

Ho, T. V. T., Woodley, S., Cottrell, A. & Valentine, P. 2014. A multilevel analytical framework for more-effective governance in human-natural systems: a case study of marine protected areas in Vietnam. *Ocean & Coastal Management*, 90, 11–19.

Hollowed, A. B., Bax, N., Beamish, R., Collie, J., Fogarty, M., Livingston, P., et al. 2000. Are multispecies models an improvement on single-species models for measuring fishing impacts on marine ecosystems? *ICES Journal of Marine Science*, 57(3), 707–719.

Howell, K. L., Holt, R., Endrino, I. P. & Stewart, H. 2011. When the species is also a habitat: comparing the predictively modelled distributions of *Lophelia pertusa* and the reef habitat it forms. *Biological Conservation*, 144(11), 2656–2665.

Hyder, K., Rossberg, A. G., Allen, J. I., Austen, M. C., Barciela, R. M., Bannister, H. J., et al. 2015. Making modelling count – increasing the contribution of shelf-seas community and ecosystem models to policy development and management. *Marine Policy*, 61, 291–302.

Ingram, R. J., Oleson, K. L. & Gove, J. M. 2018. Revealing complex social–ecological interactions through participatory modeling to support ecosystem-based management in Hawai'i. *Marine Policy*, 94, 180–188.

Inniss, L., Simcock, A., Ajawin, A., Alcala, A., Bernal, P., Calumpong, H., et al. 2016. *The First Global Integrated Marine Assessment: World Ocean Assessment I*. New York, NY: United Nations.

IPBES. 2016. *The Methodological Assessment Report on Scenarios and Models of Biodiversity and Ecosystem Services*. Bonn: Secretariat of the Intergovernmental Science-Policy Platform on Biodiversity and Ecosystem Services.

IPCC. 2018. Global warming of 1.5°C www.ipcc.ch/report/sr15/

IUCN. 2017. IUCN Position on SDG14 – Call for Action.

Kaplan, I. C., Horne, P. J. & Levin, P. S. 2012. Screening California current fishery management scenarios using the Atlantis end-to-end ecosystem model. *Progress in Oceanography*, 102, 5–18. www.sciencedirect.com/science/article/pii/S0079661112000262

Karanci, A., Berglund, E. & Overton, M. 2017. An agent-based model to evaluate housing dynamics of coastal communities facing storms and sea level rise. *Coastal Engineering Proceedings*, 1(35), 23.

Katona, S., Polsenberg, J., Lowndes, J., Halpern, B. S., Pacheco, E., Mosher, L., et al. 2017. *Navigating the Seascape of Ocean Management: Waypoints on the Voyage Toward Sustainable Use*. Seattle, WA: OpenChannels.

Kelble, C. R., Loomis, D. K., Lovelace, S., Nuttle, W. K., Ortner, P. B., Fletcher, P., et al. 2013. The EBM-DPSER conceptual model: integrating ecosystem services into the DPSIR framework. *PLoS ONE*, 8(8), e70766.

Koné, N. V., Machu, E., Penven, P., Andersen, V., Garçon, V., Fréon, P., et al. 2005. Modeling the primary and secondary productions of the southern Benguela upwelling system: a comparative study through two biogeochemical models. *Global Biogeochemical Cycles*, 19(4).

Kwiatkowski, L., Yool, A., Allen, J., Anderson, T., Barciela, R., Buitenhuis, E., et al. 2014. iMarNet: an ocean biogeochemistry model inter-comparison project within a common physical ocean modelling framework. *Biogeosciences Discussions*, 11(7), 10,537–10,569.

Landuyt, D., Broekx, S., D'hondt, R., Engelen, G., Aertsens, J. & Goethals, P. L. 2013. A review of Bayesian belief networks in ecosystem service modelling. *Environmental Modelling & Software*, 46, 1–11.

Lauria, V., Vaz, S., Martin, C. S., Mackinson, S. & Carpentier, A. 2011. What influences European plaice (*Pleuronectes platessa*) distribution in the eastern English Channel? Using habitat modelling and GIS to predict habitat utilization. *ICES Journal of Marine Science*, 68(7), 1500–1510.

Le Pape, O., Delavenne, J. & Vaz, S. 2014. Quantitative mapping of fish habitat: a useful tool to design spatialised management measures and marine protected area with fishery objectives. *Ocean & Coastal Management*, 87, 8–19.

Legrand, S., Deleersnijder, E., Hanert, E., Legat, V. & Wolanski, E. 2006. High-resolution, unstructured meshes for hydrodynamic models of the Great Barrier Reef, Australia. *Estuarine, Coastal and Shelf Science*, 68(1), 36–46.

Levin, P. S., Fogarty, M. J., Murawski, S. A. & Fluharty, D. 2009. Integrated ecosystem assessments: developing the scientific basis for ecosystem-based management of the ocean. *PLoS Biology*, 7(1), e1000014.

Levin, S. A. & Lubchenco, J. 2008. Resilience, robustness, and marine ecosystem-based management. *AIBS Bulletin*, 58(1), 27–32.

Levine, A. S. & Feinholz, C. L. 2015. Participatory GIS to inform coral reef ecosystem management: mapping human coastal and ocean uses in Hawaii. *Applied Geography*, 59, 60–69.

Link, J. S., Fulton, E. A. & Gamble, R. J. 2010. The northeast US application of ATLANTIS: a full system model exploring marine ecosystem dynamics in a living marine resource management context. *Progress in Oceanography*, 87(1–4), 214–234.

Link, J. S., Gamble, R. J. & Fulton, E. A. 2011. NEUS–Atlantis: construction, calibration, and application of an ecosystem model with ecological interactions, physiographic conditions, and fleet behavior. NOAA Technical Memo NMFS NE, 218(247), 02543–1026.

Liquete, C., Piroddi, C., Drakou, E. G., Gurney, L., Katsanevakis, S., Charef, A., et al. 2013. Current status and future prospects for the assessment of marine and coastal ecosystem services: a systematic review. *PLoS ONE*, 8(7), e67737.

Luettich Jr, R. A., Westerink, J. J. & Scheffner, N. W. 1992. ADCIRC: an advanced three-dimensional circulation model for shelves, coasts, and estuaries. Report 1. Theory and methodology of ADCIRC-2DDI and ADCIRC-3DL. Technical report.

Maes, J., Egoh, B., Willemen, L., Liquete, C., Vihervaara, P., Schägner, J. P., et al. 2012. Mapping ecosystem services for policy support and decision making in the European Union. *Ecosystem Services*, 1(1), 31–39.

Marzloff, M., Shin, Y.-J., Tam, J., Travers, M. & Bertrand, A. 2009. Trophic structure of the Peruvian marine ecosystem in 2000–2006: insights on the effects of management scenarios for the hake fishery using the IBM trophic model Osmose. *Journal of Marine Systems*, 75(1–2), 290–304.

Mason, E., Molemaker, J., Shchepetkin, A. F., Colas, F., Mcwilliams, J. C. & Sangrà, P. 2010. Procedures for offline grid nesting in regional ocean models. *Ocean Modelling*, 35(1–2), 1–15.

McCall, R. T., De Vries, J. V. T., Plant, N., Van Dongeren, A., Roelvink, J., Thompson, D., et al. 2010. Two-dimensional time dependent hurricane overwash and erosion modeling at Santa Rosa Island. *Coastal Engineering*, 57(7), 668–683.

McMichael, A., Scholes, R., Hefny, M., Pereira, E., Palm, C. & Foale, S. 2005. *Linking Ecosystem Services and Human Well-being*. Washington, DC: Island Press.

Mendoza, E., Oderiz, I., Martinez, M. L. & Silva, R. 2017. Measurements and modelling of small scale processes of vegetation preventing dune erosion. *Journal of Coastal Research*, 77, 19–27.

Millennium Ecosystem Assessment (MEA). 2005. *Current State and Trends*. Washington, DC: Island Press.

Moloney, C. L. & Field, J. G. 1991. The size-based dynamics of plankton food webs. I. A simulation model of carbon and nitrogen flows. *Journal of Plankton Research*, 13(5), 1003–1038.

Mongin, M., Baird, M. E., Tilbrook, B., Matear, R. J., Lenton, A., Herzfeld, M., et al. 2016. The exposure of the Great Barrier Reef to ocean acidification. *Nature Communications*, 7, 10732.

Moosavi, S. 2017. Ecological coastal protection: pathways to living shorelines. *In*: Hajdu, M. & Skibniewski, M. E. (eds.) *Creative Construction Conference 2017*, pp. 930–938. Oxford: Elsevier.

Morris, R. L., Konlechner, T. M., Ghisalberti, M. & Swearer, S. E. 2018. From grey to green: efficacy of eco-engineering solutions for nature-based coastal defence. *Global Change Biology*, 24, 1837–1842.

Narayan, S., Beck, M. W., Reguero, B. G., Losada, I. J., Van Wesenbeeck, B., Pontee, N., et al. 2016. The effectiveness, costs and coastal protection benefits of natural and nature-based defences. *PLoS ONE*, 11(5), e0154735.

Narayan, S., Beck, M. W., Wilson, P., Thomas, C. J., Guerrero, A., Shepard, C. C., et al. 2017. The value of coastal wetlands for flood damage reduction in the northeastern USA. *Scientific Reports*, 7, 9463.

Nature Conservancy. 2018. Coastal Resilience toolkit http://coastalresilience.org/natural-solutions/toolkit/

Nesshöver, C., Assmuth, T., Irvine, K. N., Rusch, G. M., Waylen, K. A., Delbaere, B., et al. 2017. The science, policy and practice of nature-based solutions: an interdisciplinary perspective. *Science of the Total Environment*, 579, 1215–1227.

Niemeijer, D. & De Groot, R. S. 2008. A conceptual framework for selecting environmental indicator sets. *Ecological Indicators*, 8(1), 14–25.

Nordhaus, W. 2014. Estimates of the social cost of carbon: concepts and results from the DICE-2013R model and alternative approaches. *Journal of the Association of Environmental and Resource Economists*, 1(1/2), 273–312.

Nordhaus, W. D. 2017. Revisiting the social cost of carbon. *Proceedings of the National Academy of Sciences of the United States of America*, 114, 1518–1823.

Novak, A. B. & Short, F. T. 2012. *Creating the Basis for Successful Restoration: An Eelgrass Habitat Suitability Model in GIS for Plum Island Sound, Massachusetts*. Fall River, MA: Office of Energy and Environmental Affairs (Massachusetts). www.mass.gov/eea/docs/mbp/publications/eelgrass

Nowacki, D. J., Beudin, A. & Ganju, N. K. 2017. Spectral wave dissipation by submerged aquatic vegetation in a back-barrier estuary. *Limnology and Oceanography*, 62(2), 736–753.

O'Donnell, J. E. D. 2016. Regulatory issues for implementing living shorelines. *National Wetlands Newsletter*, 38(2). www.eli.org/sites/default/files/nwn/issue/38.2_Odonnell.pdf

Osorio-Cano, J., Osorio, A. & Peláez-Zapata, D. 2019. Ecosystem management tools to study natural habitats as wave damping structures and coastal protection mechanisms. *Ecological Engineering*, 130, 282–295.

Ostrom, E. 2009. A general framework for analyzing sustainability of social–ecological systems. *Science*, 325(5939), 419–422.

Pauly, D., Christensen, V. & Walters, C. 2000. Ecopath, Ecosim, and Ecospace as tools for evaluating ecosystem impact of fisheries. *ICES Journal of Marine Science: Journal du Conseil*, 57(3), 697–706.

Pendleton, L., Donato, D. C., Murray, B. C., Crooks, S., Jenkins, W. A., Sifleet, S., et al. 2012. Estimating global 'blue carbon' emissions from conversion and degradation of vegetated coastal ecosystems. *PLoS ONE*, 7(9), e43542.

Piroddi, C., Teixeira, H., Lynam, C. P., Smith, C., Alvarez, M. C., Mazik, K., et al. 2015. Using ecological models to assess ecosystem status in support of the European Marine Strategy Framework Directive. *Ecological Indicators*, 58, 175–191.

Plagányi, É. E. 2007. *Models for an Ecosystem Approach to Fisheries*. Technical Paper No. 477. Rome: Food & Agriculture Organization.

Plaganyi, E. & Butterworth, D. 2004. A critical look at the potential of Ecopath with Ecosim to assist in practical fisheries management. *African Journal of Marine Science*, 26(1), 261–287.

Pontee, N., Narayan, S., Beck, M. W. & Hosking, A. H. 2016. Nature-based solutions: lessons from around the world. *Proceedings of the Institution of Civil Engineers-Maritime Engineering*, 169(1), 29–36.

Radach, G. & Moll, A. 2006. Review of the three-dimensional ecological modelling related to the North Sea shelf system – Part 2: model validation and data needs. *Oceanography and Marine Biology; an Annual Review*, 44, 1–60.

Randall, D. A., Wood, R. A., Bony, S., Colman, R., Fichefet, T., Fyfe, J., et al. 2007. Climate models and their evaluation. *In*: *Climate Change 2007: The Physical Science Basis. Contribution of Working Group I to the Fourth Assessment Report of the IPCC (FAR)*, pp. 589–662. Cambridge: Cambridge University Press.

Reddy, S. M., Guannel, G., Griffin, R., Faries, J., Boucher, T., Thompson, M., et al. 2016. Evaluating the role of coastal habitats and sea-level rise in hurricane risk mitigation: an ecological economic assessment method and application to a business decision. *Integrated Environmental Assessment and Management*, 12(2), 328–344.

Rizvi, A. R. & Van Riel, K. 2013. *Nature Based Solutions for Climate Change Adaptation–Knowledge Gaps*. Gland: IUCN. www.iucn.org/sites/dev/files/eba_knowledge_gaps.pdf. Accessed: October 2018.

Roberts, C. M., O'Leary, B. C., McCauley, D. J., Cury, P. M., Duarte, C. M., Lubchenco, J., et al. 2017. Marine reserves can mitigate and promote adaptation to climate change. *Proceedings of the National Academy of Sciences of the United States of America*, 114, 1518–1523.

Rockström, J. & Tyrrell, T. D. 2017. Nature-based solutions for better climate resilience: the need to scale up ambition and action. Expert Perspective for the NDC Partnership. www.ndcpartnership.org/sites/default/files/NDCP_Expert_Perspectives_SRC_Climate_Action_v5.pdf. Accessed: October 2018

Roelvink, D., Reniers, A., Van Dongeren, A., Van Thiel De Vries, J., Lescinski, J. & McCall, R. 2010. XBEACH model description and manual. UNESCO–IHE Institute for Water Education, Deltares and Delft University of Tecnhology Report, 21 June 2010.

Rooper, C. N., Zimmermann, M., Prescott, M. M. & Hermann, A. J. 2014. Predictive models of coral and sponge distribution, abundance and diversity in bottom trawl surveys of the Aleutian Islands, Alaska. *Marine Ecology Progress Series*, 503, 157–176.

Ruardij, P., Veldhuis, M. J. & Brussaard, C. P. 2005. Modeling the bloom dynamics of the polymorphic phytoplankter *Phaeocystis globosa*: impact of grazers and viruses. *Harmful Algae*, 4(5), 941–963.

Ruckelshaus, M., Mckenzie, E., Tallis, H., Guerry, A., Daily, G., Kareiva, P., et al. 2015. Notes from the field: lessons learned from using ecosystem service approaches to inform real-world decisions. *Ecological Economics*, 115, 11–21. www.sciencedirect.com/science/article/pii/S0921800913002498

Schueler, K. 2017. Nature-based solutions to enhance coastal resilience. Inter-American Development Bank: 13. https://publications.iadb.org/bitstream/handle/11319/8526/Nature_based_solutions_to_enhance_coastal_resilience.pdf?sequence=1&isAllowed=y

Schulze, J., Müller, B., Groeneveld, J. & Grimm, V. 2017. Agent-based modelling of social–ecological systems: achievements, challenges, and a way forward. *Journal of Artificial Societies and Social Simulation*, 20(2), 8.

Seppelt, R., Dormann, C. F., Eppink, F. V., Lautenbach, S. & Schmidt, S. 2011. A quantitative review of ecosystem service studies: approaches, shortcomings and the road ahead. *Journal of Applied Ecology*, 48(3), 630–636.

Shin, Y.-J. & Cury, P. 2001. Exploring fish community dynamics through size-dependent trophic interactions using a spatialized individual-based model. *Aquatic Living Resources*, 14(2), 65–80.

Shin, Y.-J., Shannon, L. & Cury, P. 2004. Simulations of fishing effects on the southern Benguela fish community using an individual-based model: learning from a comparison with ECOSIM. *African Journal of Marine Science*, 26(1), 95–114.

Smallegan, S. M., Irish, J. L. & Van Dongeren, A. R. 2017. Developed barrier island adaptation strategies to hurricane forcing under rising sea levels. *Climatic Change*, 143(1–2), 173–184.

Spalding, M. D., Ruffo, S., Lacambra, C., et al. 2014. The role of ecosystems in coastal protection: adapting to climate change and coastal hazards. *Ocean & Coastal Management*, 90, 50–57.

Stark, J., Plancke, Y., Ides, S., Meire, P. & Temmerman, S. 2016. Coastal flood protection by a combined nature-based and engineering approach: modeling the effects of marsh geometry and surrounding dikes. *Estuarine Coastal and Shelf Science*, 175, 34–45.

Stelzenmüller, V., Lee, J., Garnacho, E. & Rogers, S. 2010. Assessment of a Bayesian belief network–GIS framework as a practical tool to support marine planning. *Marine Pollution Bulletin*, 60(10), 1743–1754.

Stock, C. A., Alexander, M. A., Bond, N. A., Brander, K. M., Cheung, W. W., Curchitser, E. N., et al. 2011. On the use of IPCC-class models to assess the impact of climate on living marine resources. *Progress in Oceanography*, 88(1–4), 1–27.

Storlazzi, C., Reguero, B., Lowe, E., Shope, J., Gibbs, A., Beck, M., et al. 2017. Rigorously valuing the role of coral reefs in coastal protection: an example from Maui, Hawaii, USA. *Coastal Dynamics*, 2017, 665–674.

Sutton-Grier, A. E., Wowk, K. & Bamford, H. 2015. Future of our coasts: the potential for natural and hybrid infrastructure to enhance the resilience of our coastal communities, economies and ecosystems. *Environmental Science & Policy*, 51, 137–148.

SWAN. n.d. http://swanmodel.sourceforge.net/

Tallis, H., Ricketts, T., Guerry, A., Nelson, E., Ennaanay, D., Wolny, S., et al. 2011. *InVEST 2.1 Beta User's Guide*. Stanford, CA: The Natural Capital Project.

TELEMAC-MASCARET. n.d. open TELEMAC-MASCARET: the mathematically superior suite of solvers www.opentelemac.org/

Temmerman, S., Meire, P., Bouma, T. J., Herman, P. M., Ysebaert, T. & De Vriend, H. J. 2013. Ecosystem-based coastal defence in the face of global change. *Nature*, 504(7478), 79.

Thorslund, J., Jarsjo, J., Jaramillo, F., Jawitz, J. W., Manzoni, S., Basu, N. B., et al. 2017. Wetlands as large-scale nature-based solutions: status and challenges for research, engineering and management. *Ecological Engineering*, 108, 489–497.

Tolman, H. L. 2009. User manual and system documentation of WAVEWATCH III TM version 3.14. Technical note, MMAB Contribution, 276: 220.

Travers, M., Shin, Y.-J., Shannon, L. & Cury, P. 2006. Simulating and testing the sensitivity of ecosystem-based indicators to fishing in the southern Benguela ecosystem. *Canadian Journal of Fisheries and Aquatic Sciences*, 63(4), 943–956.

UNFCCC. 2015. Decision 1/CP.21: Adoption of the Paris Agreement. FCCC/CP/2015/10/Add.1. Bonn: UNFCCC Secretariat.

United Nations. 2015. *Sustainable Development Goals Report 2015*. https://sustainabledevelopment.un.org/content/documents/1758GSDR%202015%20Advance%20Unedited%20Version.pdf. Accessed: October 2018.

UN-Water. 2018. *The United Nations World Water Development Report 2018: Nature-based Solutions for Water. UN World Water Assessment Programme (WWAP)*. Paris: UNESCO.

van Wesenbeeck, B. K., de Boer, W., Narayan, S., van der Star, W. R. & de Vries, M. B. 2017. Coastal and riverine ecosystems as adaptive flood defenses under a changing climate. *Mitigation and Adaptation Strategies for Global Change*, 22(7), 1087–1094.

Vaudrey, J. M., Eddings, J., Pickerell, C., Brousseau, L. & Yarish, C. 2013. *Development and Application of a GIS-based Long Island Sound Eelgrass Habitat Suitability Index Model*. Storrs, CT: University of Connecticut Department of Marine Science.

Verutes, G. M., Arkema, K. K., Clarke-Samuels, C., Wood, S. A., Rosenthal, A., Rosado, S., et al. 2017. Integrated planning that safeguards ecosystems and balances multiple objectives in coastal Belize. *International Journal of Biodiversity Science, Ecosystem Services & Management*, 13(3), 1–17.

Vichi, M., Masina, S. & Navarra, A. 2007. A generalized model of pelagic biogeochemistry for the global ocean ecosystem. Part II: numerical simulations. *Journal of Marine Systems*, 64(1–4), 110–134. www.sciencedirect.com/science/article/pii/S0924796306001096

Villa, F., Bagstad, K. J., Voigt, B., Johnson, G. W., Portela, R., Honzák, M., et al. 2014. A methodology for adaptable and robust ecosystem services assessment. *PLoS ONE*, 9(3), e91001.

Vitolo, C., Elkhatib, Y., Reusser, D., Macleod, C. J. & Buytaert, W. 2015. Web technologies for environmental Big Data. *Environmental Modelling & Software*, 63, 185–198.

Vuik, V., Jonkman, S. N., Borsje, B. W. & Suzuki, T. 2016. Nature-based flood protection: the efficiency of vegetated foreshores for reducing wave loads on coastal dikes. *Coastal Engineering*, 116, 42–56.

Wallcraft, A., Carroll, S., Kelly, K. & Rushing, K. 2003. Hybrid Coordinate Ocean Model (HYCOM) Version 2.1. User's Guide https://apps.dtic.mil/docs/citations/ADA588120. Accessed: October 2018.

Wallcraft, A., Metzger, E. & Carroll, S. 2009. Software design description for the Hybrid Coordinate Ocean Model (HYCOM) Version 2.2 https://apps.dtic.mil/docs/citations/ADA494779. Accessed: October 2018.

WAMDI Group. 1988. The WAM model – a third generation ocean wave prediction model. *Journal of Physical Oceanography*, 18(12), 1775–1810.

Weijerman, M., Gove, J. M., Williams, I. D., Walsh, W. J., Minton, D. & Polovina, J. J. 2018. Evaluating management strategies to optimise coral reef ecosystem services. *Journal of Applied Ecology*, 55(4), 1823–1833.

Westerink, J. J., Luettich, R. A., Feyen, J. C., Atkinson, J. H., Dawson, C., Roberts, H. J., et al. 2008. A basin-to channel-scale unstructured grid hurricane storm surge model applied to southern Louisiana. *Monthly Weather Review*, 136(3), 833–864.

White, C., Halpern, B. S. & Kappel, C. V. 2012. Ecosystem service tradeoff analysis reveals the value of marine spatial planning for multiple ocean uses. *Proceedings of the National Academy of Sciences of the United States of America*, 109, 4696–4701.

Wilson, A. M. W. & Forsyth, C. 2018. Restoring near-shore marine ecosystems to enhance climate security for island ocean states: aligning international processes and local practices. *Marine Policy*, 93, 284–294.

World Bank & UNDESA. 2017. *The Potential of the Blue Economy: Increasing Long-term Benefits of the Sustainable Use of Marine Resources for Small Island Developing States and Coastal Least Developed Countries*. Washington, DC: World Bank.

Wylie, L., Sutton-Grier, A. E. & Moore, A. 2016. Keys to successful blue carbon projects: lessons learned from global case studies. *Marine Policy*, 65, 76–84.

XBEACH. n.d. XBeach Open Source Community. https://oss.deltares.nl/web/xbeach/

Yemane, D., Shin, Y. J. & Field, J. G. 2009. Exploring the effect of marine protected areas for the dynamics of fish communities in the southern Benguela ecosystem: an individual based modelling IBM approach. *ICES Journal of Marine Science*, 66, 378–387.

Yscbaert, T., Jansen, H. M. & Poelman, M. 2017. Coastal protection and seafood security in Bangladesh: food for thought. Presented at The Ocean/Blue Economy for Bangladesh Workshop, Dhaka, 23–23 November 2017.

Zedler, J. B. 2017. What's new in adaptive management and restoration of coasts and estuaries? *Estuaries and Coasts*, 40(1), 1–21.

Zhou, J., Wang, Q., Zhao, W., Yu, D. & Guan, S. 2016. Habitat suitability analysis of eelgrass *Zostera marina* L. in the subtidal zone of Xiaoheishan Island. *Chinese Journal of Oceanology and Limnology*, 34(1), 69–78.

6 Coastal and Freshwater Flood Models: A Review in the Context of NBS

Neil Sang

6.1 INTRODUCTION

With much of the world's population already concentrated into cities, many of which are in low-lying coastal areas or near to rivers, and urbanisation continuing apace, adaptation to climate change is of significant concern to urban planning and managing flooding from both sea inundation and rain storms is a particularly salient and pressing problem. This review aims to discuss some of the key models available today with regards to these two issues.

Although the economic gain of green infrastructure (e.g. in protection from flood damage) is of much interest, the review will not address how various methods explicitly quantify financial aspects because valuing environmental services in economic terms is a complex and controversial approach which requires more nuanced discussion than the space here allows. While the flow of water is an important first step in understanding how sediment and pollutants move and accumulate, there are many other factors specific to each pollutant which cannot be covered here. Readers interested in this are directed as a first step to the reviews of Fallahshorshani et al. (2012), Zhou (2014) and Kaykhosravi et al. (2018), as well as Chapters 3 and 4 in this book. Here the focus will be on how to model where the water goes, possibly how deep a flood that represents, and what can be included with respect to the water management functions of NBS from the perspective of preventing or reducing flooding.

6.2 MODELLING SEA INUNDATION AND STORM WATER: SIMILARITIES AND DIFFERENCES

Sea inundation and storm water management may seem like two rather distinct subject areas and it is certainly true that domain knowledge of quite different disciplines is required to parameterise these models for each purpose. From a modelling point of view, however, they have much in common. Abhas et al. (2011, p. 110) give three spatial categories of flood model (1D, 2D, 3D) which intersect three categories of method (lumped, distributed and hydraulic); in other words, does the model provide a single answer for a whole area such as a stretch of coastline or a catchment (lumped) or account for the spatial variance therein (distributed), and if the latter does it consider the physical properties of the system such as fluid dynamics (hydraulic). Within this they highlight calculation differences 'for example linear models and non-linear models, finite element, finite difference and finite volume models, coupled models and nested models'. Abhas et al. (2011) and Teng et al. (2017) give recent reviews comparing these from a scientific viewpoint. Here the focus is on the practicality of methods and tools commonly in use, selected as representative of examples of four key aspects:

- whether the model is truly 3D, i.e. considers subterranean conduits, or vertical movement through a water column;
- whether the model is fluid dynamic or simply considers the geometric flow of the water regardless of the real capacity of that space and accumulation of volume over time (i.e. can it model water volume or only flow rate, because these are two different management issues);
- whether the model assumes impermeable, frictionless surfaces or considers absorption and friction effects of the surface material and objects thereon (i.e. aspects where design can influence the system); and
- whether the model calculates the potential of the water to change the landscape as it moves, e.g. through force of pressure or erosion (critically important to evaluating risk to life, structural damage and NBS resilience).

The models are reviewed principally as to whether they are informative for how to manage the water itself, as it accumulates on the surface in volumes which impact physical planning. The chemical and ecological components of the water will not be addressed in any detail, nor slower processes such as groundwater. However, a longer-term perspective will be provided in the section on Integrated Assessment Models.

6.3 SEA INUNDATION

Both coastal and freshwater floods are commonly estimated in terms of the level expected during a given interval of years, e.g. a 10-year event or a 50-year event, as measured from a stated baseline year. For example, a 50-year event is the highest sea level or rainfall level expected every 50 years given the current climate, i.e. it may occur tomorrow or in 30 years, but it is expected to occur within 50 years. That is not necessarily the maximum level which is to be expected given the climate which might pertain in 50 years from today. Arguably, simply saying 'there is currently a 1 in 50 chance per year of such a flood level' is less misleading, but the terminology is well established. This review will deal primarily with how to model the sea inundation spatially once the maximum sea-level rise has been calculated, rather than delve into the complexities of how those sea-level scenarios may be generated (e.g. Bardet et al., 2011).

6.3.1 *Basic GIS Coastal Inundation Models*

The simplest model for sea inundation is the so-called 'bath-tub' approach, whereby the predicted sea level is measured against a terrain model of the area (Digital Terrain Model, DTM) based on digital elevation data (a Digital Elevation Model, DEM). The chief advantage is that a bath-tub model is trivial to implement and easy to understand. It is feasible to use a high-resolution DTM on a desktop computer within most Geographical Information Systems (GIS), even for large spatial extents. It also does not imply any sophistication, so limitations are easily described and intuitive to understand. The

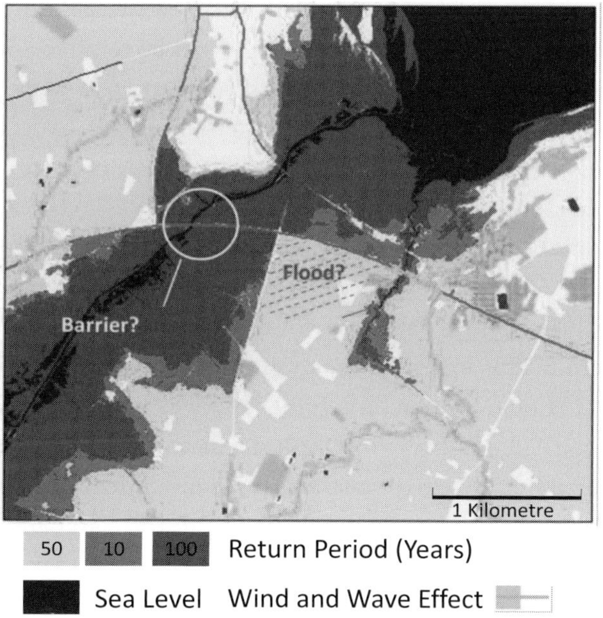

FIGURE 6.1 Flood predictions and the significance of barrier representation. (Source: Flood model in Höganas peninsula, Sweden, from the 'Rising Sea Levels' project, funded by the Swedish Civil Contingencies Agency, MSB.) (A black and white version of this figure will appear in some formats. For the colour version, please refer to the plate section.)

principal limitation is that this model will flood areas which are below the projected sea level but isolated from the sea by higher land (Figure 6.1). It is also an 'all or nothing' result, simply modelling the spatial distribution of a 'lumped' model of the sea-level rise or storm height (e.g. the historical average from local monitoring stations) assuming this to be the same for the entire coastline. Flood depth can be obtained as the difference between flood height and terrain height, but individual models must be made to distinguish between permanent submersion due to sea-level rise and temporary inundation by storms. As such it is perhaps most suited as a 'quick and dirty' check for possible issues, for example if considering whether salinisation from repeated floods may pose a threat to an NBS, rather than as a means for evaluating NBS as a coastal flood mitigation strategy.

Depending on the terrain and the size of the area of interest, flooded ground not connected to the sea might be removed on a case-by-case basis or by using a masking layer, but for larger or more complex terrain the decision as to which cases are hydrologically disconnected from the sea may not be obvious. A relatively simple approach to resolve the issue of flood connectivity is to use a series of 'cost-path' analyses,[1] assigning a high cost to routes which pass over higher ground than the predicted sea level and only allowing flooding to occur if a route from the sea is found which does not exceed that cost threshold. This approach was used in Figure 6.1 to exclude the area marked 'Flood?', where low-lying land was protected by a raised road. Alternatively, so-called 'Simple Dynamic Inundation Models' (SDIM; Mcleod et al., 2010) achieve the same effect by simulating inundation one grid cell at a time. Both of these are arguably of little more relevance to NBS than the simple bath tub. However, the SDIM (while requiring some programming skills to implement) does also provide the potential to include other heuristic variables on effect of land-cover type whereby NBS could begin to provide options to e.g. influence expected friction.

Either approach raises a more difficult question, however, with respect to data accuracy which is particularly exacting in urban areas. Elevation models are usually only available as 2.5D surfaces seen from above, so, for example, a bridge would appear to form a dyke wall. Some adjustment must be made to this DEM to allow for water to pass under objects, which may require fieldwork to verify when such an adjustment should be applied. In Figure 6.1 a small channel was introduced to the DEM in the area circled in yellow as the bridge did not create a real barrier to the river. Had this channel not been created most of the river valley would have been apparently isolated from the sea. Because fieldwork did not reveal any connecting channels for the area highlighted in dashed lines the road here is considered to form a dyke and so is not modelled as flooded. Note, however, that adding such a channel to the

1 Cost path analysis: http://wiki.gis.com/wiki/index.php/Cost_Path_Analysis.

DEM would misdirect the flow of rain storm water over the terrain, which is one simple example of how integrating several models may not be as simple as just 'chaining' them together and applying them to common data.

In an urban area the problem is particularly exacting not only due to the number of complex 3D terrain features and drains, but because some buildings will act as barriers to water flow while others will allow water to pass through them and this may depend on the volume of water and length of time involved. So even assuming an accurate DEM of high precision which includes buildings, this is not a simple issue to model. Inaccuracies in the DEM or how elevation data are used to create the DTM out of that elevation data may also create barriers which do not exist or remove those which do, although this is now less common with the advent of higher-resolution data sets.

A further issue is the rate at which a given volume of water can flow through a given aperture. This issue is acute in urban areas where connectivity may be by small drain pipes and culverts. Even in modelling of sea inundation where the total volume of water is very large, this may be relevant as it can determine whether an object is to be treated as a barrier; over time, a small leak can create a large flood. After the need to calculate forces on infrastructure in the path of floods and additional flood reach due to momentum pushing floodwater uphill, it is perhaps the principal reason why models of flooding extent might demand a fluid dynamic approach.

6.3.2 *Hydraulic Models for Coastal Flooding*

Mcleod et al. (2010) provide a helpful overview of coastal inundation models. Their view (at that time) was that 3D mathematical models were unproven and demanded higher levels of data and expertise to calibrate than 2D, plus significantly more processing time. No doubt the respective development teams would counter this conclusion by pointing out the greater potential for precision with this approach and the recent introduction of cloud-processing to deal with extra processing demands. However, given that calibration of the hydraulic properties of NBS are particularly difficult because these change dramatically with the condition of the vegetation as it grows (Passeri et al., 2015), the emphasis here will be on the longer-standing 2D models. Emphasis must also be given to the need for a precautionary principle in estimating the benefits from a given NBS (Vuik et al., 2016), particularly as regards to the kind of problem where hydraulic models might be of most value, e.g. storm surge, and so the key question is whether these can be calibrated to factor in NBS properties accurately.

The two leading commercial packages are MIKE Flood and TUFLOW. MIKE Flood has a long history of development and is widely used (www.mikepoweredbydhi.com). It permits a flexible spatial resolution (via quad-tree-raster or TIN) which provides the potential for including areas of detail within a wider study area. Flow is modelled as an incompressible liquid using dynamic drivers and as such it is relevant to complex terrain with funnel effects. In terms of coastal inundation, it further provides: a built-in storm surge model; inland flooding and overland flow modelling; momentum dispersion; and tidal potential. MIKE thus provides some indication of not only where land may flood, but how quickly and with what force. Parameterising this, however, is a skilled process requiring DEM, wind data (the software has its own wind generator if needed and has data links to NCEP and NOAA for calibration), bathymetry and tides. The model can also then be further calibrated to consider sea bed resistance, the momentum dispersion coefficients of different land covers and wind friction factors (among others). TUFLOW Classic is arguably the closest commercial competitor to MIKE in that it too models hydraulic processes for both coastal flooding and river/urban drainage by combining 2D and 1D models. Readers are directed to Néelz and Pender (2013) for a detailed comparison, but the basic parameters which might be relevant to model NBS for coastal flood management, such as friction and momentum dispersion coefficients, are similar (www.tuflow.com). Both companies have also introduced models for modelling movement in 3D water columns (MIKE 3D/TUFLOW FV), which could be relevant to marine NBS. However, no specific case studies were found applying that functionality to NBS for coastal flooding in either software. The UNDP used hydraulic modelling as part of its work on the Bangladesh coast (see Case Study 6.1), but it is not clear if this was to ascertain the mitigating effect of the NBS or simply for identifying the locations at risk.

TELEMAC is a powerful open-source alternative (www.opentelemac.org/). From the point of view of accessibility the fact that the software is freely available and open-source is positive, but training is charged for and would certainly be requisite because it is mostly a command-line interface[2] with up to 14 different parameters to consider. The core functions of TELEMAC are written in the Fortran programming language, but most scientific components are written in Python, which means that TELEMAC is (in theory) easily adapted to work with other models and GIS. That in turn might suggest it to be an obvious route to begin developing more NBS tailored functionality.

Stark et al. (2016) apply TELEMAC to model the potential of marshlands (Figure 6.2) to provide an NBS approach to storm surge management in the Netherlands, concluding that not only does the scale of any such intervention play an important role, but also its geometry. That information is clearly highly relevant to design and planning decisions around where marsh should be protected and restored, which shows the potential benefit of modelling the hydraulic characteristics of different NBS designs.

The dearth of applied examples of using hydraulic models to simulate the effect of NBS for coastal flooding may reflect a need for more scientific data to calibrate the protective effect of different NBS, perhaps due to the novelty of the NBS concept. Given the prima facie relevance of the core functions of these models, use can be expected to grow as calibration data accumulate from studies such as that of Stark et al. (2016) and processing costs continue to fall. However, there are many different circumstances for which such calibration data are

2 Limited GUI support is supplied by third-party developers Blue Kenue, https://nrc.canada.ca/en/research-development/products-services/software-applications/blue-kenuetm-software-tool-hydraulic-modellers.

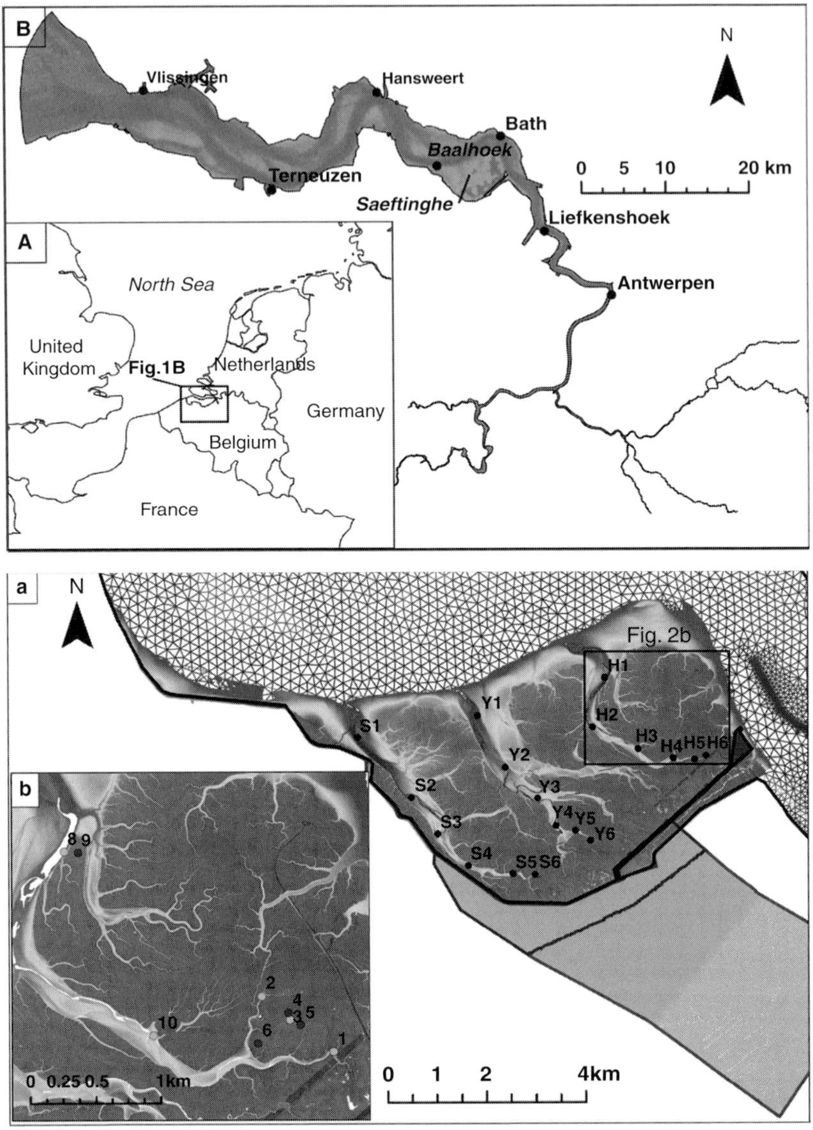

FIGURE 6.2 Saeftinghe marsh, Netherlands, modelled in TELEMAC2D (Stark et al., 2016). (A black and white version of this figure will appear in some formats. For the colour version, please refer to the plate section.)

needed. Furthermore, the complexity of the calibration process will remain a challenge for institutions without the necessary skills in-house or funds to hire consultants.

6.3.3 Integrated Impact Models

Not strictly flood models, although some incorporate this, Integrated Impact Models may serve to provide the larger-scale scenarios to which more detailed local flood models can respond.

DIVA was an integrated assessment model which has gained some popularity (Vafeidis et al., 2008; Hinkel & Klein, 2009; Hinkel et al., 2010, 2013; Brown et al., 2016). DIVA is open-source, but the model does not seem to be currently available;[3] it is included nonetheless because it was widely used until recently and has a number of relevant characteristics which, arguably, should be included in future models if they are to be relevant to designing NBS for flood management.

The inundation model is a simple hydrologically linked terrain model. The coastline is segmented with regards to how it responds to the inundation model according to a range of parameters (flooding, erosion, etc.). Results are then saved into a database to allow end-users to combine different scenarios of high water and additional data such as population to estimate potential vulnerability. The spatial resolution is coarse, but the data structure is divided at break points in relation to the response variables. That could be quite accurate for some locations, but its utility for any given location may only be determined on a per-case basis. Nonetheless, DIVA provides an example of how models can be structured for participatory planning because new scenarios can be investigated easily and tested against a model where most of the complex parameterisation and calculation is hidden and pre-calculated. Because all data are contained within the model, the user need only select scenarios. Of course, therein also lies a possible critique: should end-users be

3 https://climate-adapt.eea.europa.eu/metadata/tools/dynamic-interactive-vulnerability-assessment-model-diva.

invited to trust the results of models the inner mechanisms of which they do not see and may not fully understand?

In terms of NBS, what DIVA lacks in sophistication with respect to the flood model is compensated with functionality for estimating impacts on natural systems such as primary production, biodiversity, erosion and nutrient levels, plus adaptation strategies such as installation of dykes. This makes it potentially very helpful for geodesign of NBS because options can be selected and feedback calculated quickly over a variety of relevant topics. Access to global estimates is useful when local data are unavailable, but it would be of questionable relevance for local-scale problems with design choices between spatially detailed options. The IPCC (Wong & Losada, 2014) reports a range of studies using DIVA to make regional assessments of the impact from sea-level rise, noting, however, that these reflect mostly studies of hard structure defences for flood protection and do not generally consider what was then termed 'ecosystem-based adaptation (EBA)' (Wong & Losada, 2014, p. 35). The discontinuation of DIVA leaves a gap to be filled in the NBS modelling toolbox.

SIMClim is a modelling framework which is designed to run at a range of spatial scales. It provides built-in data for some scales, but users can add detailed local data. It thus provides one general global climate model, with many sectoral submodels on impact (e.g. water, agriculture, ecology) in relation to those pre-calculated climate models. SIMClim provides an in-built estimator for Extreme Events Analysis. Coastal flooding does not seem to be its main use, however. Inland flooding, drought and agricultural models are more commonly reported uses. The inundation model is briefly documented in CLIMSystems (2017); it applies a simple estimator for how the coastline will change based on the 'Brunn rule', which considers not only where the water will be, but how dunes will change as the shoreline moves. In addition, it takes into account the storminess of the sea, but it does not model storm surge hydraulically. Instead, the tool[4] focuses on ease of use for

[4] www.climsystems.com.

estimating other impacts of this shifting shoreline over longer time periods through providing in-built models and data to select from, including local sea-level rise models. The choice of in-built models is backed by a global scientific advisory board, but verification of the suitability of each model to a specific scenario would be advisable.

SIMClim is a modelling framework rather than a model itself, so the inputs depend on the application. In this context it appears to use shoreline response time (in years), closure distance from the shoreline (m) and DEM. It can also respond to depth of material exchange or closure depth (m), dune height (m) and residual shoreline movement (m $year^{-1}$) and is MAGICC and IPCC data-compatible.

Initially these approaches may appear to be the most immediately relevant to NBS because they explicitly address the effect of interactions between societal and biophysical systems. One study from the UK shows that modelling work represents a substantial upfront cost for NBS projects but the longer-term maintenance was relatively low (McKenna et al., 2015). Case Study 6.1 provides a well-documented example from Bangladesh of an NBS approach to flood management that sought to deliver other environmental and social benefits and where the successful outcome of one is interdependent with the other. These are the kind of complex interventions where strategic 'gaming' of likely outcomes using an Integrated Assessment Model may help a team think through possible strategies and thus avoid longer-term costs. However, it is worth noting that while the Bangladesh team did use hydrological models to assess coastal vulnerability (UNDP, 2008, pp. 34–35) this was against a background of climate scenarios prepared by the National Adaptation Program for Action (NAPA) for Bangladesh who found downscaling Global Circulation Models to the regional level was problematic. It is thus interesting to note that the greater risk to long-term decision-making from model inaccuracy may be that stemming from uncertainty in the underpinning scenarios rather than the specifics of the hydrological models used to estimate spatially distributed impacts. So wrapping such downscaling processes in an easy-to-use framework comes at the risk of lowering awareness of the problems they entail.

Mcleod et al. (2010) argue that the more complex 'Ecological Landscape Spatial Simulation Models' 'may create over-confidence among users who may assume that the increased data and feedbacks incorporated in the model provide more robust outputs. These models can be difficult to validate and calibrate due to the high level of aggregation, the dynamic long term nature of the model, and the complexity of the subsystems and their interactions, thus their primary application is for research'. Of course, misinterpretation of results is user error rather than inherent to the model and might also be stated with regard to the mathematical models where they incorporate additional dynamic impact assessments for different sectors (Andersen, 2003). Individual models may be amenable to the use of confidence intervals or Monte Carlo simulation to investigate uncertainty in scenarios, but it is hard to factor out all the sources of error in multiple models chained together. That being so, it is particularly important that such models be accompanied by expert advice on the interpretation of the results and therefore availability of sufficient breadth of domain expertise must be considered a significant limitation for their wider adoption as decision support tools for NBS.

Strategic plans at the regional scale addressing the complex set of possible paths over 50–100 years may benefit from using Integrated Assessment Models. For near-term and local spatial planning, selecting relevant scenarios from these results and applying simpler models in a geodesign process can help narrow down the parameter space of design options locally. Once the general principle has been determined (e.g. where to place protective measures, where to provide floodplains, etc.), mathematical models can help to calibrate the extent of the intervention needed (e.g. area of marshland to designate). However, a typical local planning agency would need guidance as to which scenarios from Integrated Assessment Models are likely to apply to their case and accessible calibration data on the effects of NBS would be needed to design a response.

CASE STUDY 6.1 ICBA-AR: Integrating Community-based Adaptation into Afforestation and Reforestation Programmes

Bangladesh faces frequent flooding due to cyclones bringing heavy rain and storm surge. To protect its coast, the country has a target to plant 30,000 ha of mangrove forest by 2020 (Figure 6.3). An ICBA-AR project is focusing on Patuakhali, Barguna Bhola and Noakhali and aims to deploy NBS not only as a means of coastal protection but also a means of income diversification for the local population leading to more sustainable, longer-term management.

FIGURE 6.3 Mangrove forests for storm surge defence and as an economic resource (image by kind permission of ICGB-AR). (A black and white version of this figure will appear in some formats. For the colour version, please refer to the plate section.)

Coastal flood models were used to estimate the likely risk of flooding and the protective effect of mangrove forest (UNDP, 2008, pp. 34–35); however, downscaling global scenarios of climate change to assess the necessary scale of intervention is difficult:

CASE STUDY 6.1 **(cont.)**

> Downscaling coarse resolution GCM model data using statistical dynamic downscaling techniques by different RCM models are still inadequate or results are not consistent to represent regional or local conditions. Letham (2009) found out that the process involves a long chain of assumptions and simplifications, and a corresponding propagation of, and increase in, uncertainty. Other than this, large scale uncertainty involved with the natural and human activity may not represent the true dimension and extent of climate change impact. (Nishat & Mukherjee, 2013)

What makes this case particularly interesting is that mangrove forest was already being planted in the area; however, climate change models suggest that the monoculture nature of this plantation would make it vulnerable to other environmental stressors, such as increasing salinity, but also economic pressure to return forest to agriculture as other land is lost to sea-level rise.

> There are evident and substantive problems in establishing and sustaining new greenbelt structures as protective buffer zones from climate-induced stresses, which need to be addressed by additional activities, such as: a) Changing the mix of mangrove and non-mangrove species to increase the natural adaptive capacity of coastal forests; b) Providing economic incentives for communities to nurture, protect and conserve newly planted greenbelt structures; and c) Developing long-term benefit sharing agreements between communities and the national government for the selective logging of economic tree varieties. (UNDP, 2011)

Thus, from a modelling point of view, efforts to improve downscaling of the climate change scenarios or how these translate to potential flooding extent must be set in a cost–benefit with effort expended on ensuring the right range of interventions are being modelled given economic and societal factors. Particularly with respect to NBS, the anticipated management of the intervention is often critical, so model selection should reflect this balance before focusing too much effort seeking the most precise results for any one component process.

6.4 RAIN STORM WATER MODELLING

Early catchment-scale models represented the catchments and sub-catchments as a single 'curve number', with water flow at specific locations referring to a distribution curve representing the flow rate out of that catchment to be expected a given time interval after a given amount of rainfall (Broughton, 1989). In some respects this is a pragmatic and effective approach, as each location is calibrated against historical data for that location. It therefore takes into account the land covers and soil types which pertain to that catchment. While the concept may have been overused (Garen & Moore, 2007), within the constraints of its intended purpose it remains an effective approach used in models such as MIKE 11. Calibration of this approach requires a skilled hydrologist, but attempts have been made at automatic calibration (Madsen, 2000) and data-mining approaches are starting to supersede the method as more complex questions are considered such as urban water quality (May & Sivakumar, 2009). Additional information, such as groundwater recharge levels and overground flow, are deduced from the equation rather than being estimated mechanistically. The impact of land-cover change is therefore not incorporated, nor do curve numbers offer a firm basis to extrapolate to more extreme climatic events: for this, a spatial simulation is required. As such, curve numbers are of limited utility in predicting the impact of NBS interventions, but may provide a low-cost way to monitor their impact at the catchment scale and thus a means to accrue empirical evidence to feed into other methods.

6.4.1 *Basic GIS Flow Models*

In the simplest 2D model, flooding may be estimated by assuming a completely impervious surface with no friction or absorption; thus, all water which falls on one location at the first time step will immediately flow into the adjacent downhill unit. One may then consider either 'total accumulation' (if there is no outlet from the study area) or 'peak flow', whereby a state is reached at which the total water flowing through a location is that accumulated from all the upstream area, plus its own rainfall. Peak flow assumes the rainstorm lasts sufficiently long for this scenario to arise. Most GIS packages will provide the basic functionality to calculate either of these two outcomes for a given precipitation rate. Once issues of DEM resolution and modelling of buildings as solid objects are taken into account, this would provide a reasonable 'worst-case' scenario in an urban area once all permeable surfaces are saturated and all storm drains have exceeded their capacity. It is not, however, a particularly realistic guide to less than the worst-case scenario given that a typical cloud burst would not last long enough for water to flow from the top of a large catchment to its outlet within that duration. Furthermore, urban areas contain sinks for water both via the drainage network and via urban green space, which may have substantial capacity to redirect or retain water before saturation point is reached. Given that NBS for water management are often focused more on a distributed approach to avoiding worst-case events rather than resolving them once in flood, this basic modelling method has little to offer to that end.

A further option available within standard GIS packages (e.g. within the Hydrology toolset of ESRI ArcGIS) is to provide absorption rates based on land cover as a layer representing the proportion of the water entering a cell which flows downstream and the proportion which remains. Various absorption rates have been suggested for different land covers, but ultimately such a model requires calibration with local data. For a high-resolution DEM, processing times can be lengthy on a standard desktop machine, so calibration is hard to achieve in practice. Nonetheless, as a first step to assessing the impact of NBS, absorption-only models certainly represent a pragmatic option and heuristic rules of thumb as to how much water a given soil type and vegetation mix may hold can be found in the literature (although more biotope-specific data are needed). However, it does not explicitly account for the dynamic nature of NBS, the hydrological properties of the vegetation and soil will change significantly with drought, age, erosion, management and many other factors. So to get a picture of how the system might function in the future would require building multiple such models carefully calibrated to represent expected changes.

6.4.2 *Hydraulic Models for Rain Storm Flooding*

Testing against multiple scenarios using different assumptions of absorption is a feasible option for strategic planning when several different options need to be considered, but only a general indication is needed to decide between these. What it cannot do is to address how a specific flood event develops, or what happens when water has sufficient momentum to force its way through or over barriers. In the worst case this might substantially change the most fundamental assumption of the simple models – that water flows downhill – and dramatically alter the result. To address this requires hydraulic models.

The UK Environment Agency (EA) conducted a two-step review of leading software packages which model hydraulics, first based on reported usage by their staff (Néelz & Pender, 2009) and then via a series of benchmark tests set by the EA but carried out by the respective software developers (Néelz & Pender, 2013). That review covers both coastal and freshwater flooding and the interaction of the two. The focus is on 2D rather than 1D models because 'it is not generally the case that floodplains may be reasonably represented as networks of well-defined channels and therefore 1D floodplain modelling is rarely appropriate' (Néelz & Pender, 2009). The authors also state that 1D models still have advantages in some circumstances (e.g. upstream, where the channel is narrow or in pipes).

It is worth noting that of the 20 experts surveyed in step 1, only one thought 2D flood inundation models to be essential for questions such as: capital maintenance planning for asset management; extreme coastal flood outline; flood risk assessment; flood risk mapping; modelling for appraisal; probabilistic flood risk models; wide area flood prediction (100s km^2) (Néelz & Pender, 2009, figure 3.3). This suggests that 1D models combined with non-hydraulic distributed models in GIS were still the 'go-to' method for many of the kinds of questions to which NBS apply, such as designation of large sacrificial floodplains.

Of the seven software developers which the EA review as having products that implement full models of Shallow Water Equations (SWE) and which integrate these with 1D models, only three will be looked at in any detail here[5]; MIKE Urban and TUFLOW are arguably the industry leaders with the most complete packages, FloodModeller Pro (formerly known as ISIS 2D when tested by the EA, but now rebranded after being acquired by Jacobs) is partnered with TUFLOW, but also produces some interesting models which fill the gap between simple flow accumulation and full SWE: ISIS Fast and ISIS Dynamic.

MIKE Flood is one of two commercial packages which specifically integrate coastal storm surges, estuaries, river and urban drainage (the other being TUFLOW). MIKE Urban integrates 1D (for urban drains) and 2D (for the floodplain). Fluid dynamic equations can be solved and a specific package models groundwater so longer-term fluctuations can be considered with regard to how they interact with short-term flood events. By providing the 2D models with the ability to operate on a multi-resolution grid, it allows more detailed simulation in key areas but saves time in more open or simple regions, which allows uncertainty from spatial resolution to be balanced against computation time. This could be considered advantageous for models where extensive NBS such as forest influence detailed urban areas. Computation can also be outsourced to MIKE's cloud computing services (for a fee). The recently released MIKE 3D adds functionality for larger bodies of water and would thus allow analysis of processes within larger rivers, lakes and coastal waters which would principally be of relevance to marine and freshwater ES (i.e. processes *within* the water bodies) rather than flood management.

5 The others being packages by Micro Drainage Ltd (XPSTORM), University of Exeter (UIM), Deltares (SOBEK) and University of Bristol (LISFLOOD FP).

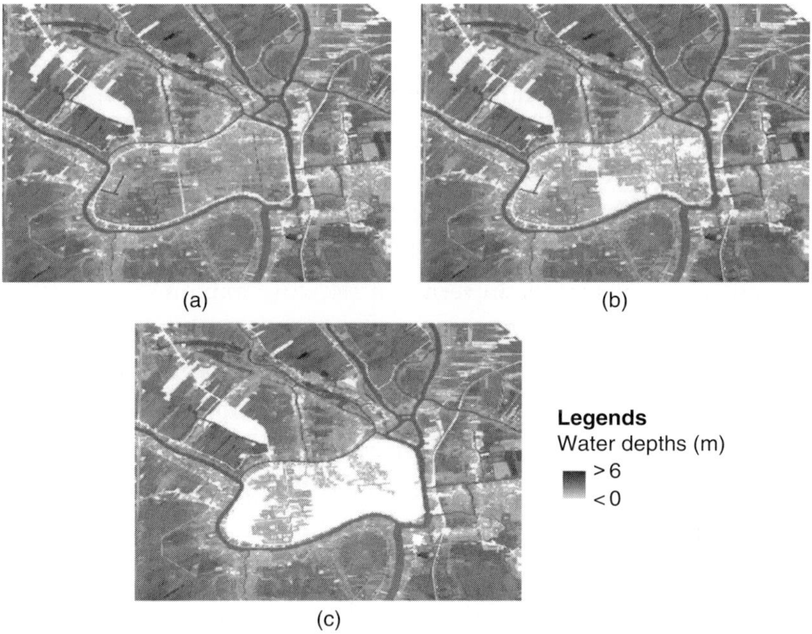

FIGURE 6.4 Simulated flood levels from MIKE based on different scenarios reinstating cultural ecosystem services (Vojinovic et al., 2017). (a) Current situation – Scenario 1, or 'business as usual'; (b) a combination of measures – Scenario 4 (increase of the U-Thong Road dyke height and reinstatement of ancient canals (local measures); and (c) a combination of measures – Scenario 7 Ayutthaya bypass channel + increasing dyke height + ponds + ancient canals (combination of regional and local measures). (A black and white version of this figure will appear in some formats. For the colour version, please refer to the plate section.)

Vojinovic et al. (2017) deploy MIKE Flood to model flooding impact on ecosystem services and cultural ecosystem services in Ayutthaya Island (an urbanised inland river island) in Thailand, to model the efficacy of different response strategies (Figure 6.4).

These models were then integrated into a geodesign process with community participation to reach consensus options for mitigation, including a mix of strategies from green infrastructure and restoration of traditional canals to hard landscaping such as additional dykes. Modelling thus helped find solutions with multiple benefits while having some confidence that a sufficient degree of flooding protection had been achieved.

TUFLOW Classic also integrates 1D and 2D models, including some aspects of momentum transference between the two, making it suitable where overland flow, urban sewers and natural streams are all involved. TUFLOW does not use multi-core CPU processing, but instead opts for GPU processing. Benchmarks show generally similar results in terms of flooding maxima and similar performance to MIKE (Néelz & Pender, 2013, table 4.13). TUFLOW uses adaptive time steps (Hunter et al., 2005) which, theoretically, could be advantageous for modelling NBS where a more frequent time step is needed to locally determine precisely how the NBS responds to a flood, when saturation is reached and thus how much water spills onward thereafter. However, given a typical time step can be as short as 10–20 seconds, any advantage would likely be small relative to the uncertainty from other assumptions. TUFLOW have also recently released a full 3D modelling system, TUFLOW FV; as with MIKE 3D, this is principally aimed at understanding processes within the water body such as 'hydrodynamics, sediment transport and water quality processes in oceans, coastal waters, estuaries, rivers and floodplains' (TUFLOW, 2016).

TUFLOW also produce FLIKE, which predicts frequency of flood events using Extreme Value Theory to assess trends in previous flooding event frequencies (requiring local historical data) and the company also offers a 'model review service' for those who wish to double-check their model with an expert.

The EA benchmarking tests were all on small–medium size test areas where no model took more than 10 minutes to run (Néelz & Pender, 2013). No direct comparisons were found for larger case studies; however, processing times can be lengthy with larger extents or high-resolution models. For example, TUFLOW states that for a grid of 18,750,000 cells (*c.* 8.5 km^2 at 2-m cell size) using one GPU takes over 11 hours and even with 8 GPU this takes 2.9 hours (Huxley, 2016). Liu et al. (2018) confirm the time-saving capacity of multiple GPU approaches for larger models; however, this requires maintaining such high-end computing capacity or buying time on cloud services. Either is likely to be beyond the capabilities and/or means of typical local planning offices and also presents something of a barrier for use of these models in geodesign workshops at present. The benefits of parallel processing aside, because processing time increases exponentially with extent and resolution, if the price of using a hydraulic model is a smaller extent or lower resolution then this needs to be weighed against the lower processing needs of simpler models. Both MIKE and TUFLOW packages can work with flexible mesh (e.g. triangular) rather than a fixed-grid resolution, which could help reduce processing times if, for example, considering large rural areas affecting flooding in an urban area within the same simulation. However, taking advantage of a full 3D model increases processing time at least threefold (Néelz & Pender, 2013, table 4.2.3).

FloodModeller Pro also integrates 1D and 2D flows and managed to outpace both TUFLOW and MIKE on some of the EA benchmarking tests even with half the time step of the latter and despite not fully supporting multi-core processing (e.g. Néelz & Pender, 2013, table 4.2.3). This is an interesting example where efforts to improve processing speed for large-scale problems may be counterproductive to small-scale ones. In other tests (e.g. Néelz & Pender, 2013, table 4.6) with larger models the fully multi-core packages were far faster, but it neatly illustrates why no single package can be considered best for all tasks. Other benefits are the option of a free licence with functionality principally limited by a maximum data size of 100,000 cells, a rental licence for shorter periods and (as with MIKE and TUFLOW) the option to run models in the cloud.

6.4.3 *Simplified SWE and Volume Spreading Models*

Sitting between the basic flow accumulation and SWE models are a wide variety of models which consider how water moves as a volume [volume spreading model (VSM)] with or without a simplified calculation of the effect the momentum of that water may have.

For those with a momentum model included, the EA concludes these models 'generally produced predictions of water levels and inundation dynamics (velocities) comparable with those of the full SWE models at least in situations characterised by low momentum and/or slowly varying flow conditions' (Néelz & Pender, 2013). However, it is not clear when these models might be of most use, as 'it is recommended that this class of model be used cautiously where accurate velocity predictions are required' (Néelz & Pender, 2013), yet the computational reduction is not dramatic compared with full SWE.

There are very large computational savings with the simple VSM models, as well as a simpler calibration process. However, these models predict only the maximum water level while the others provide a time series and, at least in the example below, although the spatial extent is largely consistent, predicted flow rate tends to be less consistent (Figure 6.5).

ISIS Fast produces 'approximate predictions of "final" inundation distributions' (Néelz & Pender, 2013). Of course, this begs the question how 'approximate' these predictions are, as all models are approximate, including SWE. The EA conclude:

> their use is limited to some large-scale applications where final water levels only are required . . . and dynamic effects are insignificant and/or not of interest (that is, as can be the case in national and regional flood risk assessment, and catchment flood management planning). (Néelz & Pender, 2013)

'With the exception of catastrophic floods (e.g. dam-break scenarios), two-dimensional flow over inundated plains is most often a slow, shallow phenomenon' (Hunter et al., 2005), so in a situation where the aim is to geodesign NBS to either absorb water before it accumulates volume and momentum, or to act as sacrificial floodplains where water may be allowed to lie for some time, VSM

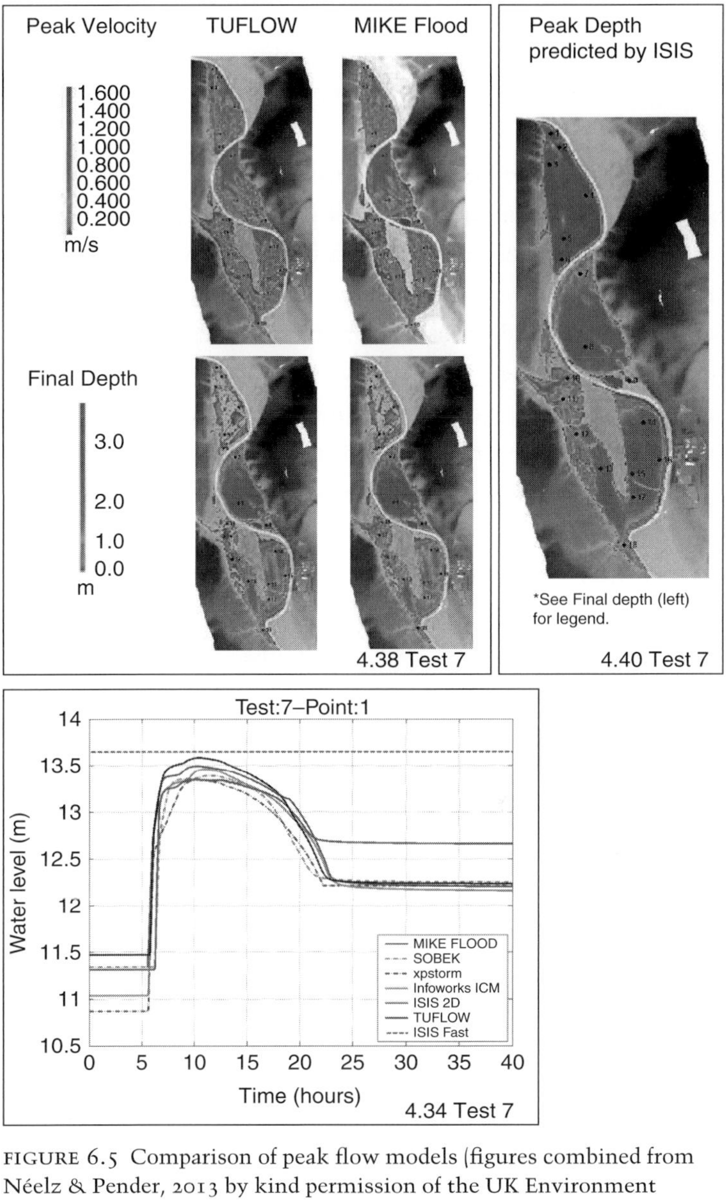

FIGURE 6.5 Comparison of peak flow models (figures combined from Néelz & Pender, 2013 by kind permission of the UK Environment Agency). (A black and white version of this figure will appear in some formats. For the colour version, please refer to the plate section.)

may be a reasonable modelling option for providing an approximate picture of flood extent and depth quickly and thus estimating the capacity of different designs, but the final design should be checked with a full SWE model.

Returning to the questionnaire results from Néelz and Pender (2009), of the applications where the experts considered 2D models to be important, it is clear that the key difference was the need to model the hydraulics of larger water volumes, and thus mostly of a nature which would require hard infrastructure or major landscaping to protect life and property. Two applications where NBS can make a contribution are urban drainage design and catchment management planning, because both principally depend on preventing flow accumulation. In both cases rate (absorption rates, rainfall rates, flow rates) rather than volume is often the key factor and when volume does matter, but not necessarily momentum, VSM can be useful. Hydraulic models are thus primarily of use to establish where water will go in the worst-case scenario, i.e. when NBS cease to be effective, saturation has occurred and so water accumulates volume and momentum.

6.4.4 *Agent-based Flood Modelling*

There are examples of agent-based models (ABMs) being used to simulate land-cover change and this then providing the scenarios for modelling impact on ecosystem services (including flood prediction) via other modelling software either as a framework approach (Murray-Rust et al., 2014) or through closely chaining models, e.g. CLAIM combines agent-based modelling with MIKE Flood (Abebe et al., 2019). A somewhat different approach to the implementation of flow models themselves is to give 'agency' to the individual cells in the terrain. Rather than applying a procedural model in a stepwise manner as water flows down the catchment picking up properties from the cells the water passes over, each cell activates routines to determine how it responds when inundated with water, e.g. to add or reduce water momentum, to flow it onward to the next cell, and so on. So the actual progress of the water is the accumulation of these responses. If the only interest is in modelling the properties of the water itself, or its local physical impact such as erosion and sediment transport, then the distinction between this and traditional process models is likely small. However, modelling the water itself within an agent-based modelling framework provides the potential to integrate systems more closely in a fully dynamic manner, e.g. Taillandier provides an open-source simple finite-volume model in the GAMA modelling environment (available on Github[6]). An agent-based modelling framework allows more complex dynamic systems to be investigated, for example Liu et al. consider how human behaviour and physical structures influence the chance of survival of a flood in a complex urban environment (Liu et al., 2009). Alternatively, the aim may be not to create a spatially detailed flood model, but rather to find the critical thresholds for NBS to provide a range of ecosystem services, including sufficient flood protection (Schneiders et al., 2012).

6.5 SUSTAINABLE URBAN DRAINAGE SYSTEMS

Simply establishing the baseline criterion for what constitutes the 'best' hydrological model is not straightforward (see Kalantari et al., 2015), but none of the models considered so far places much emphasis on the active role of NBS in water management. NBS approaches to water management tend to focus less on the redirection of water and instead on its retention and use, with the intention of reducing the rate of accumulation downstream while also supporting other services locally, such as rain gardens, green roofs and 'grey' water reuse. Globally, such systems have a range of terms attached to them: Sustainable Urban Drainage System (SUDS) being a common term in Europe, Low Impact Development (LID) (Dietz, 2007; Kaykhosravi et al., 2018) more common in North America with, argues Zhou, a greater emphasis on 'conserving and using natural features' for water management (Zhou, 2014). In the NBS context this distinction is somewhat moot, as NBS relates to both extant natural services and man-made services which

6 Taillandier, P., Flood Simulation Hydrological Model, https://github.com/gama-platform/gama/wiki/Flood-Simulation-Hydrological-Model.

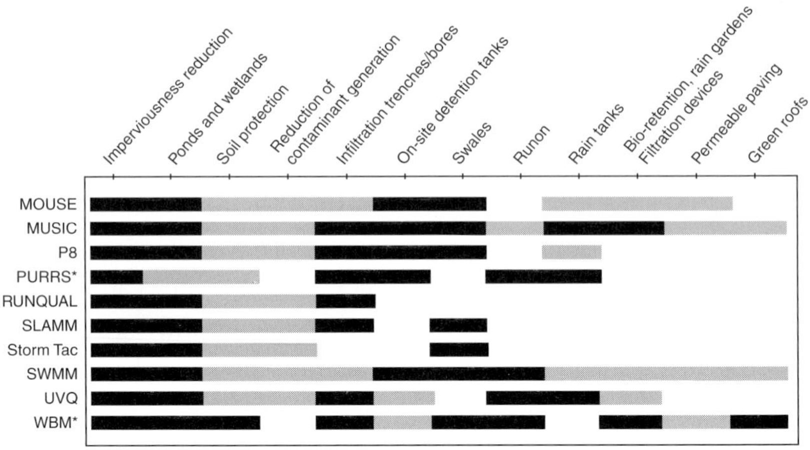

FIGURE 6.6 LID devices and measures included in the selected models. Grey shading indicates that the model does not explicitly address the device, but could be used to model the device. Models with an asterisk do not address water quality (Elliot & Trowsdale, 2007, figure 5).

draw on natural processes. Certainly, most approaches to development for Sustainable Urban Water Management aim to include a range of biological systems, extant or introduced, to that end. Apart from man-made absorbent materials, this principally means retaining water in various forms of soil, vegetation, underground vaults or surface ponds (Dietz, 2007) and reducing some of the eventual downstream load with slow release or evapotranspiration. Elliot and Trowsdale (2007) review 10 models with respect to their ability to model LID interventions such as wetlands, ponds and filter strips (Figure 6.6).

From Figure 6.6 it can be seen that most models will handle collection of water in ponds and other surface reservoirs or its diversion via trenches. Key NBS solutions such as green roofs, bioretention, filtration devices and soil protection are mostly rated as only partial modelling solutions (if any provision is made at all) in the sense that some other parameter might be used as a proxy. If the device is not part of the logical model, it is less likely that suitable parameter data will be available to characterise its precise response, at which point the question must be asked as to whether other aspects of the model are

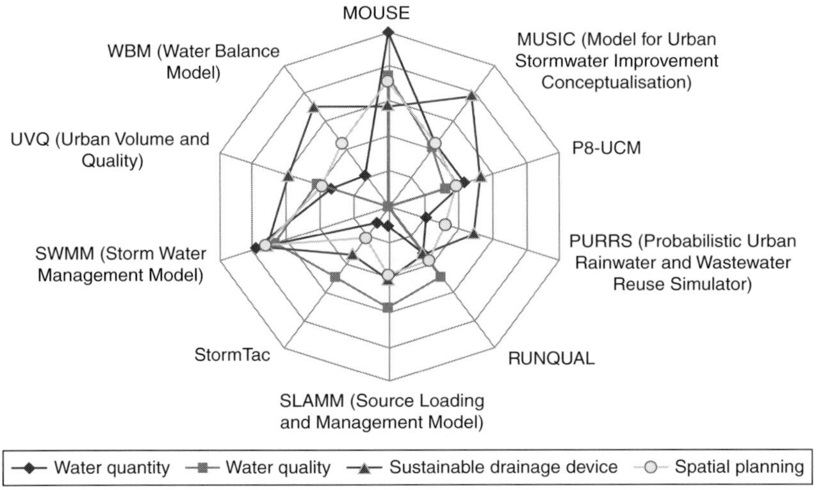

FIGURE 6.7 Potential uses for selected LID models (Zhou, 2014, adapted from Elliot & Trowsdale, 2007). (A black and white version of this figure will appear in some formats. For the colour version, please refer to the plate section.)

still needed or if a more generic model will supply similar estimates of the LID effect by deploying the same proxy variable.

Behind the general assessment in Figure 6.6, Elliot and Trowsdale note significant differences in how these aspects can be modelled and the respective assumptions being used. For example, 1D models leave more computational power available to represent high-frequency time steps, and thus more accurately consider when the capacity of rain tanks would be exceeded and for how long, so how much overspill to expect. Higher-dimension models are forced to use a coarser time step to reduce computation. Because there does not yet appear to be a 'one-size-fits-all' solution, selecting which model to apply depends on which NBS tools are planned, which in turn depends on the range of scale and application areas envisaged (Figure 6.7).

Elliot and Trowsdale (2007) conclude that: 'None of the ten models … reviewed are intended for the full spectrum of uses that could be demanded of a model in relation to LID. The models most commonly address the middle ground of planning and preliminary design levels of use'. However, while:

> the models differ in the types of LID device that are included explicitly . . . all the models can represent the effects of reducing imperviousness or improving soil infiltration properties, all but one can model ponds, all the contaminant models can represent reduction of contaminant generation, most of the models can be used for infiltration devices, and the majority of the models can represent on-site detention tanks . . . In many cases, a device which is not represented explicitly in the model can still be modeled indirectly by altering the parameters of other devices or combining other devices. (Elliott & Trowsdale, 2007)

While LID/SUD models are not as yet matured to an industry standard, given the multiple benefits for LID this might be expected to rapidly develop, but one way in which devices might be modelled indirectly is by representing absorption as run-off coefficient, as described at the start of this chapter. The problem with respect to estimating flood-risk reduction from NBS is not that many of the existing models could not be adjusted to approximate the processes, but rather the complexity of calibrating those processes. Human-designed materials and basins have clearly defined properties when dry and when saturated. Plants, soils and similar have various properties in both states depending on how dry or how saturated they are and for what period. A more recent review by Zhou (2014) (Figure 6.7) adapts Elliot and Trowsdale's figure and highlights that while a few models consider other SUDS such as rain gardens (MUSIC and WBM) and green roofs (WBM) only MIKE Urban and UrbanCycle allow sub-hourly time steps, which is important for urban drainage applications. Arguably it would also be important for considering how the properties of NBS change over different timescales (e.g. reflecting climate or as a flood progresses), but as NBS are also often dependent on significant spatial extent to have much effect, we see how challenging NBS are to current modelling methods.

Zhou also points out that use of GIS in modelling SUDS remains limited and that much of the work required in setting up SUDS models would be significantly reduced by greater GIS integration. However, this assumes suitable access to information, e.g. via a suitable Spatial Data Infrastructure (see Chapter 8). Until calibration information is easily available, and data available via SDI, it would seem that modelling of SUDS beyond simple absorbency coefficients added to the types of models reviewed above will remain 'tedious and time-consuming [due to the time required] to obtain the huge amount of input data for each sub-model' (Zhou, 2014), particularly when multiple types of SUDS are being deployed to target an integrated set of NBS.

Kaykhosravi et al. (2018) provide an up-to-date review with specific focus on models of Green Infrastructure for LID, considering 11 models. Their table 3 and the related section in that review provide a handy summary as to the provision each model has for in-built GI options (i.e. Bioretention with underdrain; Raingarden without underdrain, Porous pavement, Swale, Green roof; Cistern and rain barrel; Infiltration trench and box planter tree canopy) and whether the model supports layered approaches (e.g. tree canopy, surface and subterranean). In doing so it also provides a quick summary of the functioning of the different GI options as NBS for managing storm water. One innovation has been the conversion of the Storm Water Management Model (SWMM) into a web tool by the US Environmental Protection Agency, the Green Values National Storm Water Calculator (http://greenvalues.cnt.org/national/calculator.php). This is a good example of the kind of work necessary to improve access to modelling tools. Overall, however, the paper concludes that there is still work to be done to support modelling of GI solutions:

> despite the recent updates of existing LID models, several important features are still missing and need improvement. These features include the ability to model: multi-layer subsurface media,

> tree canopy and processes associated with vegetation, different spatial scales, snow melt and runoff calculations. (Kaykhosravi et al., 2018)

Another aspect to accessibility is ensuring data can be easily imported and providing results in a spatially explicit, visually intuitive way. Unfortunately, Kaykhosravi et al. (2018) confirm that the problem of a lack of GIS integration noted by Zhou (2014) persists, with only three of the 11 LID models they review having significant GIS integration (MIKE Urban, PCSWMM and SWAT) (Kaykhosravi et al., 2018). Most recently, the GIS support which Kaykhosravi et al. (2018) noted as being under development for Win-SLAMM and HEC-HMS have also both been completed.[7]

With respect to flood modelling, protecting life and property against the 'worst-case scenario' is often a primary goal. In such a scenario, the upper limits to volume and force of water will be of primary concern, so a 'sealed surface' assumption is still commonly used in urban areas. So while it is important to collect more calibration data for SUDS (Dietz, 2007), perhaps even more pressing is the need to model sustainable water management NBS in rural areas, in order to make the economic case for protecting the ecosystem services they provide and thus reducing the severity and frequency of worst-case floods downstream. In that context, absorption and retention coefficients linked to soil type, land cover and land use are likely sufficient to the task (Sonaje, 2013) and certainly easier to come by (although finding a study with results calibrated to the local context may be harder).

Indeed, due to the complexity and variety of urban environments, for whichever approach is used, considerable effort is likely to be required to calibrate the model to each specific case. The question which then arises is when one might decide to undertake the more sophisticated models if specifically addressing NBS for storm water management. Given the dynamic nature of NBS and the range of possible responses from different combinatorial setups for urban trees,

7 ArcSLAMM: www.winslamm.com/ArcSLAMMPlus.html; HEC GeoHMS: www.hec.usace.army.mil/software/hec-geohms/

ground vegetation, built structures, mechanical animal and human disturbance and so on, the calibration of process models of NBS for stormwater management is daunting.

In deciding what modelling approach to use the question must be asked whether more complex models will deliver qualitatively different results, or merely greater precision around the same general picture? Will this difference lead to operationally different conclusions? If not then one needs to consider whether effort might be better spent on other implications of different drainage designs. For example, in some regions loss of forest near to cities not only impacts drainage but has also been associated with increased risk of infectious disease (Robbins, 2016), so from a cost–benefit view simple models which are sufficient to estimate the retention capacity of that forest and which leave time to consider ecological factors may present a preferable method with which to justify their protection than models necessary for downstream management of the flooding which would otherwise result from deforestation. On the other hand, upstream solutions may not be readily available, so the question of how to safely divert, retain or disperse water which has already accumulated may well require understanding its momentum, not only where this could be too high and thus a risk to life or property but also if it could become too slow. Introduction of wetlands into urban areas or slow-release floodplains, while it can help manage flooding and provide habitats for other species, can also present risks, such as providing habitats for disease vector-carrying insects near to people's homes (Haase, 2017). NBS place such trade-offs centre stage by offering to provide several ecosystem services as part of a wider ecological system. Consequently, the biggest challenge for modelling NBS is the choice of model to use with respect not only to whether it represents a specific aspect to a given accuracy and precision but also how well it can incorporate that wider context, which may well create feedbacks with greater significance than the additional precision of a using a more complex model.

6.6 CONCLUSION

The relevance or otherwise of particular models is highly dependent on the spatial and temporal scale of application as well as whether the results are to be used to inform specific planning decisions, for strategic regional planning or guiding policy development nationally. Selecting a model from the range available can be confusing and while guidelines do exist (e.g. WMO, 2013) these tend to be focused only on the flooding issue, rather than the wider policy context in which NBS necessarily sit. Therefore, it is worth noting some general principles which might be drawn from the models and examples considered in this review.

In both coastal flooding and storm water flooding, there are simple models which will deliver much of the information at relatively little effort. The question is whether the results of this model can be used with confidence to inform a particular decision. In some cases it will be immediately obvious that a risk is present, or that the area is safe from flooding, and no reasonable change in parameters between precautionary or conservative would affect that decision, in which case there is little benefit from investing further time refining the precision of the result. If, however, the result appears more 'borderline' or there is reason to suspect the dynamics of the system would substantially change the picture (i.e. water might carry enough momentum to run uphill), then in both domains mathematical models exist which will provide greater precision to the result. However, even with the more complex models the same basic principle will apply: a coastal inundation model with conservative settings such as for land-cover friction parameters will provide a precautionary 'worst-case' picture, as will a storm water flow model based on an assumption of sealed surfaces. For low-velocity problems, decisions around parameterisation of the effect of NBS can be at least as significant as modelling method. Mathematical models are important when terrain could cause large concentrations of flow, or when two flows (storm surge and storm water) meet. They could also be very useful when considering NBS that form barriers which break up or redirect the water's momentum (e.g. mangrove forest), but are arguably of less benefit when the process is fundamentally slower, i.e. infiltration processes from SUDS. In the latter case calibration data are hard to find compared with flow absorption coefficients which can be more quickly and easily included with simple methods available in many GIS packages. Time saved modelling one aspect of NBS is time which can be spent modelling another aspect, and simple models may be used during the geodesign stage but more precise models deployed to look at the implications of the outcome of that design process before committing to a plan.

REFERENCES

Abebe, Y. A., Ghorbani, A., Nikolic, I., Vojinovic, Z. & Sanchez, A. 2019. A coupled flood–agent–institution modelling (CLAIM) framework for urban flood risk management. *Environmental Modelling & Software*, 111, 483–492.

Abhas, J., Bloch., R. & Lamond, J. 2011. *Cities and Flooding: A Guide to Integrated Urban Flood Risk Management for the 21st Century*. Washington, DC: World Bank.

Andersen, R. 2003. Mike info *Coast* – a GIS-based tool for coastal zone management. *In*: Green, D. R. & King, S. D. (eds.) *Coastal and Marine Geo-Information Systems*, pp. 467–472. Dordrecht: Springer.

Bardet, L., Duluc, C.-M., Rebour, V. & L'Her, J. 2011. Regional frequency analysis of extreme storm surges along the French coast. *Natural Hazards and Earth System Sciences*, 11, 1627–1639.

Broughton, W. 1989. A review of the USDA SCS curve number method. *Australian Journal of Soil Research*, 27(3), 511–523.

Brown, S., Nicholls, R. J., Lowe, J. A. & Hinkel, J. 2016. Spatial variations of sea-level rise and impacts: an application of DIVA. *Climatic Change*, 134, 403–416.

CLIMSYSTEMS. 2017 SimCLIM 4.0 for Desktop Essentials [Online]. http://documents.climsystems.com/SimCLIM%204.0/SimCLIM%204.0%20Essentials.pdf

Dietz, M. E. 2007. Low impact development practices: a review of current research and recommendations for future directions. *Water, Air, and Soil Pollution*, 186, 351–363.

Elliott, A. H. & Trowsdale, S. A. 2007. A review of models for low impact urban stormwater drainage. *Environmental Modelling & Software*, 22, 394–405.

Fallahshorshani, M., André, M., Bonhomme, C. & Seigneur, C. 2012. Coupling traffic, pollutant emission, air and water quality models: technical review and perspectives. *Procedia – Social and Behavioral Sciences*, 48, 1794–1804.

Garen, D. & Moore, D. 2007. Curve number hydrology in water quality modeling. *Journal of the American Water Resources Association (JAWRA)*, 41(2), 377–388.

Haase, D. 2017. Urban wetlands and riparian forests as a nature-based solution for climate change adaptation in cities and their surroundings. *In*: Kabisch, N., Korn, H., Stadler, J. & Bonn, A. (eds.) *Nature-based Solutions to Climate Change Adaptation in Urban Areas: Linkages between Science, Policy and Practice*. Cham: Springer International Publishing.

Hinkel, J. & Klein, R. J. T. 2009. Integrating knowledge to assess coastal vulnerability to sea-level rise: the development of the DIVA tool. *Global Environmental Change*, 19, 384–395.

Hinkel, J., Nicholls, R. J., Tol, R. S. J., Wang, Z. B., Hamilton, J. M., Boot, G., et al. 2013. A global analysis of erosion of sandy beaches and sea-level rise: an application of DIVA. *Global and Planetary Change*, 111, 150–158.

Hinkel, J., Nicholls, R. J., Vafeidis, A. T., Tol, R. S. & Avagianou, T. 2010. Assessing risk of and adaptation to sea-level rise in the European Union: an application of DIVA. *Mitigation and Adaptation Strategies for Global Change*, 15, 703–719.

Hunter, N. M., Horritt, M. S., Bates, P. D., Wilson, M. D. & Werner, M. G. F. 2005. An adaptive time step solution for raster-based storage cell modelling of floodplain inundation. *Advances in Water Resources*, 28, 975–991.

Huxley, C. 2016, GPU – the next generation modelling for catchment flood plain management. Presentated at the ASFPM Conference, Grand Rapids, USA, June 2016. www.tuflow.com/Download/Presentations/2016/GPU%20-%20Next%20Generation%20Modeling%20for%20Catchment%20Floodplain.pdf

Kalantari, Z., Lyon, S.W., Jansson, P. E., Stolte, J., French, H. K., Folkeson, L., et al. 2015. Modeller subjectivity and calibration impacts on hydrological model applications: an event-based comparison for a road-adjacent catchment in south-east Norway. *Science of the Total Environment*, 502, 315–329.

Kaykhosravi, S., Khan, U. & Jadidi, A. 2018. A comprehensive review of low impact development models for research, conceptual, preliminary and detailed design applications. *Water*, 10, 1541.

Liu, Q., Quin, Y. & Guodong, L. 2018. Fast simulation of large scale floods based on GPU parallel computing. *Water*, 10, 589.

Liu, Y., Okada, N., Shen, D. & Li, S. 2009. Agent-based flood evacuation simulation of life-threatening conditions using vitae system model. *Journal of Natural Disaster Science*, 31, 33–41.

Madsen, H. 2000. Automatic calibration of a conceptual rainfall–runoff model using multiple objectives. *Journal of Hydrology*, 235, 276–288.

May, D. B. & Sivakumar, M. 2009. Prediction of urban stormwater quality using artificial neural networks. *Environmental Modelling Software*, 24, 296–302.

McKenna, D., Krüger, I. & Hinzmann, M. 2015. Coastal protection and suds – nature-based solutions. Recreate Policy Brief No. 4. Berlin.

Mcleod, E., Poulter, B., Hinkel, J., Reyes, E. & Salm, R. 2010. Sea-level rise impact models and environmental conservation: a review of models and their applications. *Ocean & Coastal Management*, 53, 507–517.

Murray-Rust, D., Robinson, D. T., Guillem, E., Karali, E. & Rounsevell, M. 2014. An open framework for agent based modelling of agricultural land use change. *Environmental Modelling & Software*, 61, 19–38.

Néelz, S. & Pender, G. 2009. *Desktop Review of 2D Hydraulic Modelling Packages*. Bristol: Environment Agency.

Néelz, S. & Pender, G. 2013. *Benchmarking the Latest Generation of 2D Hydraulic Modelling Packages*. Bristol: Environment Agency.

Nishat, A. & Mukherjee, N. 2013. Climate change impacts, scenario and vulnerability of Bangladesh. *In*: *Climate Change Adaptation Actions in Bangladesh*. New York, NY: Springer.

Passeri, D., Hagen, S., Medieros, S., Bilksie, M., Alizad, K. & Wang, D. 2015. The dynamic effects of sea level rise on low-gradient coastal landscapes: a review. *Earth's Future*, 3, 159–181.

Robbins, J. 2016. *How Forest Loss is Leading to a Rise in Human Disease*. New Haven, CT: Yale School of Forestry and Environmental Studies.

Schneiders, A., Van Daele, T., Van Landuyt, W. & Van Reeth, W. 2012. Biodiversity and ecosystem services: complementary approaches for ecosystem management? *Ecological Indicators*, 21, 123–133.

Sonaje, N. 2013. Modeling of infiltration process – a review. *Indian Journal of Applied Research*, 3, 226–230.

Stark, J., Plancke, Y., Ides, S., Meire, P. & Temmerman, S. 2016. Coastal flood protection by a combined nature-based and engineering approach: modeling the effects of marsh geometry and surrounding dikes. *Estuarine, Coastal and Shelf Science*, 175, 34–45.

Teng, J., Jakeman, A. J., Vaze, J., Croke, B. F. W., Dutta, D. & Kim, S. 2017. Flood inundation modelling: a review of methods, recent advances and uncertainty analysis. *Environmental Modelling & Software*, 90, 201–216.

TUFLOW. 2016. *TUFLOW User Manual Build 2016–03-AA*. TUFLOW.

UNDP. 2008. *Community-based Adaptation to Climate Change through Coastal Afforestation in Bangladesh*. www.thegef.org/project/community-based-adaptation-climate-change-through-coastal-afforestation

UNDP. 2011. Community-based adaptation to climate change through coastal afforestation in Bangladesh. Bangladesh Project Identification Form (23 November 2011).

Vafeidis, A. T., Nicholls, R. J., McFadden, L., Tol, R. S. J., Hinkel, J., Spencer, T., et al. 2008. A new global coastal database for impact and vulnerability analysis to sea-level rise. *Journal of Coastal Research*, 244, 917–924.

Vojinovic, Z., Keerakamolchai, W., Weesakul, S., Pudar, R., Medina, N. & Alves, A. 2017. Combining ecosystem services with cost-benefit analysis for selection of green and grey infrastructure for flood protection in a cultural setting. *Environments*, 4(1), 3.

Wong, P. & Losada, I. 2014. Coastal systems and low-lying areas. *In*: *WGII AR5*. Geneva: IPCC.

WMO. 2013. Intercomparison of flood forecasting models for review. Decision-Support Tool for the Selection of Flood Forecasting Model Working Group, Koblenz, Germany. www.wmo.int/pages/prog/hwrp/documents/FFI/Intercomparison_of_flood_forecasting_models_for_review.pdf

Vuik, V., Jonkman, S. N., Borsje, B. W. & Suzuki, T. 2016. Nature-based flood protection: the efficiency of vegetated foreshores for reducing wave loads on coastal dikes. *Coastal Engineering*, 116, 42–56.

Zhou, Q. 2014. A review of sustainable urban drainage systems considering the climate change and urbanization impacts. *Water Air and Soil Pollution*, 6, 976–992.

7 Nature-based Solutions to Urban Microclimate Regulation

Johanna Deak Sjöman and Erik Johansson

7.1 MICROCLIMATE

Understanding the microclimate in a given site influences the preconditions of sustainable development in many ways. Cold and strong winds in the winter will, for example, intensify the energy use in buildings depending on the air tightness of the building enclosure (Bagge et al., 2011), and in areas close to the seafront strong salty winds may also increase the wear and tear on building materials. High wind speed during winter also affects outdoor recreation, and the likelihood of people walking or cycling to local commerce and social activities subsides if the area is subject to highly uncomfortable wind speed (Glaumann & Nord, 1993). Thermal comfort during winter time is thus integrated in how people will access and use facilities in their local communities. Wind turbulence and funnel effects between buildings and along streets also occur to a greater extent in cities compared to rural settlements, although wind speed in general is stronger in the countryside (Oke, 1987), illustrating the importance of scale in modelling the urban environment. In Sweden, especially during winter time, strong winds help lower the air temperature by several degrees and thus contribute to uncomfortable physical conditions (Glaumann & Westerberg, 1988).

On the other hand, in the summer, high temperatures and lack of shade will increase the need for cooling – in buildings as well as in outdoor public areas where people visit. In contrast to winter time, moderate wind speed might be necessary in order to increase thermal comfort. The need to address thermal comfort in the future is accentuated in a report issued by the European Commission (2014). According to a report by the European Environment Agency, 70,000 premature deaths were attributed to the heatwave of 2003 in Europe

(EEA, 2017). With predictions of increased heatwaves and warmer weather conditions due to climate change, incidents like this will unfortunately increase, and with that the expenditure to cover health-care costs with regards to heat exhaustion (EEA, 2017).

Although contemporary urban planning is well abreast with the necessity to build sustainably and to plan the urban environment with regards to climate adaptation and mitigation, it is still surprising how little climate knowledge is actually incorporated into contemporary urban development. For instance, the spatial layout of buildings and infrastructure will strongly affect the urban climate. A grid plan (the most recurring spatial layout in current urban development) is more likely to result in higher wind speeds throughout an area than is an irregular plan. In terms of pollution and particle removal, this is beneficial. In terms of energy use in buildings and encouraging people to spend time outdoors, this plan is problematic in cold climates – especially in development schemes next to the seafront. Tall and box-shaped buildings with protruding corners and sharp angles will accentuate wind turbulence while a more aerodynamic contour will reduce the likelihood of turbulence occurring. Also, the thermal properties and albedo (the whiteness of surfaces and subsequent reflection of incoming solar radiation) of building materials have a great effect on the urban climate (Erell et al., 2011; Oke et al., 2017). With predominantly dark surfaces and materials absorbing incoming solar radiation during the day, nighttime temperatures in towns and cities increase compared to the surrounding countryside – a process known as the urban heat island effect. In turn, lower humidity in the air and soil (from e.g. soil sealing) further contributes to a warmer urban environment, as do high-rise buildings and narrow streets which lessen the 'sky view factor' and thereby prevent absorbed heat radiating back into space (Eliasson et al., 2011; Oke et al., 2017).

Green infrastructure – and specifically trees – can be used strategically in order to ameliorate different climate conditions. In comparison to other building materials trees are flexible and dynamic with qualities which change over the seasons and throughout the entire life cycle.

These are useful qualities that can advance thermal comfort and reduce building energy use if appropriate species, conditions and strategic location are taken into account. Different species also have different architectural makeup of branches and foliage – traits to consider in design for shade in summer and wind regulation in winter. Shading from trees in summer can lower surface temperatures by up to 19°C (Armson et al., 2012). Comparing areas with no trees to areas with trees, the difference in Physiologically Equivalent Temperature (PET, see p. 255) can be as much as 13°C. Using vegetation, and particularly trees, thus helps provide a comfortable microclimate during hot days while reducing energy use in buildings equipped with air conditioning (Sawka et al., 2013).

In summary, many aspects and complex combinations will influence the urban microclimate. In new development schemes, but also within existing built-up areas, it may almost be impossible to intuitively comprehend the pattern and movement of different climate conditions over a given time frame. This is why the use of microclimate models plays an important role, as they can help the urban planner and architect to better assess future scenarios and reflect this in more sustainable design, spatial layout, use of building materials and vegetation for a site. Incorporating modelling of this kind into the planning and building processes will also help practitioners recognise urban green structures as important components of nature-based solutions.

7.2 MODELS

The review concentrates on three microclimate models, ENVI-met (Huttner et al., 2008), SOLWEIG (Lindberg et al., 2016) and RayMan (Matzarakis et al., 2007). All models are designed to simulate microclimatic variables in complex urban settings, i.e. areas with a complex geometric layout of buildings, streets and vegetation. The makeup of each model varies and so does the level of complexity, i.e. type of input data, temporal and spatial resolutions, length of time to run simulations and the characteristics of the output data. All models are used daily in practice and research in Sweden as well as internationally. It is possible to download and run the ENVI-met, SOLWEIG and RayMan software programs on an ordinary PC as long as they are compatible with Windows NT/2000/XP/Vista/7 and 64-bit platforms (Bruse, 2009; Urban Climate Group, 2013).

The models represent three completely different model designs and constitute different focus specialties (discussed in the following sections). Nonetheless, one key output parameter included in all models is mean radiant temperature (Tmrt) – the combined and total sum of short-wave and long-wave radiation fluxes to which the human body is exposed. The mean radiant temperature is normally calculated for a standing person, typically modelled as a vertical cylinder. As such, mean radiant temperature has very strong influence on thermal comfort and it is necessary to retrieve it from a given site to be able to calculate thermal comfort indices which describe how the human body physiologically perceives heat or cold.

7.2.1 *ENVI-met*

The most complex model of the three is ENVI-met, which exists in three versions: a limited freeware version called Basic, a research version called Science and a professional version called Business (ENVI-met, 2017). This chapter reviews mainly the earlier version of ENVI-met (version 3.1) but to some extent also version 4.4, which includes a broader range of analyses and usage options. The model simulates all variables related to the urban microclimate: air temperature, humidity, short-wave and long-wave radiation, mean radiant temperature, temperature of surfaces, wind speed and direction, etc. In addition, ENVI-met also simulates air pollution dispersal (gas and particles). ENVI-met is a CFD (Computational Fluid Dynamics) model simulating air flow, but as such it also takes longer to run compared to RayMan and SOLWEIG. The ENVI-met model is composed of a relatively simple and one-dimensional soil model, a vegetation model and a radiative transfer model (Bruse, 2009). Jointly these comprise a three-dimensional model with a special focus on the surface–plant–air interaction. In order to process the simulation, the user first needs to map the study area on to a grid cell interface (Figure 7.1).

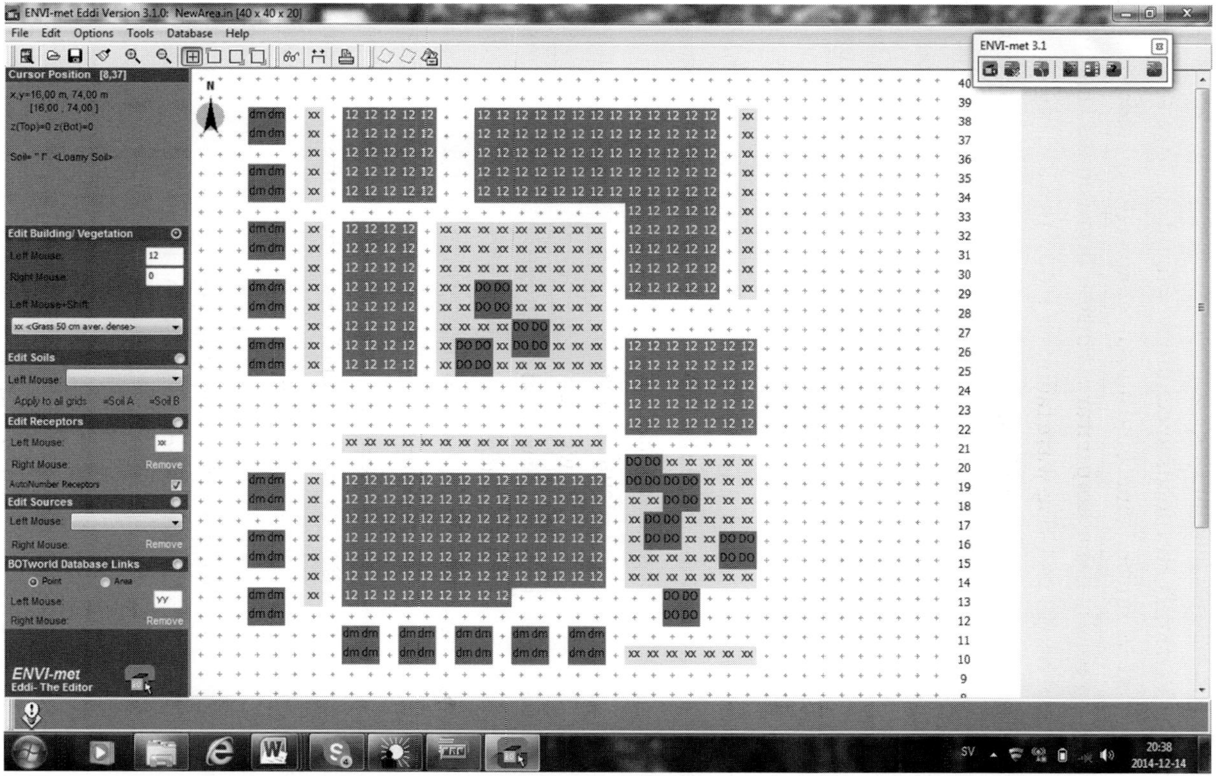

FIGURE 7.1 Screenshot of ENVI-met version 3.1 input data.

Buildings, type of vegetation, surface cover and soil type are thus assembled as input data on the interface. The horizontal extension of the model area is limited to 100 × 100 grid cells for the Basic version, whereas the Science and Business versions go up to about 250 × 250 grid cells. Vertically the maximum number of grids is 40 in the Basic versions and 30 in the Science/Business versions (ENVI-met, 2017). Each cell typically has a horizontal extension between 0.5 and 10 m and vertical height of 1–5 m (depending on study area and objectives) (Huttner et al., 2008). However, vertical so-called telescoping grids, whose size increase with height, make it possible to simulate areas containing high-rise buildings. This limitation means it is not possible to run simulations of extensive areas, such as entire cities, at a suitable resolution. Instead, the simulations need to be broken down into smaller fragments of individual areas and neighbourhoods. The time frame for simulations for models in ENVI-met usually ranges from 24 to 48 hours, covering diurnal and nocturnal conditions. As regards temporal resolution, simulations have a time step of typically 1–2 s (Ozkeresteci et al., 2003; ENVI-met, 2017).

7.2.2 *SOLWEIG*

Besides mean radiant temperature, SOLWEIG simulates three-dimensional radiation fluxes and shadow patterns (Lindberg et al., 2016). The input data consist of meteorological data (direct and diffuse shortwave radiation, air temperature and relative humidity), geographical information (latitude, longitude and elevation), surface properties (albedo and emissivity) of ground, walls and the human body and morphological data. The time resolution is optional. The morphological data consist of digital surface models (DSM) of both buildings (footprint and height) and vegetation, which are included in separate raster grids. Three-dimensional vegetation is included both as a canopy DSM, representing the top of the vegetation, and a trunk zone which describes the bottom of the vegetation (see Lindberg & Grimmond, 2011). The output data are presented either as two-dimensional maps or as specific points in the simulation domain. Since

2016, SOLWEIG has been incorporated in Urban Multi-scale Environmental Predictor (UMEP), a tool designed for researchers and professionals to be used for various applications including outdoor thermal comfort (Lindberg et al., 2018).

7.2.3 *RayMan*

Compared to ENVI-met and SOLWEIG, RayMan is the model requiring fairly simple and straightforward data input. The basic inputs include geographical location (latitude and longitude) and meteorological data, which are limited to global short-wave radiation, the ratio between direct and diffuse short-wave radiation, albedo and cloud cover. The morphological data are usually in the form of a text file containing raster data or the RayMan obstacle file, which will require a manual input on to the RayMan interface (Fröhlich & Matzarakis, 2013). The model is two-dimensional, although limited 3D data can be included by adding fish-eye photographs, drawings of solid elements in a hemispherical perspective and the geometric dimensions of e.g. buildings and trees (Matzarakis, 2009). These data are added as reference points (x, y and z) on to a grid. RayMan is developed primarily to calculate the radiation fluxes and mean radiant temperature. The output from RayMan is limited to one point in the studied area. The time frame in RayMan can cover hours to days, months and even years (as used in the study by Fröhlich & Matzarakis, 2013) and the time resolution when running the model is 1 hour. The model can be used for very small-scale calculations to estimations on a regional level (Matzarakis et al., 2007).

Today, researchers and practitioners worldwide use the three reviewed models (see e.g. Elnabawi et al., 2013; Puliafito et al., 2013). In Sweden, ENVI-met was applied for microclimate studies of the Norra Sorgenfri project in Malmö (Kronvall & Johansson, 2011) and the SOLWEIG program has been used for projects in Djurgårdshamnen, Stockholm (Lindberg & Grimmond, personal communication). In the following sections, both input and output data will be compared in detail.

7.3 DATA

In both SOLWEIG and RayMan, buildings and the ground are modelled as geometric objects without thermal mass. Surface properties consist of albedo and emissivity. RayMan has one albedo value for all materials whereas SOLWEIG has different albedo and emissivity for walls and ground. In the current version of ENVI-met (version 4), on the other hand, buildings are defined by the indoor temperature and walls and roofs are built up in three layers, each having thermal properties such as thermal conductivity and specific heat. This means that heat transmission through walls and roof as well as thermal storage in the building envelope is taken into account. Albedo and emissivity values can be given individually for each wall and roof. Ground surface covers can be defined as bare soil, asphalt, concrete, etc. with a range of different underlying soil types (Bruse, 2009).

The required and additional input data thus vary between the models, although all will incorporate a data input which calculates mean radiant temperature, short-wave radiation (direct and diffuse), long-wave radiation, shade and sky view factor (Huttner et al., 2008; Lindberg et al., 2008; Matzarakis et al., 2010). There are, however, several key differences in both the initial and additional output data when comparing the three models, as will be discussed in the following sections.

7.4 MEAN RADIANT TEMPERATURE AND THERMAL COMFORT INDICES

As already mentioned, mean radiant temperature constitutes a key output for all models and is an important parameter for estimating thermal comfort (or discomfort) of the human body. Although most weather reports will provide information on air temperature and wind speed, the radiative environment is not known. Radiation from the sun, the sky and from materials in our surrounding environment plays a decisive role to whether the human body will experience thermal stress or not. In the ENVI-met model, radiation fluxes are calculated from the sky and buildings ('upper hemisphere') and from ground level ('lower hemisphere') (Lindberg et al., 2008). In SOLWEIG, calculations of radiant fluxes incorporate six angles of six long-wave and short-wave radiation fluxes (upward, downward and from the four cardinal points) (Lindberg et al., 2008).

Due to the technological improvement in ameliorating indoor climate in the 1950s and 1960s with air conditioning, the following decades contributed to research deriving various calculations into the thermal energy balance of human bodies from which the 'predicted mean vote' (PMV) developed by Fanger (1970) still forms a sound foundation in contemporary assessments. However, compared to the stable indoor climate in space-conditioned buildings for which PMV was designed, thermal comfort and stress in outdoor environments is the result of several additional attributes and climate conditions. As such, Physiologically Equivalent Temperature (PET) was derived to better assess thermal stress in complex outdoor urban environments (Mayer & Höppe, 1987; Honjo, 2009). For the same reason, the Universal Thermal Climate Index (UTCI) was recently developed (Jendritzky et al., 2012).

PET, which takes wind speed, radiation, humidity and air temperature into account and is expressed in °C, helps define the heat budget of the human body in a way that is easily interpretable by both professionals and laypeople (Höppe, 1999). It provides a basis for how the thermal conditions in a particular environment could be adjusted to mitigate physical discomfort (Mayer & Höppe, 1987). The UTCI, which is based on the same meteorological variables as PET, is also expressed in °C. However, whereas PET refers to an indoor environment with light clothing and low activity (a sitting person), the insulation value of the clothing for UTCI increases with decreasing outdoor temperature and the activity corresponds to walking at a speed of 1.1 m s^{-1}.

Several factors contribute to how the human body will physiologically experience climate and weather conditions. For example, the surrounding materials in a compact urban setting will store solar energy and re-radiate heat that will affect the thermal perception. For example, in a street canyon surrounded by brick buildings and

CASE STUDY 7.1 Use of Vegetation to Improve Outdoor Thermal Comfort in Hot, Dry Damascus, Syria

The aim of this study was to see how street trees and overhead shading devices could be used to improve thermal comfort in streets in Damascus, Syria. Damascus has hot, dry summers with a mean maximum temperature of 36°C and fairly cold winters with a mean maximum temperature of 12°C.

As in many parts of the Middle East, the urban design in contemporary areas is generally not adapted to the climate. The distance between buildings is large and there are few elements of shade, which results in high amounts of solar radiation in summer. The combination of high air temperature and radiation from the sun and from warm surfaces such as streets and the facades of buildings creates very hot environments. In this study the microclimate of a typical residential street having 15-m high buildings situated 18 m apart was simulated with ENVI-met version 3.1. The thermal conditions expressed as the PET – a thermal index which takes air temperature, humidity, radiation and wind speed into account – in the street is shown in Figure 7.2. During this season PET can reach 60°C in areas exposed to solar radiation. The addition of shading trees and shading devices, which were put along the street so that pedestrians walking on the pavements had continuous shade, improved the thermal conditions in the hot summer radically; in the shaded pavements PET decreased by up to 19°C during the hottest part of the day (see Figure 7.2d). In winter the added trees and shading devices also led to more shade in the street, but due to the lower solar angles the PET values on the sunny side of the street were similar to the case without shading. The study concluded that landscape elements such as street trees and shading devices can greatly improve human comfort conditions in urban areas in Damascus. However, trees should be deciduous and shading devices moveable in order to allow for sufficient solar access in winter (Yahia & Johansson, 2014).

CASE STUDY 7.1 **(cont.)**

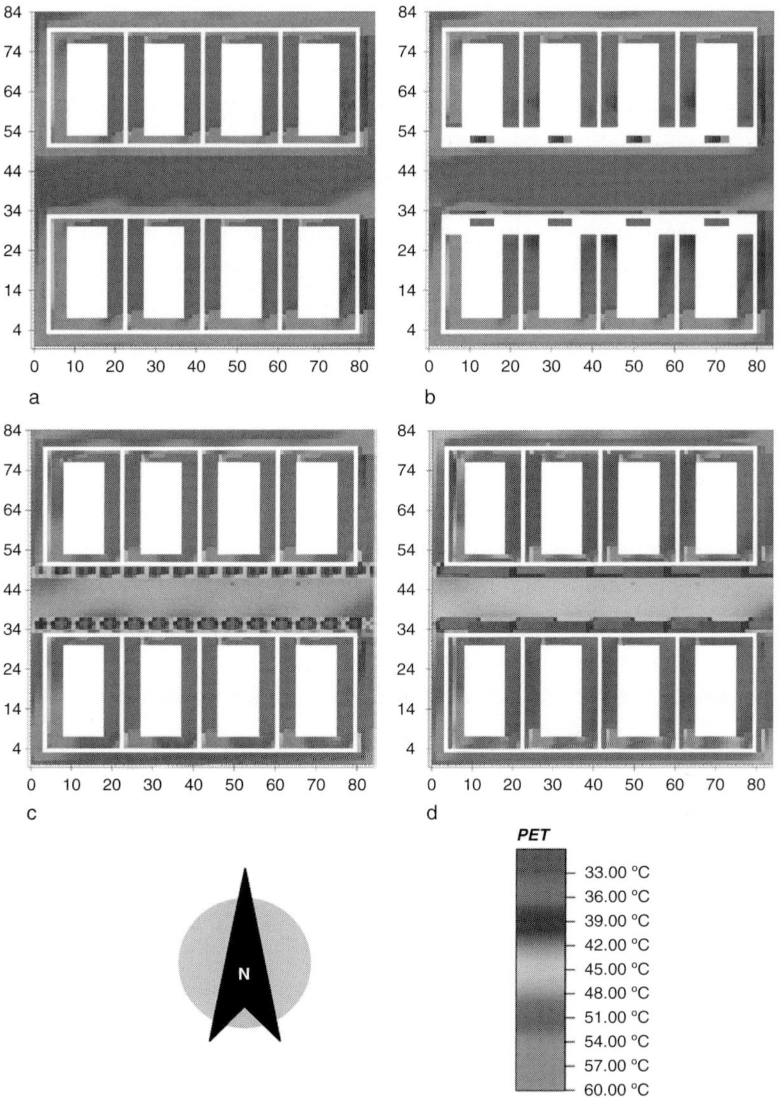

FIGURE 7.2 Calculated maximum PET values (2 pm) for the summer for a street (a) without any shade, (b) changed urban morphology, (c) with street trees and (d) with street trees and horizontal shading devices over the pavements. (A black and white version of this figure will appear in some formats. For the colour version, please refer to the plate section.)

ground surfaces covered with asphalt, the likelihood of thermal stress on a warm day will be greater compared to a planted area with mature trees. Strong winds will have a cooling effect on the human body (wind chill effect) and this could be problematic during winter in areas subject to very low air temperatures, or beneficial during summer when cool breezes will help ameliorate thermal qualities in very hot areas (Oke, 1987).

RayMan includes the possibility of calculating PET and is therefore often used in combination with the other models, where the mean radiant temperature retrieved from either SOLWEIG or ENVI-met can be converted fairly easily in the RayMan spreadsheet (Fröhlich & Matzarakis, 2013; Lindberg & Grimmond, personal communication). The professional version of ENVI-met version 4 allows calculation of both PET and UTCI. By modelling the mean radiant temperature and subsequent calculation of PET or UTCI, planners and architects may, beforehand, understand which urban areas may be subject to severe heat stress or intensely cold situations. Such information may also be retrieved for future scenarios involving measures of climate change adaptation.

7.5 SOLAR RADIATION, SHADE AND SKY VIEW FACTOR

The incoming solar radiation, both direct and diffuse, is calculated by all three models (Huttner et al., 2008; Lindberg et al., 2008; Matzarakis, 2009). This can be simulated for any time and day throughout the year independent of geographical location and sky view factor. Access to sunlight and how this will vary depending on time of year is a significant factor with regard to sustainable development. In winter, passive solar gain in buildings is important to lessen the energy use and heating bills (Littlefair, 2001). However, shade from structures or adjacent buildings is often not considered for new development plans, nor its effect on subsequent building energy use (Sawka et al., 2013). By simulating the horizontal and vertical angles of the sun's position in microclimate models it is therefore possible to assess how existing and new developments impact on sunlight and shading patterns. Access to sunlight during winter is also beneficial for the public good in terms of well-being and recreation – in indoor as well as outdoor environments (Ne'Eman, 1974). RayMan also calculates the sunshine duration in the studied point of the urban area (Matzarakis, 2009). In fact, RayMan is the only software reviewed in this chapter that calculates sunshine duration. This can be simulated for any day throughout the year independent of geographical location and sky view factor.

In so-called urban canyons, the visual access to the upper hemisphere – sky view factor – is limited, especially if buildings are tall and streets are narrow. With irregular geometry of horizontal and vertical surfaces the high-rise buildings and deep streetscape help contribute to trapped heat and to the nighttime phenomenon of the urban heat island (Eliasson et al., 2011). The sky view factor thus provides an estimation of which areas within the urban fabric of buildings, streets and open spaces may increase certain climate conditions such as absorption and reflection of short-wave radiation, incoming and outgoing long-wave radiation, wind turbulence, shading and so on. However, the sky view factor is mainly linked to estimations of the mean radiant temperature and the urban heat island effect (Gál et al., 2009).

The ENVI-met model will calculate the sky view factor from the three-dimensional model built on to the grid interface. It does not incorporate image data such as fish-eye photographs or GIS vector data files to the model. Both RayMan and SOLWEIG can use GIS-based sky view silhouette files (as long as the vector files are converted to raster files for the SOLWEIG model) (Lindberg & Grimmond, personal communication). Raster data files (e.g. photographs and other pixelated imagery) will not project sharp and clear objects when zoomed into a more detailed scale; this is less of a problem for vector files (Matzarakis & Matuschek, 2011) and the difference may be significant for very local shading effects. The possibility of integrating municipal GIS or digital models of construction plans is highly beneficial as it provides a fairly quick assessment of how existing and future development will affect the sky view factor (Matzarakis & Matuschek, 2011). In this respect, SOLWEIG and RayMan have an advantage over ENVI-met.

CASE STUDY 7.2 Effect of Urban Design and Greenery on Outdoor Thermal Comfort in Warm, Humid Dar es Salaam, Tanzania

Dar es Salaam, Tanzania, has a warm–humid climate characterised by maximum temperatures of up to 32°C during the warm period of the year. However, both air temperature and humidity are high throughout the year and temperature variations between day and night are small. In such a climate it is important to protect against solar radiation as well as allowing for air movements. However, in Dar es Salaam, consideration of climate in urban design has received little attention. Variables such as building heights, street orientation and spaces between buildings strongly affect solar access as well as wind speed and direction in urban areas. This study examined the relationship between urban design and outdoor thermal comfort in four neighbourhoods with different urban design: Kariakoo, a dense neighbourhood with many high-rise buildings, narrow streets and almost no vegetation; the city centre, a dense area with varying building heights and sparse vegetation; Upanga, a lush area with low- and medium-rise buildings; and Manzese, a dense, low-rise informal settlement with sparse vegetation. Microclimatic variables such as air temperature, humidity, wind and radiation were simulated with ENVI-met version 3.1. PET, the thermal index, was calculated in order to compare the thermal comfort conditions in the studied areas in order to highlight strengths and weaknesses of the existing design (see Figure 7.3). The study showed that due to differences in building height, spaces between buildings and street orientation, the average wind speed varied significantly between the areas. Although wind speeds in general were low, low-rise Manzese had twice as high a wind speed as high-rise Kariakoo.

Moreover, areas with low-rise buildings such as Manzese lead to more stressful urban spaces than areas with high-rise buildings such as the city centre and Kariakoo due to high solar radiation (see Figure 7.3). It was also shown that the use of dense trees, as in the neighbourhood Upanga, helps enhance the thermal comfort conditions by reducing heat stress (Figure 7.3). However, vegetation reduces wind speed and to improve the current situation by reducing heat stress in Dar es Salaam it was recommended to

CASE STUDY 7.2 (cont.)

increase shade by adding street trees or other forms of shading, for example overhead shading devices. It was also concluded that street trees should have large and dense crowns but high stems in order not to block air movement (Yahia et al., 2018).

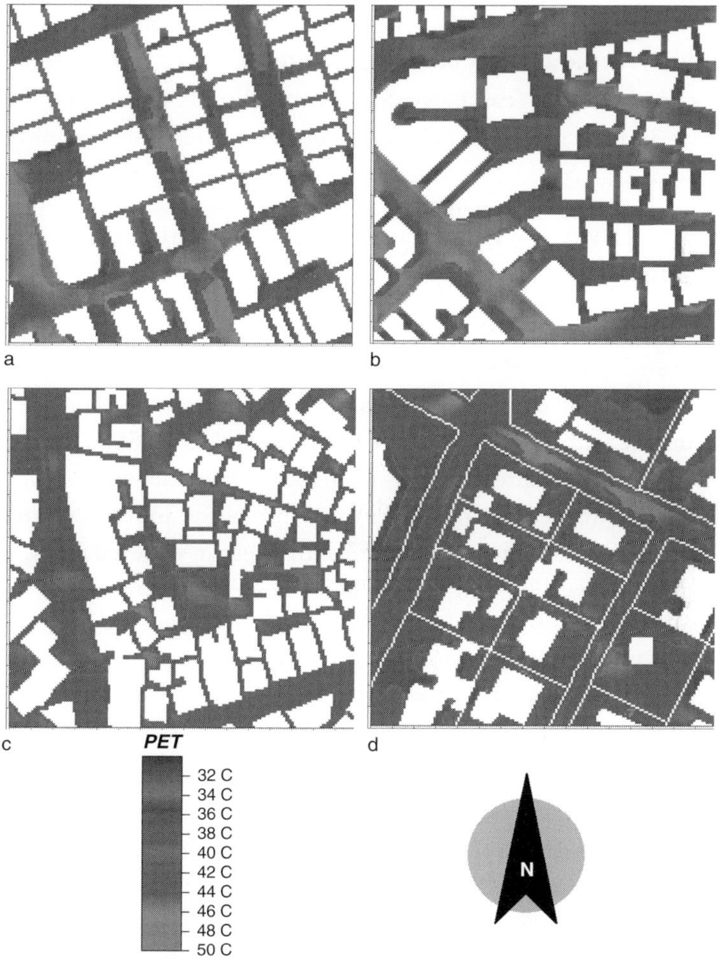

FIGURE 7.3 Spatial variation of the physiologically equivalent temperature for the simulated areas during the hottest time of the day in the hottest month (February at 2 pm) for (a) Kariakoo, (b) city centre, (c) Manzese and (d) Upanga. (A black and white version of this figure will appear in some formats. For the colour version, please refer to the plate section.)

7.6 WIND

Of the three models, only ENVI-met calculates air flow in the area of study. As such, it is possible to use the ENVI-met program to assess how existing or future development will contribute to stronger or lesser wind speed and how the wind flow pattern will move throughout the area. As illustrated in Figure 7.4, the small green squares in the lower image (b) represent a green structure which is reducing wind speed.

Fluid dynamic air flow simulations are, however, very complex processes for a model to calculate. Simulations in ENVI-met can take a long time and the accuracy largely depends on the resolution of the

CASE STUDY 7.3 **Wind Simulations for Lomma Harbour, Sweden**

As part of an overall strategy in developing a new neighbourhood with regards to environmental goals of sustainability, Lomma Harbour, Sweden, became the case study for a simulation in ENVI-met in order to examine the role of vegetation in regulating wind. Located by the sea on a former industrial site, the new neighbourhood is subject to strong winds throughout the year. In winter the wind speed can reach up to 10 $m\ s^{-1}$, creating an accentuated wind chill effect in targeted areas. Modifying wind speed in winter to help create a more comfortable microclimate and with possible benefits to indoor energy use is thus of interest for the developers and by the local council, and ultimately the users and the community.

Several simulations were processed with different combinations of vegetation including variations of tree species and layers of shrubs and trees. Figure 7.4 shows two of the five simulations, indicating the difference in wind speed in the neighbourhood with no vegetation included (upper) and with extended vegetation targeting, e.g. street corners and the seafront area. The results were later discussed in a workshop with municipality officials, tree planners and developers and consequently opened up for a more progressive attitude in how to incorporate green infrastructure as nature-based solutions in tandem with built structures.

CASE STUDY 7.3 **(cont.)**

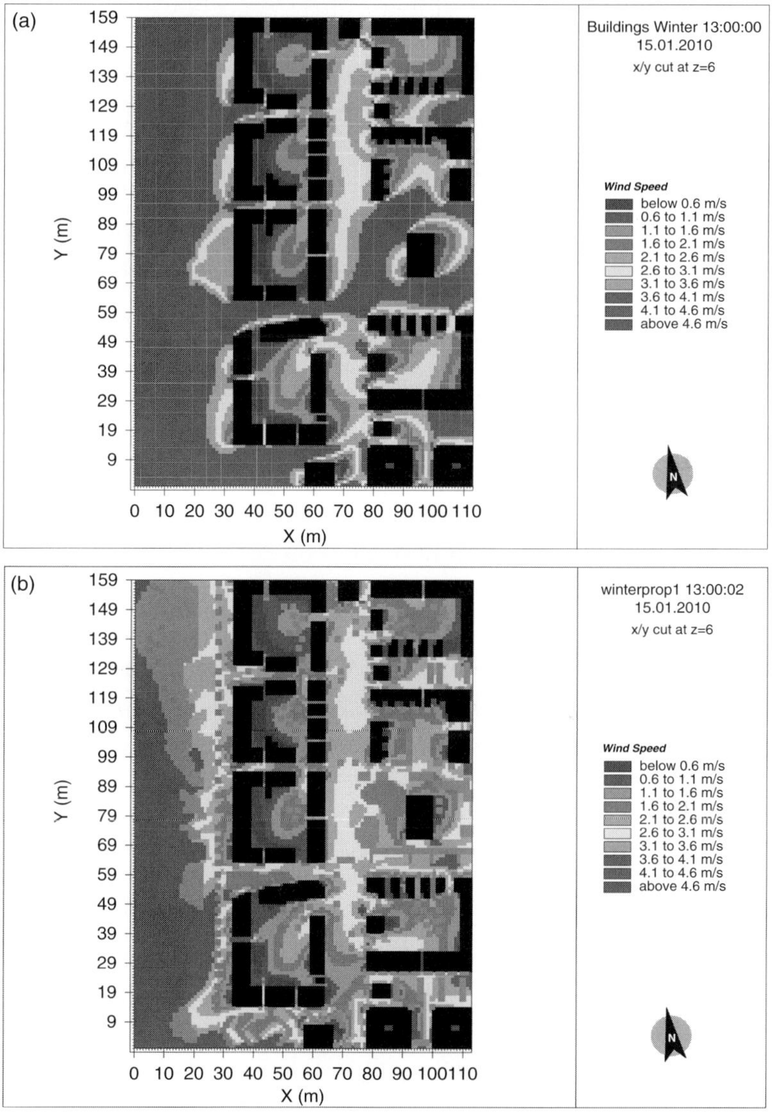

<Left foot> <Right foot>

FIGURE 7.4 Wind speed output from ENVI-met without trees (a, upper) and with trees (b, lower). (A black and white version of this figure will appear in some formats. For the colour version, please refer to the plate section.)

model. Because ENVI-met uses raster data where all cells are equally large there is no possibility of refining the grid cells around critical parts of the model. In ENVI-met there is thus no use of nested grids within the digital model. This has brought some criticism to the output results when it comes to wind speed and air flow (Lindberg & Grimmond, personal communication). Turbulent effects around corners, behind buildings and around protruding objects, for instance, will not show correctly. There are, however, more advanced CFD models where such effects can be simulated and where interlaced nested grids exist throughout the modelled area. Examples of such models are the commercially developed FLUENT (ANSYS, 2014), and OpenFOAM (Lohmeyer, 2014). These models are complicated to process and also take a long time to run; they are thus relevant to model impact around specific buildings but of less use for planning over larger areas and iterative, geodesign-type processes. Due to its ability to replicate and process wind speed and air flow, ENVI-met simulations take longer when compared to RayMan and SOLWEIG. It is possible to run simulations of radiation fluxes on a much shorter time frame in the RayMan and SOLWEIG programs than in ENVI-met (Lindberg & Grimmond, personal communication) and thus they are more easily incorporated into iterative design methods.

7.7 VEGETATION

Vegetation, and particularly trees, constitutes a valuable asset in the urban landscape in terms of ameliorating climate conditions and the mitigation and adaptation to climate change. As mentioned previously, trees provide for multifunctional benefits when it comes to a wide range of ecosystem services – i.e. benefits to human health, recreational values, storm water control, lower energy use in buildings, etc. (Akbari et al., 2001; Xiao & Wedd, 2002; Grahn et al., 2003; Borja et al., 2008; Katzschner, 2011). Studies in warm climates have shown that trees can lower both the mean radiant temperature and the ground surface temperature by up to 20°C compared to an unshaded asphalt surface (Johansson et al., 2013; Yahia et al., 2018).

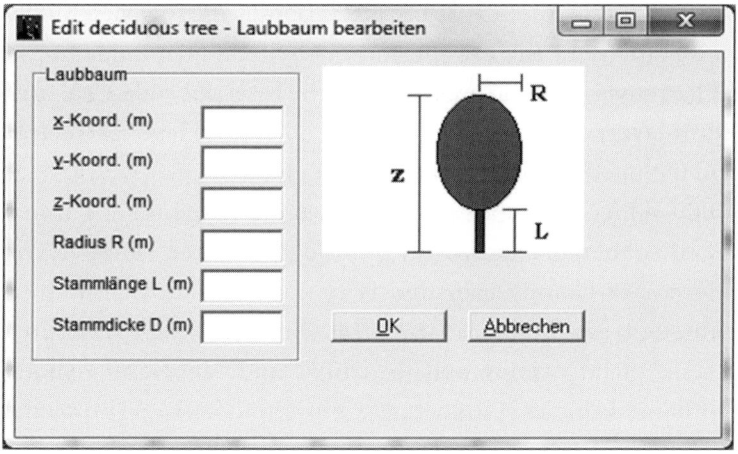

FIGURE 7.5 Designing the tree model in RayMan.

Evapotranspiration contributes less to this effect than the shading from the tree canopy (Lindberg & Grimmond, 2011). However, different trees will provide different qualities depending on species and time of year. Shading depends on the foliage and architectural makeup of branches – features that may have a very different makeup depending on species. How to take advantage of these qualities in terms of shade and wind regulating effects is thus an important design issue (Deak Sjöman et al., 2016). Simulations of how trees affect the mean radiant temperature (but also additional microclimate conditions) thus require a sound understanding of the different qualities of different species throughout the year.

With regards to the input data required on vegetation, all models – ENVI-met, SOLWEIG and RayMan – require different information. The most simple information input is that of RayMan, where two types of trees are distinguished – coniferous and deciduous. Tree input data consist of the basic information on tree height, stem height (from ground level to lowest branch) and radius of canopy (Figure 7.5). The deciduous tree has full leaf cover even during wintertime simulations, the alternative being to run the model without trees and so also losing trunk and branch structure (Matzarakis, personal communication). The input data on vegetation in the RayMan model contain no porosity in the canopy and neither leaf area index (m^2 of projected leaf cover) nor leaf area density (the total one-sided leaf area (m^2) per unit layer of volume (m^3), for each horizontal layer of the tree crown) are included when creating the tree elements.

In SOLWEIG the input data for trees are based on the transmissivity of solar radiation coming through the tree canopy. The measurements of canopy transmissivity consider both coniferous and deciduous trees (Media et al., 2014). Trees are then simulated in a division of (a) canopy and (b) trunk, and represent visually conical or domed shapes (Lindberg & Grimmond, 2011). The model assumes that the surface temperature of the vegetation is equal to the air temperature, that the transmissivity through the foliage for short-wave and long-wave radiation is 20% and 0%, respectively, and that the albedo and emissivity of the foliage are 0.20 and 0.95, respectively. Similarly to the input data of buildings and hard surface cover, a mean value of deciduous trees and a mean value of coniferous trees are subsequently used as tree input parameters in the SOLWEIG model (Lindberg & Grimmond, personal communication).

ENVI-met allows a more detailed input database of vegetation compared to the RayMan and SOLWEIG models. All vegetation data, from turf and grasses to shrubs and trees, are based on a leaf area density value. Each tree (or vegetation species) can be given individual leaf area density values and as such reflect both shape and specific species, with or without full leaf cover. Additional input on vegetation data considers stomata resistance and background CO_2 concentration (Bruse, 2009). ENVI-met could therefore be regarded as the most advanced microclimate model of the reviewed models when it comes to the interaction of vegetation and urban microclimate. By including vegetation in the models it is possible to evaluate the influence of vegetation on mean radiant temperature. This is considered in all three models reviewed in this chapter. In the ENVI-met model it is also possible to retrieve output data on how e.g. trees affect relative humidity, wind speed, surface temperatures, etc. (Bruse, 2009). In addition to the unidimensional vegetation available in old versions of ENVI-met, version 4 allows complex, three-dimensional trees and bushes (ENVI-met, 2017).

CASE STUDY 7.4 Simulating Vegetation with Different Seasonal Qualities

In parts of the world with a temperate climate vegetation plays a dynamic role in tandem with changing seasons. In summer, shading from trees provides cooler microclimates and becomes particularly important in areas where people congregate and e.g. in children's play areas. However, depending on the architectural attributes of trees, different species may influence the microclimate and the thermal comfort differently. In fact, a group of trees with high leaf area index can create thermal discomfort because dense canopies reduce airflow and a much-needed breeze during hot summer days. The cooling effect from wind in summer and how surrounding buildings are spatially arranged are also important elements to consider. This not only concerns microclimate conditions but also the movement and dispersal of air pollution.

Different species will develop and drop their leaves at different times in spring and autumn. Depending on the place-specific qualities and site use it may be beneficial to e.g. avoid trees with early leafing out in areas where solar radiation will provide an enhanced microclimate in spring (Figure 7.6). In ENVI-met it is possible to simulate the different architectural attributes of trees due to the 10 layers of leaf area density required for the plant's input data. This allows for specific input with regards to different species and time of year. However, the ENVI-met model calculates leaf area density values only – i.e. trees with leaf cover. Simulating trees in ENVI-met with consideration to winter conditions thus means that the tree value being calculated includes leaves (albeit with a very low value). This gives rise to certain inaccuracies where e.g. the latent heat fluxes from transpiration would not occur during defoliated conditions. On the other hand, using ENVI-met for simulating e.g. the effect of trees on wind speed in winter will give an appropriate estimate of how different species affect wind flow in complex urban

CASE STUDY 7.4 **(cont.)**

settings. As different trees will display different qualities in terms of architectural attributes and seasonal qualities, ENVI-met provides for a method to assess how to best accommodate trees depending on site-specific situations. In temperate parts of the world, climate-responsive design needs to include both summer and winter seasons.

FIGURE 7.6 In temperate climates it is important to consider how different architectural attributes vary among different tree species. An ideal urban tree has low transmissivity in summer when thermal heat stress occurs and high transmissivity in winter when sunshine is limited. Placing trees of high branch area density (e.g. *Carpinus betulus* 'Fastigiata', left) close to south- and west-facing building facades will, for instance, create negative effects on the thermal conditions in and around that building. Low solar azimuth angles and limited hours of solar radiation mean that trees with less branch area density (e.g. *Ginkgo biloba*, right) are better suited in close approximation to buildings or in places where people visit. In situations where the chill effect from wind is of particular concern, trees with a denser makeup of branches can be used strategically to block out wind. This may involve using e.g. columnar hornbeam or oak in strategic places (i.e. street corners) (Deak Sjöman et al., 2016). (A black and white version of this figure will appear in some formats. For the colour version, please refer to the plate section.)

7.8 COMPARATIVE CRITIQUE AND FUTURE DEVELOPMENT

The microclimate models ENVI-met, SOLWEIG and RayMan present three highly compatible models for estimating microclimate conditions in a complex urban environment, albeit comprising different levels of input data and simulation mechanisms. As such the models also represent different levels of user-friendliness where the model-building and input data for RayMan could be regarded as the most user-friendly of the three. That said, it is still important to consider what kind of output data emerge in the end and how readily readable these data will be (Lindberg & Grimmond, personal communication). The output data of RayMan are for only one single point in the model and constitute a text file, which in turn needs to be transcribed into a more visually accessible format – especially if the results are to be presented to laypersons or decision-makers without expertise in microclimate simulations. Although ENVI-met is a more complex software program which requires detailed input data, manual input of building cells on to the model interface and takes a longer time to simulate, the output data can be very easily depicted and visualised to laypeople or to other professional groups. Other advantages are the CFD models incorporated into ENVI-met and the LEONARDO software program which help visualise the output results into either sections or two- or three-dimensional illustrations. That functionality needs to be set against the scale of applications, however. All three provide a fixed total grid size, the more complex the model the smaller the grid. It is possible to run whole cities in the RayMan model, but large areas need to be broken down into smaller districts or quarters in SOLWEIG and ENVI-met. However, in the RayMan 1.2 software (free to download) the size of the obstacle file is limited to 1.6 × 1.6 km.

As already mentioned, wind simulations in ENVI-met have been criticised due to the lack of accuracy (Lindberg & Grimmond, personal communication). Thorsson et al. (2007) also question both

RayMan and ENVI-met when it comes to the input parameters for the calculation of mean radiant temperature. For example, the RayMan model has been shown to underestimate the mean radiant temperature at low solar elevations. At such elevations multiple reflections of short-wave radiation and emittance of long-wave radiation have a big impact on the estimation of mean radiant temperature and it is not clear how RayMan takes these aspects into account (Thorsson et al., 2007). ENVI-met divides the hemisphere into upper and lower divisions for radiant fluxes – parameters which according to Thorsson et al. (2007) will not project accurately when it comes to long-wave radiation, a criticism which was further validated in a study by Ali-Toudert (2005).

The input parameters of vegetation also present substantial variation in the functionality which can be incorporated. According to Lindberg (personal communication), the studies undertaken by the Urban Climate Group at the Physical Geography, Earth Sciences Centre at Gothenburg University show little differences between species performance when it comes to affecting the mean radiant temperature. On the other hand, the different architectural and vertical makeup of branches between species in winter do have an impact on e.g. wind speed depending on strategic placement (Deak Sjöman et al., 2016). This in turn influences mean radiant temperature, physiologically equivalent temperature and building energy use (Höppe, 1999; Matzarakis, 2009; Nikoofard & Fazli, 2011). The default input data for vegetation in ENVI-met could be questioned, however, as they provide set values for a range of trees which present relatively high (in some circumstances unrealistically high) leaf area index. As such it is important for any user to understand that it may be relevant to customise leaf area index and leaf area density to a more species-specific index corresponding to the situation (growth shape and time of year). This requires retrieving the leaf area index and dividing it into 10 layers of leaf area density, then replacing each value in the edit plant database with a known value for the species.

Further questions could be raised with regards to the input data on buildings and other horizontal and vertical surfaces. For example, in SOLWEIG a mean value for all buildings and surface covers is used regardless of its actual colour and other thermal properties. However, RayMan, SOLWEIG and ENVI-met are all models in a constant process of improvement and of validation (e.g. Ozkeresteci et al., 2003; Ali-Toudert, 2005; Gulyás & Matzarakis, 2006; Matzarakis et al., 2010; Lindberg & Grimmond, 2011; Unger et al., 2011). For instance, the next SOLWEIG software aims to incorporate the calculation of PET which also means an estimate of wind speed (Urban Climate Group, 2013) as well as specific material properties.

REFERENCES

Akbari, H., Pomerantz, M. & Taha, H. 2001. Cool surfaces and shade trees to reduce energy use and improve air quality in urban areas. *Solar Energy*, 70, 295–310.

Ali-Toudert, F. 2005. Dependence of outdoor thermal comfort on street design. *Berichte des Meteorologischen Institutes der Universität Freiburg*, November No. 15. 2005 SRC – Google Scholar.

ANSYS. 2014. RE: FLUENT 6. Ansys, 2006. FLUENT 6-3 Getting Started Guide. http://users.abo.fi/rzevenho/ansys%20fluent%2018%20tutorial%20guide.pdf

Armson, D., Striner, P. & Ennos, A. R. 2012. The effect of tree shade and grass on surface and globe temperatures in an urban area. *Urban Forestry & Urban Greening*, 11, 245–255.

Bagge, J., Gaida, J. E., Danielson, P., Alfredson, H. & Forsgren, S. 2011. Physical activity level in Achilles tendinosis is associated with blood levels of pain-related factors: a pilot study. *Scandinavian Journal of Medicine & Science in Sports*, 21, e430–e438.

Borja, A., Bricker, S. B., Dauer, D. M., Demetriades, N. T., Ferreira, J. G., Forbes, A. T., et al. 2008. Overview of integrative tools and methods in assessing ecological integrity in estuarine and coastal systems worldwide. *Marine Pollution Bulletin*, 56, 1519–1537.

Bruse, M. 2009. RE: ENVI-met 3.1 Online Manual. www.envi-met.info/documents/onlinehelpv3/helpindex.htm

Deak Sjöman, J., Hirons, A. & Sjöman, H. 2016. Branch area index of solitaire trees – understanding its significant in regulating ecosystem services. *Journal of Environmental Quality*, 45(1), 175–187.

EEA. 2017. Climate change, impacts and vulnerability in Europe 2016. An indicator-based report. No. 1/2017. Copenhagen: European Environment Agency.

Eliasson, I., Erell, E., Pearlmutter, D., Williamson, T. & Earthscan, I. 2011. Urban nocturnal temperatures, street geometry and land use. *Atmospheric Environment*, 30, 379–392.

Elnabawi, M. H., Hamza, N. & Dudek, S. 2013. Use and evaluation of the ENVI-met model for two different urban forms in Cairo, Egypt. Measurements and model simulations. Presented at the 13th Conference of the International Building Perfomance Simulation Association, Chambéry, France, 26–28 August 2013.

ENVI-met. 2017. *Microclimate Simulations with ENVI-met Version 4*. Essen: ENVI-MET GmbH.

Erell, E., Pearlmutter, D. & Williamson, T. 2011. *Urban Microclimate – Designing the Spaces between Buildings*. London: Earthscan

European Commission. 2014. The European Union explained: climate action. Report. 16 pp. DOI:10.2775/83031

Fanger, P. O. 1970. *Thermal Comfort: Analysis and Applications in Environmental Engineering*. Copenhagen: Danish Technical Press.

Fröhlich, D. A. & Matzarakis, A. 2013. Modeling of changes in thermal bioclimate: examples based on urban spaces in Freiburg, Germany. *Theoretical and Applied Climatology*, 111, 547–558.

Gál, T., Lindberg, F. & Unger, J. 2009. Computing continuous sky view factors using 3D urban raster and vector databases: comparison and application to urban climate. *Theoretical and Applied Climatology.*, 95, 111–123.

Glaumann, M. & Nord, N. 1993. *Uteklimat. Stad & Land*, Vol. 133. Report from the Swedish University of Agricultural Sciences and Statens Institut för Byggnadsforskning.

Glaumann, M. & Westerberg, U. 1988. *Klimatplanering Vind*. Gävle: Statens institut för Byggnadsforskning.

Grahn, P., Unger, J. & Matzarakis, A. 2003. Landscape planning and stress. *Urban Forestry and Urban Greening*, 2, 1–18.

Gulyás, Á., Unger, J. & Matzarakis, A. 2006. Assessment of the microclimatic and thermal comfort conditions in a complex urban environment: modelling and measurements. *Building and Environment*, 4, 1713–1722.

Honjo, T. 2009. Thermal comfort in outdoor environment. *Global Environmental Research*, 13, 43–47.

Höppe, P. J. 1999. The physiological equivalent temperature – a universal index for the biometeorological assessment of the thermal environment. *International Journal of Biometeorology*, 43(2), 71–75.

Huttner, S. & Bruse, M. 2009. Numerical modeling of the urban climate – a preview on ENVI-met 4.0. Presented at the 7th International Conference on Urban Climate ICUC-7, Yokohama, Japan.

Huttner, S., Bruse, M. & Dostal, P. 2008. Using ENVI-met to simulate the impact of global warming on the microclimate in central European cities. *In*: Mayer, H. & Matzarakis, A. (eds.) *Berichte des Meteorologischen Instituts der Albert-Ludwigs-Universität Freiburg Nr. 18 (2008): 5th Japanese-German Meeting on Urban Climatology*, pp. 307–312. Freiburg: Meteorologischen Institut.

Jendritzky, G., De Dear, R. & Havenith, G. 2012. UTCI – why another thermal index? *International Journal of Biometeorology*, 56, 421–428.

Johansson, E., Spangenberg, J., Gouvea, M. L. & Freitas, E. D. 2013. Scale-integrated atmospheric simulations to assess thermal comfort in different urban tissues in the warm humid summer of São Paulo, Brazil. *Urban Climate*, 6, 24–43.

Katzschner, L. 2011. Urban climate strategies against future heat stress conditions. *In*: Otto-Zimmermann, K. (ed.) *Resilient Cities*. Dordrecht: Springer.

Kronvall, G. A. & Johansson, E. 2011. Sommaren är längre i kvarteret Spårvägen! *PLAN*, 65, 33–36.

Lindberg, F. A. & Grimmond, C. S. B. 2011. The influence of vegetation and building morphology on shadow patterns and mean radiant temperatures in urban areas: model development and evaluation. *Theoretical and Applied Climatology*, 105, 311–323.

Lindberg, F., Grimmond, C. S. B., Gabey, A., Huang, B., Kent, C.W., Sun, T., et al. 2018. Urban Multi-scale Environmental Predictor (UMEP) – an integrated tool for city-based climate services. *Environmental Modelling & Software*, 99, 70–87.

Lindberg, F., Holmer, B. & Thorsson, S. 2008. SOLWEIG 1.0 – modelling spatial variations of 3D radiant fluxes and mean radiant temperature in complex urban settings. *International Journal of Biometeorology*, 52, 697–713.

Lindberg, F., Onomura, S. & Grimmond, C. S. B. 2016. Influence of ground surface characteristics on the mean radiant temperature in urban areas. *International Journal of Biometeorology*, 60, 1439–1452.

Littlefair, P. 2001. Daylight, sunlight and solar gain in the urban environment. *Solar Energy*, 70, 177–185.

Lohmeyer. 2014. *OpenFOAM* [Online]. www.lohmeyer.de/en/node/529

Matzarakis, A. 2009. Additional features of the RayMan model. Presented at the Seventh International Conference on Urban Climate, Yokohama, Japan, 29 June–3 July 2009.

Matzarakis, A. & Matuschek, O. 2011. Sky view factor as a parameter in applied climatology – rapid estimation by the SkyHelios model. *Meteorologische Zeitschrift*, 20, 39–45.

Matzarakis, A., Rutz, F. & Mayer, H. 2007. Modelling radiation fluxes in simple and complex environments – application of the RayMan model. *International Journal of Biometeorology*, 51, 323–334.

Matzarakis, A., Rutz, F. & Mayer, H. 2010. Modelling radiation fluxes in simple and complex environments: basics of the RayMan model. *International Journal of Biometeorology*, 54, 131–139.

Mayer, H. & Höppe, P. 1987. Thermal comfort of man in different urban environments. *Theoretical and Applied Climatology*, 38, 43–49.

Media, B. V., Konarska, J., Lindberg, F., Larsson, A., Thorsson, S. & Holmer, B. 2014. Transmissivity of solar radiation through crowns of single urban trees – application for outdoor thermal comfort modelling. *Theoretical and Applied Climatology*, 117, 363–376.

Ne'Eman, E. 1974. Visual aspects of sunlight in buildings. *Lighting Research and Technology*, 3, 159–164.

Nikoofard, N. & Fazli, H. 2011. Free-energy barrier for electric-field-driven polymer entry into nanoscale channels. *Physical Review E*, 83(5 Pt 1), 050801.

Oke, A. F. 1987. *Boundary Layer Climates*. 2nd ed. London: Methuen.

Oke, T. R., Mills, G., Christen, A. & Voogt, J. A. 2017. *Urban Climates*. Cambridge: Cambridge University Press.

Ozkeresteci, I., Crewe, K., Brazel, A. J., Bruse, M. & South, D. 2003. Use and evaluation of the ENVI-met model for environmental design and planning: and experiment on linear parks. Presented at the 21st International Cartographic Conference ICC, 10–16 August 2003.

Puliafito, S. E., Bochaca, F. R., Allende, D. G. & Fernandez, R. P. 2013. Green areas and microscale thermal comfort in arid environment. A case study in Mendoza, Argentina. *Atmospheric and Climate Sciences*, 3, 372–384.

Sawka, M., Millward, A. A., McKay, J. & Sarkovich, M. 2013. Growing summer energy conservation through residential tree planting. *Landscape and Urban Planning*, 113, 1–9.

Thorsson, S., Lindberg, F., Eliasson, I. & Holmer, B. 2007. Different methods for estimating the mean radiant temperature in an outdoor urban setting. *International Journal of Climatology*, 27, 1983–1993.

Unger, J., Matzarakis, A., Hämmerle, M. & Gál, T. 2011. Comparison of models calculating the sky view factor used for urban climate investigations. *Theoretical and Applied Climatology*, 105, 521–527.

Urban Climate Group. 2013. *SOLWEIG – a Climate Design Tool. User Manual for Version A.* Gothenburg: Urban Climate Group, Department of Earth Sciences, University of Gothenburg.

Xiao, Z. & Wedd, A. G. 2002. A C-terminal domain of the membrane copper pump Ctr1 exchanges copper(I) with the copper chaperone Atx1. *Chemical Communications (Cambridge, England)*, 588–589.

Yahia, M. W. & Johansson, E. 2014. Landscape interventions in improving thermal comfort in the hot dry city of Damascus, Syria – the example of residential spaces with detached buildings. *Landscape and Urban Planning*, 125, 1–16.

Yahia, M. W., Johansson, E., Thorsson, S., Lindberg, F. & Rasmussen, M. I. 2018. Effect of urban design on microclimate and thermal comfort outdoors in warm-humid Dar es Salaam, Tanzania. *International Journal of Biometeorology*, 62, 373–385.

8 Data Mining, Machine Learning and Spatial Data Infrastructures for Scenario Modelling

Neil Sang and Matthew Aitkenhead

8.1 INTRODUCTION

The models discussed in other chapters in this book relate (generally) to some form of simulation or representation in a formal modelling language. The range of computational or technological complexity involved is variable, but in most cases a very high degree of domain knowledge is also required with respect to the system under investigation. This presupposes that such expertise is available, and indeed that it is sufficient to understand and represent a particular system. For large coupled systems with a wide range of socio-economic, ecological and biophysical systems interacting, this may not be feasible. As with nature itself, NBS are often part of a complex web of interdependent systems so this chapter explores data mining as a pragmatic alternative/complementary approach when systems are insufficiently well described by current theory or where domain expertise is in short supply. Examples are provided in Table 8.1.

A key distinction in modelling approaches is between inductive and deductive approaches. In scenario models that might be considered the primary distinction is between the simulation component whereby a response is 'deduced' from scientifically understood principles, and components which rely on 'externalities' – parameters provided a priori such as a future climate scenario that has to be been inductively estimated from historical trends. Where simulation is impractical (perhaps because the system is not sufficiently well understood) a pragmatic scenario may still be inferred, but it must be recognised that the trends upon which such predictions rest are also changing.

Externalities are often used to maintain simplicity by focusing modelling time only on the response of the phenomena of interest rather than contextual factors. It may be appreciated that these 'external' parameters and trends do, in fact, respond to the model phenomena over some other spatial or temporal scale, but simulating that reciprocal response is deemed impossible or unnecessary. In situations where a sophisticated Integrated Assessment Model (Refsgaard et al., 2006) is desired, feedback loops can be incorporated between different environmental systems and human behaviour by chaining together several models; however, the output can quickly become impossible to verify. Various strategies have been suggested to try to assess their utility, such as multiple competing models (Refsgaard et al., 2006), but given that every additional model used adds another layer of complexity to be supplied with data, parameterised, computed and assessed, it is hard to see such an approach being feasible in an applied setting. Emulating (rather than mechanistically simulating) some of these models (those of lesser interest or which are less well understood) with a statistical approximation established from observed relationships between coupled systems can be one means to limit the spread of error and so keep subsequent modelling stages operating on realistic input scenarios. For example, 'mechanistic fire modelling across large landscapes may be inherently intractable' (Cushman et al., 2006), so it may not be possible to simulate precisely where a fire will spread, but it is possible to predict the total burnt area (Safi & Bourami, 2013) and then use GIS to identify likely spatial scenarios. As a means to design NBS with the aim of ensuring the long-term sustainability of the ecosystem, this is still a useful piece of information.

Traditionally, inference of a relationship between two or more parameters would be achieved from statistical analysis of observed data. Machine learning broadens the range of techniques available such that one need not assume an underlying theoretical statistical distribution. Instead, the approach is to leverage iterative optimisation algorithms to explore the entire parameter space for relationships and so predict patterns which are too complex to be represented by analytical equations.

Data mining, the practice of seeking patterns without a prior hypothesis as to what kind of relationship one is expecting to find, has grown in popularity due to the advent of 'big data', a fashionable term referring to the development of data sets which are so large even very finely nuanced effects reflecting a small proportion of the data set can be identified with statistical significance. Data fishing refers to the problem that, given enough data, entirely spurious relationships are likely to be found simply through random chance, particularly if one does not begin the enquiry with a specific null hypothesis (Webb, 2007). Statistically sound association discovery (Webb, 2007) reduces the danger of finding spurious relationships, but does not abrogate the user from the responsibility of considering whether inferring a causal connection is realistic.

> Data mining derives its name from the similarities between searching for valuable business information in a large database ... and mining a mountain for a vein of valuable ore. Both processes require either sifting through an immense amount of material, or intelligently probing it to find exactly where the value resides. (Sumathi & Sivandam, 2006)

The challenge for many applied NBS projects is the breadth of domain expertise needed to explore the many dimensions of the issue. Of course, deploying data-mining methods also requires a type of expertise which is increasingly in demand, but the key difference is that this expertise is not domain-specific. It can be deployed to sift material on a range of subject matter, including cases where scientific theory has no more intelligent solution to offer.

8.2 SEVEN COMMON CLASSES OF DATA-MINING TASK[1]

Anomaly detection identifies outliers, i.e. unusual data or potential errors requiring further attention. For example, analysing satellite imagery of forest disturbance due to disease or pests (Chávez et al.,

1 Adapted from Fayyad, U., Piatetsky-Shapiro, G. & Smyth, P. 1996. From data mining to knowledge discovery in databases. *AI Magazine*, Fall, 37–54 (with examples added).

2019), aiding planning for both short-term responses and long-term probable disturbance scenarios.

Association rule learning finds relationships within data which suggest that, if given conditions are met, some further outcome is statistically likely to occur, e.g. tourists are likely to visit sites X and Y if they stayed at hotel of type Z (Versichele et al., 2014), aiding planning for public transport and tourism promotion.

Clustering group observations based on similarity. This might be based on characteristics, e.g. demographic information for people, or heights of trees, etc. Alternatively, it could be grouping based on context, e.g. where or when the data were observed. Clustering is useful for identifying subsystems at work and for identifying comparison scenarios (e.g. to validate if a model predicts all observed circumstances equally well; Fung et al., 2010).

Classification involves generalising into a particular structure (classes) in order to emphasise a certain relevant aspect. IT communications can be classified in real time to monitor perceived environmental issues (e.g. eutrophication; TWC, 2012). Land cover can be classified to represent land use (e.g. for forestry in Sweden see Reese, 2011) or land capability for a particular purpose such as agriculture (Bibby et al., 1991).

Regression determines a function which models a trend in the data by minimising the difference between the value of the function and the value of the observed data. Regression methods include quantitative (linear, multi-linear, non-linear, geographically weighted) or frequentist (logistic) which assume an underlying analytical distribution, or Bayesian which seek to estimate an underlying distribution through Monte Carlo simulation (Zurr et al., 2007). For example Dramstad and colleagues (Dramstad & Sang, 2010; Sang et al., 2014) use a combination of linear, logistic and geographically weighted regression to explore the system of farmland ownership in Norway and the possible risk that abandonment presents to landscape as an NBS for tourism. It is worth mentioning here also the role of Extreme Value Theory, which focuses on the 'tail' of a distribution to calculate the probability that rare but extreme events may occur, as it is often these (peak temperature, 1000-year flood level, etc.) which pose the greatest risk when they happen (e.g. Mudersbach & Jensen, 2010).

Interpolation estimates the implications of known parameters in one place or time for those of another place or time based on believed common explanatory variables. For example, it could be used to spatially predict the utility of an NBS given its proximity to possible users (Mokondoko et al., 2018).

Summarisation provides a brief set of descriptors that give an overview of the data. This may be mathematical (i.e. descriptive statistics such as mean and variance) or visual via graphs, maps and report generation. Indicators combine several dimensions into one measure, for example different kinds of vegetation into a general value for biodiversity, but it is critical that each component metric can be measured in a comparable way for all cases because the underlying calculations may become obscured. Temporal summarisation – e.g. average rainfall over a given time period – can provide an easier comparison between two time periods or allow the trend to emerge from noisy data. Spatial summaries apply the same principle within spatial units showing trends over space, including NBS-relevant metrics such as tree canopy density. For example, the city of Dublin, Ireland, is using dashboards to help summarise for its citizens how NBS support their lives (www.dublindashboard.ie/pages/index).

8.3 SEVEN COMMON DATA-MINING TECHNIQUES[2]

Artificial neural networks (ANNs): Maps inputs to output through a network of weightings that are altered through repeated training by

[2] This list of techniques is an adaption and extension of those discussed in the white paper 'An introduction to data mining: discovering hidden value in your data warehouse' by Kurt Thearling (2003). At the time of press a copy is available here: http://akira.ruc.dk/~bulskov/undervisning/E2003/data_mining.pdf.

comparison between examples of input and expected output in order to reduce error rates. A generalisable approach which can predict highly non-linear outcomes, but that can be hard to interpret in order to understand the relationships between input and output parameters.

> The main advantages of using ANNs are their flexibility and ability to model non-linear relationships. The neural network is an alternative to the parameter-intensive physically based models in applications that do not rely on the subjacent physics of the system dynamics. (Kankal & Yüksek, 2012)

The examples found tended to use ANNs to address problems where a mechanistic model was either too time-consuming or too hard to calibrate. Common applications include predicting the response of populations (e.g. Wei et al., 2001; Sholahuddin et al., 2015) to environmental and anthropogenic drivers and, perhaps due to the tempting but limited parallel with the human brain, in modelling human perception and cognition both individually and as a collective, e.g. in relation to environmental Common Pool Resource Problems (Frey & Rusch, 2013). Because they operate by weighting a decision surface using 'Case-based Reasoning' about whether the predicted outcome is 'correct', ANNs present one method of eliciting expert knowledge from which to emulate decisions even when the experts themselves may not have a clear view of what drives their decisions (so-called 'tacit' knowledge) (Nemati et al., 2003). It is arguable that their use has been something of a 'catch-all' solution where more informative models have failed:

> There is little doubt that ANNs have the potential to be a useful tool for the prediction and forecasting of water resources variables ... ANNs need to be viewed as alternatives to more traditional approaches in certain situations and not as '... a remedy for all existing computational failings' (Flood and Kartam, 1994).
> (Maier & Dandy, 2000)

For applied purposes, Maier and Dandy's concern for theoretical rigour is perhaps less compelling, provided the predictions can be demonstrated to be accurate and the input parameters are both logical and amenable to policy changes. On the other hand, ANNs rely on translating between inputs and outputs using continuous functions, which means that they cannot model discrete relationships as effectively as other approaches. There is also often a stated concern about the risk of 'over-fitting' such that the responses within the known parameter space may no longer apply to future scenarios for which there is not yet training data available. However, ANNs do not over-fit any more than other methods described here if used correctly, and this concern can be obviated using appropriate data set splitting and training approaches (e.g. *k*-fold cross-validation). Nonetheless, ANNs are probably better suited to predicting responses to limited changes in current scenarios rather than longer-term future scenarios which historical training data may not encompass.

Decision trees: Structures that represent sets of decisions where each 'branch' shows a different decision path history, thus creating a 'tree'. Helpful for seeing the possible outcomes of different decisions and grouping decisions at different scales (for example, when classifying an image – Grass/Tree > Deciduous/Coniferous > Species of Coniferous) or clustering together net predicted outcomes of different policy decisions.

Decision trees can be applied to a wide range of applications across all the domains of interest here. Examples were commonly found where discrete differentiation is required between a hierarchy of circumstances leading to a likely outcome. It is unsurprising, therefore, to see the use of decision trees for rule induction, trying to 'step back' through the decisions which have been made in determining a given land use and thus hope to infer future decision-making strategies of land owners (Pal & Mather, 2003; Aalders & Aitkenhead, 2006).

Genetic algorithms (GAs): Optimisation techniques that start with many possible algorithms and combine or slightly alter them at random, maintaining only those that are most successful, thus mimicking natural selection.

The main applications of GAs are to situations where multiple parameters exist and the parameter space is complex and non-linear. They are suitable for finding local 'good' solutions within the parameter space (or for finding a slightly better solution than the existing one) and less so when the best 'global' solution needs to be found. Examples in environmental modelling include calibration of process models, identification of sample point distribution patterns, or resource distribution planning for management decisions (Aitkenhead & Aalders, 2009).

Fuzzy classification: A technique that classifies each record in a data set based on a combination of the classes of those records most similar to it in a historical data set such that likely outcomes might be inferred by looking at previous outcomes from similar, but not identical, circumstances.

This approach allows an 'unknown' piece of evidence to be related to known data using metrics of distance within the phase-space of the parameters used. The fuzzy membership allocates a measure of similarity to each record or cluster of records, and can be used to give a measure of membership of each cluster/class or to provide a 'crisp' classification to a single cluster. A number of comparison approaches exist, ranging from the most simple (nearest neighbour) to more sophisticated methods taking into account the distribution of values within each parameter (fuzzy *k*-means with expectation-maximisation algorithm).

Dimensional analysis: Structuring data so that they can be queried or visualised as a dimension of change. The purpose of dimensional analysis is to simplify the relationships between variables by reducing the range of units, and it is thus a somewhat similar idea to factoring of fractions. It is a more general case of normalisation, and is important to allow display of key relationships between variables via Principle Component Analysis (PCA) and Redundancy Analysis (RDA), which in turn provide methods to 'exclude' less important dimensions of variance from the analysis.

Bayesian belief networks: Incorporating expressed beliefs as to how components of a systems interact within a quantitative model.

Not strictly a data-mining approach, but included here as a means of structuring the data-mining process (Aitkenhead & Aalders, 2009), and including stakeholder or expert beliefs within that structure. Bayesian mathematics is a branch of statistics which aims to avoid assuming a given distribution model, such as the Gaussian or Poisson distribution. Instead, a general form of an equation is developed with a given number of parameters and 'prior beliefs' (operators) as to the possible relations between them. The shape of the distribution is estimated based on these beliefs and compared with empirical evidence (Troldborg et al., 2013). In many cases the empirical evidence is only available for parts of a complex system, but experts or other stakeholders with experience of that system are able to indicate other relevant factors and estimate the strength of relationships between these factors and those which can be empirically measured. By comparing the outcome of the overall system with that predicted given the experts' beliefs, one can then begin to objectively consider whether those beliefs are correct. BBN are thus a means to represent beliefs within a model, but also a technique for qualitative rule induction (Marcot et al., 2006).

Geographically weighted regression: GWR is a powerful tool for analysing and visualising the spatially dependent relationship between two or more variables (Fotheringham et al., 2002). This helps to take into account spatial autocorrelation (Borrough & McDonnel, 1998), which may confound standard regression because two apparently independent variables may appear to be statistically correlated (e.g. vegetation type and house price) when they are in fact only co-dependent on an unidentified third variable (e.g. terrain aspect).

GWR can also help us to understand how regionality affects relationships between variables; for example, the relationship between changes in farm ownership structure and rates of farm abandonment may be altered by other factors such as landscape type or the presence of a significant urban area. GWR helps to separate out the different regional systems at work (Sang et al., 2014). Geographically weighted versions of PCA have also been developed (Lloyd, 2010). It therefore provides a powerful tool for understanding what factors are in play where, and therefore how NBS might be either deployed as a solution or face future threats to their functions (Case Study 8.1).

CASE STUDY 8.1 Modelling the NBS of Agricultural Land; Examples from the Norwegian Institute of Bioeconomy Research (NIBIO)

Farming represents perhaps the single most important way in which humans harness nature to our own purpose, providing not only food, fuel and fibre but also cultural ecosystem services such as landscape recreation. The process may be highly industrialised in many places, but it is nonetheless a continual management of natural systems and as such, should that management cease, a number of natural systems will begin to reassert themselves with potentially complex consequences which are dependent on *where* this takes place.

For example, agricultural land represents just 3% of the surface area of Norway. That rarity makes it an important component of biodiversity resources by providing a home to species not found in the largely forest and moorland ecology elsewhere. Furthermore, while natural forest is generally considered to provide an NBS to counter rising atmospheric CO_2, forest regrowth in some parts of Norway may in fact negatively impact climate change due to the warming effects of the dark colour of the natural forests (de Wit et al., 2014) compared with grass and rock exposed by grazing.

Given the significant role of production subsidies to the Norwegian agricultural system this may appear to provide a simple mechanism to counter such effects. However, agricultural land management presents an increasingly complex web of actors, with some areas being managed by a single business as a large number of tenancies (Dramstad & Sang, 2010). Whether tenanting contributes greater resilience to – or greater vulnerability to – land abandonment is complex and spatially

CASE STUDY 8.1 **(cont.)**

dependent. GWR can be applied to understand where rising tenancy rates may indicate land is at risk of abandonment (Figure 8.1) (Sang et al., 2014).

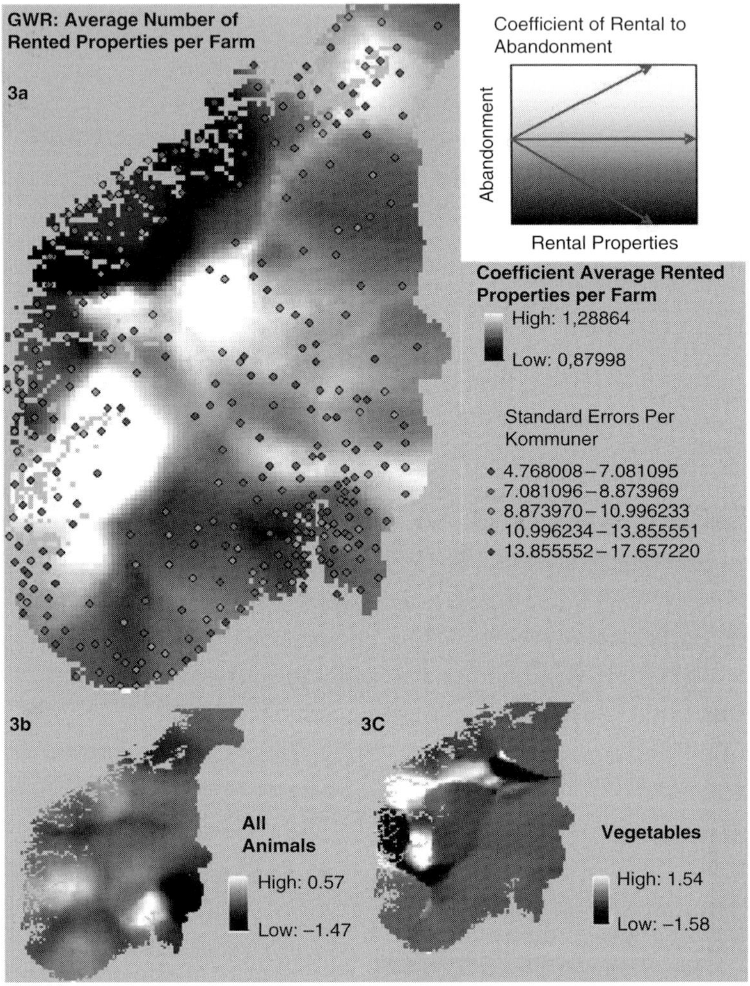

FIGURE 8.1 Geographically weighted regression of farm production data in 2000 against rate of farm abandonment in 2010 (Sang et al., 2014). (A black and white version of this figure will appear in some formats. For the colour version, please refer to the plate section.)

CASE STUDY 8.1 **(cont.)**

The net balance of benefits and risks from agricultural land abandonment are highly dependent on what network effects may result with e.g. greater habitat disruption from one pattern of abandonment than another (Zozaya et al., 2012). However, maintaining up-to-date maps for ecologically relevant land-use characteristics is extremely expensive because only a limited range of these can be obtained from satellite or areal photography. Fieldwork is usually only possible on a sample basis, which is insufficient to properly describe the habitat connectivity. So Aune-Lundberg and Bryn (2018) are deploying Maximum Entropy models to predict species distribution from the field sample data. This would allow landscape planners to ensure that development (or indeed natural regrowth) is not inadvertently allowed to break the vital corridors which provide habitat at the landscape scale.

A notable recent extension to this is Geographical and Temporal Weighted Regression (GTWR) (Fotheringham et al., 2015). The time dimension is particularly important to NBS, which are inherently dynamic systems. Climate change is a good example where the weightings between cause and effect have been changing over time as feedback effects come into play. So if NBS are to be dimensioned for a future point in time, models of the impact they could have needs to take this into account.

8.4 SUPPORTING NBS WITH SPATIAL DATA INFRASTRUCTURES

Data mining, as with all forms of scientific enquiry, benefits greatly from straightforward access to data. Accessing a greater range of data can, assuming a statistically sound approach to association, improve a model by providing explanatory factors to confounding issues. For example, information on anthropogenic pressure across a woodland may not exist in an ecology database, but data collected for an entirely separate purpose such as car park maintenance planning might serve as a proxy to explain spatial variance in the ecological observations due to anthropogenic disturbance.

For complex integrative models, one of the largest costs may be sourcing the necessary data for each component model. This is particularly so when components demand data produced and held by institutions and people outwith the personal networks of the modeller. In these circumstances it is often difficult to even know what information is available outwith one's field of expertise, let alone where to source it.

The primary purpose of a Spatial Data Infrastructure (SDI) is to simplify the identification and locating of data via provision of metadata in a standardised form. Metadata provide a summary of what information a database contains, such as subject, the location and time period and data owner. Ideally some indication will also be given as to the provenance of the data, quality of the observations, spatial scale and so forth.

In order for data mining to make the best use of the available data resources, it is necessary for this metadata system to operate to common standards to allow a computer algorithm to find the relevant data. It must also be connected to a system of automated access to the data resources so that algorithms may draw on all the available data as required. However, this entails some system of access control to ensure only those entitled to access may do so, and possibly some form of payment mechanism where data have commercial value. The development of data distribution mechanisms is thus an organisational challenge as much as a technological one. In principle, however, automated access should both save money directly as this need no longer be undertaken manually, and leverage greater use from the investment the data represent.

Access to data alone is not sufficient to leverage the benefits of data mining. The data themselves must bear some degree of compatibility. Where two different sources are being used to compile a larger data set (e.g. soil data in adjacent regions) classification may appear to be similar, but do the terms used refer to the same thing and is this also what the end-user understands it to mean? To some degree interpolation methods and classification look-up tables may be used to make data comparable (Feiden et al., 2012), but it can also introduce errors and artefacts such that false relationships are found and real relationships hidden (Sang et al., 2005; Swift et al., 2008; Briant et al., 2010; Su et al., 2011; Mitra & Buliung, 2012; Sabel et al., 2013; Houston, 2014). Mining 'big data' is thus not an alternative to employing statistical skills, but rather requires careful and knowledgeable scrutiny.

Ultimately, comparable data require coordination at the collection stage, and that entails collaboration and cooperation between collecting agencies which they may not support (Sang et al., 2005). For example, ensuring the representation of 'spatial minorities' – rare populations or unusual geographical contexts – is in some respects contradictory to the drivers of commercial funding models of data collection.

A key choice when considering how to develop an SDI is the balance between 'products' and 'processes' (Rajabifard et al., 2003; Williamson et al., 2003). Products are specific services, such as common databases. They are usually managed by a 'Single Coordinating Body' (Sang et al., 2005) able to control the upload of data and thus both ensure their quality and manage access rights. While such an approach provides for a product which can be tailored to a particular end-user's requirements, it requires funding for staff time and equipment to support the process as well as the ability to persuade data collection agencies to participate. For this reason, product SDI are usually limited to state-managed data, the TIGER data set run by the US Geological Service being one of the oldest and best-known examples (www.census.gov/geo/maps-data/data/tiger.html). The Swedish Geodata Portal also represents the beginning of such a product approach (www.geodata.se/). Beyond providing a central access point, such SDI need to provide a commitment to maintain an Application Programming Interface for access to the data sets, and a common statistical base, to fully utilise data mining.

'Process' SDIs do not seek to create single databases. Rather, they are a managerial approach whereby interested parties begin to negotiate common standards which allow their data to be more easily identified, accessed and ultimately become more compatible and intraoperative. How far down that road the process reaches, and what kinds of data become available, is thus dependent on the interest of participants. Some coordinating body is still required to manage that process, and perhaps provide some core architecture to host metadata, but they do not direct the process. Rather, agencies which collect data as part of their own operational purpose see a mutual benefit to contributing to the system, perhaps in order to gain access to other's data or create a wider user base for their own. Realistically, unless the parties are interested in funding this work, success depends on achieving some mutual benefit without impeding each participant's core activities. For example, compliance with the INSPIRE (http://inspire.ec.europa.eu/) legislation when collecting and storing data should result in less additional work when providing environmental data to the European Union.

GEOSS is a global project providing one example of how a process may be implemented for gradually improving coordination, which ultimately can produce products such as a portal with API access (www.geoportal.org/), but it is worth noting coordinating efforts have received direct institutional and financial support from national governments, European Union and United Nations sources.

The same principles that determine data availability also apply to models themselves. In theory, decisions could be made more effectively and models developed more cheaply if some means existed to allow their use to be shared (Nativi et al., 2013). Models as a Service (MaaS) approaches which deliver the modelling capability via web portals offer one means of improving access to modelling resources at a local level. In particular, it could allow sourcing several competing models for comparison (see, for example, the UncertWeb project; Bastin et al., 2013). However, it requires central resourcing both in terms of IT infrastructure and support to end-users. In the case of both data and software, the issue with their wider distribution is threefold: how to identify their existence and capabilities; how to manage access and intellectual property rights; and how to provide end-user support services.

8.5 SDI FOR NBS

The oldest and arguably most complete SDI is the National Spatial Data Infrastructure (NSDI) in the USA (www.fgdc.gov/nsdi). This includes most of the Earth Observation data from both NASA (e.g. Landsat (https://landsat.usgs.gov/) and NOAA (e.g. https://www.goes.noaa.gov). The length of time for which data are available is of critical value when monitoring change in large-scale systems. For example, artificial intelligence (AI) has been applied to Landsat data to monitor and/or model a wide range of NBS from monitoring drought risk for the whole continent of Africa in order to direct mitigation measures (Vicente-Serrano et al., 2012) to mapping Land Use Land Cover change in the Himalayas via tree-based ensemble classification (Chakraborty et al., 2016). It can also be applied to more detailed scales such as measuring Leaf Area Index for the city of Terre Haute (Indiana, USA) with neural networks where vegetation may be hard to statistically distinguish from the complex urban fabric without very high-resolution imagery (Jensen et al., 2009). Of course this need not always require AI; human interpretation of imagery can also yield useful results – for example, helping to understand the effect of armed conflict as a driver of migration and urban expansion in areas where fieldwork is hard to access (Pech & Lakes, 2017).

Importantly, the NSDI also provides, within the USA, a Topologically Integrated Geographic Encoding and Referencing (TIGER) (Carbaugh & Marx, 1990) system which helps ensure other forms of data (e.g. census) are collected to a nested set of Basic Spatial Units (BSUs) (Sang et al., 2005), allowing information from multiple sources to be compared without introducing artefacts due to non-nesting statistical units (Openshaw, 1984). BSUs are especially important if AI is to be used for more speculative data mining in order to fulfil what Professor Stan Openshaw termed the 'moral imperative …

to use the information for the betterment of people's lives' (Openshaw, 1996b) once it has been collected. This imperative to analyse the data resources we have is arguably still not being sufficiently addressed (or at least not in the way we may have then hoped; Openshaw, 1996a).

The European INSPIRE project also sought to achieve a degree of harmonisation, particularly in respect of environmental data (e.g. Geodata Services Soil; Feiden et al., 2012). With respect to socio-economic data the Nomenclature of Territorial Units for Statistics (NTUS) system provides a common basis for statistical reporting, but only down to 'small regions' covering perhaps one county, municipality or arrondissement with far greater variation in definition compared with the US TIGER Line files which support the USGS National Census (USGS, 2018). However, the EU through its Earth Observation and research-data collation networks GEOSS (Nativi et al., 2014) and COPERNICUS (Hřebíček et al., 2015) has placed particular emphasis on not only monitoring of threats to ecosystem services such as heavy metal pollutants (Nativi et al., 2014) but applying this knowledge within Horizon 2020 projects to test methods such as renaturing cities (European Commission, 2015). This said, it is notable that in projects aiming to provide greater decision support for those tasked with planning at larger scales, e.g. for management of natural resources in cities (e.g. www.bridge-fp7.eu/), considerable effort is still required in the initial data acquisition and harmonisation steps, particularly because more detailed spatial data are still often restricted by licensing issues at the national level (Sang & Ode-Sang, 2015) and lack a 'single coordinating body' to ensure pan-European harmonisation (Sang et al., 2005).

The problem is particularly acute in countries without extensive national mapping and environmental monitoring systems. The United Nations supports efforts to develop national-level SDI (www.unsdi.nl/) and to coordinate SDI effort on global systems such as food supply

(FAO2016 I5322E/1/01.16; www.fao.org/3/a-i5322e.pdf), but data access and harmonisation remains a significant problem facing attempts to use data more effectively in support of NBS globally. While this remains so, it seems unrealistic to expect that time-pressed local authorities will opt to use more than simple models in their spatial planning (Sang & Ode-Sang, 2015). However, that means models which are simple to set up and use, rather than simplistic in nature. So machine learning methods such as ANN and tacit knowledge capture approaches such as Bayesian belief networks can also help to fill gaps in data by 'learning' from local knowledge.

8.6 SEMANTIC ANALYSIS AND SPATIAL INDEXING

A key difference between SDI for environmental modelling in general and SDI for participatory planning in particular is that much of the data relating to planning proposals are not quantitative and are not held within databases. The planning system tends to generate written reports wherein qualitative information on stakeholder responses is quoted directly, or statistically summarised to tables within these documents. Other information such as proposed development areas may be encoded in symbolic representation and presented only within pictorial maps – i.e. the information has never been formally digitised as a geographical object which is machine-readable.

Semantic analysis methodologies can go some way to extracting relevant information from traditional planning documentation held online (Brasethvik & Atle Gulla, 2001; Punitha & Punithavalli, 2012). Adoption of semantic web standards for information generation can help in collating operational data such as Building Information Modelling (BIM) (Abanda et al., 2013). This will also improve interoperability between types of software, such as GIS, BIM and simulation models.

Less ambitious technologically, but requiring some organisational and procedural standardisation, is to spatially index this information such that all relevant information pertaining to a particular location may be retrieved (Hill, 2006).

8.7 SUMMARY

Data-mining techniques can be useful in addressing NBS because they allow (a) inductive solutions to problems for which science has yet to provide a reliable theoretical model, and (b) deductive solutions to problems where scientific knowledge is sufficient but expertise is in short supply. It will not, generally, be a stand-alone solution as expertise is still needed to check the results are reasonable and provide interpretation, but it allows those experts to oversee more projects by reducing the workload. Key methods and NBS applications can be found in Table 8.1. The most important distinction to note is that of the *organisational* scale at which they might be used; these techniques require expert knowledge to calibrate but some can be made self-calibrating, while output from some calibrated models may be understood with domain expertise in the relevant environmental or planning field. Because these techniques principally rely on identifying trends and relationships in historical data, they are of limited use for future scenarios where new circumstances are expected (e.g. climate change) but are very useful for impact analysis in complex integrated scenarios.

Investment in a comprehensive and accessible SDI allows all modelling techniques to consider the widest range of factors possible by saving staff time in project design, data gathering, calibration and maintaining data currency. As such it increases the chances of modelling being deployed at all, and indeed is a valuable resource even where an NBS implementation is being planned in a traditional way without reference to computational models because resolving the related intellectual property and accessibility issues also allows more organisations and individuals to contribute to, and benefit from, available information.

Table 8.1 *Selected examples of data mining with NBS-relevant applications*

Example reference	Software used	Task/technique	NBS relevance	Goal
Mcleod et al. (2010)	MATLAB (Palani et al., 2008)	Clustering/ANN	Urban/perception	Prediction and grouping of factors by relative importance to net perceived service quality in public transport given data from a survey of passengers. 'ANN are proposed in this research because of its numerous advantages over more traditional parametric models (such as regression models, structural equation models or logit/probit models), but also over other non-parametric models, such as decision trees. ANNs provide higher fits of the phenomenon under study ... The main disadvantage of this approach is the duration of the calculus, since a large number of ANN must be trained and tested' (McLeod et al., 2010)
McLeod et al. (2010)	Xu et al. (2014)	Interpolation/ANN	Marine/ eutrophication	Prediction of water quality (salinity, temperature, dissolved oxygen and chlorophyll-a concentrations) in non-monitored locations of Singapore coastal waters both temporally and spatially using continuous weekly measurements of water quality variables at different stations

Table 8.1 (*cont.*)

Example reference	Software used	Task/technique	NBS relevance	Goal
TWC (2012)	GPKernel	Interpolation/ANN & GP	Marine/ eutrophication	Comparison of variable selection between ANN, GA and deterministic techniques, when predicting algal bloom in marine environment. Contains a particularly useful section on model variable selection methods
Webb (2007)		Regression and classification/ decision trees	Landscape/wildfire	Modelling the anthropogenic component of wildfire ignition. Comparison with linear regression
Reese (2011)		Classification	Marine/oil pollution	Comparison of seven different classifiers for detecting oil spills based on radar satellite imagery. NB: ANN do not perform well in this example
Maier and Dandy (2000)	NA	REVIEW/ANN	Marine/freshwater	This paper is an early review of the role of ANN in marine and freshwater modelling including a summary of 45 papers on the subject up to 1998
Langella et al. (2010)		Interpolation/ANN	Soil	Downscaling of precipitation for use in soil–vegetation–air transfer models. Comparison with geostatistics
Malekmohamadi et al. (2011)		Classification and interpolation/ANN, ANFIS	Marine/wave height	Compares several alternative machine learning algorithms for the estimation of wave height based on spatially sparse wave height data and temporally frequent wind speed data

Olawoyin (2013)	(GoldenSoftware, 2012) – visualisation and kriging only	Interpolation/ ANN, SOM	Marine/oil pollution	Uses ANN, self-organising maps and geostatistics to map likely exposure to various oil pollutants with respect to the manner of their absorption into the human body
Suryanarayana et al. (2008)		REVIEW: classification, interpolation. ANN, fuzzy logic, wavelets	Marine/fisheries	Reviews use of machine learning in fisheries research 1978–2008. 'Forecasting in fisheries covers distribution of eggs, recruitment, fish growth/age, biomass and fish catch. Other major areas are identification, abundance and food products, environmental factors and collapse of fishery industry.'
Alonso Fernández et al. (2014)		Regression (multivariate adaptive regression splines)	Freshwater/ eutrophication	Predicts eutrophication in a reservoir some days ahead based on monitored parameters. MARS fits polynomial regression splines to different sections of the data, thus allowing the function to change between system states
Areerachakul et al. (2013)		ANN	Freshwater	Prediction of dissolved oxygen content via supervised and unsupervised ANN to model impact of pollution
Ferrarini and Tomaselli (2010)		Association rules	Landscape	Modelling land-cover patch spatial adjacency for ecological networks. Association rules allow inference as to the probability of an ecological network of landscape patches based on how many relevant adjacencies there are between different types of land cover

Table 8.1 *(cont.)*

Example reference	Software used	Task/technique	NBS relevance	Goal
Levers et al. (2014)		Decision trees	Landscape/forestry	Uses boosted regression trees to spatially predict forest harvesting intensity across Europe based on biophysical and socio-economic explanatory variables
Marcot et al. (2006)		BBN		Review of the use of BBN in ecological modelling
Aitkenhead and Aalders (2009)	Netica	BBN, GA	Landscape/forestry	Combines genetic algorithms with Bayesian belief networks to predict land-use/land-cover change
Troldborg et al. (2013)		BBN	Soil	Uses BBN to identify risk to soil

REFERENCES

Aalders, I. H. & Aitkenhead, M. J. 2006. Agricultural census data and land use modelling. *Computers, Environment and Urban Systems*, 30, 799–814.

Abanda, F. H., Tah, J. H. M. & Keivani, R. 2013. Trends in built environment semantic Web applications: where are we today? *Expert Systems with Applications*, 40, 5563–5577.

Aitkenhead, M. J. & Aalders, I. H. 2009. Predicting land cover using GIS, Bayesian and evolutionary algorithm methods. *Journal of Environmental Management*, 90, 236–250.

Alonso Fernández, J. R., García Nieto, P. J., Díaz Muñiz, C. & Álvarez Antón, J. C. 2014. Modeling eutrophication and risk prevention in a reservoir in the Northwest of Spain by using multivariate adaptive regression splines analysis. *Ecological Engineering*, 68, 80–89.

Areerachakul, S., Sophatsathit, P. & Lursinsap, C. 2013. Integration of unsupervised and supervised neural networks to predict dissolved oxygen concentration in canals. *Ecological Modelling*, 261–262, 1–7.

Aschwanden, G. D. P. A., Haegler, S., Bosché, F., Van Gool, L. & Schmitt, G. 2011. Empiric design evaluation in urban planning. *Automation in Construction*, 20, 299–310.

Aune-Lundberg, L. & Bryn, A. 2018. Spatial transferability of vegetation types in distribution models based on sample surveys from an Alpine region. *Journal of Geographic Information Systems*, 10, 111–141.

Bastin, L., Cornford, D., Jones, R., Heuvelink, G. B. M., Pebesma, E., Stasch, C., et al. 2013. Managing uncertainty in integrated environmental modelling: the UncertWeb framework. *Environmental Modelling & Software*, 29, 116–134.

Bibby, J. S., Douglas, H. A., Thomasson, A. J. & Robertson, J. S. 1991. *Land Capability Classification for Agriculture*. Aberdeen: The Macaulay Land Use Research Institute.

Borrough, P. & McDonnel, R. 1998. *Prcinciples of Geographical Information Systems: Spatial Information Sysems and Geostatistics*. Oxford: Oxford University Press.

Brasethvik, T. & Atle Gulla, J. 2001. Natural language analysis for semantic document modeling. *Data & Knowledge Engineering*, 38, 45–62.

Briant, A., Combes, P. P. & Lafourcade, M. 2010. Dots to boxes: do the size and shape of spatial units jeopardize economic geography estimations? *Journal of Urban Economics*, 67, 287–302.

Carbaugh, L. & Marx, R. 1990. The TIGER system: a census bureaux innovation serving data analysts. *Government Information Quarterly*, 7(3), 285–306.

Chakraborty, A., Sachdeva, K. & Joshi, P. K. 2016. Mapping long-term land use and land cover change in the central Himalayan region using a tree-based ensemble classification approach. *Applied Geography*, 74, 136–150.

Chávez, R. O., Rocco, R., Gutiérrez, Á. G., Dörner, M. & Estay, S. A. 2019. A self-calibrated non-parametric time series analysis approach for assessing insect defoliation of broad-leaved deciduous *Nothofagus pumilio* forests. *Remote Sensing*, 11, 204.

Cushman, S., Mckenzie, D., Peterson, D., Littell, J. & McKelvey, K. 2006. Research agenda for integrated landscape modeling. Presented at the 21st Annual Symposium of the United States Regional Chapter of the International Association for Landscape Ecology, San Diego, CA, 28–31 March 2006. www.fs.fed.us/rm/pubs_other/rmrs_2006_cushman_s002.pdf

De Wit, H. A., Bryn, A., Hofgaard, A., Karstensen, J., Kvalevag, M. M. & Peters, G. P. 2014. Climate warming feedback from mountain birch forest expansion: reduced albedo dominates carbon uptake. *Global Chang Biology*, 20, 2344–2355.

Dramstad, W. E. & Sang, N. 2010. Tenancy in Norwegian agriculture. *Land Use Policy*, 27, 946–956.

European Commission. 2015. *Towards an EU Research and Innovation Policy Agenda for Nature-based Solutions & Re-naturing Cities. Final Report of the Horizon 2020 Expert Group on 'Nature-based Solutions and Re-naturing Cities'*. Brussels: European Commission.

Feiden, K., Kirchenbauer V., Kruse, F., Englisch, M., Leitgeb, E., Reiter, R., et al. 2012. Discover INSPIRE compliant harmonised soil data and services. Assessment and Strategic Development of INSPIRE compliant Geodata-Services for European Soil Data. ECP_2008_GEO_318004.

Ferrarini, A. & Tomaselli, M. 2010. A new approach to the analysis of adjacencies: potentials for landscape insights. *Ecological Modelling*, 221, 1889–1896.

Fotheringham, A. S., Brunsdon, C. & Charlton, M. 2002. *Geographically Weighted Regression: The Analysis of Spatially Varying Relationships*. Chichester: Wiley.

Fotheringham, A. S., Crespo, R. & Yao, J. 2015. Geographical and temporal weighted regression (GTWR). *Geographical Analysis*, 47, 431–452.

Frey, U. J. & Rusch, H. 2013. Using artificial neural networks for the analysis of social–ecological systems. *Ecology and Society*, 18, 40.

Fung, C., Yau, P., Lam, C., Yu, P. & Yu, L. 2010. Clustering analysis of air quality model performance. *In*: Steyn, D. G., Builtjes, P. J. H. & Timmermans, R. M. A. (eds.) *Air Pollution Modelling*. Dordrecht: Springer.

GoldenSoftware. 2012. Surfer Mapping Systems, User's Guide, Version 11.00.

Hill, L. 2006. *The Geographic Associations of Information*. Cambridge, MA: MIT Press.

Houston, D. 2014. Implications of the modifiable areal unit problem for assessing built environment correlates of moderate and vigorous physical activity. *Applied Geography*, 50, 40–47.

Hřebíček, J., Jensen, S. & Steenmans, C. 2015. The framework for environmental software systems of the European Environment Agency. *In*: Denzer, R., Argent, R. M., Schimak, G. & Hřebíček, J. (eds.) *Environmental Software Systems. Infrastructures, Services and Applications*, pp. 44–55. Cham: Springer.

Jensen, R. R., Hardin, P. J., Bekker, M., Farnes, D. S., Lulla, V. & Hardin, A. 2009. Modeling urban leaf area index with AISA+ hyperspectral data. *Applied Geography*, 29, 320–332.

Kankal, M. & Yüksek, Ö. 2012. Artificial neural network approach for assessing harbor tranquility: the case of Trabzon Yacht Harbor, Turkey. *Applied Ocean Research*, 38, 23–31.

Langella, G., Basile, A., Bonfante, A. & Terribile, F. 2010. High-resolution space–time rainfall analysis using integrated ANN inference systems. *Journal of Hydrology*, 387, 328–342.

Levers, C., Verkerk, P. J., Müller, D., Verburg, P. H., Butsic, V., Leitão, P. J., et al. 2014. Drivers of forest harvesting intensity patterns in Europe. *Forest Ecology and Management*, 315, 160–172.

Lloyd, C. D. 2010. Analysing population characteristics using geographically weighted principal components analysis: a case study of Northern Ireland in 2001. *Computers, Environment and Urban Systems*, 34, 389–399.

Maier, H. R. & Dandy, G. C. 2000. Neural networks for the prediction and forecasting of water resources variables: a review of modelling issues and applications. *Environmental Modelling & Software*, 15, 101–124.

Malekmohamadi, I., Bazargan-Lari, M. R., Kerachian, R., Nikoo, M. R. & Fallahnia, M. 2011. Evaluating the efficacy of SVMs, BNs, ANNs and ANFIS in wave height prediction. *Ocean Engineering*, 38, 487–497.

Marcot, B., Steventon, J., Sutherland, G. & McCann, R. 2006. Guidelines for developing and updating Bayesian belief networks applied to ecological modeling and conservation. *Canadian Journal of Forest Research*, 36, 3063–3074.

Mcleod, E., Poulter, B., Hinkel, J., Reyes, E. & Salm, R. 2010. Sea-level rise impact models and environmental conservation: a review of models and their applications. *Ocean & Coastal Management*, 53, 507–517.

Mitra, R. & Buliung, R. N. 2012. Built environment correlates of active school transportation: neighborhood and the modifiable areal unit problem. *Journal of Transport Geography*, 20, 51–61.

Mokondoko, P., Manson, R. H., Ricketts, T. H. & Geissert, D. 2018. Spatial analysis of ecosystem service relationships to improve targeting of payments for hydrological services. *PLoS ONE*, 13, e0192560.

Mudersbach, C. & Jensen, J. 2011. An advanced statistical extreme value model for evaluating storm surge heights considering systematic records and sea level rise scenario. *Coastal Engineering Proceedings*, 32(10).

Nativi, S., Mazzetti, P., Craglia, M. & Pirrone, N. 2014. The GEOSS solution for enabling data interoperability and integrative research. *Environmental Science and Pollution Research*, 21, 4177–4192.

Nativi, S., Mazzetti, P. & Geller, G. N. 2013. Environmental model access and interoperability: the GEO Model Web initiative. *Environmental Modelling & Software*, 39, 214–228.

Nemati, H., Steiger, N., Steiger, D. & Herschel, R. 2003. Knowledge warehouse: an intelligent analysis platform for enhancing management decision process. *In*: Mora, M., Forgionne, G. A. & Gupta, J. N. D. (eds.) *Decision Making Support Systems: Achievements, Trends, and Challenges for the New Decade*. Hershey, PA: Idea Group Inc. (IGI).

Olawoyin, R. 2013. Exploration of the spatial-Composite Risk Index (CRI) for the characterization of toxicokinetics in petrochemical active areas. *Chemosphere*, 92, 1207–1213.

Openshaw, S. 1984. *The Modifiable Areal Unit Problem*, Norwich: Geo Books.

Openshaw, S. (ed.) 1996a. *A Lot of Fuss about Very Little That Matters and Not Enough about That Which Does!* Santa Barbara, CA: NCGIAUCSB.

Openshaw, S. 1996b. Some ideas about the exploratory spatial analysis technology required for massive databases. *In*: Committee on Applied and Theoretical Statistics, Board on Mathematical Sciences, & National Research Council (eds.) *Massive Data Sets: Proceedings of a Workshop*. Washington, DC: The National Academies Press.

Pal, M. & Mather, P. M. 2003. An assessment of the effectiveness of decision tree methods for land cover classification. *Remote Sensing of Environment*, 86, 554–565.

Palani, S., Liong, S.-Y. & Tkalich, P. 2008. An ANN application for water quality forecasting. *Marine Pollution Bulletin*, 56, 1586–1597.

Pech, L. & Lakes, T. 2017. The impact of armed conflict and forced migration on urban expansion in Goma: introduction to a simple method of satellite-imagery analysis as a complement to field research. *Applied Geography*, 88, 161–173.

Punitha, S. C. & Punithavalli, M. 2012. Performance evaluation of semantic based and ontology based text document clustering techniques. *Procedia Engineering*, 30, 100–106.

Rajabifard, A., Feeney, M. & Williamson, I. 2003. Spatial data infrastructures: concept, nature and SDI heirarchy. *In*: Williamson, I., Rajabifard, A. & Feeney, M. (eds.) *Developing Spatial Data Infrastructures: From Concept to Reality*. New York, NY: Taylor and Francis.

Reese, H. 2011. Classification of Sweden's forest and Alpine vegetation using optical satellite and inventory data. PhD thesis, Swedish University of Agricultural Sciences.

Refsgaard, J. C., Van Der Sluijs, J. P., Brown, J. & Van Der Keur, P. 2006. A framework for dealing with uncertainty due to model structure error. *Advances in Water Resources*, 29, 1586–1597.

Sabel, C. E., Kihal, W., Bard, D. & Weber, C. 2013. Creation of synthetic homogeneous neighbourhoods using zone design algorithms to explore relationships between asthma and deprivation in Strasbourg, France. *Social Science & Medicine*, 91, 110–121.

Safi, Y. & Bouroumi, A. 2013. Prediction of forest fires using artificial neural networks. *Applied Mathematical Sciences*, 7, 271–286.

Sang, N., Birnie, R. V., Geddes, A., Bayfield, N. G., Midgley, J. L., Shucksmith, D. M., et al. 2005. Improving the rural data infrastructure: the problem of addressable spatial units in a rural context. *Land Use Policy*, 22, 175–186.

Sang, N., Dramstad, W. E. & Bryn, A. 2014. Regionality in Norwegian farmland abandonment: inferences from production data. *Applied Geography*, 55, 238–247.

Sang, N. & Ode-Sang, A. 2015. *A Review on the State of the Art in Scenario Modelling for Environmental Management*. Stockholm: Naturvårdsverket.

Sholahuddin, A., Ramadhan, A. P. & Supriatna, A. K. 2015. The application of ANN-linear perception in the development of DSS for a fishery industry. *Procedia Computer Science*, 72, 67–77.

Su, M. D., Lin, M. C. & Wen, T. H. 2011. Spatial mapping and environmental risk identification. *In*: Nriagu, J. O. (ed.) *Encyclopedia of Environmental Health*. Burlington, MA: Elsevier.

Sumathi, S. & Sivanadam, S. 2006. *Introduction to Data Mining and Its Applications*. New York, NY: Springer.

Suryanarayana, I., Braibanti, A., Sambasiva Rao, R., Ramam, V. A., Sudarsan, D. & Nageswara Rao, G. 2008. Neural networks in fisheries research. *Fisheries Research*, 92, 115–139.

Swift, A., Liu, L. & Uber, J. 2008. Reducing MAUP bias of correlation statistics between water quality and GI illness. *Computers, Environment and Urban Systems*, 32, 134–148.

Troldborg, M., Aalders, I., Towers, W., Hallett, P. D., McKenzie, B. M., Bengough, A. G., et al. 2013. Application of Bayesian belief networks to quantify and map areas at risk to soil threats: using soil compaction as an example. *Soil and Tillage Research*, 132, 56–68.

TWC. 2012. *Demo for citizen scientist extension to the water quality portal* [Online]. New York, NY: Rensselear Polytechic Institute. http://tw.rpi.edu/web/Courses/AdvancedSemanticTechnologies/2012/CitizenScientist/Demo

USGS. 2018. TIGER/Line® Shapefiles Technical Documentation.

Versichele, M., De Groote, L., Claeys Bouuaert, M., Neutens, T., Moerman, I. & Van De Weghe, N. 2014. Pattern mining in tourist attraction visits through association rule learning on Bluetooth tracking data: a case study of Ghent, Belgium. *Tourism Management*, 44, 67–81.

Vicente-Serrano, S. M., Beguería, S., Gimeno, L., Eklundh, L., Giuliani, G., Weston, D., et al. 2012. Challenges for drought mitigation in Africa: the potential use of geospatial data and drought information systems. *Applied Geography*, 34, 471–486.

Webb, G. I. 2007. Discovering significant patterns. *Machine Learning*, 68, 1–33.

Wei, B., Sugiura, N. & Maekawa, T. 2001. Use of artificial neural network in the prediction of algal blooms. *Water Research*, 35, 2022–2028.

Williamson, I., Rajabifard, A. & Feeney, F. (eds.) 2003. *Developing Spatial Data Infrastructures: From Concept to Reality*. London: Taylor and Francis.

Xu, L., Li, J. & Brenning, A. 2014. A comparative study of different classification techniques for marine oil spill identification using RADARSAT-1 imagery. *Remote Sensing of Environment*, 141, 14–23.

Zozaya, E. L., Brotons, L. & Saura, S. 2012. Recent fire history and connectivity patterns determine bird species distribution dynamics in landscapes dominated by land abandonment. *Landscape Ecology*, 27, 171–184.

Zurr, A., Leno, E. & Smith, G. 2007. *Analysing Ecological Data*. New York, NY: Springer.

9 Can Geodesign Be Used to Facilitate Boundary Management for Planning and Implementation of Nature-based Solutions?

Sarah Gottwald, Ron Janssen and Christopher Raymond

9.1 INTRODUCTION

Ecosystem-based approaches are vital to addressing environmental issues and are crucial to buffering human communities against the adverse effects of climate change (Jones et al., 2012). The impacts of ecosystem-based projects have been considered within a range of societal challenge areas, such as wetland management (Max Finlayson et al., 2011), as well as across cross-cutting challenges of biodiversity conservation, public health and well-being (Kloos & Renaud, 2016). In most instances, researchers have drawn upon the ecosystem services framework for assessing the biophysical or economic value of ecosystem-based approaches (Liquete et al., 2015; Green et al., 2016), and for examining the potential for synergies and trade-offs between bundles of ecosystem services (Mouchet et al., 2017).

Ecosystem service assessments are now informing urban and regional policy and planning across the world. The European Commission, through MAES (Mapping and Assessment of Ecosystems and their Services), is assisting member states in the process of mapping and assessing ecosystems and their services and incorporating these values into EU and national accounting and reporting systems (European Union, 2013). The Intergovernmental Panel on Biodiversity and Ecosystem Services (IPBES) is drawing upon a wider nature's benefits for people framework in recognition that different types of values need to be promoted in environmental decision-making, including ecosystem services and concepts associated with other worldviews on human–nature relations and knowledge systems, such as 'nature's contributions to people' (Pascual et al., 2017).

However, multiple impacts of ecosystem-based management approaches are currently missing from social innovations projects. These include tools for assessing the co-benefits of solution-oriented interventions across geographic and temporal scales, and processes for engaging with businesses and multiple stakeholders to commercialise and upscale the benefits of ecosystem-based management strategies (Raymond et al., 2017).

In response, the European Commission developed the nature-based solutions umbrella term to combine aspects of social innovation with environmental management in a solutions-oriented process (European Commission, 2015). Nature-based solutions (NBS), referred to as solutions to societal challenges that are inspired and supported by nature, bring together established ecosystem-based approaches such as 'ecosystem services', 'green–blue infrastructure', 'ecological engineering', 'ecosystem-based management' and 'natural capital' (Nesshöver et al., 2016; *Nature*, 2017). NBS have global appeal given their potential to initiate strategies that provide environmental, social and economic benefits, and help build climate resilience (European Commission, 2015). While the strength of the term rests in its potential to integrate knowledge on living solutions and to provide multidisciplinary, evidence-based strategies to address societal challenges (Nesshöver et al., 2016; *Nature*, 2017), important questions remain about how to define NBS and how to engage multiple stakeholders in the assessment of NBS within and across different societal challenges (Raymond et al., 2017).

To clarify how to define NBS, Albert et al. (2019) recommended that an NBS should fulfil three criteria. It should: (1) address a relevant societal challenge, such as human well-being and climate adaptation; (2) be based on ecosystem processes, e.g. through restoration, creation or protection of wetlands; and (3) be realisable through viable business or governance models. All three criteria call for an approach integrating various stakeholders and transdisciplinary knowledge (Nesshöver et al., 2016; Raymond et al., 2017). Science and technology arguably is crucial to support planning and implementation of NBS as they deliver knowledge on ecosystem process and facilitate stakeholder integration. Raymond et al. (2017) recommend a seven-stage process for implementing NBS comprising: (1) identify the problem; (2) assess and choose NBS options; (3) design NBS implementation; (4) implement NBS; (5) inform policy makers about results; (6) transfer and upscale NBS; and (7) monitor and evaluate co-benefits. Systematic implementation of NBS requires the monitoring and evaluation of co-benefits across all stages.

However, landscape development is a complex task and challenged by boundaries existing between different social groups with different interests and knowledge frames (e.g. scientific knowledge vs. local knowledge), and between different institutional approaches (government vs. self-governance) (Westerink et al., 2017). Taking a multiple evidence-based approach, the combination of these different knowledge systems potentially leads to a richer picture of the situation than focusing on a single knowledge system, taking into account their complementarities, synergies and contradictions (Tengö et al., 2014). Boundary management, which addresses the facilitation of social or institutional boundaries, e.g. between stakeholder groups, such as scientists, practitioners or interest groups, has shown to be beneficial for a successful integration of science and policy (Cash et al., 2003). It is comprised of communication, translation and mediation (Cash et al., 2003). In more recent times, the boundary management approach has been built upon using the term knowledge weaving involving mobilising, translating, negotiating and synthesising different forms of knowledge across actors, institutions and processes (Tengö et al., 2017).

While there are many processes for conceptualising boundary management and knowledge weaving, NBS require a participatory planning support tool facilitating the communication between stakeholders from science and practice. Geodesign tools provide the interface between stakeholders and spatial information and is defined as 'a design and planning method which tightly couples the creation of design proposals with impact simulations informed by geographic contexts, systems thinking and digital technology' (Steinitz, 2012, p. 12). Geodesign may act as a boundary management process between science and practice by translating information and promoting a common understanding and conflict mediation (Wissen Hayek et al., 2016) for NBS planning and implementation. It provides new opportunities to address complex planning tasks and facilitate the communication of trade-offs between NBS and grey solution planning. While definitions and approaches differ widely among the variety of reported geodesign workshops, we would like to focus on those employing digital maps and using impact simulations and evaluation methods of design input by participants (Flaxman, 2010; Steinitz, 2012; Eikelboom & Janssen, 2017). These geodesign tools provide features such as mapping, sketching, analysing (e.g. multi-criteria analysis, impact simulation models) and representation/visualisation (GIS) (Ervin, 2011; Raumer & Stokman, 2013; Janssen et al., 2015). Using the maps as a common interface facilitates exchange of ideas, promotes explicit statements and avoids the need for specialised jargon. Practical cases demonstrate the process to be multidisciplinary, collaborative, dynamic, responsive, iterative and non-linear (Ervin, 2011; Ballal & Steinitz, 2015; Janssen et al., 2015; Nyerges et al., 2016). Thus in spatial planning processes geodesign workshops can serve as mediators between science and practice and between conflicting stakeholder interests. Geodesign workshops and outputs potentially highlight advantages of NBS compared to conventional rather than technical solutions that otherwise may seem preferable applying conventional economy-based decision support tools.

Despite the research efforts in the past years and increasing technical advances in planning support systems in general and geodesign in particular, there is still a mismatch between the provision of tools and their actual use in practice (Vonk et al., 2007; Vonk & Geertman, 2008; Currier & Couclelis, 2014; Pelzer et al., 2015a, 2015b). Current research is rather substantive, presenting tools and highlighting insights from distinct case studies, than comprehensive by contributing to the general concept of geodesign (Campagna, 2015). The NBS approach offers the opportunity to learn from the past and avoid the separate views from the planning requirement perspective (NBS) and the method and tool perspective (geodesign).

Therefore, our aim is to critically and systematically analyse the potential of geodesign tools and workshops for boundary management in NBS planning. To do so, we will (1) explore how geodesign workshops facilitate translation, communication and mediation in planning processes, (2) present a geodesign case study which facilitated planning of solutions ranging from technical to NBS, and (3) discuss for this case if and how the geodesign tool and workshops could be seen as a boundary management process. Finally, lessons learnt are drawn from the analysis to guide future work on geodesign and NBS.

9.2 GEODESIGN AS BOUNDARY MANAGEMENT

We propose geodesign as one 'innovation [which] is turning knowledge into design for landscape change that protects earth's life-support system for the long term while respecting societal values' (Nassauer & Opdam, 2008, p. 635). There are several definitions and understandings of geodesign tools and workshops all highlighting the design aspect and the integration in a spatial context. Lee et al. (2014) define geodesign to be an 'iterative design and planning methods whereby an emerging solution is influenced by (scientific) geospatial knowledge derived from geospatial technologies'. Schwarz-v.Raumer and Stokman (2011) locate geodesign 'somewhere between mapping, modelling, sketching, visioning, planning, generating, constructing and engineering' (p. 108), pointing out the attributes of intuition, creativity and emotion which in geodesign influence the data analysis and representation. Many geodesign applications refer to the geodesign framework developed by Carl Steinitz (2012) (Yang et al., 2014; Janssen et al., 2015; Campagna et al., 2016; Slotterback et al., 2016; Wissen Hayek et al., 2016), which emphasises a decision-driven over a data-driven approach (Steinitz, 2014).

While using Steinitz's framework as a workshop guide, in this chapter, geodesign tools are seen as a subset of planning support tools. They are based on digital devices (e.g. interactive digital mapping devices such as Touch Tables) that can be used in the workshop by the participants to explore, design and negotiate land-use changes and their potential impacts (Arciniegas & Janssen, 2009; Eikelboom & Janssen, 2013). Geodesign tools make use of different types of maps such as topographical maps, value maps, impact maps, etc. Further, geodesign tools facilitate an interactive process, such as on-the-fly impact assessments for designed land-use changes (Arciniegas et al., 2011). The workshops in which these tools are used are based on an active exchange between participants and device.

In order to explore the potential of geodesign workshops as boundary management work, the three functions of boundary management are analysed in more depth. With boundary management we refer to the facilitated integration of different stakeholder groups' or disciplines' knowledge systems. Cash et al. (2003) underline that effective science and technology integration requires a management of boundaries enhancing the perceived salience, credibility and legitimacy of process and outcome. While they summarise the functions of boundary management as communication, translation and mediation, these have been built upon and further developed in recent research introducing five tasks for successful communication across knowledge systems, which are mobilisation, translation, negotiation, synthetisation and application (Tengö et al., 2017). However, the following analysis draws upon the three initial dimensions and uses the five tasks for further explanation and discussion. Figure 9.1 presents the three dimensions of boundary management and boundary objects as a result (circles) allocated over the process of the geodesign workshop, including the preparation phase and the outcome. The light

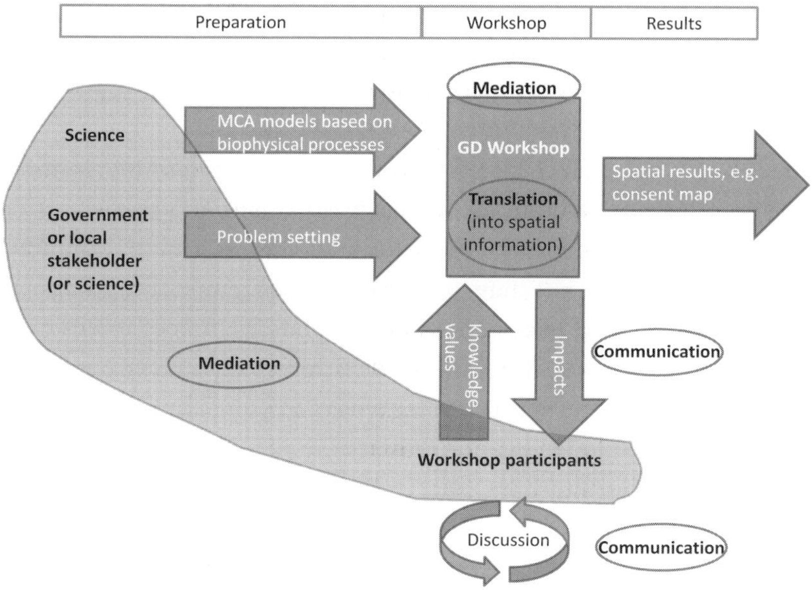

FIGURE 9.1 The three dimensions of boundary management (circles) within the geodesign process.

grey area encloses all process participants which are active either during the workshop or in the preparatory phase. These can be different types of stakeholders representing the affected public and depending on the context and they can be the same or different in the preparation and during the workshop (Figure 9.1).

9.2.1 *Translation*

Planning of NBS requires the integration of various knowledge frames, methods and concepts, such as engineering science for the design of NBS, natural science for evaluation of ecological benefits and social and economic science for evaluation of socio-economic benefits, but also knowledge from local stakeholders (Nesshöver et al., 2016). Bringing together different knowledge frames can be seen as very beneficial, but at the same time carries some inherent challenges. Local stakeholder, scientific experts and decision-makers possess different languages, jargons, experiences with and conceptions of landscapes and approaches to convey ideas, which is challenging for successful communication (Cash et al., 2003; Nassauer, 2015). The mobilisation of diverse knowledge systems, as described by Tengö et al. (2017), and the translation into a 'language' of mutual comprehension deliver an enriched information basis for planning practice. Geodesign tools enable the translation of different types of information into spatial information (Figure 9.1). While scientists may integrate their models in the setup of the geodesign tool, the workshop participants can actually assign values to different locations of the study area. Further, translation to spatial information or visualisation of facts enables us to see what you cannot imagine, such as inventions for future landscapes (Nassauer, 2015).

9.2.2 *Communication*

Communication should be active, iterative and inclusive, which means all stakeholders should be able to communicate between and among different hierarchical levels and knowledge systems. Further, communication should be frequent and various stakeholders have to perceive themselves as included in the process (Cash et al., 2003). Nesshöver et al. (2016) point out the involvement of multiple stakeholders and the wider public as a crucial element of NBS projects. Planning workshops in general serve as a platform for communication. The advantage of the geodesign workshop is the common language (the spatial translation). Additionally, the tool facilitates the communication between scientific knowledge translated into the input to the geodesign tool and the workshop participants through for example multi-criteria assessments (Figure 9.1). Participants comment on each other's input and additionally receive instant feedback by the tool based on scientifically sound models.

9.2.3 *Mediation*

By bringing together different stakeholders, conflicting views and opinions may arise. This requires an analysis of common or contradicting knowledge systems (Tengö et al., 2017). These can be mediated by the instant feedback the geodesign tool provides (Figure 9.1). The geodesign tools and workshops presented in this chapter allow for the mediation of trade-offs of different solution options, e.g. technical or natural solutions, but also between different opinions. The impact assessments or valuation provided by the tool decrease the space for speculation and potentially increasing fact-based over power-based argumentation. Further, Cash et al. (2003) highlight the need of professional mediation between the three criteria of successful science technology projects, namely perceived salience, credibility and legitimacy of the process. These three criteria can be conflicting, when for example the sound scientific results (credibility) do not reflect the needs or values of the local stakeholder to whom they should apply (Cash et al., 2003). If the models in the geodesign tool do not meet the requirements of the participants the success of the whole workshop is at risk as the impact assessment or valuation results will not have the power to influence the discussion. Whether the problem at stake is salient depends on the design and focus of the workshop. However, workshops addressing salient challenges are more likely to motivate various stakeholders to participate. Geodesign tools are based on scientific models and input aiming for credible results. Combining the different knowledge frames and allowing the public to take part in the workshops increase the legitimacy of the results. In successful projects the trade-offs between legitimacy, credibility and salience are mediated.

9.2.4 Boundary Objects

Results of geodesign workshops are spatially visualised design options or decisions based on spatial designs. The resulting maps are a product of the communication between the scientific models in the backend of the geodesign tool resulting in on-the-fly impact assessments and the communication among workshop participants, also responding to the impacts. Ideally, the output maps represent a synthesis of the commonly accepted knowledge which integrates the different knowledge systems

(Tengö et al., 2017). Therefore, one could argue that they are or should be understandable for all participants including the scientists responsible for model building and setup (Figure 9.1). The resulting maps could be seen as boundary objects, which stakeholders of different knowledge frames can adapt (Star & Griesemer, 1989; Cash et al., 2003). They represent a common framework for further communication. The use of the maps as a means of communication is the essence of geodesign.

CASE STUDY 9.1 Developing a Spatial Adaptation Strategy for Friesland

Dutch peatlands have been subsiding due to peat decomposition, shrinkage and compression, since their reclamation in the eleventh century. Currently, subsidence amounts to 1–2 cm year^{-1}. Water management in these areas is complex and costly, greenhouse gases are being emitted, and surface water quality is poor. Regional and local authorities and land owners responsible for peatland management have recognized these problems. In the Province of Friesland about 850 km^2 are peat meadows (Figure 9.2). To make the area suitable for agricultural use, large parts of this area are drained mechanically. The region is currently mainly used for commercial dairy farming but is also important for its high natural, cultural and historical values. Important problems in the region caused by soil subsidence are damage to buildings and infrastructure, deterioration of landscape values, inefficient water management and poor water quality (Provincie Friesland, 2011).

THE GEODESIGN WORKSHOPS

A planning process including diverse stakeholders has been initiated by the Province and Water Board of Friesland to develop an adaptation strategy. They invited stakeholders to the geodesign workshops based on prior involvement in the planning process. Some participants had a direct stake in the planning process as they owned a farm or house in the region; others represented interest groups such as farmers or nature conservationists.

CASE STUDY 9.1 **(cont.)**

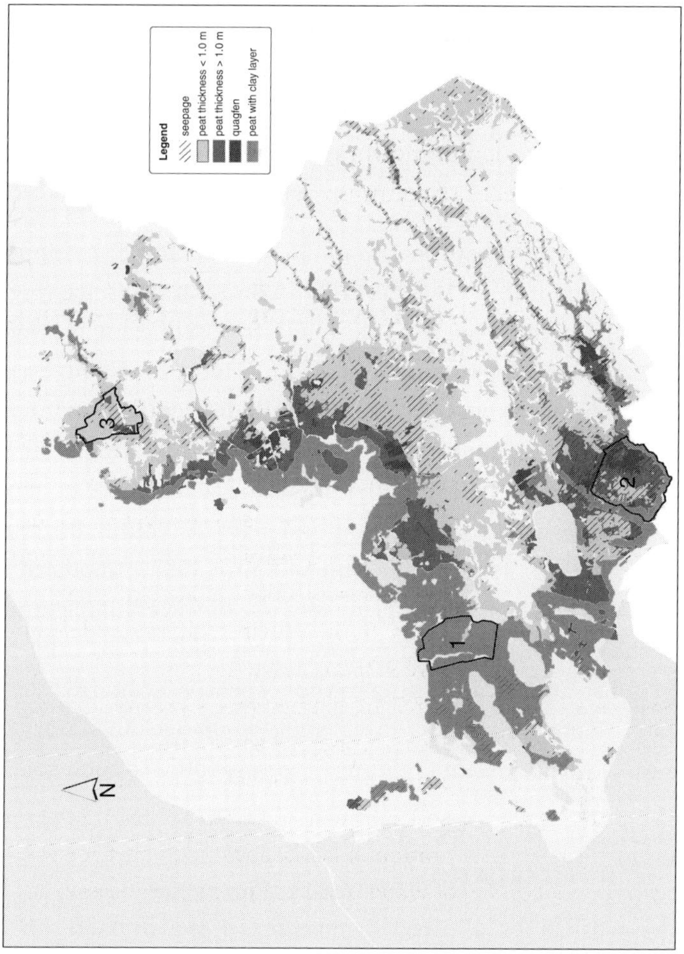

FIGURE 9.2 Map of the province of Friesland (north-west Netherlands) showing the three communes where the workshops took place and different types and densities of peatland (Brouns et al., 2015). (A black and white version of this figure will appear in some formats. For the colour version, please refer to the plate section.)

Three workshops were organised to develop spatial plans for three areas in different parts of the Friesland province (Figure 9.2). The selection of these areas was based on their representativeness

CASE STUDY 9.1 **(cont.)**

of the Friesland province related to type and thickness of the peat layer. All three examples face similar challenges as described above. The workshops employ scenarios previously developed by the Province and Water Board of Friesland. The workshops were exploratory and did not involve a case choice for one of the scenarios. Each workshop involved six to eight stakeholders representing the various interests in the plan. An interactive mapping device (the 'Touch Table') was used as a common interface (Figure 9.3). The use of the Touch Table made it possible for participants to have direct access to tools and information and provided a common platform for discussion. The geodesign application included an evaluation tool and a design tool. The evaluation tool included simplified models linking land use and water level to agricultural productivity, soil subsidence and natural values (Brouns et al., 2015). Both tools were dynamic and provided immediate feedback on the effects of any change in land use or water management made by the participants (Figure 9.4). These tools were used to design spatial strategies according to the respective scenario by allocating water management measures, such as changes in water levels and drainage systems, and land-use types specific to each scenario.

GEODESIGN WORKSHOPS IN FRIESLAND, THE NETHERLANDS

The workshops allowed discussion of the impacts on different scenarios with more or less strong nature-based measures. They employed a Touch Table using a GIS-based software and models generating immediate feedback to the participants' input. Responses were given for three main indicators or objectives: agriculture, soil and nature. The models are characterised by different degrees of complexity; while soil models were relatively complex, models for nature and agriculture were more simplified. The workshops were highly interactive, facilitated by the research staff in

CASE STUDY 9.1 **(cont.)**

charge. While the input models were based on scientific data, the workshops facilitated the design of the spatial scenarios and their deliberate evaluation. As a result, knowledge exchange between participants and between participants and researchers could be observed. The created maps represent consent for each scenario reached through interaction with the Touch Table and the models behind them and vivid discussion.

FIGURE 9.3 Workshop participants around the Touch Table. (A black and white version of this figure will appear in some formats. For the colour version, please refer to the plate section.)

The workshops followed the steps of the geodesign framework as defined by Steinitz (2012). Steinitz distinguishes three iterations through the framework phrasing the questions as 'Why?' questions in the first iteration, as 'How?' questions in the second iteration and as 'What, where and when?' questions in the third and final iterations. Each workshop started with an introduction to the region and communication of information needed for the assignments. The complicated relations between land use,

CASE STUDY 9.1 **(cont.)**

groundwater level and soil subsidence were communicated by an exercise where participants experimented by changing land use and water levels and observed the result on soil decline. Only very simple models were used to model the relations between water management, soil decline, nature and agriculture. This made it possible to explore and even adapt all model relations during the workshop. About half of the available time was used to communicate all information. The second half was used for three assignments where participants were asked to design three spatial strategies for each area.

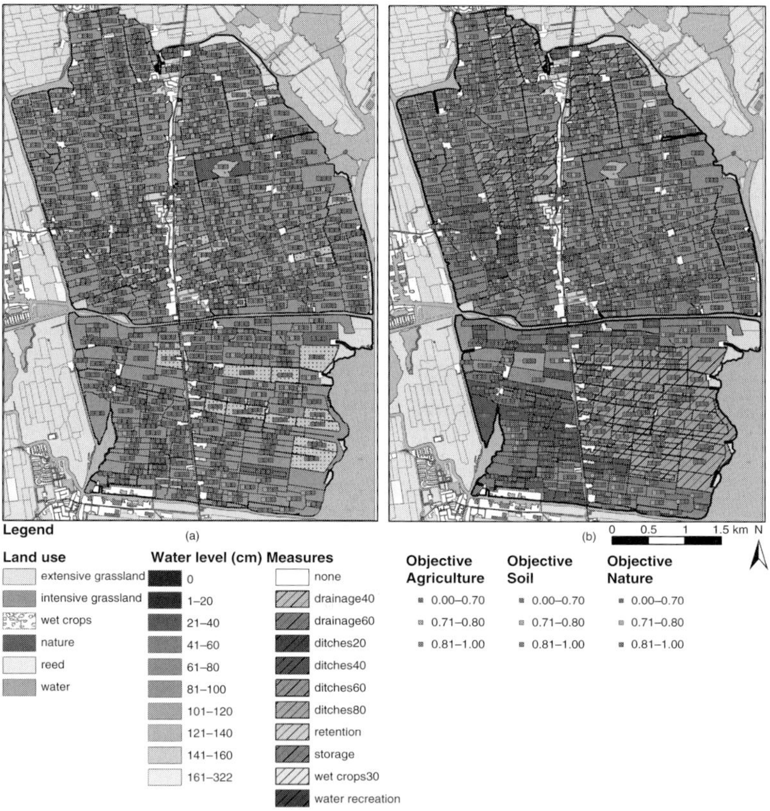

FIGURE 9.4 Use of the design tool for the region 'Hommerts': combined with land use (a) and water levels (b). (A black and white version of this figure will appear in some formats. For the colour version, please refer to the plate section.)

9.3 PLANNING OF NBS

The Province and Water Board of Friesland had decided to develop a long-term adaptation strategy for the peat meadow area of the province in cooperation with stakeholders (Provincie Friesland, 2011). They described three strategies in general terms.

1. Business as usual: low-impact technical measures only, no changes in land use.
2. Parallel tracks: create buffers to separate conflicting functions.
3. New horizons: introduction of new crops, large changes in land use and water management.

The workshops in Case Study 9.1 are based on these three predefined scenarios including different approaches towards agriculture and water management. The workshops took place in 2013 when the term 'NBS' was not yet commonly used and thus they were not explicitly framed around it. Nevertheless, looking at the scenarios, NBS are clearly part of the set of solutions. Definitions of NBS are rather vague and allow for some interpretation. Different solutions can be found on a grey to green solution continuum (van der Nat et al., 2016).

The scenarios developed by the regional water board comprise various measures to deal with soil subsidence. The 'business as usual' scenario aims at keeping the existing agricultural policy as is and adjusting the water supply using technical measures (drainage, gauges) to reduce soil subsidence. These technical measures could only be applied if they did not create limitations for agriculture. Similarly, the 'parallel development' strategy aims at maintaining and enhancing the agricultural conditions, but additionally other land uses should be developed in designated zones and the water management adapted according to the respective needs. It is based on zoning and separation of the different types of land use separated by buffer zones. The 'new horizons' scenario aims at transforming the existing land uses, including agriculture, according to the natural hydrological conditions. Even though water management, including technical measures, is still required, the use of technical measures such as pumps can be reduced due to the introduction of new adapted crops and the implementation of recreation as an additional source of income for farmers (Table 9.1). None of these scenarios included a spatial allocation of the proposed measures (Provincie Friesland, 2011, 2015).

The NBS identified in the scenarios are: (1) the restoration of peatland, which is the indigenous vegetation of this landscape and adapted to the natural hydrological patterns, and (2) the introduction of new crops adapted to existing wet conditions. Further, one could consider the implementation of recreation as a further NBS measure that alleviates the agricultural pressure on the soil. It could be argued that although the usage of pumps is clearly a technical measure, it enhances ecosystem processes and therefore on a natural to technical solution scale should be placed somewhere between.

The three scenarios include two main types of changes: change of crops and change of water management. Figure 9.5 shows the relative share of these two types in the scenarios (red dotted boxes) and includes where these could be placed on a continuum between technical and nature-based solutions (bottom triangle). New horizons includes a large share in new crops, a reduction in water management and therefore large share of NBS. Parallel development includes current crops combined with a small reduction in water management and therefore some solutions tend rather towards NBS. It provides some NBS for soil compaction such as re-establishment of peatland, but because the agricultural productivity is a priority, solutions are less diverse and more conservative. In the business as usual (BAU) scenario nothing changes and solutions are rather technical, such as intense water management (Figure 9.5).

In order to characterise the NBS approach in this planning process, the three criteria established by Albert et al. (2019) are employed. We argue that the NBS, such as peatland restoration or introduction of adapted crops, are addressing a relevant societal challenge (criteria 1). Soil subsidence is considered as a major threat to the region which is

Table 9.1 *Strategies established by the regional water board, which served as input for the geodesign workshop*

	Business as usual	Parallel development	New horizons
Guiding principle	Agriculture: no limitations – orientation on the world market	Agriculture: no limitations – orientation on the world market Separate agriculture, housing and nature (zoning)	Transformation Adaptation to local hydrological conditions
Adaptation of	Water management	Water management Land use	Agriculture (land use) Water management
New features	None	Development of new functions and hydrological buffer zones	New crops (adapted to hydrological conditions) Recreation (additional source of income) Peatland (natural vegetation)
Technical measures	Regulate water supply (gauge and drainage) Increase of drainage in wet season and water input in dry season	Adapted and appropriate water management for every land-use type Predominantly in agricultural areas and hydrological buffer zones: regulate water supply (gauge and drainage)	Less intense as the land use is more adapted to natural hydrological patterns

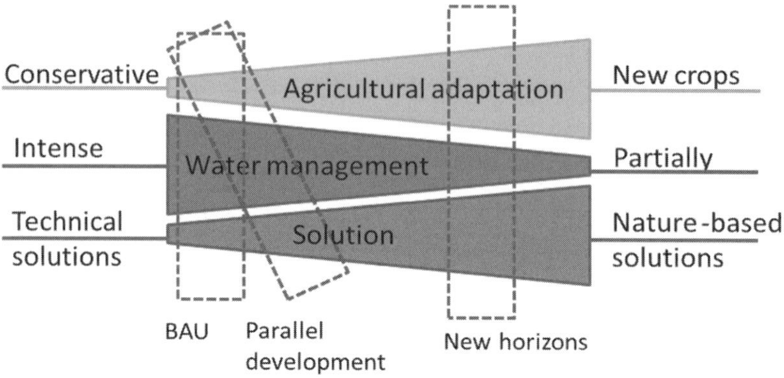

FIGURE 9.5 The share of NBS within the three scenarios. (A black and white version of this figure will appear in some formats. For the colour version, please refer to the plate section.)

due to water mismanagement and causes damages to infrastructure, landscape values and water quality (Eikelboom & Janssen, 2013; Janssen et al., 2015). Further, the proposed solutions which are then further defined in the geodesign workshop are based on scientific evidence on ecosystem processes (criteria 2). The effects of rewetting or renaturing agricultural land into peatland are calculated using soil and hydrological models in the geodesign tool (Brouns et al., 2015). Finally, a viable governance and business model can be assumed for some of the solutions (criteria 3). The third scenario ('new horizons'), for example, which includes a public fund supporting land-use change and recreation is highlighted as an alternative income for farmers (Provincie Friesland, 2011) (Table 9.2).

9.3.1 *Boundary Management*

Two main boundaries can be observed during the workshops: first, the different knowledge frames and experiences of the stakeholder groups, e.g. researcher, farmer, representatives of the tourism sector, regional government and other local citizens; and second, the different views on agriculture. According to the experience of the stakeholders (e.g. years working as a nature conservationist, years active in that region)

Table 9.2 *Criteria of NBS (Albert et al., 2019)*

Relevant societal challenge	Soil subsidence
Based on ecosystem processes	Impacts based on scientific models
Viable governance or business models	Public funding for new land uses Encouragement for recreation as additional source of income for farmers Decision on the water levels is made by a democratically elected board

people possess different types of knowledge (Raymond et al., 2010) and further their professional backgrounds frame their usual usage and interpretation of maps (Carton & Thissen, 2009). Groups or individuals hold different contextual values regarding the topics at stake, such as the adaptation of agriculture and water management.

To overcome these boundaries and integrate different perspectives in the final scenario maps, the workshops' assignments requested the participants to translate the three pre-established scenarios into spatial strategies using the geodesign tool. Thus every opinion and interest, e.g. need for more peatland, had to be 'translated' into specific spatial decisions on the map, which were discussed among the participants. Additionally, the input of the scientists (in the form of scientific models) was translated into impacts responding to the land-use or water-level changes made by the participants. The on-the-fly impact assessments informed further discussions.

This highlights the two types of communication in the workshop, namely the communication among the participants and the communication between the geodesign tool, and thus indirectly the scientists, and the participants. As the developers of the tool (scientists) were also present in the workshop, participants could address them directly with questions. For every predefined objective (agricultural productivity, soil subsidence and natural values), the land parcels in the geodesign tool obtained a value according to its land use and water level (Figure 9.4). Changing land use and water level, the values of the objectives would change accordingly. Workshop participants commented on each other's ideas, which was informed and enhanced by the feedback they received from the tool application after translating them into a spatial decision. Feedback from the participants indicated that they found exchange of information very important. The opportunities to switch between maps and for learning by doing were considered useful. Participants reported an increased understanding of the underlying mechanisms, a raised awareness of the perspectives of other participants as well as a feeling of joint ownership of the plans produced (Janssen et al., 2013, 2015; Brouns et al., 2015; Eikelboom & Janssen, 2015; Eikelboom et al., 2015).

Integrating the impact assessment of the geodesign tool into the workshop as a 'neutral referee' was found to be useful for discussion and conflict mediation. The initial maps and the feedback were critically analysed by participants. Participants' comments on the received spatial information therefore provided feedback to the scientists, e.g. they judged the predicted groundwater levels to be too high in the south-west corner of the Groote Veenpolder. This corner borders on a very deep polder, which creates seepage to this polder, which according to the participants was not properly addressed in the current model. Perceptions on how realistic each of the scenarios are changed during the workshop (Figure 9.6). Before the workshops, most people considered the 'new horizon' scenario most realistic and after the workshops half of the participants considered the 'parallel development' most realistic. There were fewer people voting for the business as usual scenario. Geodesign supports the understanding of scenario impacts. These are relatively easy to grasp for business as usual as participants bring their experience from practice. For the other scenarios the geodesign workshops allowed learning about and discussion of potential impacts. Additional to this, a shift

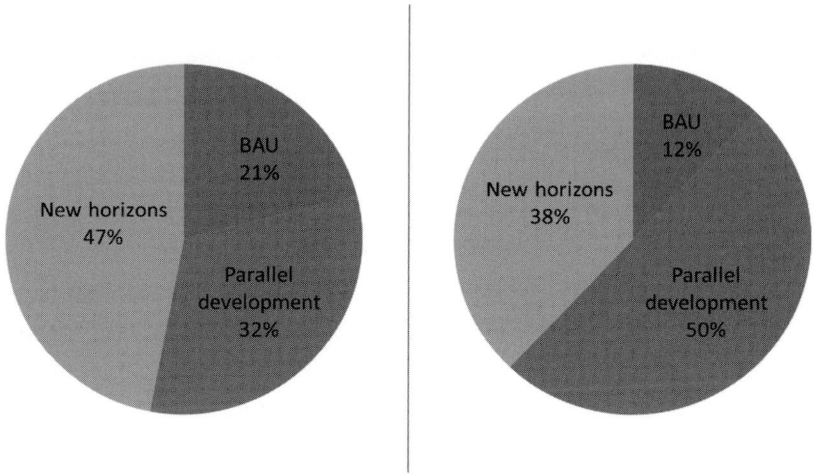

FIGURE 9.6 'What do you consider the most realistic scenario?' – responses before (left) and after (right) the workshop (n = 19). (A black and white version of this figure will appear in some formats. For the colour version, please refer to the plate section.)

towards another scenario could be observed, and the distribution of preferences is more uneven after the workshops. Geodesign may promote consensus here.

As Cash et al. (2003) point out, active mediation is crucial to solve conflicts between salience, credibility and legitimacy. In this special case, the workshop's content was informed by the regional water board and workshop participants agreed on the salience of the problem of soil compaction. Whether process and results are legitimate is arguable. However, the water board responsible for the implementation of the water management decisions is elected democratically. Further, workshop participants represented interests of agriculture, tourism, local citizens, regional government and science.

9.4 DISCUSSION

The aim of this chapter was to critically and systematically analyse the potential of geodesign workshops for boundary management in

NBS planning. The two main considerations are: (1) the workshop setting and how it can manage boundaries, and (2) the opportunity of using scenarios. Here we discuss the future role of geodesign as a boundary management tool, and how to integrate NBS into geodesign workshops.

9.4.1 Geodesign as a Boundary Management Tool

From the critical analysis of the potential of geodesign for boundary management taking into account a distinct case study, five major lessons can be learnt.

1. The wide range of definitions and operationalisations of the geodesign concept necessitates that the term be used with much care and that conclusions can only be extrapolated to comparable approaches (e.g. map-based, digital, combination of design and impact or multi-criteria assessment, interactive).
2. The geodesign tool should be as simple as possible to be understandable and transparent for its users and to be able to address socio-ecological processes.
3. The geodesign concept provides just a tool and a platform, professional mediation responding to difficult conflicts and power relations remains crucial.
4. Geodesign has a strong potential to harness the strengths of both deliberative and instrumental value assessment.
5. Maps are the main result of geodesign workshops representing the synergy of different knowledge systems and a broad agreement.

Figure 9.7 illustrates how the tool and the workshop are interwoven in the geodesign approach and each can be described by different characteristics which need to be selected.

What type of geodesign? Will a digital, responsive and/or interactive approach work best?

Which way to go – simple or complex? Regarding these two elements, Figure 9.7 shows the decision challenge arising between a more simplistic approach which is easier to replicate and transparent in the workshops but does not represent the complex reality.

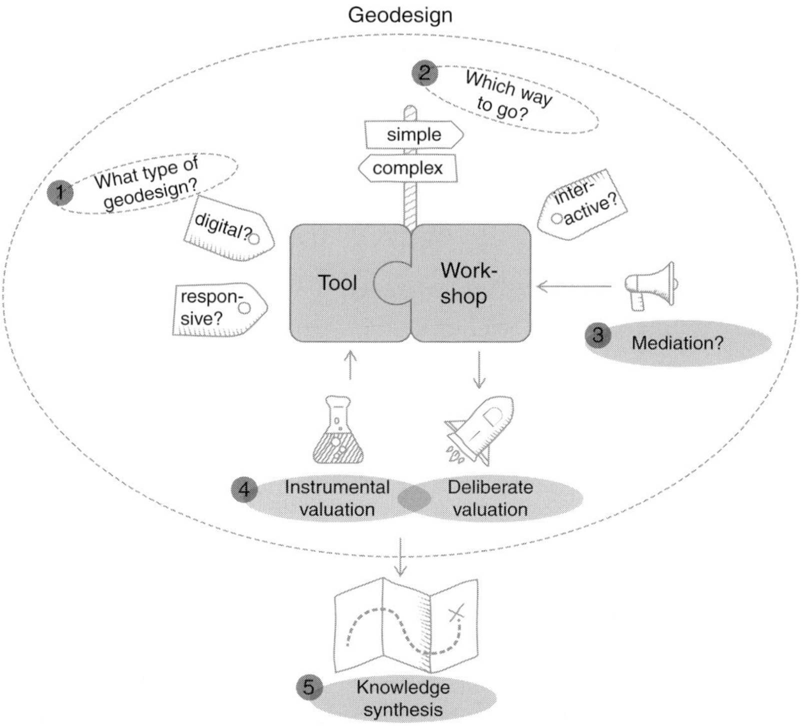

FIGURE 9.7 Major lessons to be learnt from geodesign approaches.

Mediation? Although the tool is an essential part of the workshop, it will not replace certain general workshop requirements such as traditional mediation.

Instrumental valuation or deliberative valuation? The combination of the two elements, which are the tool and the workshop, may present challenges, but certainly offers opportunities such as the combination of instrumental and deliberate valuation.

Knowledge synthesis. Finally, the figure illustrates the outcome of the whole process as a synthesis of different knowledge systems which were fed in to the tool and contributed during the workshop.

9.4.1.1 Lesson 1. Geodesign Cases Differ Substantially in Their Operationalisation, Which Impedes Drawing Conclusions for Geodesign as Such

Geodesign provides new opportunities to address complex planning tasks, such as NBS implementation. It provides an integrative approach which combines 'concerns of ecological balance, cultural values and human needs' (Xu, 2015, p. 202). We could indeed find that geodesign workshops have potential to be used as boundary management for planning NBS. They enable translation of various knowledge systems into spatial information, communication of these among workshop participants and between them and the tool and hence mediation of conflicts. Nevertheless, a very narrow definition of geodesign was taken into account. Other geodesign applications are realised without workshops, with less emphasis on communication or without impact assessment and using paper maps (Rambaldi et al., 2007; Recatalá Boix & Zinck, 2008; Marimbaldo et al., 2012; Campagna et al., 2016; Littaye et al., 2016). Therefore, any conclusions drawn from this chapter have to be carefully applied to geodesign applications, which are interactive, map-based and digital and combining design with on-the-fly impact assessment.

The existence of different approaches on geodesign may partly explain the lack between the availability of geodesign tools and experiences and their scarce application in practice (Vonk et al., 2007; Vonk & Geertman, 2008; Currier & Couclelis, 2014; Pelzer et al., 2015a, 2015b). Concentrating on conclusions of very distinct geodesign case studies has been shown to fall short in contributing to a more general understanding of geodesign (Campagna, 2015). The application of the boundary management concept addresses this shortcoming and highlights the potential of geodesign tools and workshops and clearly characterises the type of geodesign used. Therefore, we argue that future research should emphasise the approach they take on geodesign by addressing the questions: (1) What type of geodesign approach is taken, e.g. degree of interactivity or use of digital tools? There exist other participatory mapping tools and workshops using public participation GIS (PPGIS), raising the question on the similarities and differences between these approaches and geodesign. (2) Which general and comprehensive conclusions can be drawn not for geodesign as a whole but for this specific type?

9.4.1.2 Lesson 2. It is a Challenge to Set Up a Geodesign Tool as Simple as Possible and as Complex as Needed

Communication is a key element in workshops and should be the focus, which requests the geodesign tool not to be too complex, but to provide understandable communication support. An understandable tool as opposed to a 'black box' triggers trust in the tool and the workshops as such. In order to reach an effective use of the tools (measured by correct completion of the assignment) the tools should be kept simple, only providing the information absolutely necessary (Eikelboom & Janssen, 2015). Use of on-the-fly impact simulations proved an effective way of communicating the underlying mechanisms of the simulation models used. Geodesign has the potential to be applied in practice as well as in research, but especially for application in practice the workload for the tool set up should be reasonable. Eikelboom and Janssen tested different interactive spatial support tools (drawing, evaluation, simulation) using the geodesign approach and concluded the necessity to adapt these to the regional context. They also stress that time and effort of the adaptation processes may limit the application of the tools in real-life planning (Eikelboom & Janssen, 2013).

Using more complex models (e.g. applying a genetic algorithm) may create valid and useful results (credibility), but provides challenges in terms of acceptance by the stakeholders (legitimacy) (Eikelboom et al., 2015) and final use in practice. Therefore, we suggest that future research focus more on the need of the actual beneficiaries of geodesign tools and workshops, which are planners, decision-makers, but also partly the civil society by asking (1) what requirements do the stakeholders have for the geodesign tool and workshops; and (2) what kind of tool and workshop setting fits the planning task?

9.4.1.3 Lesson 3. The Geodesign Tool Does Not Replace the Need for Professional Mediation

Geodesign workshops provide a space for mediation and the tool supports such efforts by enabling translation of information and communication. The tool informs the discussion and acts as a 'neutral referee', presenting the impacts of spatial decisions. However, power relations and questions of legitimisation are not automatically taken care of and require attention, starting with the mobilisation of the knowledge systems (Tengö et al., 2017). The tool is embedded in a workshop setting where diverse stakeholders with regards to their knowledge backgrounds and interests are present. Therefore, professional facilitation is beneficial to cope with power relations and the different stakeholder values (Reed et al., 2018). The tool supports the mediation process, but does not replace an active engagement with stakeholders and conflict solutions.

It is crucial to perceive geodesign as a combination of the tool and the workshop, which cannot be separated. As previous studies show, the preparation of the workshop is as crucial as the preparation of the tool itself. For future research, we suggest to have a closer look at the mediation potential of both tool and workshop. This relates to questions such as (1) how did the geodesign tool support the mediation of conflicts of interest; and (2) what aspects of salience, legitimacy and credibility (Cash et al., 2003) were mediated by the tool and the workshop facilitator?

9.4.1.4 Lesson 4. Geodesign Harnesses the Strengths of Deliberative and Instrumental Value Assessments

Although workshops such as the analysed example follow a deliberative paradigm of value assessment, the geodesign tool allows the integration of various types of information, such as data from surveys (instrumental paradigm). While the input to the geodesign tool or workshops presented in this chapter was based on scientific knowledge only, it provided the basis for discussion, and the discussion of trade-offs between stakes was informed by the input of the geodesign tool. This pragmatic paradigm (instrumental → deliberative) combines the strengths of large amount of data, e.g. from surveys – or in this case scientific models, with deliberative discussion of trade-offs (Raymond et al., 2014). This potential of the geodesign approach responds to the need for the integration of various knowledge bases, stakeholder engagement and communication of co-benefits and trade-offs (Nesshöver et al., 2016; Raymond et al., 2017).

Therefore, we argue that geodesign would provide a very suitable empirical case for investigating further the challenges and benefits of combining instrumental and deliberate value assessments. Additionally, the integration of results from surveys, especially public participation GIS (PPGIS) surveys, including a larger range of stakeholders than a workshop setting allows would increase the legitimacy of the whole process. Equally, the results of the geodesign process could be the basis of a survey to gain feedback on the generated consensus maps. Related research questions could be (1) how to integrate survey data into a geodesign workshop; and (2) how to evaluate geodesign results using a survey approach?

9.4.1.5 Lesson 5. Geographical Maps Synthesise the Knowledge Systems of the Participants and are the Main Results of the Geodesign Workshop

Finally, the main and most important output of any geodesign workshop are maps. They represent the synthesised knowledge systems of all participants involved in creating the maps either in the preparatory phase or during the workshops and can therefore be used and adopted by all stakeholders for further planning processes. However, using maps creates a new boundary as some participants may not be familiar with reading or working with maps or are used to interpret maps very differently according to their knowledge frame (Carton & Thissen,

2009). Further, different users prefer different scales, e.g. landscape planners use a catchment or local farmers use the region around their farm, and different map types, e.g. planners usually work with topographical maps, and farmers with areal picture. Here the use of digital tools such as the Touch Table makes it possible to accommodate these requirements. Eikelboom and Janssen (2013) found in a row of geodesign workshops including a wide range of participants (e.g. farmer, decision-maker, scientist) that most of the participants (86%) considered the use of the Touch Table as 'fairly easy', although some had no experience of using spatial support tools (55%). The use of maps, preferably using the same legend (e.g. values from 1 to 10), proved effective to communicate a large amount of information in a short time. Thus, translating different arguments into spatial information is a potentially suitable method to integrate local and scientific knowledge (Raymond et al., 2010).

For future research it would be highly interesting to investigate these maps further: (1) how are the different knowledge systems reflected in this map? Geodesign Hub©, for example, allows negotiating the integration of different proposals per interest group (Ballal & Steinitz, 2015; Campagna et al., 2016; Nyerges et al., 2016) and compares the different inputs according to their divergence or convergence. Further, we could ask (2) how are these geodesign maps implemented in the final plan? Maps are a strong means of communication and as such have the potential to influence the further planning process. However, empirical evidence is needed to reveal opportunities and challenges these maps offer.

9.4.2 Using Scenarios and Implicitly Integrating NBS in Geodesign Workshops

Apart from the potential to integrate different knowledge systems, which is a crucial component for NBS planning and implementation (Nesshöver et al., 2016), geodesign as presented here offers an advanced tool to compare scenarios and analyse trade-offs of different NBS, technical or hybrid solutions. In the three workshops participants translated the verbal scenarios into spatial scenarios. This permitted visualising and comparing the impacts of different land-use and water-level changes in every scenario and across scenarios. The presented geodesign case showed the same strengths as other participatory scenario planning cases, which are the dialogue between local and technical knowledge and the strengthening of relationships between local stakeholder, scientists and land managers, a co-learning process between science and society or engagement of creative thinking (Oteros-Rozas et al., 2015). This is in line with the processes for designing projects that implement NBS as described by Nesshöver et al. (2016), which include multidisciplinary and transdisciplinary knowledge and the development of common understandings of multifunctional solutions.

Using NBS implicitly in the workshops may be of advantage in avoiding misleading discussions of definitions and preserving the neutral role of the workshop organisers. The workshops took place in 2013, when NBS was not yet such a prominent concept in research and policy-making. Nevertheless, we provided arguments that NBS had been included in some of the scenarios. The scenarios illustrate the rather vague definition of NBS and its blurry limit to technical solutions. The technical solutions in question include pumping of water in different intensities for rewetting and drainage. While the measures themselves may be seen as technical, they are enhancing natural processes. This highlights the difficulty to clearly distinguish nature-based from technical solutions, which arguably supports the use of the NBS concept implicitly in the workshop. For future research the articulation of NBS concepts in the context of geodesign could be improved.

However, there is no case known to the authors of this chapter that used the geodesign approach as presented for NBS planning, explicitly naming the concept and including it in the discussion. The geodesign approach has been shown to be applicable for NBS planning, especially as it has the potential to engage and synthesise different knowledge systems. Therefore, for future research it would be of interest to investigate how valuable geodesign tools and workshops are when explicitly using the NBS term.

9.5 CONCLUSION

In this chapter we have critically and systematically analysed the potential of geodesign workshops for boundary management in NBS planning using the three functions of boundary management: translation, communication and mediation. The case study highlighted the crucial role of the geodesign tool in translating knowledge into spatial information, the communication aspect between tool and participants and among participants, and the mediation effect of discussions informed by on-the-fly responses of the tool. Further, we highlighted five key lessons learnt to successfully apply geodesign tools and workshops for NBS planning, which included: type of geodesign, simple versus complex approaches, workshop mediation, instrumental and deliberate valuation, and knowledge synthesis. In particular, the scenario approach supported by geodesign provides the advantage to contrast the benefits of different intensities of nature- and technical-based solutions. As the focus is on the spatial information, it is not necessary to explicitly name the NBS term.

In conclusion, geodesign potentially offers a valuable approach for NBS planning. The five key lessons identified from geodesign applications support the use of this potential. The tool allows integration of state-of-the-art scientific knowledge on ecosystem processes and to calculate on that basis the impacts of land-use changes. It supports scenario-based planning and facilitates the synthesis of different knowledge systems of diverse stakeholders. Therefore, geodesign, as described and discussed in this chapter, can be used to facilitate boundary management for planning and implementation of NBS.

ACKNOWLEDGEMENTS

Funding for the preparation of this book chapter was provided by the German Ministry for Education and Research (BMBF) through the Junior Research Group PlanSmart (funding code: 01UU1601A).

The geodesign workshops were organised by Tessa Eikelboom and Ron Janssen. Their research was funded by the 'Knowledge for Climate' research programme of the Netherlands. The participants are acknowledged for their contribution to the success of the workshops.

REFERENCES

Albert, C., Schröter, B., Haase, D., Brillinger, M., Henze, J., Herrmann, S., et al. 2019. Addressing societal challenges through nature-based solutions: how can landscape planning and governance research contribute? *Landscape and Urban Planning*, 182, 12–21.

Arciniegas, G. A. & Janssen, R. 2009. Using a touch table to support participatory land use planning. *In*: Anderssen, R. S., Braddock, R. D. & Newham, L. T. H. (eds.) *18th World IMACS Congress and MODSIM09 International Congress on Modelling and Simulation: Interfacing Modelling and Simulation with Mathematical and Computational Sciences*, pp. 2206–2212. Nedlands, Western Australia: University of Western Australia.

Arciniegas, G., Janssen, R. & Omtzigt, N. 2011. Map-based multicriteria analysis to support interactive land use allocation. *International Journal of Geographical Information Science*, 25, 1931–1947.

Ballal, H. & Steinitz, C. 2015. A workshop in digital geodesign synthesis. *In*: *Proceedings of Digital Landscape Architecture*, pp. 400–407. Berlin: Herbert Wichmann.

Brouns, K., Eikelboom, T., Jansen, P. C., Janssen, R., Kwakernaak, C., van den Akker, J. J. H., et al. 2015. Spatial analysis of soil subsidence in peat meadow areas in Friesland in relation to land and water management, climate change, and adaptation. *Environmental Management*, 55, 360–372.

Campagna, M. 2015. Geodesign as a process: from modelling to enactment. *In*: *Proceedings of Digital Landscape Architecture*, pp. 276–283. Berlin: Herbert Wichmann.

Campagna, M., Clara, A., Moura, M., Borges, J. & Cocco, C. 2016. Future scenarios for the Pampulha region: a geodesign workshop. *Journal of Digital Landscape Architecture*, 2016, 292–301.

Carton, L. J. & Thissen, W. A. H. 2009. Emerging conflict in collaborative mapping: towards a deeper understanding? *Journal of Environmental Management*, 90, 1991–2001.

Cash, D. W., Clark, W. C., Alcock, F., Dickson, N. M., Eckley, N., Guston, D. H., et al. 2003. Knowledge systems for sustainable development. *Proceedings of the National Academy of Sciences of the United States of America*, 100, 8086–8091.

Currier, K. & Couclelis, H. 2014. Geodesigning 'from the inside out'. *In*: Lee, D. J., Dias, E. & Scholten, H. J. (eds.) *Geodesign by Integrating Design and Geospatial Sciences*, pp. 287–298. Cham: Springer International Publishing.

Eikelboom, T. & Janssen, R. 2013. Interactive spatial tools for the design of regional adaptation strategies. *Journal of Environmental Management*, 127, S6–S14.

Eikelboom, T. & Janssen, R. 2015. Comparison of geodesign tools to communicate stakeholder values. *Group Decision and Negotiation*, 24, 1065–1087.

Eikelboom, T. & Janssen, R. 2017. Collaborative use of geodesign tools to support decision-making on adaptation to climate change. *Mitigation and Adaptation Strategies for Global Change*, 22, 247–266.

Eikelboom, T., Janssen, R. & Stewart, T. J. 2015. A spatial optimization algorithm for geodesign. *Landscape and Urban Planning*, 144, 10–21.

Ervin, S. 2011. A system for geodesign. *In*: *Proceedings of Digital Landscape Architecture*, pp. 145–154. Berlin: Herbert Wichmann.

European Commission. 2015. *Towards an EU Research and Innovation Policy Agenda for Nature-based Solutions & Re-naturing Cities. Final Report of the Horizon 2020 Expert Group on 'Nature-based Solutions and Re-naturing Cities'*. Brussels: European Commission.

European Union. 2013. *Mapping and Assessment of Ecosystems and Their Services. An Analytical Framework for Ecosystem Assessments under Action 5 of the EU Biodiversity Strategy to 2020*. Luxembourg: Publications Office of the European Union.

Flaxman, M. 2010. Geodesign: fundamentals and routes forward. Presented at Geodesign Summit, Redlands, CA.

Green, T. L., Kronenberg, J., Andersson, E., Elmqvist, T. & Gómez-Baggethun, E. 2016. Insurance value of green infrastructure in and around cities. *Ecosystems*, 19, 1051–1063.

Janssen, R., Eikelboom, T., Brouns, K. & Jansen, P. 2013. Verslag workshops Friese Veenweidevisie. Utrecht.

Janssen, R., Eikelboom, T., Verhoeven, J. & Brouns, K. 2015. Using geodesign to develop a spatial adaptation strategy for Friesland. *In*: Lee, D., Dias, E. & Scholten, H. J. (eds.) *Geodesign by Integrating Design and Geospatial Sciences*, pp. 103–116. Cham: Springer International Publishing.

Jones, H. P., Hole, D. G. & Zavaleta, E. S. 2012. Harnessing nature to help people adapt to climate change. *Nature Climate Change*, 2, 504–509.

Kloos, J. & Renaud, F. G. 2016. *Overview of Ecosystem-based Approaches to Drought Risk Reduction Targeting Small-scale Farmers in Sub-Saharan Africa*, pp. 199–226. Cham: Springer International Publishing.

Lee, D. J., Dias, E. & Scholten, H. J. 2014. Introduction to geodesign developments in Europe. *In*: Lee, D. J., Dias, E. & Scholten, H. J. (eds.) *Geodesign by Integrating Design and Geospatial Sciences*, pp. 3–9. Cham: Springer International Publishing.

Liquete, C., Kleeschulte, S., Dige, G., Maes, J., Grizzetti, B., Olah, B., et al. 2015. Mapping green infrastructure based on ecosystem services and ecological networks: a pan-European case study. *Environmental Science & Policy*, 54, 268–280.

Littaye, A., Lardon, S. & Alloncle, N. 2016. Stakeholders' collective drawing reveals significant differences in the vision of marine spatial planning of the western tropical Pacific. *Ocean & Coastal Management*, 130, 260–276.

Marimbaldo, F. J. M., Corea, F. V. G. & Callejo, M. Á. M. 2012. Using 3D geodesign for planning of new electricity networks in Spain. *Lecture Notes in Computer Science (including subseries Lecture Notes in Artificial Intelligence and Lecture Notes in Bioinformatics)*, 7333 LNCS (PART 1), 462–476.

Max Finlayson, C., Davidson, N., Pritchard, D., Randy Milton, G. & MacKacy, H. 2011. The Ramsar convention and ecosystem-based approaches to the wise use and sustainable development of wetlands. *Journal of International Wildlife Law and Policy*, 14 (3–4), 176–198.

Mouchet, M. A., Paracchini, M. L., Schulp, C. J. E., Stürck, J., Verkerk, P. J., Verburg, P. H., et al. 2017. Bundles of ecosystem (dis)services and multifunctionality across European landscapes. *Ecological Indicators*, 73, 23–28.

Nassauer, J. I. 2015. Commentary: visualization verisimilitude and civic participation. *Landscape and Urban Planning*, 142, 170–172.

Nassauer, J. I. & Opdam, P. 2008. Design in science: extending the landscape ecology paradigm. *Landscape Ecology*, 23, 633–644.

Nature. 2017. Natural language: the latest attempt to brand green practices is better than it sounds. *Nature*, 541, 133–134.

Nesshöver, C., Assmuth, T., Irvine, K. N., Rusch, G. M., Waylen, K. A., Delbaere, B., et al. 2016. The science, policy and practice of nature-based solutions: an interdisciplinary perspective. *Science of the Total Environment*, 579, 1215–1227.

Nyerges, T., Ballal, H., Steinitz, C., Canfield, T., Roderick, M., Ritzman, J., et al. 2016. Geodesign dynamics for sustainable urban watershed development. *Sustainable Cities and Society*, 25, 13–24.

Oteros-Rozas, E., Martín-López, B., Daw, T. M., Bohensky, E. L., Butler, J. R. A., Hill, R., et al. 2015. Participatory scenario planning in place-based social–ecological research: insights and experiences from 23 case studies. *Ecology and Society*, 20(4), 32.

Pascual, U., Balvanera, P., Diaz, S., Pataki, G., Roth, E., Stenseke, M., et al. 2017. Valuing nature's contributions to people: the IPBES approach. *Current Opinion in Environmental Sustainability*, 26–27, 7–16.

Pelzer, P., Arciniegas, G., Geertman, S. & Lenferink, S. 2015a. Planning support systems and task–technology fit: a comparative case study. *Applied Spatial Analysis and Policy*, 8, 155–175.

Pelzer, P., Geertman, S. & van der Heijden, R. 2015b. Knowledge in communicative planning practice: a different perspective for planning support systems. *Environment and Planning B: Urban Analytics and City Science*, 42, 638–651.

Provincie Friesland. 2011. *Achtergrondrapport Startnotitie Veenweidevisie* [in Dutch]. Leeuwarden: Provincie Friesland.

Provincie Friesland. 2015. *Veenweidevisie, Een duurzame toekomst voor het Friese Veenweidegebied* [in Dutch]. Leeuwarden: Provincie Friesland.

Rambaldi, G., Muchemi, J., Crawhall, N. & Monaci, L. 2007. Through the eyes of hunter-gatherers: participatory 3D modelling among Ogiek indigenous peoples in Kenya. *Information Development*, 23(2–3), 113–128.

Raumer, H. S. & Stokman, A. 2013. GeoDesign – Herausforderungen an einen verständigen Umgang mit GIS [GeoDesign – a challenge to improve communicating of GIS applications]. *In*: *Proceedings of Digital Landscape Architecture*, pp. 311–321. Berlin: Herbert Wichmann.

Raymond, C. M., Fazey, I., Reed, M.S., Stringer, L. C., Robinson, G. M. & Evely, A. C. 2010. Integrating local and scientific knowledge for environmental management. *Journal of Environmental Management*, 91, 1766–1777.

Raymond, C. M., Frantzeskaki, N., Kabisch, N., Berry, P., Breil, M., Nita, M. R., et al. 2017. A framework for assessing and implementing the co-benefits of nature-based solutions in urban areas. *Environmental Science & Policy*, 77, 15–24.

Raymond, C. M., Kenter, J. O., Plieninger, T., Turner, N. J. & Alexander, K. A. 2014. Comparing instrumental and deliberative paradigms underpinning the assessment of social values for cultural ecosystem services. *Ecological Economics*, 107, 145–156.

Recatalá Boix, L. & Zinck, J. A. 2008. Land-use planning in the Chaco plain (Burruyac, Argentina): Part 2: generating a consensus plan to mitigate land-use conflicts and minimize land degradation. *Environmental Management*, 42, 200–209.

Reed, M. S., Challies, E., de Vente, J., Frewer, L., Hohenwallner-Ries, D., Huber, T., et al. 2018. A theory of participation: what makes stakeholder and public engagement in environmental management work? *Restoration Ecology*, 26(S1), S7–S17.

Schwarz-v.Raumer, H. G. & Stokman, A. 2011. GeoDesign – approximations of a catchphrase. *In*: *Proceedings of Digital Landscape Architecture*, pp. 106–115. Berlin: Herbert Wichmann.

Slotterback, C. S., Runck, B., Pitt, D. G., Kne, L., Jordan, N. R., Mulla, D. J., et al. 2016. Collaborative geodesign to advance multifunctional landscapes. *Landscape and Urban Planning*, 156, 71–80.

Star, S. L. & Griesemer, J. R. 1989. Institutional ecology, 'translations' and boundary objects: amateurs and professionals in Berkeley's Museum of Vertebrate Zoology, 1907–39. *Social Studies of Science*, 19, 387–420.

Steinitz, C. 2012. *A Framework for Geodesign: Changing Geography by Design*. Redlands, CA: ESRI.

Steinitz, C. 2014. Which way of designing? *In*: Lee, D., Dias, E. & Scholten, H. J. (eds.) *Geodesign by Integrating Design and Geospatial Sciences*, pp. 11–40. Cham: Springer International Publishing.

Tengö, M., Brondizio, E. S., Elmqvist, T., Malmer, P. & Spierenburg, M. 2014. Connecting diverse knowledge systems for enhanced ecosystem governance: the multiple evidence base approach. *AMBIO*, 43, 579–591.

Tengö, M., Hill, R., Malmer, P., Raymond, C. M., Spierenburg, M., Danielsen, F., et al. 2017. Weaving knowledge systems in IPBES, CBD and beyond – lessons learned for sustainability. *Current Opinion in Environmental Sustainability*, 26–27, 17–25.

Turner, K. G., Odgaard, M. V., Bøcher, P. K., Dalgaard, T. & Svenning, J.-C. 2014. Bundling ecosystem services in Denmark: trade-offs and synergies in a cultural landscape. *Landscape and Urban Planning*, 125, 89–104.

van der Nat, A., Vellinga, P., Leemans, R. & van Slobbe, E. 2016. Ranking coastal flood protection designs from engineered to nature-based. *Ecological Engineering*, 87, 80–90.

Vonk, G. & Geertman, S. 2008. Improving the adoption and use of planning support systems in practice. *Journal of Applied Spatial Analysis and Policy*, 1(3), 21.

Vonk, G., Geertman, S. & Schot, P. 2007. A SWOT analysis of planning support systems. *Environment and Planning A*, 39, 1699–1714.

Westerink, J., Opdam, P., van Rooij, S. & Steingröver, E. 2017. Landscape services as boundary concept in landscape governance: building social capital in collaboration and adapting the landscape. *Land Use Policy*, 60, 408–418.

Wissen Hayek, U., von Wirth, T., Neuenschwander, N. & Grêt-Regamey, A. 2016. Organizing and facilitating geodesign processes: integrating tools into collaborative design processes for urban transformation. *Landscape and Urban Planning*, 156, 59–70.

Xu, P. 2015. Applying systems thinking: geodesign structure provides general models integrating architecture with landscape planning and design to create a sustainable environment. *In*: *Proceedings of Digital Landscape Architecture*, pp. 195–204. Berlin: Herbert Wichmann.

Yang, P. P.-J., Quan, S. J., Castro-Lacouture, D., Rudolph, C. & Stuart, B. 2014. Performance metrics for designing an algae-powered eco urban district: a geodesign perspective. *Energy Procedia*, 61, 1487–1490.

10 Integrating Models into Practice – Recommendations

Neil Sang, Ioanna Akoumianaki, Matthew Aitkenhead, David Miller and Åsa Ode-Sang

10.1 INTRODUCTION

The modelling techniques set out in this book provide a powerful array of methods to help understand what the state of our environment is, what may be driving changes in that state, and how future scenarios may look given current trends or policies. They also, however, present a significant challenge in terms of deciding what approach to apply where, resourcing that approach with data and skills and educating others in how to engage with such modelling methods and understand the results. As part of the review upon which much of this book has been based, a survey was conducted as to the current use of computational models by local planning agencies within Sweden. Responses showed a recognition of the need for knowledge which modelling can provide but also the importance of simplicity in terms of how that can be obtained given the skills of those who need to engage with this knowledge, the resources available to do so and the often time-pressured nature of the work:

> There is generally a need for a simple way to get a good basis for decisions. The demands are constantly increasing for risk analysis of various kinds while demands for fast processes and simplicity increases elsewhere. Good tools are important to meet these different types of expectations. (Translated from Swedish, see Q13, appendix 3 in Sang & Ode-Sang, 2015, for original survey response)

Improving access to this knowledge and the utility of the models themselves is no simple task. It necessitates coordinated changes to current practice at many levels; from the working practices of individual researchers and practitioners to the organisations which employ them such as universities, software companies and consultancies, plus those local government and national agencies which might directly support such work. It also entails strategic changes to government policy in terms of development of NSDI and national and supranational legal frameworks which enable or frustrate access to data.

The solutions must be context-sensitive; for example, even within Sweden it was clear from this survey (Sang & Ode-Sang, 2015) that there was considerable variance in the financial resources, skills and requirements of different local authorities. This said, there are also certain issues in common which we believe will have some general relevance elsewhere, at least in so far as some hierarchy of government exists whereby local government has responsibility for granting or denying permission to specific developments of smaller scale and national authorities are involved in decisions over key infrastructure and strategic planning as well as regulatory and financial frameworks. Not all the suggestions will fit equally to all domains, such as land versus marine, but we hope, in bringing together the views of the authors here, to provide some general principles by which greater capacity for scenario modelling may be built. Of course, these represent the views of modellers and academics, albeit ones with considerable collective experience of working with practitioners, policy makers, citizens and other stakeholder groups. Some of these recommendations may be 'easier said than done' and few are exclusively the responsibility of any one party, efforts must be coordinated, but we nonetheless believe it is of value to set out as plainly as possible the tasks at hand and where these might be most fruitfully begun.

10.2 A HIERARCHY OF MODEL COMPLEXITY REQUIRES A HIERARCHY OF SUPPORTING SERVICES

As Figure I.2 set out in the Introduction, different stakeholders may have quite different requirements as to model output, not only in terms of the theme but also as to the level of precision required in order to base decisions upon that information. This is often, but not necessarily, correlated with spatial scale.

Generally speaking there is a trade-off between precision (in terms of location or degree of effect) and accuracy. Because accuracy is defined relative to precision (i.e. an accurate model contains less error than the degree of precision needed), the more precise the prediction the harder it is to deliver accurately. Critical decisions, such as where life may be at risk, require high degrees of accuracy; that is, the predictions they make must be consistently correct to within the error margin deemed acceptable.

For example, a regional development agency may seek, by some consultative process, to determine what level of risk from flooding society is willing to accept (i.e. insure, support with disaster relief, etc.). This done, an accurate model of future storm size and frequency is important to determine the conditions from which a water flow model might then estimate risk to one part of the region compared with another. The probability of rainfall over that region may vary with low spatial precision, but it is sufficient to set development policies graduated towards favouring the lower-risk areas for development or estimating the amount of NBS, such as planting woodland, required to mitigate flooding in the higher-risk areas.

It may be much harder to precisely model where the boundaries between each risk zone should fall. This lack of precision could be accommodated by 'erring on the side of caution' and thus ensuring, at the regional scale, a minimum exposure to risk with reasonable confidence. However, such caution may meet strong resistance if, for example, it limits valuable and necessary development opportunities, in which case it may become necessary to demonstrate the risk to particular locations with greater spatial precision by applying more precise flood models to the locales of interest. It is likely, however, that the driving model for rainfall becomes less accurate at higher spatial resolution, so the spatial precision may be gained at the expense of wider error margins. In which case, the question for the decision-maker is whether, given those wider error margins, the acceptable risk threshold is breached.

The more complex the range of systems to be considered and the longer the timescale of prediction, the greater sacrifice of spatial precision needed to achieve a desired degree of accuracy, which is why complex chained models linking e.g. global climatic and land-use systems with models of human behaviour tend to focus on large spatial scales. Furthermore, as the various sources of uncertainty combine within complex systems, predictions are more likely to reach 'equifinality', i.e. several different sets of pathways combine to different but similarly likely (or unlikely) outcomes. Thus, chained models tend to be about exploring and comparing potential narratives rather than strongly guiding specific decisions and so also tend to be of more interest to authorities attempting to shift societal goals at organisational levels with a large spatial remit (regional–national–international).

Complicating this general picture is the fact that some systems are 'emergent', i.e. the general implications arise from detailed local dynamics, an issue touched on by several authors in this book. Nonetheless, most models considered in this book do follow the general trend that (for a given model) accuracy becomes harder to achieve as spatial precision increases and (for a given precision) computation more challenging as spatial extent increases. Furthermore, this book shows how the decision-making process is also spatially scaled, with different modelling approaches suitable/feasible for different levels of decision-making. Generally speaking, those decisions become more strategic in nature as spatial extent increases. So while there are many exceptions to the rule, we believe it is reasonable to use spatial scale of application as a frame of reference when making a general point about the kinds of models which are useful for different tasks across diverse application domains. Moreover, the link between spatial scale of model, type of decision and decision-making body also serves as a pointer towards where the primary responsibility lies to facilitate the use of models.

10.2.1 *Stepping Up Modelling*

In Figure 10.1 we set out four general types of modelling in an approximate ordering as to the nature of the output from the specific to the strategic which, as argued above, tends (with many exceptions) to also be applied over increasing spatial extent. The ordering also tends to reflect increasingly specialised and/or broad-ranging skills which are thus increasingly scarce. As regards providing modelling resources, a distinction should perhaps be drawn between models which can be entirely implemented with 'standard' GIS software and those which require more simulation or statistical software. The reason for this distinction is that GIS are a common technology not only for many models but also for data collection, management, visualisation and traditional planning processes, as well as supporting the day-to-day logistics of managing municipalities. As such, many planning departments have at least basic GIS software and skills available or, failing this, can access cheap or free online GIS tools. Most GIS software

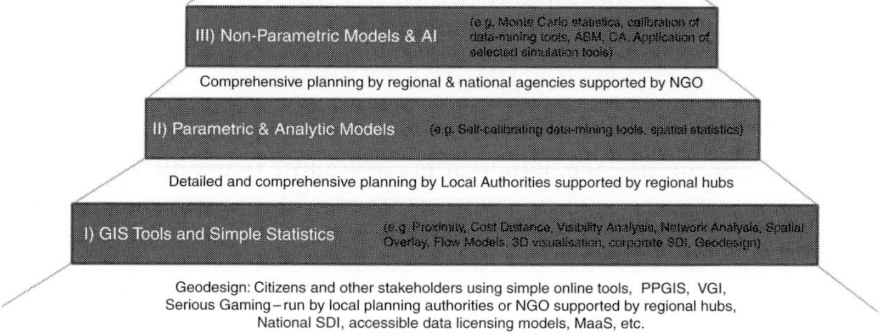

FIGURE 10.1 Types of models, scale of use and key actors. (A black and white version of this figure will appear in some formats. For the colour version, please refer to the plate section.)

provide analytical tools which, used judiciously, can go a long way towards providing modelling functionality as well as being a means to obtain necessary data from sources such as satellite imagery.

With respect to GIS-based scenario development there is considerable potential for adoption at the local authority level. However, for less well-resourced local authorities even this may require outside investment, while for very small authorities investment in software and data is expensive for the number of cases undertaken. In particular, the requirement to pay fees to access national data sets could be a barrier in such cases.

I. 'On the ground' at some individual municipalities, it is clear that there is often a practical issue as to the time currently used by GIS staff on data collation and map production which might be undertaken by other staff if appropriate training, organisational SDI and simplified mapping tools are in place. However, a deeper reason is perhaps uncertainty as to the value of GIS-based analytical methods compared with expert judgement, and their appropriate use. As one respondent to the survey commented:

> We are very understaffed, so we would have the most benefit from simple models (easy to handle). However, this would be a great help when needing to relatively quickly produce a forecast, and we do not want to deliver all data to the consultant, then wait for an answer, and then still have to revise. As to more extensive investigations we must probably continue to hire a consultant, but it is still a great advantage in having one's own knowledge of the models, so that you know what to order and can view [the] result. (Translated from Swedish; see Q13, appendix 3, Sang & Ode-Sang, 2015, for original)

At this level there two related but distinct issues: how to support the use of simple models for fast, iterative (and thus necessarily in-house) impact assessment; and how to commission and/or interpret the implications of more complex scenario models. The issue is perpetuated by lack of time between ongoing work to learn and evaluate the methods as a team. Higher education also has a role to play here in ensuring that graduates from programs in landscape architecture, planning, geography and related fields have a sound understanding of basic GIS analyses.

Access to necessary software and training is no longer the barrier it once was given the availability of open-source GIS and free online training. However, making this learning a priority within busy schedules requires leadership at the departmental level, but also higher levels which may include local political support. Even where a case can be made that this will save time and lead to better decision-making in future, there is an upfront cost in staff time.

Access to data remains a problem for many local authorities, even in well-resourced areas of the world. This may be because the licensing model is a one-size-fits-all 'full-access' approach, which is too expensive for occasional use, or because the data do not exist in free data sets (e.g. Open Street Map depends on local citizens with the time, knowledge and facilities to contribute). Satellite imagery is increasingly available at relevant resolutions for urban planning, but classification requires knowledge of remote sensing and the kinds of map which can be extracted may not fulfil the needs of many models. This is an area where national governments and international organisations have a role to play by (a) ensuring accessible SDI and (b) creating relevant data sets for areas which cannot do this themselves, including modelled risk maps at a range of scales. Scientists also have a responsibility in this respect to consider not only how best to model the phenomenon of interest ever more precisely with the best data available to them, but how to do so to *sufficient* accuracy given the data available to local authorities around the world.

II. Some municipalities and NGOs have the capacity to use GIS for impact assessment and simple multi-criterion analysis (MCA) types of model, for example basic flood models, statistical trend analysis, accessibility models, site selection, spatial 'hotspot' identification, and remote sensing classification in various applications. If an appropriate agreement could be established between neighbouring municipalities, supported by regional agency funding, this capacity could be expanded to support those which do not and perhaps include more sophisticated modelling tools, to the mutual benefit of all the municipalities involved. An alternative to locating such facilities within a 'hub' municipality could be a third-party organisation such as an appropriately constituted regional government agency, NGO or landscape observatory. Some municipalities reported using such a strategy already:

> As a single municipality, it is difficult and expensive to develop your own data and models. We draw today from things that have been undertaken in a framework of regional and local authorities in cooperation. Examples are flood scenarios for the river … (Translated from Swedish, see Q13, appendix 3, of Sang & Ode-Sang, 2015, for original)

As the quotation shows, many environmental management and planning problems are not limited to the spatial boundaries of one municipality (or indeed country), so regional cooperation is logical. This needn't take the form of a single institutional 'hub', but simply a coordinated training network that trains staff across agencies so the skills can be shared. However, education is a long-term solution; with respect to specifically the modelling of NBS, the immediate need is for sources of authoritative information on relevant parameters ready for use in simple models such as absorption/run-off coefficients for local soil types in relevant land use and climatic conditions.

III. In the Swedish survey (Sang & Ode-Sang, 2015) no municipality identified themselves as having significant capacity for predictive scenario modelling (rather than responding to a presented future scenario) or for downscaling global scenarios. If this work was undertaken at all it was outsourced to agencies such as the Swedish Environmental Protection Agency or to private consultancies. The appropriate knowledge to commission this work is also limited, particularly for smaller municipalities. Thus it is unrealistic, at present, to expect planning processes at this scale to undertake modelling of possible future response to complex systems. However, even simple outputs of such models would be useful, e.g.:

> Flood mapping (data) based on 10, 20, 50 and 100 year rain would be good. How secondary drainage is working would be good to know, and what happens if a greater degree of surface sealing occurs. (Translated from Swedish, see Q13, appendix 3, of Sang & Ode-Sang, 2015, for original)

While some respondents mentioned working with universities on specific problems, it is also, perhaps, unrealistic to expect those who develop modelling tools for their own research to play a large role in repeatedly applying these models in various municipalities and regions.

Countries such as Sweden may be able to build on the existing specialist networks of regional planning agencies to support alliances with Higher Education Institutions (HEIs) at a regional scale. Such a network could draw together the skills needed to apply (if not necessarily develop) models for downscaling the implications of scenarios generated at national scale. However, this requires a substantial commitment from the central government and a cultural shift in the role of HEIs. For countries that lack a sufficient skill base and infrastructure at the HEI or regional planning level, it would be impossible without international support. Given the demand for such skills including from the private sector, even richer countries would struggle to create and sustain such a network.

One possible approach is provided by the EU Copernicus platform, which not only hosts a wide range of data, but is beginning to provide modelled output layers based on this. Thus far, Copernicus has tended to focus on modelled output which can be delivered at a European scale, but the US EPA's National Storm Water Calculator provides a good example of how national data sources can be turned into a Model as a Service (MaaS) tool for local application to planning NBS. International organisations could pool resources to validate models for use in specific regions and provide these as freely available MaaS tools. However, this would require a wider context, such as commitment from contributing countries to standardise relevant data sets and ensuring models be made available, e.g. by insisting that models built with public research funds be open-access in the same manner as is increasingly required of publications.

IV. The most sophisticated models, particularly those which predict broad future scenarios from integrated subsystems, require for the most part expertise, data or facilities which are only available in limited numbers nationally or even internationally. These resources are generally within academia, in government agencies or specialist research institutes. There is no single, tried and tested approach for bringing such diverse resources to bear on national planning systems. Indeed, different modelling disciplines and individuals within each discipline do not all agree as to how complex and integrated a model it is useful or wise to create. The IPCC is arguably the largest environmental modelling assessment exercise ever attempted. Its recent report (IPCC, 2018) represents something of a new departure by placing the focus on (relatively short-term) impacts rather than on long-term models of climate change itself. In doing so it brings together the work of many researchers globally, covering a wide range of disciplines, which is to be welcomed. Other initiatives, such as the UN Global Land Programme (https://glp.earth/), have sought to bring the global scientific community with many related disciplines together into a concerted effort. SDI are slowly making data more accessible, and data portals from agencies such as NASA (https://data.nasa.gov/) and ESA (https://scihub.copernicus.eu/) are providing more and more freely available data. Yet there remains a notable utility gap between models which address various dimensions of change in complex systems at extensive spatial scales and the disparate planning systems attempting to manage that change one local decision at a time. Models from levels I, II and III are useful in the search for solutions, but knowing what questions to ask of them depends on having accessible tools and map libraries that translate the level IV models into tractable, locally contextualised, scenarios. For example, establishing local implications of sea-level rise can be undertaken with modelling at levels I and II. However, because SLR will vary significantly around the globe for a given global average, local planning agencies need tools to downscale the global model to their region. Such tools often do exist (www.adaptationclearinghouse.org/; https://climate-adapt.eea.europa.eu/), the problem is for local agencies to be able to find and use them. Ideally, international agencies such as the UN and EU will host more MaaS, but there is also a role for national governments and scientific funding agencies to place greater priority on filling this gap. (Bullet points I–IV adapted from Sang & Ode-Sang, 2015)

10.3 CONCLUSION

One reason why it may be difficult to implement the kinds of change suggested is that often making a process feasible for the level below requires the active attention of decision-makers at higher organisational levels. This is obvious in terms of, for example, development of SDI to supply data, but other actors such as individual scientists operate within wider institutional and cultural settings, which may limit their ability to attend to these issues even where they recognise the need. For example, academia prioritises the production of new knowledge, not the re-implementation of existing knowledge, and even the most single-minded researcher needs to acknowledge the priorities of their department. Departments must acknowledge the priorities of the university and the university those of its funders and governments. Thus, at every level, a choice is required as to whether to redirect effort (e.g. via funding and assessment criteria) or fund some additional process of knowledge transfer. Research funding has, not uncontroversially, made a significant shift towards applied purposes, for example with the 'Innovation' calls in the EU Horizon 2020 programme. However, such efforts continue to produce a disparate body of knowledge with a proliferation of tools, and these tools too often reflect the information and skill resources available to researchers at well-resourced universities because this is where much of the necessary scientific and modelling knowledge resides. We argue that the urgency of the challenges requires the second approach: a specific effort to operationalise environmental modelling knowledge at every level.

REFERENCES

IPCC. 2018. Global warming of 1.5C. *In*: Masson-Delmotte, V., Zhai, P., Pörtner, H-O., Roberts, D., Skea, J., Shukla, P., et al. (eds.). Geneva: Intergovernmental Panel on Climate Change.

Sang, N. & Ode-Sang, A. 2015. *A Review on the State of the Art in Scenario Modelling for Environmental Management*. Stockholm: Naturvårdsverket.

Appendix: List of Models/ Software

NB: This list covers those discussed in the text, not those only listed in tables.

Analytical/Data Mining/Artificial Intelligence

anomaly detection
Artificial Intelligence for Ecosystem Services (ARIES)
Artificial Neural Network (ANN)
Association Rule Learning (ARL)
Bayesian belief network (BBN)
classification
clustering
decision tree
dimensional analysis (DA)
fuzzy classification
genetic algorithm (GA)
geographically weighted regression (GWR)
interpolation
regression
summarisation

Freshwater

BASINFORM
CATCHMOD
CurveNumber
Green Values National Storm Water Calculator
HSPF
Hydrologic Simulation Program-Fortran (HSPF)
INCA (Integrated Catchment Model)
MIKE SHE/MIKE 11
MyLake
National Hydrological Instrument (NHI)
phosphorus indicators tool

Root Zone Water Quality Model (RZWQM)
SAGIS (source apportionment GIS)
SIMCAT (simulation catchment)
SPACSYS
SPARROW (SPAtially Referenced Regression On Watershed)
SWAT (Soil and Water Assessment Tool)
WaSim
WASP (Water Analysis Simulation Program)
SWMM

Freshwater/Soil

DRAINMOD-DSSAT
WATEM (Water and Tillage Erosion Model)

Freshwater/Storm Water Management

Arc SLAMM
FloodModeller Pro
ISIS 2D
ISIS Fast
ISIS Dynamic
MIKE Flood
MUSIC
PCSWMM
SWAT
TUFLOW
USGS Green Values National Storm Water Calculator
WBM
Win SLAMM

Landscape/Integrative Assessment

ATOMIS
CHOICE
GEPARD
ITE^{2}M
LandSFACTS
ProF
Spatial Information Exploration and Visualisation Environment (SIEVE)
SWAT

Marine and Coastal

ADvanced CIRCulation Model (ADCIRC)
Atlantis NEUS
bath tub model
Coastal Resilience Tool
Cost-Path
DIVA
Dynamic Integrated model of Climate and the Economy (DICE)
European Regional Seas Ecosystem Model (ERSEM)
General Estuarine Transport Model (GETM)
HEC-HMS
HYbrid Coordinate Ocean Model (HYCOM)
IBIS (Integrated Biosphere Simulation) Integrated Assessment
Integrated Marine Valuation of ES and Trade-offs (INVEST)
MarineMap
MBL-GEM (Marine Biological Laboratory General Ecosystem Model)
OSMOSE
PCSWMM
Risk and Vulnerability Assessment Methodology Development Project (RiVAMP)
SIMClim (Integrated Assessment)
Simple Dynamic Inundation Models (SDIM)
Simulating Waves Nearshore (SWAN)
TELEMAC 2D
XBEACH

Soil

AnnAGNPS (Annualised Agricultural Nonpoint-Source Pollution)
CarboSOIL
CENTURY
CREAMS (Chemicals, Run-off and Erosion from Agricultural Management Systems)
DAYCENT
DNDC (Denitrification–Decomposition)
DSSAT (Decision Support System for Agrotechnology Transfer)
EUROSEM (European Soil Erosion Model)
export coefficient
MAGIC
MONICA (Model for Nitrogen and Carbon in Agroecosystems)

Roth-C
SCOPE (Soil, Canopy Observation, Photochemistry and Energy fluxes)
TOPMODEL

Urban Climate

ENVImet
OpenFOAM
RayMan
SOLWEIG
Urban Multi-scale Environmental Predictor (UMEP)

Other Models

Building Information Model (BIM)
CLAIM
FARMSCOPER
Marxan
ProLand
Geographical Information System (GIS)

Index